PACKAGING POLITICS

| Political
| Communications
in Britain's Media
| Democracy

Second Edition

BOB FRANKLIN

ARNOLD

First published in Great Britain in 1994
Second edition published in 2004 by
Arnold, a member of the Hodder Headline Group,
338 Euston Road, London NW1 3BH

http://www.arnoldpublishers.com

Distributed in the United States of America by
Oxford University Press Inc.,
198 Madison Avenue, New York, NY10016

British Library Cataloguing in Publication Data
A catalogue record for this book is available from the British Library

Library of Congress Cataloging-in-Publication Data
A catalog record for this book is available from the Library of Congress

ISBN 0 340 76194 6

1 2 3 4 5 6 7 8 9 10

Typeset in 9.5 on 13pt Baskerville Book by Phoenix Photosetting, Chatham, Kent
Printed and bound in Great Britain by The Bath Press, Bath

What do you think about this book? Or any other Arnold title?
Please send your comments to feedback.arnold@hodder.co.uk

There has been much complaint of late years of the growth, both in the world of trade and in that of the intellect, of quackery, and especially of puffing; but nobody seems to have remarked that these are the inevitable fruits of immense competition; of a state of society where any voice not pitched in an exaggerated key is lost in the hubbub. Success in so crowded a field depends not upon what a person is but upon what he seems; mere marketable qualities become the object instead of substantial ones, and a man's labour and capital are expended less in doing anything than in persuading other people that he has done it. Our own age seems to have brought this evil to its consummation. For the first time, arts for attracting public attention form a necessary part of the qualifications even of the deserving; and skill in these goes farther than any quality towards ensuring success.

J.S. Mill, *Essay on Civilisation*, 1836

Performance, the theatre of politics, is an essentially supplementary activity. It is not – or, at least it should not be – an end in itself. Yet, increasingly, journalists judge politicians, and politicians judge each other, according to what are euphemistically called 'communication skills'. When that happens, politics qualifies for the criticism that Stephen Sondheim makes of grand opera: 'What sort of show is it that regards the singer as more important than the song?'

Roy Hattersley, *James Cameron Memorial Lecture*, 1996

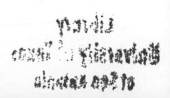

This book is dedicated to the people
who decided to protest their opposition
to the government's policy on war with Iraq
by marching and gathering at Hyde Park in London
on 15 February 2003, instead of staying at home
and watching the demonstration, packaged by
spin doctors, pundits and journalists on
the early evening television news

Contents

Acknowledgements

Writing a book can be a lonely business: at worst, a long and solitary slog. But by the time the acknowledgements are written, the project is all but over and the next book is already behind schedule. The hope that the book will prove useful to students of political communication and political journalism casts a mellifluous and obscuring haze over what until very recently had been a stressful, overdue commitment.

The loneliness of the long-distance writer is unthinkable without the routine support of friends and colleagues, as well as the contribution of specialist knowledge by a host of communication professionals who are not only willing to be interviewed about their involvement in political communications, but are enthusiastic about the prospect. I am very grateful to the many journalists and editors in local, regional and national media, the local and national politicians and their election agents, the local government public relations officers and the members of the Government Information and Communications Service (GICS) and the Government News Network (GNN) who have given me so much of their time across the last fifteen years to discuss the growing significance of media in political life.

I am also eager to thank the 'usual suspects', as well as some new colleagues, who have been willing to discuss ideas, offer support and invariably lift my spirits with their energy and industry as well as their horror stories about work schedules sometimes further behind than my own. In this respect a good deal is owed to Jay Blumler, Peter Cole, Simon Cottle, John Corner, Chas Critcher, James Curran, David Deacon, Peter Golding, Tony Harcup, Martin Harrison, John Horgan, Richard Keeble, Brian McNair, David Miller, Geoff Mungham, David Murphy, Ralph Negrine, Tom O'Malley, Julian Petley, Greg Philo, Rod Pilling, John Richardson, Colin Seymour Ure, James Stanyer, Granville Williams, Kevin Williams, Brian Winston and Dominic Wring.

Students too demand a vote of thanks for the unique support they provide by showing their interest and enthusiasm for what is on offer in lectures: but also for their curiosity and criticism in seminars. The students in the departments of Sociological Studies and, more recently Journalism Studies, at the University of Sheffield who have taken my options on 'Manufacturing Consent', 'Media and Social Policy' and 'Political Communications', have been amazingly kind and helpful; thanks particularly to Ioannis

Kolovos for his remarkable energy and the constant supply of cuttings and websites he has kindly steered me towards. To those students who have chosen to become working journalists or public relations specialists working in political communications, I hope the course provided insights that proved helpful.

The biggest debts should be repaid last: and that's my intention. My weekly 'lunch appointments' for beans on toast, a good old-fashioned gossip and routine ruminations on the problems confronting higher education with labour historian, political scientist and my good friend Steve Ludlam have been great fun as well as very valuable. Finally, love and thanks to Annie for keeping me company and so much more.

Bob Franklin
April 2003

List of Tables

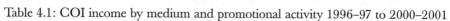

Part 1
Political communications and packaging politics

Chapter One

PACKAGING POLITICS: ☐
AN OVERVIEW OF THE ARGUMENT

On 11 September 2001, within minutes of the attack on the World Trade Center in New York, government spin doctor Jo Moore circulated an email to her colleagues in the press office at the Department of Trade and Industry suggesting, 'it's now a very good day to get out anything we want to bury' (*Daily Telegraph*, 10 October, p. 2). When the email was leaked to the press, members of the public, journalists and politicians expressed their concern at such a cynical and opportunist attempt to manage the news: especially by a publicly funded civil servant. Older and wiser journalistic counsels offered more seasoned appraisals. 'Spin of this kind isn't new', Peter Preston suggested. On the contrary, 'it is as old as politicians in a jam. Proclaim bright triumphs from the rooftops and slip out the garbage via the back door ... it's what these advisers are there for' (Preston, 2001, p. 17). A reader's letter from a retired press officer in the Government Information and Communication Service (GICS) during the previous Conservative administration, confirmed that 'this kind of news manipulation was standard practice ... On the day of the appalling Dunblane shootings, my colleagues and I were instructed by our chief press officer to release any "bad" news stories for the very reason that they would be overlooked or "buried" in the next day's coverage of events' (*Guardian*, 10 October 2001, p. 23). As if to underscore the routine character of Moore's news management suggestion, her email carried the standard GICS heading 'Media Handling'.

While this incident attracted widespread media attention and understandable public opprobrium, the significant revelation of this story was not the moral misjudgement or culpability of an individual government spin doctor, but the extent to which politicians' determination to set the news agenda, to use media to inform, shape and manage public discourse about policy and politics, have become crucial components in a modern statecraft which I wish to describe as the packaging of politics. Others have preferred different labels to characterise essentially the same development in contemporary political processes and institutions of governance. For Jay Blumler these trends form part of the 'modern publicity process' (Blumler, 1990) which reflects and, in turn, shapes the growing 'crisis in public communication' (Blumler and Gurevitch, 1995). Others have characterised these developments as 'designer democracy' (Scammell, 1995), the activity of the 'public relations state' (Deacon and Golding, 1994), the workings of the newly established 'public relations democracy' (Davis, 2002), the 'Americanization' of British political communications (Negrine, 1996), or the 'politics of Labour camp' where, following Susan Sontag, camp is defined as 'the consistently aesthetic experience of the world ... which incarnates a victory of "style" over "content"' (Bayley, 1998, p. 7). The extent of politicians' commitment to the packaging of politics, as central to the processes of governance in Britain, was exemplified by press reporting of Alastair Campbell's resignation as Labour's Director of Communications on 29 August 2003. Coverage was extensive and highlighted Campbell's crucial role in the success of the Labour government. The *Mirror* headline described him as 'The Most Powerful Man in Britain' (*Mirror*, 30 August 2003) while the *Sun* acknowledged Campbell as the 'The King of Spin' and the 'Deputy Prime Minister': for Tony Blair, Campbell's departure was akin to 'having his brain removed' – 'Blair without Campbell is like fish without chips, unimaginable!' (*Sun*, 30 August 2003, p. 14). The story of Campbell's resignation formed the front-page lead in every broadsheet newspaper and editorial: 'Exit The Spinmeister' – *The Independent*; 'Campbell's Farewell to Downing Street' – *Telegraph*; 'Campbell is To Quit Number Ten' – *Financial Times*; 'The End of Labour's Spin Cycle?' – *The Times*; and 'Time for Labour to Jump off Spin Roundabout?' – *Guardian*).

Significantly, despite widespread press criticism of the news management structures which Campbell had created in government and at Number Ten, his 'battle' with the BBC over his alleged role in 'sexing up' the 'dodgy' dossier about weapons in Iraq, the death of David Kelly (the source for journalist Andrew Gilligan's story about the dossier), as well as the continuing Hutton inquiry, political journalists were sceptical about the suggestion that these events and Campbell's departure might signal the end of spin. Hugo Young, for example, argued that news management and spin have become so deeply embedded in the structures of governance that 'it is fanciful to imagine that spinning will come to an end in the post Campbell utopia ... in the struggle to capture the public mind, spinning is the most elementary weapon' (Young, 2003, p20). The *Financial Times*' political editor confirmed Young's assessment, suggesting 'the idea that there can be a return to a golden era of spin-free politics will almost certainly prove false' (*Financial Times* 30 August 2003, p. 13). But the Labour party used Campbell's departure to announce precisely this, according to the *Mirror*, 'Tony Blair was preparing to re-launch New Labour as a "spin-free zone"' (*Mirror*, 30 August 2003, p. 4). Ironically, a number of newspapers reported that Campbell had been 'counselled' about how best 'to finesse his departure' in ways which would permit 'No. 10 to hail the end of spin', by Peter Mandelson, believed by many to be the architect of New Labour's media strategy and the consummate practitioner of the 'black art' of spin (*Guardian*, 1 September 2003, p. 2; *Daily Express*, 30 August 2003, p. 7).

Politicians' preoccupation with using the media to win approval for their policies and senior politicians is, of course, not a new feature of the British political landscape: it is as old as politicians' love of kissing babies. In the Labour party, the first Press and Publicity Department was established in 1917 (Hollins, 1981, p. 46), while debates within the party about whether election campaigns should be 'image' or 'issue' driven, began in the 1920s

(Wring, 1997, pp. 13–14). As part of that continuing debate, Tony Benn criticised Aneurin Bevan for his apparently 'absurd idea that all publicity is unimportant and that all you need is the right policy' (Benn, 1994, p. 190). Throughout the 1960s, Harold Wilson, who exploited his media image to great political effect, remarked with tongue-in-cheek but a growing accuracy, that 'most of politics is presentation and what isn't is timing' (quoted in Mitchell, 1982, p. 207). What is undoubtedly new in contemporary political communications is the belief that the presentation of policy, whether by government, political party or interest group, is at least as significant as any substantive policy content. 'What they can't seem to grasp', a Labour spin doctor announced after the 1997 election, 'is that communications is not an after thought to our policy. It's central to the whole mission of new Labour' (Gaber, 1998, p. 13).

It was the election of the first Thatcher administration during the late 1970s which marked a radical shift in both the extent and nature of politicians' enthusiasm for targeting the media to present themselves and their policies to the public. During the 1980s and 1990s, enthusiasm became obsession as politicians tried to influence and regulate the flow of political information and messages via mass media to an unprecedented degree. In this process, politicians and policies have become 'packaged' for media presentation and public consumption. Lord Young, who was Minister at the Department of Trade and Industry in 1988 announced, in a phrase which captured the mood of the time, 'the government's, policies are like cornflakes, if they are not marketed they will not sell' (*PR Week*, 16 March, 1988).

The thesis concerning the packaging of politics is informed by three broad assumptions. First, politicians in government and political parties have revealed a growing commitment to using the media to market their policies and their leaders to the public. In the words of columnist Matthew Parris 'politicians run on publicity like horses run on oats' (*Sun*, 14 February, 1998). It is difficult to overstate the centrality of media to politicians' identity and their perception of what it means to engage with the political world. Labour Minister John Battle, for example, claimed 'to be in the media is to exist as a politician. Politicians see themselves as another consumer product and anxiously ask: "Are they still buying me?" In other words, there is a temptation for my whole political existence to be determined by media coverage, constantly living in a world of the immediate, superficial and easily consumable concepts' (John Battle MP, *The Catholic Post*, 1992, cited in Garner and Short, 1998, p. 181).

Second, governments are increasingly adept at using media to package politics and devote expansive financial and human resources to the enterprise. The prime minister's official spokesperson briefs the lobby twice daily delivering the government's spin on key political issues to the 200 most senior political journalists at Westminster. Governments similarly enjoy access to the 1200 press and public relations specialists in the GICS, the 300 officers in the Government News Network (GNN), the Strategic Communications Unit (SCU), the Number Ten press office and the growing band of special advisers in the various departments of state (Jones, 2002). Governments also employ marketing consultants and advertising staff to design and implement specific policy campaigns as well as the 'Forth-bridge-style' activity of preening the government's public image. Such grooming is a costly business: in 2001, the government's advertising expenditure reached an unprecedented £295 million making it the largest purchaser of advertising services in the UK. Labour's budget for a single advertising campaign designed to tackle benefit fraud, matched MacDonald's advertising spend to promote Big Macs (Chapter 4).

Third, this ambition to package politics poses a number of challenges to democracies. The relationship between government and media can become unduly collusive yet asymmetrical, with the media acting as little more than conduits for government policy messages, drafted by press officers and special advisers but mistaken by readers and viewers as the work of independent journalists (Franklin, 1997, p. 19). In these circumstances, the role of media in informing the public sphere and creating the 'informed citizen' who makes 'rational' policy choices may be substantially diminished as governments try to set the media agenda in ways which exclude certain policy options rather than offering audiences the widest possible policy agenda (Franklin, 1999, p. 9).

A number of political and media developments have encouraged this increasing emphasis on the packaging of politics. First, the current generation of politicians does not suffer the instinctive estrangement from television so typified by Churchill, but feels at ease with television and understands its characteristic discourse. While Attlee's replies to interviewers' questions were so famously monosyllablic that it was once said of him that 'Conversation should be like a game of tennis, but with Clem it's like tossing biscuits to a dog' (Benn, 2001, p. 337), Ken Livingstone acknowledges that he 'grew up watching television. I watched everything that was on from 1956 when I was eleven until joining the Labour Party and being out every evening. I *think* in soundbites' (Fountain, 1993, p. 14). Tony Benn adapted to the changing requirements of his trade: party media advisers taught him how! 'I can do a soundbite' he claims with a hint of pride in his voice, 'I've been trained, I can give you twenty seconds on any known subject – because I'd rather I edited it than they [the media] did' (Benn, 2001, p. 336). Consequently, in 1997, voters who knew little else of Labour's plans for government, understood their intention to be 'Tough on crime and tough on the causes of crime' along with their commitment to 'Education, Education, Education' (Franklin, 1998).

Second, there has also been a growing professionalisation of the presentation of politics (Franklin, 1999; Kavanagh 1995; Norris *et al.*, 1999). The 1980s witnessed a dramatic expansion in political parties' communication staffs and their commitment to developing communication and marketing strategies: an expansion which has been sustained into the new millennium. The trend has been replicated in central and local government with consequent increases in press and communication staffs (Chapters 2, 3, 4 and 5) along with unprecedentedly high advertising budgets (Chapters 4 and 5).

Third, the sheer burgeoning of media outlets including the Internet, but especially the rapid increase in radio and television services – prompted by new satellite, cable and digital delivery systems and government policy ambitions for de-regulation – means there are greater opportunities for politicians to make media appearances. In 2001, 40,000 hours of programming was broadcast every week, while the existence of 250 channels with the resulting audience fragmentation, creates for the first time opportunites for targeting 'niche audiences' (DTI and DCMS, 2000, para 1.1.2).

Fourth, politics has become populist with politicians keen to appear on television chat shows as well as political programmes; many believe the former may be more significant. Charles Kennedy, for example, argues that 'A programme like *Have I Got News For You?* has a gigantic audience compared with *On The Record* or *Newsnight* and you're getting exposure with people who never watch politics. It's important in that marketing sense' (Fountain, 1993, p. 14). Sir Gordon Reece promptly persuaded Mrs Thatcher to eschew appearances on the *Today* programme or *P.M.* in favour of the presentational benefits to be gleaned from *Jimmy Young Programme*, while Tony Blair's appearances on *Richard and Judy* suggest he is also aware of the political rewards to be derived from reaching the substantial audiences for day-time entertainment programmes. A potentially troublesome consequence of such populism for democratic polities has been the growing tendency of successive American and British, among other governments, to promote social and welfare issues by incorporating policy messages into prime time soap opera storylines: it is uncertain whether these inclusions inform, persuade or merely 'soft-soap the public' about policy concerns (Franklin, 1999; Brennen, 2000; see Chapter 4).

Fifth, the growth in media outlets combined with the availability of four 24-hour news channels, has triggered a substantial expansion in news and current affairs programming, although audiences remain modest (Hargreaves and Thomas, 2002), except in times of war: *Al Jazeera*, for example, recorded 4 million new European subscriptions during the first week of the war against Iraq (*Guardian*, 24 March 2003). Television reporting of the 2001 election was more typical. Coverage was slightly reduced on terrestrial channels compared to 1997 but, despite viewer apathy, remained considerable (Deacon, *et al.*, 2001, p. 104; Harrison, 2002, p. 133–4). It is sobering to recall that television reporting of elections only began in 1959 (the 'first television election') when confronted by the current and extensive election coverage.

Finally, media are constantly gaining access to political arenas from which they were previously excluded. The press won the right to report local council and committee meetings in 1960 and 1972 respectively. March 2003 marked the 25th anniversary of journalists' access to Parliament for radio broadcasting of proceedings, while television cameras began to broadcast from the House of Lords in January 1985 but were denied access to the Commons until November 1989: live uninterrupted webcasting from the Commons began in 2002 (see Chapter 8).

PACKAGING PARTIES, GOVERNMENTS AND PARLIAMENT

The packaging of politics is evident in the operation of many political institutions and processes, although the activities of political parties during general elections offer perhaps the clearest example. Parties have recruited small armies of media advisers to develop strategies for promoting electorally favourable media images of their leaders and key policies. Internationally distinguished film directors like Hugh Hudson, Mike Newell and Stephen Frears have been commissioned to transform the humble party election broadcasts (PEBs) of the early 1970s into expensive, slick and persuasive agitprop productions. Political communications has become an expensive business. It is estimated that the political parties spent £25,949,685 on the 2001 election campaign (Watt and Tempest, 2001, p. 14). But politicians and pundits of every kind have come to believe that the way media report the election campaign and the ability of parties to incorporate their messages into media coverage is crucial to the election result (see Chapter 6).

At the constituency level, local parties have adopted the media-based campaigning strategies of their national counterparts. In the run up to local, European, but especially general, elections local parties establish a communications team with a brief to devise a media strategy combining both news management and advertising elements. Locally, parties target the local and regional press: nationally, television is the preferred medium for campaigning. At the constituency level, parties believe that packaging political messages for media dissemination is considerably more effective in winning electoral support than direct 'face-to-face' meetings with voters. The columns of the local rag have superseded election meetings in draughty village halls as the locus classicus for winning the hearts and minds of voters (see Chapter 7).

Politicians in central government can draw on the advertising, marketing and campaigning skills of the specialist press and information officers working in the GICS to promote their policies. The 1990s witnessed a phenomenal growth in government advertising budgets with campaigns focused on the NHS, the reduction of benefit fraud and the prevention of teenage pregnancy: in the 1980s the focus for advertising was the privatising of nationalized industries, 'Action For Jobs' and public health information campaigns about HIV/AIDS. Between 1982 and 1989 government publicity expenditure rocketed from £60.5 to £200 million (Cobb, 1989a, p. 12). Expenditure reduced under the Major governments but since 1997 and the election of new Labour, it has reached record levels: the government spent £97 million on advertising in the three months prior to the 2001 election (Chapter 4). This expansion in government advertising, whether by Conservative or Labour governments, has proved contentious because of the high levels of public expenditure involved, as well as the claims of opposition politicians that the government has too frequently crossed the line which divides 'government information' from 'government propaganda' (Chapters 3 and 4).

There are other media management opportunities for politicians in government. The prime minister's official spokesperson's daily briefings with the lobby help to structure and inform the political news in the television and radio bulletins of the day and newspapers' political coverage on the following day. Since October 2003, David Hill, Alastair Campbell's successor chairs the daily 9 a.m. communications meeting with the SCU, special advisers and senior press officers from Whitehall departments, designed for 'rapid rebuttal', preparation for the 11 a.m. lobby and the resolution of any problematic media management issues arising from the first editions of the newspapers. Again these arrangements have proved contentious with officials in the GICS, opposition politicians and senior journalists alleging that the government manipulates news media to an unacceptable degree and in ways which challenge democratic protocols (Ingham, 2003; Oborne, 1999): government relations with journalists are judged to be so manipulative, that the designation of the government as 'control freaks' has become relatively commonplace (Jones, 2002).

In local government too there has been a growing preoccupation with the presentation and packaging of politics. The vast majority (85 per cent) of the larger authorities (London boroughs, metropolitan authorities and unitary authorities) have established public relations departments which, in the case of one unitary authority employs almost 50 staff with one London borough enjoying a budget of just less than £4 million (Chapter 5). The 1980s witnessed a rapid expansion, both in terms of staffing and budgets, in these locally based public relations departments which has continued to the present. Typically staffed by ex-local journalists, with a detailed knowledge of both the political and media scene locally, the key brief for these departments is news management of local and, occasionally, national media. Local newspapers and to some extent local radio, hard pressed for financial but especially journalistic resources, have in many cases become overly reliant on what Gandy terms 'information subsidies' emanating from local government press offices (Gandy, 1982). These public relations specialists are so successful in influencing the news agenda in local newspapers that they have been dubbed 'the last bastion of good municipal journalism' (Harrison, 1998, p. 168). It is unclear, however, if readers of the local rag are aware of the extent to which the newspaper's coverage of local government and politics has been inspired or even drafted by a press officer in the employment of the local authority, rather than a local journalist. During the late 1980s, local government public relations officers' success in manipulating local media news agendas, especially during the campaign against abolition of the Greater London Council, prompted conflict with politicians in central government. A war was waged for communications supremacy in the local political arena. Central government emerged the victor, but only after it had legislated to restrict and censor many aspects of local government's communications practices (see Chapter 5).

The arrival of cameras in the Commons since 1989 has created further media-management opportunities for politicians. For its part, the public enjoys new opportunities to see politicians perform in the House at close quarters. Gaffes committed at the despatch box are relayed promptly to millions of viewers watching the six o'clock news. But politicians receive training from their party or by officers of the House, depending on their seniority, in how to 'perform' successfully before the cameras. The televising of proceedings offers parties and individual MPs considerable, if highly variable, communication possibilities. The government's prominence in House proceedings, combined with its role in driving the business of the House, guarantees the party of government communication advantages over the various opposition parties. In the run up to the 2001 general election, politicians attempted to exploit television coverage to electoral advantage. At PMQs the television cameras offered Tony Blair and William Hague a shop window in which to present their leadership qualities, along with their policy portfolios, to the electorate. More Machiavellian news manipulation is also possible with carefully drafted questions, placed by the whips with compliant back-benchers, allowing the prime minister opportunities to make a statement about an area of policy success. In the constituency setting, MPs are eager to appear in regional parliamentary programming which help to establish incumbent MPs' identity with local voters giving them potential electoral advantage over a new challenger (see Chapter 8).

Changes to media as well as political structures have encouraged this packaging of politics. The development of local and national newspaper monopolies, the concentration of local press ownership in substantial national and international media corporations, the increasing willingness of some newspaper editors to barter their newspaper's political support for a knighthood, politicians' growing demands for statutory press regulation, the growth of free newspapers with their editorial reliance on non-journalistic sources of news and the emergence of local 'municipal' or 'civic' free papers published by PROs in the pay of local politicians, each signal expansive opportunities for politicians to influence the reporting of political news.

Changes in British broadcasting deriving from new technology, but especially recent government policy embodied in the Communications Act 2003, similarly create opportunities for politicians to package their communications for public consumption. The proliferation of television and radio services both locally and nationally, the fragmentation of audiences, the emergence of a market driven multi-channel broadcast system, changing interpretations and commitments to the idea of public service broadcasting, changing commitments to content regulation and the de-regulation of media ownership and cross media ownership, politicians renewed enthusiasm for regulating broadcasting and a reassessment of the role, functions and finance of the BBC are some of the features of Britain's developing broadcasting system. Many of these changes have consolidated the process of packaging politics while diminishing the competence of broadcast media to operate as a fourth estate (Franklin, 2001, 1997; Chapters 6, 7 and 9).

PACKAGING POLITICS: INFORMING, PERSUADING OR MISLEADING THE PUBLIC?

This trend towards packaging politics has attracted both advocates and critics. Many politicians, broadcasters and academic observers believe it is an almost inevitable consequence of developments in media technology: there is a discernible whiff of technological determinism in the widely touted claim that 'you can't de-invent television'. But advocates argue that the packaging of politics enhances the processes of a democratic polity. Political communication via television, press and radio guarantees that people receive greater information about political issues, events and personalities: and in a more readily comprehensible and accessible form. A well-produced party election broadcast is a more effective vehicle for communicating party policy than a thousand poorly attended public meetings. The consequent growth in public awareness prompts enhanced voter interest in election campaigns and the activities of government which, in turn, increases or at least sustains voter turnout. Politicians' systematic use of media-based communication strategies expands the public's information base from which people can draw as voters to make an informed choice between political parties during elections, or as citizens to assess the competence of government and thereby render politicians accountable. In brief, packaging politics increases public knowledge, citizen participation and government accountability (McNair, 2000; Scammell, 1995, p. 18). Consequently, the new media-based politics improves the 'extent, quantity and efficiency of communications between voters and parties' (Harrop, 1990, 283). These are substantive claims.

Critics allege that the political process is being diminished by growing media involvement: the charge is that media *corrupt* as well as *communicate* political messages. The process of packaging politics *manipulates*, as well as *informs*, the public. In Britain's media democracy the presentational *form* of political communications has become more significant than the substantive policy *content*. Image has supplanted substance; the manicure is everything. In the early days of the 1997 Labour government Mandelson, in his role as coordinater of communications, was explicit. 'There are some who still denigrate the presentation of policy as a diversion from its substance, as a superficial and unnecessary coating to the main product', he argued, 'I take the opposite view ... If a government policy cannot be presented in a simple and attractive way, it is more likely than not to contain fundamental flaws and prove to be the wrong policy' (Mandelson, 16 September 1997). The election of the politically inexperienced Hollywood star Arnold

Schwarznegger to the office of Governor of California (8 October 2003), the fifth largest economy in the world, seemed to confirm the supremacy of style over policy substance. It prompted the *Guardian G2* to ask on its front page, 'Is This The End Of Politics?' (*Guardian G2*, 9 October 2003, p. 1).

Packaging politics, moreover, impoverishes political debate by oversimplifying and trivialising political communications. Negative attacks on opponents' policies have come to be preferred by many politicians, as well as judged to be more effective, to the positive elaboration of their own case. Packaging politics places a premium on personalities and presidentialism. Persistent television portrayals of a select clique of 'telegenic' politicians, mouthing pre-rehearsed slogans and automaton soundbites, has supplanted the rational and sustained advocacy of policy. Photo opportunities represent the logical conclusion of this process of packaging politics. Even the staccato soundbite is judged unduly loquacious and consequently redundant. The politicians are blessedly silent; they offer no hostages to electoral fortune. The communication specialists are happy to let the appropriate image 'speak for itself'. They have succumbed to the claims of their own cliche that 'a good photograph can say more than a thousand words'. Carefully packaged, coiffured and colour co-ordinated, but rendered silent by the communications advisers, modern politicians need only smile, look statesman-like, clasp a calf in their arms, or head a football with Kevin Keegan while offering mute endorsement of party orthodoxy. Without words, the photo opportunity attempts communication via a curious and rather eery form of body language or political mime. Effective political communications has become a harrowingly quiet business.

Given this analysis, some politicians have come to believe that the process of packaging politics threatens to *subvert*, rather than *nurture* the democratic process. Tony Benn attributes these developments to the media and the communications advisers who have risen to prominence in political parties and government in recent times. He argues that 'the media, the pollsters, the people who hype it up and the public relations people who engage in politics have taken the democratic process away from us and made it something that highly paid experts want to manage for us' (HC Debs., 1990, Col. 1264). 'The whole business of focus groups, spin doctors and rebuttal units' moreover 'proliferates the idea that there is some alternative to getting out and listening to people and talking to people ... the machinery of rebuttal – if anybody says anything about anything, the computer will tell you something he said that was different – is simply a sort of mechanism for repudiating any argument without having to listen to it' (Benn, 2001, p. 337). Benn's conclusion is that 'it'll be the media that destroys democracy. They have cultivated a little clique of politicians whose constituencies are Lime Grove North and Broadcasting House South' (quoted in Fountain, 1993, p. 15). It follows that the task for politicians is to 'recover democracy for the people from the media' (HC Debs., 1990, Col. 1264). But Benn is wrong. The media have not hijacked politics. The reverse proposition, that politicians have attempted to hijack the media, might approximate the truth more closely, but to state the matter so baldly would represent a gross oversimplification.

What remains uncontested is that packaging politics has profound implications both for politicians and citizens in a media democracy. Some of the consequences for politicians have been discussed: the emphasis on image and appearance, the constraints on political discourse which must now be conducted via soundbites, the need to become accomplished in media performance. Politicians like Michael Foot learned their considerable skills for political rhetoric and oratory at factory gate meetings and turbulent hustings, where the ability to project the voice above the heckling crowd was a prerequisite for political success. By the mid-1980s, the process of packaging politics had reduced distinguished politicians to the status of mere anachronisms and curiosities. The political skills once so crucial for devastating opponents in Parliament, building a formidable reputation for debate and making claims for political leadership, were redundant in an age of political communication via broadcast media. Some politicians were unable to accommodate their political style to the changing political communications climate. Benn recalls 'the first time Nye Bevan did a television broadcast. I took him to Broadcasting House and he couldn't sit down: we had to have a stand mike and Nye walked round addressing it' (Benn, 2001, p. 336).

The consequences of packaging politics for citizens are greater; the implications for democracy more worrying. It has resulted in a decline in the number of face-to-face encounters between politicians and the public. Political meetings even during a general election campaign have become a rarity. Politicians seem reluctant to devote two hours to rallying a room full of the party faithful when they believe that a twenty-second clip on television will prove electorally more effective. Media based campaigning has resulted in nothing less significant than 'the death of the public meeting as part of the political process' (Young, 1992, p. 23). It is remarkable how few obituaries have commented on the passing of this crucial mechanism for political communication and participation in the political process.

Few citizens now have any direct knowledge of political matters independent of the media. But audiences have grown increasingly sceptical and uninterested in media presentations of politics. Serious consequences flow from such scepticism since voters' reliance on media for knowledge of political affairs may diminish rather than promote political activity. Twenty years ago, Blumler put on record his disquiet 'that more and more people seem to be getting into a frame of mind where campaign propaganda is almost automatically expected to be off-putting ... there is even evidence that electoral participation ... may falter as respect for political talk diminishes' (Blumler, 1981, p. 59). Electoral history, which records a sustained decline in turnout for general elections since the 1970s, including the lowest voting figures recorded since 1918 for the 2001 election, signals Blumler's observation as portentous: 5 millon less voters turned out in 2001 than 1997.

The public's lack of participation and diminishing interest in politics, combined with a growing scepticism about political affairs, may eventually come to challenge the authority and legitimacy of modern government. Liberal political theory, which informs most modern democratic systems, argues that citizen obligation is rooted in consent which is expressed in the act of voting. But Pateman argues that citizens must be clear about the nature of the commitment they are making when they vote. They must also be certain about the reasons underlying their decision. But such clarity of purpose and reason are undermined by election campaigns in which 'parties and candidates are "sold" to the electorate like commodities, not for their political worth but for their commercial "image" ' (Pateman, 1979, p. 88): policies and politicians branded and marketed like cornflakes or Big Macs (Chapter 4).

In Britain's media democracy politics, like football, has become an armchair activity. Watching the match from a ringside seat at home has replaced the need to play the game. Participation in a media democracy is essentially ersatz and vicarious. In the radical and direct democracies enjoyed by Athens and advocated by Rousseau, citizen participation was crucial and encouraged; political communication was unproblematic. Everyone could attend the assembly, hear and contribute to the debate and participate in decision-making. Yet at a time when the Internet with its interactive capacity promises the possibility of remaking a public sphere in which universal participation in debate and decision making is at hand, the packaging of politics dictates a different reality. In media democracy citizens' voices are barely audible. They are as silent as the politicians featured in the photo opportunity. They speak only as the faceless mass whose aggregated opinions have been 'polled' by MORI, ICM or Gallup for the mutual convenience of media and politicians. Citizens have become passive receivers, no longer active participants, in the dialogue of democracy. For the greater part of the time they remain worryingly silent.

POLITICIANS AND THE MEDIA: ADVERSARIES OR ACCOMPLICES?

Richard Littlejohn, the *Sun* columnist, entertains few doubts about his role as a journalist: 'The job of someone like me', he claims, 'is to sit at the back and throw bottles'. Politicians constitute his favourite targets. He believes they are well placed to defend themselves. 'They employ an entire industry', he suggests, 'often using public money, to present themselves as favourably as possible and I certainly don't see it as my job to inflate the egos of little men' (*Guardian*, 22 February 1993). A more forceful advocacy of the press as a fourth estate is hard to imagine.

But everyday relationships between politicians and journalists are less adversarial than this account: indeed the typical pattern is a relationship in which the two groups work in complementary if not collusive ways. Journalists and politicians each have ambitions, interests and needs which can be achieved most readily when they can win the co-operation of the other group. Politicians, for example, need the media as conduits for their political messages to the public. They remain wary of broadcasters, but are eager to sieze the communications opportunities which news media provide. For their part, journalists understand that without at least a minimal co-operation from politicians they cannot guarantee a credible and well informed political journalism: without the 'support' of politicians, the project of political journalism may become impossible. In brief the relationship between politicians and journalists is best viewed as an exchange relationship in which insider political information and opinion is traded for coverage in news media (Ericson *et al.*, 1989). Each set of actors is crucially dependent on the other and the packaging of politics reflects and, in turn, nurtures this mutual reliance. The relationship is symbiotic, serving and meeting divergent and contrasting needs for each group, but uniting both because of the overlapping of their fundamental purposes. Recognition of this mutuality of interests has drawn the two groups closer together to the point where they become 'inextricably linked' (Blumler and Gurevitch, 1981, p. 473).

Conflicts between politicians and journalists remain not merely possible but an endemic feature of this broadly co-operative and consensual relationship, for two reasons. First, politicians and journalists hold divergent perceptions of the fundamental purposes of political communication. For journalists, political communication presents opportunities to educate and enlighten the electorate; for politicians the purpose is to persuade voters to their point of view (ibid., p. 485). The ambitions of information and propaganda seem destined to collide. Second, since the relationship is governed and regulated by mutual acknowledgement and respect for an 'unspoken' set of rules and conventions, the relationship will necessarily begin to fissure if one party 'breaks the rules'. Consequently, conflict inevitably arises if a journalist publishes an embargoed story, makes public use of an off-the-record statement, or identifies a source. Similarly, if a politician leaks a major story to another journalist, disavows a statement made previously to a journalist or denies a journalist an interview, the relationship will begin to break down. But it is in the interests of both parties to negotiate and repair any breaches to re-establish a viable way of working together; a process which has been described as 'mutual adaptation' (ibid., p. 472).

In the British setting, the lobby offers the clearest institutional expression of mutual adaptation by politicians and journalists. It allows journalists privileged access to the very heart of government. Unattributable briefings by senior politicians and press officers provide journalists with insider views on the key political issues of the day. For politicians, the lobby provides considerable opportunities to manipulate news agendas and place their particular spin on political news. Relationships between politicians and journalists are literally formalised in a handbook of rules governing lobby journalists' behaviour. But even a cursory glance at the history of the lobby, especially the period when the *Guardian*, the *Independent* and the *Scotsman* withdrew their lobby correspondents, reveals considerable conflict between politicians and journalists (Jones, 2002; Oborne, 1999). But the significant benefits which both groups derive from the lobby, guarantee that new ways of working together to overcome transient problems are developed. Mutual adaptation ensured, if not the return of each of these papers to the lobby, the continued operation of the overall system (see Chapter 2). In brief, the relationship between politicians and journalists can be characterised as a marriage of convenience, albeit a volatile marriage, which is plagued by temporary separations. Cook prefers the metaphor of journalists and politicians 'sleeping together' although the shifting balance of power within their relationship ensures that 'no one ends up being consistently dominant' (Cook, 1989, p. 30). Mancini is linguistically more measured preferring to characterise journalists' relationships with politicians as fundamentally ambivalent and oscillating between 'trust and suspicion' (Mancini, 1993, p. 33). Analysed within this framework, political news and current affairs have come to be understood not as the outcome of any adversarial encounter but as the product of a process of mutual construction by politicians and the media. 'The final draft of the newspaper article or TV news broadcast is', according to Mancini, 'the result of a long process of negotiation between journalists and politicians' (ibid., p. 34).

The process of mutual adaptation is driven by a strategic complementarity of interests. Politicians value their relationship with journalists because the media can fulfil invaluable functions for them. Politicians, for example, use the media to create and maintain a high public profile. They are essential to what Mancini describes as politicians' 'quest for fame' (ibid., p. 37). Ken Livingstone considers television appearances to be crucial in sustaining his public visibility. 'It's vital for me that the public remembers I'm still alive,' he claims. 'Going on *Have I Got News For You?* is one way of continuing to have a political base' (Fountain, 1993, p. 14).

Media may also help politicians in their efforts to stimulate public awareness and support for particular policy initiatives: essentially an agitprop function (Franklin, 1999, p. 22). In this way, the media can serve as a surrogate or complementary, arena to Parliament. Politicians also use the media to assess or anticipate public reaction to a particular proposal or policy. Kellner claims that the lobby is often used in this way. Politicians' purpose is to 'fly kites' (Kellner, 1983, p. 279). If public reaction is strong and adverse, politicians can deny their intention to implement the policy denouncing the original story as nothing more than a press rumour. The media are also used routinely by politicians to set news agendas and create a favourable climate of public opinion about particular policies and issues. Politicians' growing preoccupation with spin to set media agendas is evident in the growing numbers of press releases they issue. In the two years following the 1997 election, for example, the Labour government issued 20,000 press releases, an 80 per cent increase on the output of the Major government (Cohen, 1999b, p. 15).

Politicians are also concerned to promote favourable images of themselves, their party or their government via the media. Most MPs seem eager for promotion, to climb 'the greasy pole'. But beyond individual instrumentalism, politicians are concerned to use the media to advance and promote their political cause and, in the case of political parties, to help them secure re-election (see Chapters 6 and 7).

Significantly, politicians use the media for unequivocally propagandist purposes. The government, for example, pays for advertisements on television, local radio and in newspapers to persuade people to do (or to stop doing) a range of activities including the need to 'Think before they drink and drive', to buy a television licence, to stop defrauding the welfare benefits system (or to inform on someone who is!), to help promote adult literacy, to practice safe sex or not to become pregnant if a teenager (Chapter 4). The purpose of such advertising is unashamedly propagandist. The government, moreover, uses the media so extensively in this way that it has become one of Britain's largest purchasers of advertising. In its first year in office, new Labour spent £165 millions on advertising while the launch of 172 campaigns during the first three months of 2001, contributed to the overall annual expenditure of £295 millions which placed the government in pole position for advertising spend ahead of Unilever (2nd) and BT (3rd) (Watt, 2001, p. 13).

Finally, television is, on occasion, considered capable of fulfilling even more significant functions for politicians. Schatz, for example, argues that the reason for televising the German Parliament, following the collapse of the Nazi regime in 1945, was to popularise the Bundestag and re-establish a democratic way of life in Germany. Schatz also suggests that the extension of television coverage to include the Volkskammer, the Parliament of the German Democratic Republic in 1990, gave television an important role in the process of German reunification (Schatz, 1992, p. 234). O'Donnell similarly argues that the admission of the cameras early in the life of the European Parliament reflected politicians' belief that television would be influential in establishing the legitimacy of the new assembly (O'Donnell, 1992, p. 254).

Politicians fulfil a smaller but no less significant range of functions for broadcasters and journalists. First, politicians' activities constitute a regular and major source of stories for journalists, which are significant both for their quantity and news value. As McNair noted, 'Politics is the staple food of journalistic work' (McNair, 2000, p. 43). Second, politicians themselves, both as individuals and via institutions such as the lobby, are a major source of political news for journalists. Lobby correspondents are briefed twice daily about political events while journalists also nurture their own individual sources which they rely on greatly for insider information. In the constituency setting, many local journalists are wholly dependent on the local MP to provide them with surveillance of the political landscape at Westminster. A journalist on a Huddersfield newspaper claimed the local MPs were the paper's, 'eyes and ears at the Commons' (Franklin, 1991, p. 23).

Third, politicians are invariably the star performers on news and political programmes, whether as the subject of a single interview or as a member of a panel discussing a particular topic. It is politicians' appearances, moreover, which endow the programmes with authority and credibility. Spin doctors are increasingly conscious of this credentialising function and discipline journalists by witholding comment or denying their bids for particular politicians if journalists have been critical of them previously. It is difficult to imagine that a flagship news or current affairs programme like *Panorama* or the *Today* programme, could survive for long without the continuing involvement of senior politicians.

Finally, Mancini claims that in Italy friendships with politicians can result in promotion for journalists and broadcasters (Mancini, 1993, p. 37). In the British setting there is a discernible trend for editors whose newspapers offer political support to the party of government to be rewarded with a knighthood (Franklin, 1994, p. 41). Some observers argue that the division between journalists and politicians is breaking down, reflecting the government's growing enthusiasm to appoint special advisers to work on government–media relations. These advisers are 'hybrids', part politician part journalist: Nicholas Jones dubs them 'journo-politicos' (Jones, 2001, p. 68).

In summary, relationships between politicians and the media should not be understood as simply adversarial: although on occasion they may be highly combative. Journalists and politicians may sometimes pursue different goals but this occurs within an agreed framework which offers potential benefits to both groups. Each group requires the other, no matter how reluctantly, to prosecute its own interests and purposes. Mutuality of interests drives and sustains the relationship. Journalists and politicians have become, in Blumer and Gurevitch's phrase, mutually dependent and mutually adaptive actors, shaping and regulating each others behaviour and jointly controlling mechanisms for resolving conflicts between them (Blumler and Gurevitch, 1981). Politicians' and journalists' mutual reliance prompts a continual adjustment of their relationships to ensure continuity despite the conflict and co-operation which characterises them. Politicians and journalists are certainly *adversaries* but, on occasion, they are just as certainly *accomplices* in the enterprise of political communication.

POLITICIANS' RELATIONS WITH MEDIA, HIERARCHIES, PARTISANSHIP AND RESOURCES

Within this overall framework, it is evident that politicians enjoy a wide and radically divergent range of possible relations with the media. Some of the factors which create this diversity are purely contingent and serendipitous. Particular MPs may previously have been journalists or broadcasters who retain professional skills, as well as close personal contacts among media personnel, which create untypical opportunities for media appearances. But there are other, less contingent factors, which structure politicians' relationships with media. Three are especially significant: the existence of hierarchies within media and political structures; the extent of overlap or dissonance between politicians' and media partisan commitments; and the considerable disparities in resources available to different sectors of the media and politicians.

POLITICAL AND MEDIA HIERARCHIES

Party and parliamentary political structures offer obvious hierarchies. The prime minister, senior members of Cabinet and government spokespeople are mirrored by an equivalent hierarchy of office within the official opposition party as well as the various minority parties: parliamentary parties are divided between front and back benches. Journalists are positioned in a similar hierarchy with its parameters demarcated at one extreme by 'star' interviewers, like the Dimblebys (David and Jonathan), David Frost, Trevor MacDonald and Jeremy Paxman, who perform on prestigious television news and current affairs programmes; at the other, by the junior journalist on the local free newspaper. These two parallel hierarchies structure relationships between politicians and journalists by matching and 'pairing' politicians with 'appropriate' media partners. Humble back-benchers lack the required political gravitas to merit an appearance on *Breakfast with Frost*, but they are crucially significant to the local newspaper, radio and regional television journalists who report affairs in their constituency. The Leeds University study of television broadcasting from the Commons confirmed regional programming as the predominant arena for back-benchers' appearances (First Report, 1989–90, p. 23). Back-benchers should not entertain media ambitions above their political station and would be advised to 'forget Front bench territory, the cloudy, rarely glimpsed Sunday peaks of ... *On The Record*' (Fountain, 1993, p. 14).

News values can occasionally disrupt this institutionalised 'matchmaking' and allow a back-bencher to be courted by media suitors who would generally consider themselves above such a partner. Back-benchers who are routinely critical of their own party leadership (Dianne Abbott, Alan Simpson and Dr Ian Gibson), or who persistently criticise their party on a major policy issue (Frank Field on pensions and social security, George Galloway on foreign affairs and the war in Iraq), or who possess an unusual interest and expertise in a particular policy area (Gwyneth Dunwoody on transport and railways and Austin Mitchell on fisheries and the European Union), can break free from the usual restraints which media and political hierarchies impose and enjoy untypical media flattery and be seduced with gifts of airtime.

Journalists are also conscious of being sited in a finely gradated hierarchy which influences their access to politicians. Journalists recognise that a very senior politician is more likely to respond favourably to a request for interview from a broadcaster working on a flagship news programme than a local journalist working on the *Heckmondwike Herald*. Politicians are utilitarians whose decisions about whether to grant an interview are informed by such considerations as the size of the audience, the prestige of the interviewer and the likely impact of the interview on public opinion. Acknowledging and exploiting to the full the advantages which their position in the media hierarchy bestows, is a precondition for journalistic advancement. 'There is a hierarchy discriminating between the various organs of information', Mancini argues, 'something the journalist must come to understand if he or she is to be successful in the field of political reporting' (Mancini, 1993, p. 41).

In summary, political and media hierarchies structure relationships between the groups in two ways. First, *different* politicians enjoy very different relationships with media expressing their location in a political hierarchy: the prime minister's relations with media will be radically different from those of a back-bencher. For their part, journalists will experience an equivalent diversity of relationships reflecting their variable location in a parallel media hierarchy. Second, but equally significantly, the *same* politician will enjoy highly variable relationships with journalists depending upon the extent of 'match' between their positions in their respective hierarchies; courted lavishly by the local press, for example, the local MPs' passion for the prestigious national media may be unrequited.

MATCHING PARTISANSHIP

The degree of congruence, or lack of it, between the partisan commitments of journalists and politicians, what Seymour-Ure (1968) describes as 'press–party parallelism', is a second factor which structures the extent and character of politicians' relationships with media. Expressed broadly, when politicians and media share political sentiments there is a greater potential for relationships to be co-operative and consensual; where they differ, contacts are likely to be less frequent but more conflictual. Conservative Central Office's relations with the *Telegraph*, which offers unswerving political support for the party during and beyond election periods, will be markedly more convivial and less conflictual than with the editorial offices of the *Guardian* or the *Mirror*. In lobby briefings too, relationships based on shared political commitments are more likely to prove congenial. Campbell was always particularly attentive to *The Times* correspondent Philip Webster and Trevor Kavanagh of the *Sun* (both owned by Murdoch's News International), while George Jones of the *Telegraph*, much favoured by previous conservative administrations, found himself untypically part of 'the awkward squad' and 'starved of the oxygen of information which alone can sustain the dedicated reporter' (Oborne, 1999, p. 174; see Chapter 3).

But if relationships based on shared political commitments are more likely to be frequent and co-operative, the reverse is also true. There have been striking, if untypical examples. In 1987, the ideological 'mismatch' between Labour and sections of the media, following press allegations about Labour's 'loony left', prompted the party to abandon news conferences for the press and to focus the party's communications strategy entirely on television and radio. Mutual adaptation assured that both press and party wished to change this relationship in 1992. Similarly, the Conservative Party remains sceptical about the political independence of the BBC, believing the Corporation is inherently biased against them: or perhaps more accurately reflects the bias towards liberalism (small l) which the Conservatives believe afflicts all news media. But since the BBC constitutes the major broadcasting organisation in the UK, any boycott by politicians would be highly undesirable. This process of mutual adaptation will also help to heal the rift between the Labour government and the BBC following Alastair Campbell's objection to journalist Andrew Gilligan's claims on Radio 4's *Today* programme (29 May 2003), that Campbell had 'sexed up' an intelligence dossier detailing Iraq's potential arms threat to the West. Despite Greg Dyke's claim, in his evidence to the Hutton inquiry, that Campbell mounted a 'pre-planned attack' on the BBC to 'settle old scores' (*Guardian*, 16 September 2003, p. 5), both the BBC and the government have overriding, long term interests, in re-establishing the previous mutually beneficial, if mutually dependent, ways of working.

The influence of press–party parallelism, however, is usually less dramatic resulting in politicians avoiding, or being attracted to, individual newspapers, programmes or journalists. Ingham, for example, advised Mrs Thatcher against interviews on the *Today* programme and any engagement with Sir Robin Day: her personal favourite was Brian Walden. More recently, two special advisers working at Number Ten constructed a list of 28 senior journalists, their political views and interview styles in order to 'connect' politicians with the most favourable [parallel] interviewer (Milne and Maguire, 2001, pp. 2–3).

But the idea of press–party parallelism requires some qualification in the British setting as press allegiances have become highly complex with substantial shifts between 1997 and 2001: in 1992, the circulation gap between papers supporting Conservative and Labour peaked at 48 per cent, but by 2001 72 per cent of newspapers (by circulation) supported Labour, only 7.8 per cent Conservative. Significantly, what occurred was a de-alignment not a re-alignment: a collapse of press support for the Conservatives rather than any damascene conversion to Labour. Moreover, while the *Sun* 'Backed Blair' its editorials were hostile to Labour policy on Europe. Similarly while the *Guardian* supported Labour, 13.5 per cent of its readers shifted allegiance to the Liberal Democrats. Newspapers' partisan commitments have become highly variegated and complex. In Peter Hitchen's phrase the UK has traded the 'Tory press for the Tony press' (see Chapter 6).

JOURNALISTS, POLITICIANS AND RESOURCES

The third factor which is influential in structuring relationships between politicians and journalists is the resources which each can bring to any particular exchange. Variations in the range and nature of resources which groups can muster will alter decisively the general character of the relationship and may be influential in determining the extent to which one group is able to assert its interests above the other.

Resources are defined broadly here to include the particular qualities of politicians: their ability to perform well on television or their physical appearance and 'telegenic' qualities which may prove attractive (literally) to broadcasters and audiences. But they also include more obvious considerations such as the support provided by press officers and special advisers. Politicians, however, enjoy extremely variable access to communication resources. Senior politicians, for example, enjoy high status, considerable prestige and their published and broadcast comments are vested with an authority which reflects their office. They are also more likely to have received extensive training in media presentation techniques which allow them to engage successfully with troublesome interviewers and to present their case succinctly and clearly to camera. They will also have access to computerised information and rapid rebuttal systems like the Knowledge Network and Excalibur which provide them with the party line on particular issues and ensure they do not stray 'off message'. Government ministers enjoy access to a whole armoury of additional communication resources. The prime minister has monopoly access to special advisers who will insist on details of media interviews in advance and set down a series of requirements – that the minister has the opportunity to make the last comment in any exchange – as a condition of the politician's appearance on the programme (see Chapter 6). Other political actors such as back-bench MPs, local councillors and spokespeople for interest groups, will rarely be able to match these resources.

Journalists also confront highly variable resource situations. Some may work for prestigious national newspapers, which employ specialist and highly knowledgeable journalists and political columnists, which are financially well resourced and sustain a rigorous culture of investigative journalism which informs the paper's news-gathering activities. Local newspapers and radio services, by contrast, might more probably be 'strapped for cash' and staffed only by junior and less experienced reporters. But even within the local setting, journalistic resources are significant in shaping politician–journalist relations. A monopoly in local press reporting, for example, can be a substantial journalistic resource. A study in West Yorkshire revealed how the Labour leader of a metropolitan authority influenced reporting of local politics in the two local papers by withholding information from one while offering monopoly access to the other on clearly specified conditions which detailed not only the content of the report, but its positioning and layout within the paper. Where a local newspaper enjoys an editorial monopoly in reporting a council it is more able to adopt a critical posture towards the authority. Conditions of newspaper duopoly may shift the balance of power in politician–journalist relations significantly in favour of the former (Franklin, 1991, p. 17).

The impact of newspaper monopoly on the balance of power in journalist–politician relationships was highlighted during the 2001 election. Party agents campaigning in the constituency and trying to win coverage in the local paper, believed the existence of a newspaper monoply was crucial to their success. 'I think newspapers are in the driving seat' an agent complained. 'It has always seemed to me that we are at their mercy: completely at their mercy. It doesn't matter whether you come up with the best story and the best picture in the world. If they don't feel like covering it then they won't . . . They have the upper hand. If you want to have news reported in the local paper then you have got to work with the people that are there'. Local journalists agree. 'We don't fly the flag for any political party' an editor argued 'We don't think it is right for us to do that because we have a local monopoly. But it was "The Sun Wot Won It" and it could happen here' (see Chapter 7).

The particular mix of resources which politicians and journalists bring to a particular encounter will structure the character of the relationship between the two groups: two extreme and inverse circumstances of resource imbalance prescribe the limits of the relationship. When senior politicians, supported by professional media advisers, are dealing with under-resourced and inexperienced local journalists, it might be anticipated that the politicians' communication objectives will prevail. There is, of course, no iron rule of certainty which operates here. It is precisely the inexperienced inquisitor, perhaps even a member of the public, who may on occasion prompt even a prime minister to falter by her persistent questioning about the sinking of the Belgrano: or who may challenge a prime minister during an election walkabout concerning the quality of NHS treatment of her partner's cancer. But such exceptions seem merely to prove the rule. The reverse circumstance of resource imbalance suggests an equally predictable outcome. An inexperienced and junior politician who is interviewed on a flagship current affairs programme like *Newsnight* would be wise to anticipate at least the possibility of a serious mauling at the hands of a seasoned, well-briefed and assertive broadcaster like Jeremy Paxman.

But this formulation of the impact of resources on relationships between politicians and journalists is unduly simplistic for at least two reasons. First, the two examples given are untypical. Prestigious news and current affairs programmes show little interest in interviewing low profile, junior politicians. They prefer senior politicians whose authoritative statements can set the agenda and provide headlines in later programmes; a classic strategy for the *Breakfast with Frost* Sunday programme. Exchanges between politicians and journalists are usually characterized by a more even matching of communication resources. The process of packaging politics, however, has certainly encouraged politicians to buttress the communication resources which they bring to their encounters with journalists. Second, the examples propose an influence for resources in isolation from the operation of other factors such as the influence of political and media hierarchies, the impact of each group's political allegiances, as well as the operation of a range of contingent factors, which will each help to shape and structure relationships between politicians and journalists creating a great diversity and complexity of arrangements.

PACKAGING POLITICS: THE STRUCTURE OF THE BOOK

The following eight chapters elaborate in greater detail the case outlined above. Britain, it is argued, has become a media democracy in which politicians and policies are packaged for media marketing and public consumption. The different chapters consider the various ways in which politicians in parties, in central and local government and in Parliament, have become increasingly enthusiastic and skilled at managing and manipulating the mass media of communications to present themselves to the public. Media democracy, with its packaged politics, is characterised by an absence of direct political debate; voters have become spectators rather than participants in the democratic dialogue. What should be a rousing and deafening, if necessarily discordant chorus of democratic voices, has been reduced to a carefully orchestrated silence. Amid the hush, it is just possible to hear the autocues turning.

The argument unfolds in Chapters 2 to 8 by examining the activities of the political communicators, considering in turn: central government news management via the lobby, the prime minister's press secretary and government controls on the press which range from patronage to censorship (Chapter 2); new Labour's centralising of news management at Number Ten, the government's more robust relations with journalists and the allegations concerning the politicising of the GICS (Chapter 3); the growth in central government's use of advertising to promote its policy ambitions, especially in the run up to the 2001 general election, and the consequent questions which are raised concerning the distinction between information and propaganda (Chapter 4); local government public relations and local spin doctors' potential to set the local news agenda (Chapter 5); political parties' use, especially during elections, of news management strategies and corporate marketing and advertising techniques to communicate political messages to voters (Chapter 6); local parties' adaption and adoption of the media strategies of their national counterparts to target local media as campaigning vehicles for the promotion of policy and candidates (Chapter 7); and the arrival of television in the House of Commons, the changing character of parliamentary reporting and the potential which broadcasting on television and the Internet offers politicians and parties for packaging politics (Chapter 8).

The final chapter considers the impact of packaging politics on the public. Contrary to Norman Tebbit's suggestion concerning the public's ability to 'unwrap' political packaging, articulated in his evocative metaphor that the public 'can smell a dead rat even when it is wrapped up in a red rose', the chapter argues that audiences may increasingly be influenced by the more subtle and persuasive techniques of communications professionals, special advisers and spin doctors: the publicly funded officials who, to adopt a different metaphor, seek to 'bury bad news'.

Part 2

The political communicators

Chapter Two

CENSORSHIP, NEWS □
MANAGEMENT AND THE LOBBY

Throughout the 1980s, successive Conservative administrations systematically pursued policies resulting in the greater centralisation, regulation and control of the flow of information concerning the activities of the government. Predictably, perhaps, the media became a central focus of this broader government ambition: consequently their independence of government is less obvious than in the recent past. Governments try to regulate media news-gathering and reporting activities by: mounting sustained attacks on reporters – especially television broadcasters – involved in investigative journalism; attempting to influence appointments to senior positions in broadcasting organisations; using the financial lever of the licence fee and legislating for radical changes to the financial and organisational structures of broadcasting; and, finally, by deploying that device beloved of British governments with their traditions and culture of secrecy – good old-fashioned censorship. There is much in the recent history of government activity in the sphere of political communications to offer credence to even the wilder speculations of conspiracy theorists.

This chapter examines the growing power of the prime minister's press secretary and his changing relationship with the Parliamentary lobby which has resulted in the emergence of a system of strict and centralised control of political communications. The argument here is that successive Conservative administrations laid the foundations for such centralised controls on which subsequent Labour governments have built a robust and aggressive news management structure, prompting political journalists, government information officers, as well as politicians from across all political parties, to describe the senior politicians in the Labour party and those special advisers who staff the communication organisations based at Number Ten, as 'control freaks' (Jones, 2002, esp. Chapter 3). There is a clear line of descent connecting Bernard Ingham's 'politicising' and expansion of the office of prime minister's press secretary with Alastair Campbell's development of the media monitoring unit and the Strategic Communications Unit, designed to keep the government 'on message' and to shape media coverage of the government (Seymour Ure, 2000, p. 152; see Chapter 3): for his part, Ingham denies any such connection (Ingham, 2003). The chapter begins by reviewing governments' relations with the media and their efforts to silence the sometimes oppositional voices of journalists.

QUIETENING OPPOSITIONAL VOICES: GOVERNMENT AND MEDIA RELATIONS

REPROACHING INVESTIGATIVE JOURNALISM

Government attempts to inhibit investigative journalism from exploring facets of its operations have resulted in a number of celebrated skirmishes with journalists especially those working at the BBC. Most recently in July 2003, Alistair Campbell launched a robust attack on the BBC, alleging bias in the Corporation's coverage of the war in Iraq and demanding an apology for journalist Andrew Gilligan's use of an anonymous source to suggest that Campbell had 'sexed up' the (dodgy) security dossier concerning the military threat posed by Iraq. But on this occasion, quite untypically, the BBC Director General, the Board of Governors and Head of News Richard Sambrook, offered an equally robust reposte to Campbell's demands which were widely interpreted by journalists to be intimidatory, as well as diversionary, in intention and effect. These reactions by government to journalists' criticism constitutes the 'flak' which Herman and Chomsky identify as one of the five filters which 'cleanse' news of its radical and critical content leaving only a safe if rather bland residue behind (Herman and Chomsky, 1988, p. 27; Klaehn, 2002, p. 160). In the UK, journalists have become very conscious of their changing relationships with government. 'We are working in the context of a more powerful state, one that is brusque, authoritarian and contemptuous of alternative ideas', one journalist observed. 'Investigative journalists are by definition antagonistic to the strong state. They stand for information not propaganda.' (Leigh, 1988, p. 17). There are many examples to illustrate how government intervention undermined the journalistic enterprise, especially during the 1980s and 1990s which seemed to mark a nadir in relationships between government and the press until the summer of 2003.

The outbreak of the Falklands war in 1982, for example, revealed government sensitivities to media probing. Government's largely successful attempts to manage news reporting of the war, through the Ministry of Defence and the press office at Number Ten, have been well documented (Harris, 1983; Morrison and Tumber, 1988). In 1985 Leon Brittain, then home secretary, persuaded the BBC governors to postpone and then re-edit the *Real Lives* programme which Thatcher wanted to ban, before she had seen it, on the grounds that it would provide terrorists with 'the oxygen of publicity'. Curtis and Jempson catalogue the British government's interference in investigative journalism in Northern Ireland across more than 30 years in its efforts to smother critical opposition (Curtis and Jempson, 1993). Intervention in journalistic affairs has on occasion assumed even less subtle forms. In February 1987, journalist Duncan Campbell's series *Secret Society*, which alleged that government had deliberately misled Parliament about the funding of the new Zircon satellite, triggered a special branch raid on the offices of BBC Scotland. The raid lasted for 28 hours, resulted in the removal of private files and programme notes and in the words of Alan Protheroe, then assistant director general of the BBC, it was 'a shabby, shameful, disgraceful state sponsored incursion into a journalistic establishment' (Protheroe, 1987, p. 4).

The most injurious battle in this protracted war between politicians and broadcasters across the 1980s, concerned the 1988 Thames Television programme *Death on the Rock* which challenged the government's account of the shooting of three members of the IRA in Gibraltar who were subsequently discovered to have been unarmed. The government argued that broadcasting the programme would prejudice the inquest in Gibraltar and allegedly constitute 'trial by television'. Politicians' protests became so severe that Thames Television commissioned a special inquiry into the programme which vindicated the company and argued that the programme makers 'did not bribe, bully or misrepresent those who took part ... and did not offend against the due impartiality requirements of the IBA' (Windlesham-Rampton, 1989, p. 142). This conclusion did little to placate politicians. Downing Street immediately issued a statement announcing that the prime minister 'utterly rejected' the findings of the report.

During the 1990s the tensions between journalists and government continued. If they were slightly subdued and fewer in number, this reflected the more ameliorative approach of the Major government towards the press, the honeymoon period (post 1997) which the new Labour government enjoyed with news media, the effectiveness of Labour's news management operation, the reduction in investigative journalism prompted by the scarcity of resources for making these relatively expensive programmes and the fact that the government's use of 'flak' against broadcasters had deterred many journalists from making such programmes. But despite this apparent collegiality, outbreaks of hostility have been evident. In the run up to the 1997 election, both major parties mounted critical assaults on the BBC to 'soften them up' as part of their broader news management strategy. John Birt's response to these attacks was supine. In a speech in Dublin, Birt seemed to side with politicians as he denounced 'overbearing interviewers who sneer disdainfully at their interviewees' and suggested that 'politicians have a higher claim to speak for the people than journailsts' who should become more 'humble, dispassionate and rational' in their interviews with politicians (Cited in McNair 2000, p. 159). Birt's remarks were widely interpreted as being targeted at BBC Radio 4's *Today* programme and its leading journalist John Humphrys.

But under new Labour the criticism of journalism has typically moved away from attacks on broadcasting organisations like the BBC, to a preferred focus on particular journalists such as Andrew Gilligan (Jones, 2002 and Oborne, 2002, pp. 32–40). An internal Cabinet memo leaked to the *Guardian* in 2001, revealed that Labour keeps a dossier on political journalists which provides a 'thumbnail guide' to the 'perceived influence, reliability and political leanings of daily newspaper reporters and commentators' (Milne and Maguire,

22 January, pp. 2–3). In the late 1990s, a number of incidents revealed government sensitivities to journalists' criticisms of Labour policy. Andrew Marr, editor of the *Independent* at the time of the 1997 election was a self-proclaimed supporter of new Labour, but during the campaign, Blair published an article in the *Sun* on St George's day which struck a markedly anti-European note. 'On this day' Blair claimed 'we remember the legend that St George slayed a dragon to protect England, some will argue there is another dragon to be slayed: Europe'. Responding in an editorial, Marr claimed that Blair was speaking in bad faith and that the phrase 'some will argue' was intended to excuse an otherwise xenophobic essay. Blair was pro-European to europhile audiences but espoused anti-European 'nostalgic, flag waving Gormenghast politics' to Eurosceptics. Although critical, Marr's journalistic iron fist was softened by a velvet glove as he pronounced that 'no one is suggesting that the Labour party today is in anything like the same state as the Tories when Major became leader' (cited in Cohen 1999, p. 153–4). But his criticism prompted offence and reaction. Campbell contacted David Montgomery, chief executive of the *Independent* and demanded that Marr be sacked. Shortly after, Marr was fired.

The net effect of this running battle between journalists and politicians has been to undermine journalists' self-confidence, encourage self-censorship and create a climate which is typically hostile to investigative journalism. Briggs recalls that the BBC's response to such pressures has often been excessively timorous and that, on occasions, BBC was an acronym for 'Be Bloody Cautious'. But there seems little doubt that the complaints, requests, threats and adverse comments by government expressed in Parliament, at party conferences and in other public arenas, subvert the prospects for investigative journalism. But that, according to some observers, is precisely their purpose (Etzioni-Halevy, 1987, p. 41).

FROM APPOINTING 'ONE OF OURS' TO 'TONY'S CRONIES'

Patronage is a time-honoured device to secure political compliance from potential dissenters. Politicians have used it extensively to influence key appointments in broadcasting organisations. During the 1980s, there was a widely held suspicion that the Government was 'packing' the BBC Board of Governors with political supporters. A former managing director of BBC Television claimed 'the government has tended to put people [on the board] who are sympathetic to its views in greater numbers than has been the practice in the past. There is a question that the PM is said to ask about every appointee to a public body: "is he one of ours?" ' (*Guardian*, 25 August 1985, p. 6).

The appointment to the BBC Board of Governors of Daphne Park, the rightwing head of Mrs Thatcher's old Oxford college, as well as Sir John Boyd, a right-wing trade unionist, Malcolm McAlpine whose building company had donated substantial sums to the Conservative Party, Lord Harewood the Queen's cousin and Stuart Young (brother of Lord Young a member of the Conservative Cabinet) as chair of the governors with

William Rees-Mogg, an outspoken Conservative supporter as his deputy, prompted Lord Bonham Carter, a Liberal and vice chair of governors between 1975 and 1981, to comment that these appointments 'did seem to provide evidence that the government were politicising, or trying to politicise, the BBC' (*World in Action*, 29 February 1988). But it was the appointment of Marmaduke Hussey, the former chief executive of Times Newspapers during the period of the newspaper's 12 months of strike closure, as chair of the board of governers which prompted journalists to speculate that Hussey had been appointed to 'sort out' the BBC. Headlines in the *The Times* and *The Financial Times* on the day after his appointment reported the 'political storm over Hussey's post', and asked 'Can the duke bring the BBC to heel?' (Milne, 1988, p. 188).

The summary effect of these appointments was to create a board of governors which was more genuinely 'in tune' with government thinking about broadcasting matters than previously. But it was a board more at odds with the managers and programme makers who felt their creative autonomy was being challenged by an in-house group of critics who spoke the language of constraint. Alasdair Milne captured neatly this growing estrangement between governors and broadcasters and identified its root:

> As perceived in Number Ten, the liberal elite of the media' have become
> anathema ... nine years of [the Thatcher] premiership brought about many
> gubernatorial retirements and their replacements by Thatcher appointees.
> The governors found themselves growing apart from what they saw as a
> liberal elite who dominated the news and particularly the current affairs
> output. This was not a prescription for harmony and understanding.
>
> (ibid., p. 213)

Milne himself was not to witness the outcome of this debacle. On Thursday 29 January 1988 he was summoned to Hussey's office and dismissed (ibid., p. 202).

In the new millennium, appointments to senior posts at the BBC remain contentious and continue to trigger allegations of patronage and partisanship from politicians. The appointment of Greg Dyke to the post of director general of the BBC in June 1999 prompted a perhaps predictable outcry, not least because Dyke was a well known Labour supporter who had donated a total of £55,000 to the party. The then Conservative leader William Hague argued Dyke's 'close ties with the Labour Party ... create a problem' (*Guardian*, 29 June 1999, p. 2). Columnist Hugo Young described it as a 'shocking appointment' not because BBC journalists will behave in a less impartial way, but because they will 'be for ever vulnerable to the charge that the BBC's agenda is no longer to be trusted' (Young, 1999, p. 18). Ironically, this was Dyke's concern in his 1994 McTaggart lecture when he argued that 'we must never again be in a position where the government of the day can fill the BBC's Board of Governors with their friends and placemen as the Thatcherites did' (Cited in *Guardian*, 26 June 1999, p. 5).

A similar outcry followed the appointment of Gavyn Davies as chairman of the BBC in September 2001. Davies, a member of the Labour Party and donor to its funds, is a close friend of Gordon Brown: his wife Sue Nye runs the chancellor's private office. The Conservatives were allegedly 'apoplectic' (*Guardian*, 20 September 2001, p. 13). Party Chairman David Davis claimed that 'over the last four years Tony Blair has stuffed his cronies into every corner of public life' but now he is mounting 'a final takeover bid for the BBC' by 'packing the corporation with cronies' (*Guardian*, 19 September 2001, p. 13). A year later Lord Currie, a Labour supporter, government adviser and close friend of the chancellor, was appointed to chair the newly created and powerful media regulator OFCOM: the allegations of cronyism and partisanship followed in what had by now become a rather monotonous but not wholly unjustified fashion. Describing the appointment as a 'step back 200 years' a Conservative spokesperson claimed 'After all the commotion last year over Gavyn Davies . . . I think it is a pity that we find yet another person in a position of power who is an active Labour member . . . all these jobs [the director general of the BBC, chair of the board of governors, and chair of OFCOM] are gradually being politicised' (*Guardian*, 26 July 2002, p. 1). By 2001, some conservative politicians were alleging that BBC stood for the 'Blair Broadcasting Corporation': as McNair notes this is perhaps an improvement on the 'Bolshevik Broadcasting Corporation' although the basic message and complaint remains the same (McNair, 2000, p. 157).

But both recriminations proved incorrect in the summer of 2003 when Dyke, Davies and the entire BBC Board of Governors, without regard to their particular partisan affiliations, became deeply embroiled in the defence of the BBC's journalism – and the journalist Andrew Gilligan in particular – against Campbell's allegations of inaccurate and partisan reporting of the war in Iraq. While the historical record signals some close policy congruence between Thatcher and Hussey's ambitions for the BBC in the 1980s, the events of the summer of 2003 obliged Blair and the Labour government to learn the lesson that Lord Hill taught Harold Wilson in the 1970s. Namely, whatever a politician's motive or intentions may be when making an appointment to the chair of the BBC Board of Governors (or the office of Director General), appointees may, on occasion, forget their previous partisan commitments, 'go native' and define their role to be precisely that which is set down in the BBC's Charter: i.e. to defend the quality and independence of BBC journalism from any intrusion by economic or political influences.

CENSORSHIP

A third strategy for constraining flows of political communication is outright censorship, which can be delivered in both light- and heavy-handed fashion. The D-notice system reflects the former. Established in 1912 by the War Office and the Admiralty, it was designed to prevent newspapers from publishing military information which might be useful to 'the enemy' and became 'voluntary' in 1945. The Defence, Press and Broadcasting Advisory Committee (DPBAC), which convenes twice yearly, oversees the system and currently includes four senior government officials and twelve editors/elder statesmen from the media: Sir Kevin Tebbit, permanent under secretary of state at the ministry of defence chairs the committee and rear admiral Nick Wilkinson serves as secretary. The committee is intended to form a point of contact and liaison between the media and government on delicate issues of national security. The notices are 'intended to provide to national and provincial news-paper editors, to periodical editors, to radio and telvision organisations and to relevant book publishers, general guidance on those areas of national security which the governemnt con-siders it has a duty to protect' (www.dnotice.org.uk/system.htm).

It is no longer practice to issue individual letters asking editors not to publish. In 1971, all the 'Parkers' (as they were called after the first Press Association representative on the committee) were consolidated into 12 standing D notices giving guidance about ongoing security issues, the intelligence services, civil defence and nuclear weapons (Hodgson, 2001, p. 10): these were refined and reduced to 6 in 1993 (and to 5 in 2000) and their name changed to DA Notices (Defence Advisory Notices). So 'contrary to popular misconception, a specific notice is not slapped on a particular story' (Wilkinson, 2002). While there has been a broadening of D-notice powers to cover the reporting of domestic terrorism, most focus upon external threats to national security (McNamara, 1992, p. 8). In November 2001, for example, the committee issued a notice to newspaper editors requesting them not to report any activities of the SAS in the context of the war in Afghanistan. Editors are advised to contact the secretary and seek advice before publishing any information which falls in these broad categories.

At first glance the committee appears to be little more than a harmless curiosity, but it has a more worrying aspect. Sadler's recent academic study of national security and the D-notice system argues that the public interest is insufficiently represented in the system with the result that material may be suppressed not because it threatens national security but instead risks exposing the government to embarrassment (Sadler, 2001). Jack Straw's attempts to revise D-notices to prohibit the disclosure of details about homes and second homes owned by ministers, allegedly on ground of security, follows closely on the considerable press interest in the second homes of Lord Irvine the Lord Chancellor, Peter Mandelson's home loan from Geoffrey Robinson and environment minister Michael Meacher's ownership of 6 private houses: these circumstances seem to provide a exemplar case study of Sadler's thesis (*Guardian*, 11 November 1999, p. 2).

The heavy-handed style of censorship has, in the British setting, always found its locus classicus in the Official Secrets Act. The catch-all, censorial character of section 2 of the Act was infamous. Born in the panic of wartime, nurtured in apathy and ignorance, it eventually floundered on contempt and fell into disrepute. But the Zircon affair, the publication of Peter Wright's *Spycatcher* and successive leaks (anathema to a government so besotted with the control of information) by Sarah Tisdall, Clive Ponting and others about government 'economies with the truth' convinced government that it needed a replacement. Announced by Douglas Hurd, then home secretary, as a liberalisation of the old Act, the new legislation enacted in 1989 was more restrictive than its predecessor.

The Act specifies four categories of information – information obtained in confidence from a foreign government or international organisation, interception of communications, disclosure by former agents about the security services and certain disclosures by journalists about the security services – about which nothing may be published. Breach of the law can no longer resort to a defence based on prior publication abroad or publication being in the public interest. Key terms in the Act, moreover, are conveniently vague. 'International organisations', for example, covers the EU, the UN and the IMF, excluding vast amounts of information from legitimate publication. Additionally, the wide-ranging nature of the prohibited categories makes it very difficult for journalists and editors to decide whether a story falls into one of these categories. It also invites the obvious temptation to play safe when in doubt and self-censor. Assessing the impact of the new Act, Clive Ponting forecast that 'the government intends to virtually censor the media, stop investigative journalism and establish stricter information controls than ever before in peacetime' (Ponting, 1988, p. 15).

The sentencing of former MI5 officer David Shayler on 5 November 2002 for three breaches of the Official Secrets Act, following his disclosure of secret documents to the *Mail on Sunday*, illustrates the government's determination to enforce a strict interpretation of these four prohibited categories of information as well as the absence of any public interest defence in the revised OSA (*Guardian*, 6 November 2002, p. 2). Shayler's defence was that he had disclosed documents to reveal the illegality of secret service operations such as telephone tappings and bugging of politicians and others. But while the judge acknowledged Shayler's actions reflected his 'wish to expose illegality and inefficiency', the House of Lords had established that there was 'no public interest defence'. Moreover, the Lords had 'also ruled that the Official Secrets Act – which states that former members of the security and intelligence agencies are bound by a life-long duty of confidentiality – was compatible with the Human Rights Act which establishes the right to free expression'. MI5 said the judge 'must be protected by a shield of secrecy' (*Guardian*, 29 October 2002, p. 3).

There are other more dramatic examples of censorship. On 19 October 1988, the home secretary announced that eleven political and paramilitary groups in Northern Ireland, including the legal political party Sinn Fein, were to be banned from television and radio but, curiously, not from newspapers (Article 19, 2000). Notices were issued to the BBC and the IBA requesting that they 'refrain at all times from sending any broadcast matter which consists of or includes any words spoken ... by a person who ... represents an organisation specified ... below, or when the words support or solicit or invite support for such an organisation'. The home secretary had required broadcasters 'to refrain' on five previous occasions including the 1926 general strike (Miller, 1990, p. 34). The ban applied retrospectively and resulted in the absurdity of broadcasters having to re-edit educational programmes to remove footage of the Nationalist politician Connelly. The ban was eventually lifted in 1994.

The conditions of the ban were rather incoherent. The notice permitted the broadcasting of pictures and visual images of politicians but not their voices. The use of computer technology which synchronised actors' voices with the televisual images of politicians, seemed to underscore the absurdity of such crude censorship. As Mark Bonham Carter, a former BBC vice chair observed, 'deaf people who can lip read are exempt from the ban' (*Independent*, 12 January 1989). But the overall effect of the censorship of these groups was to deny them a voice in British media and the broad political debate (Article 19, 1989, p. 24).

A cross-national study of censorship in nine countries, including the USA and Canada, confirmed Britain's position as the most censorial government in Western Europe; Britain was 'head and shoulders above the rest' (Newton and Artingstall, 1992, p. 13). Two other findings are significant. First, incidents of censorship have grown more rapidly in Britain than in other countries with an 'unprecedented and sustained' period of growth dating from 1986 (ibid., p. 17). Secondly, the development of private censorship (i.e., by non-governmental agencies such as broadcasters) tends to grow in proportion to governmental censorship leading to what the report describes as a 'spiral of censorship'. In Britain, the 'spiral of censorship' is more developed and potentially malevolent than in other European countries (ibid., p. 19).

PAYING THE PIPER

The final strategy for influencing media has been politicians' use of a range of financial and organisational levers. The licence fee, which provides the bulk of the BBC's income, was initially intended to provide financial autonomy and independence of government, but has traditionally been used to chastise the corporation and to try to influence its broadcasting policy. The government has typically set the licence fee below the figure requested by the BBC. The BBC was threatened over the licence fee by a Conservative government at the time of Suez and subsequently by Harold Wilson, who was very dissatisfied with coverage of his administration. Tom (now Lord) McNally, political adviser to James Callaghan, described how in 1978, following a patch of 'rough treatment by the BBC especially *Newsnight*', he had met Brian Wenham, then head of BBC 2 at the Labour Party conference in Brighton and 'having eyeballed him in the way of Mohammed Ali' McNally threatened 'that hell will freeze over before you get a licence fee increase unless we get a better deal out of you' (*World in Action*, 29 February 1988). The government's retention of the licence fee in the 1994 green paper on *The Future of the BBC*, its rejection of the Davies report in favour of a digital licence fee supplement in 1998 and Chris Smith's insistence on £3bn in savings and efficiencies at the BBC in 2001, confirmed government's intention to keep a tight rein on broadcasting finance. Greg Dyke's warning about broadcasting increasingly being conducted within 'a culture of dependency' on government is perhaps appropriate given this history of disciplining the BBC via the licence fee.

But government control of the licence fee is not the only financial lever it can deploy in an effort to shape broadcasting policy. Public sector broadcasting can be pressured by proposals to introduce commercial funding either through advertising or subscription. The Peacock Committee was established by government in the spring of 1985 to explore both options. The Broadcasting Acts 1990 and 1996, which restructured the Channel 3 commercial network and introduced Channel 5, have left many regional television companies short of the financial resources necessary for expensive programming such as documentaries and current affairs (Campaign for Quality Television 1998, pp. 1–7; Franklin, 2001, pp. 61–64). The December 2000 White Paper *A New Future for Communications* and the Communications Act 2003, with the increasingly commerical, competitive, multi-channel broadcasting ecology which they envisage, will exacerbate these trends towards constraint on programme range and plurality. Many broadcasters believe that these economic and commercial pressures inhibit programme makers as much as the more direct, but sinister, hand of the censor. David Elstein claimed in his James McTaggart memorial lecture that 'government policies have paralysed ITV, threatened the survival of Channel 4 and destabilised Independent Television News' (*Guardian*, 24 August 1991, p. 8). The advantage of deploying economic mechanisms, of course, is that politicians are not seen to be overtly 'dirty handed' in decision-making about programming. They know however, that market forces limit broadcasters' choices in predictable ways. The 'invisible hand' of the market placed across a broadcaster's mouth can gag as effectively as any censor.

Governments have also used more proactive strategies in attempting to manage political news. The office of the prime minister's press secretary as well as the institution of the press lobby are significant, if not crucial, components in such strategies

THE PRIME MINISTER'S PRESS SECRETARY

George Steward, an official from the Foreign Office news department, was the first person appointed as press secretary by Ramsey MacDonald in 1931, who wanted professional advice on how to handle the Conservative dominated press (Cockerell et al. 1984, p. 37). From the outset a central brief for the post was the manipulation of media news agendas, especially in newspapers. Stewart quickly established the convention that although formally attached to the prime minister, the press secretary's briefings of lobby journalists should be understood as expressing the official position of the entire government (ibid.). This convention held predictable benefits for the prime minister. The press secretary's news management skills guaranteed that Number Ten's interpretation of events was reported in the press, enabling the prime minister to undermine the independence of the Cabinet and further centralize power in Downing Street. Chamberlain used Steward repeatedly to bypass the Cabinet and promote his policy of appeasement with Hitler (Harris, 1990, p. 74).

All subsequent prime ministers, with a single exception, found the post invaluable. In 1951, on his return to power, Winston Churchill, who had always been suspicious of journalists and broadcasters, wanted nothing to do with media, the lobby or government information officers. He ordered Reginald Bacon, the press secretary inherited from Attlee, not to speak to journalists, thereby effectively sacking him. But press coverage of the government deteriorated and began to so alarm senior conservatives that Churchill was persuaded to relent and, in May 1952, appointed Thomas Fife Clark, a press officer from the Ministry of Health to the post (Hennessy and Walker, 1987, p. 120; Ogilvy-Webb, 1965, p. 87). It was the last occasion on which a prime minister so undervalued his press secretary.

BERNARD INGHAM: PRESS SECRETARY OR MINISTER OF INFORMATION?

On 1 November 1979, Bernard Ingham was appointed press secretary to prime minister Thatcher. In constitutional terms the post was relatively new, but Ingham earned it both a prominence and notoriety not achieved by any of the previous 14 office holders (Harris, 1990, Appendix, pp. 187–9). The job of handling the prime minister's media relations and serving as spokesperson for the prime minister had always proved politically sensitive and uncertainties prevailed about whether the post should be a party political appointment or part of the civil service; at the time of Ingham's appointment it was judged to be a job with which 'the constitutional theorists have yet to catch up' (Cockerell et al., 1984, p. 63). But Ingham became so closely identified with Margaret Thatcher, her brand of conservatism and her political style, that when she resigned it seemed obvious that he should go with her. His track record in office made it unthinkable that Ingham might serve as press secretary even for the new Conservative leader John Major, much less an incoming Labour prime minister. Ingham stamped his identity on the post of press secretary and expanded the brief of the office considerably.

Assessments of Bernard Ingham varied widely: few are gracious. John Biffen, whose fall from ministerial grace had been orchestrated by Ingham, described him as a 'sort of rough-spoken Yorkshire Rasputin who is manipulating government and corroding standards of public morality' (HC Debs., 7 February 1983). Many journalists were critical of his political manoeuvring but acknowledged his effectiveness in his post. BBC correspondent Nicholas Jones claimed Ingham 'turned the central coordination of government publicity into an art form' (Jones, 1991b).

Ingham saw his role as press officer to be that of a gate-keeper controlling a two-way flow of political communication; his preferred metaphor was that of a 'bridge ... between media and government' (Ingham, 1991, p. 164). He was uniquely influential in determining the prime minister's knowledge of media reporting of government matters, but also advised her about what information to release to media. He began his working day by producing a 'warts and all' digest of press coverage of Thatcher, her government and general economic affairs, which was delivered to the prime minister's private office by 9.30 a.m. She apparently valued these summaries highly and, apart from reading *The Sunday Times* at the weekend, relied on them for her knowledge of press coverage of political affairs. No previous prime minister placed such faith in a press secretary.

But Ingham was also highly influential in structuring the prime minister's relations with media, advising her, and later her ministers, on when to speak to the media and what to say. Every detail of Thatcher's appearances on television was negotiated and agreed with broadcasters in advance. Ingham would not allow any breach of such conventions and wrote a swingeing letter of complaint to ITN, threatening to exclude them from future events 'when an ITN cameraman questioned Mrs Thatcher during a photo call at Number Ten' (*UK Press Gazette*, 6 January, 1989).

As Thatcher's reliance on Ingham grew, she rewarded him by increasing the status and salary of his post. On 9 February 1989, she took the unprecedented step of appointing Ingham to the head of the entire Government Information Service (GIS). As Harris noted, Ingham now had four separate functions:

> He was the Prime Minister's personal media adviser. He was the nonattributable spokesman for the entire government. He had responsibility for the recruitment, training and career development of 1,200 information officers. He coordinated an advertising and publicity budget of some £168 million. In any other country he would have been given the proper title: Minister of Information.
>
> (Harris, 1990, p. 170)

The lad from Hebden Bridge had come a long way. Little wonder that one political journalist described him as 'the real deputy Prime Minister' (Lawson, 1990, p. 32).

ALASTAIR CAMPBELL: 'THE DAILY VOICE OF THE GOVERNMENT'

By the time of his resignation in late July 2003 and his eventual departure from office in early October, Alastair Campbell had become the most powerful and influential Press Secretary in the history of British politics. But as his press secretary role became increasingly contentious, he preferred the designation Director of Communications which he adopted in mid-2000. Campbell was the progeny of Ingham: the latter's expansionist view of the office of press secretary undoubtedly paved the way for Campbell's further centralised control of government communications at Number Ten since 1997 (see Chapter 4; Hattersley, 1998, p. 3). Whatever Campbell's official title, he was 'in reality, chief aide, right hand man, a player and the most powerful unelected politician at the very heart of British government' he was 'the daily voice of the government and Tony Blair' (Toolis, 1998, p. 29). Campbell's control of the prime minister's and the Cabinet's relations with the media, but especially political journalists, was comprehensive and disciplined (Cockerell, 2001, p. 15; Franklin, 2003). By the end of the 1990s, one political journalist claimed,

> Blair never moves from Downing Street without Campbell. He never appears on a platform without Campbell nearby. Never makes a speech that Campbell has not read or rewritten. Never walks into an important room without Campbell close behind. Never takes a decision that Campbell has not been consulted on. Never holds a significant meeting that Campbell does not attend or at least know about. Other Cabinet ministers slavishly repeat Campbell's line on the latest twist of governmental policy in their broadcast interviews. Not vice versa ... There has never been a Chief Press Secretary like Campbell before.
>
> (Toolis, 1998, p. 31)

In one very strict and significant sense this was true. Immediately on assuming office, Tony Blair passed an order in council which bestowed an unprecedented status on Campbell allowing him to wear both a government and a party political hat: to direct Labour HQ at Millbank and permanent civil servants in Whitehall (White and MacAskill, 1999, p. 2, see also Jones, 2001, p. 242). But despite this significant difference, Campbell shares many similarities with Ingham.

Both are ex-journalists and highly skilled at their trade. Ingham worked at the *Hebden Bridge Times*, the *Yorkshire Post* and the *Guardian* before joining the Government Information Service. He was judged (even by his critics) to be an industrious and consumate professional (Harris, 1991). Campbell was similarly well regarded having worked as news editor on *Today* and later as political editor on the *Sunday Mirror* and the *Mirror*. Like Ingham, even Campbell's most ardent critics acknowledge his journalistic talents: (Cockerell, 2000, p. 7; Hagerty, 2000, p. 7; Jones, 2001, p. 182). Campbell's journalism skills have equipped him to hone finely crafted soundbites for Blair to deliver – and at short notice. It was Campbell, for example, on the morning of the death of Diana in 1997, who proclaimed her 'The People's Princess', a phrase which was 'too brilliant in its tabloid compression to have been dreamed up by Tony Blair' since 'It takes years of tabloid hackery to develop such an edge'. It was not the first, nor the last, occasion on which Campbell would assume the role of 'His Master's Voice' (Jones, 1999, p. 52; Toolis, 1998, p. 36).

Second, both Ingham and Campbell came to display an increasing disrespect and hostility towards journalists. Ingham accused journalists of 'exaggeration, speculation, oversimplification and trivialisation' in their political coverage (Ingham 1990) while Campbell routinely objected to the 'regular diet of trivia, froth, speculation and sheer invention that passess for so much political journalism these days'. Political journalists like Peter Oborne recall the many occassions on which Campbell verbally abused journalists during lobby briefings (Jones, 2001, pp. 182–207; Oborne, 1999, pp. 178–87 and 2002, pp. 32–33), while Trevor Kavanagh claimed that Campbell 'loathes the Sunday lobby' (Kavanagh, 2002, p. 14).

Third, Ingham and Campbell's briefings came to be invested with great authority by journalists because of their very close relationships with their respective prime ministers, as well as the overview of all aspects of government policy they achieved. Campbell has been described as 'a living, breathing, acessible doppelganger' for Blair (Toolis, 1998, p. 29): Ingham was 'extraordinarily close to and instinctively in tune with Thatcher' (White and MacAskill, 1999, p. 2). To some degree this empathy is inevitable and typical. Number Ten press secretaries often complement the prime ministers with whom they work. Harold Evans's unhurried style of addressing the lobby, for example, did much to reinforce perceptions of Macmillan as 'unflappable'. Gus O'Donnell, who succeeded Ingham, was likewise believed to complement John Major's reputation for being 'a nice guy' who is quiet and open to debate. After only six months in office there was allegedly 'a strong bond' between them (Jones, 1991a). But Blair and Campbell were even closer than other 'such Downing Street partnerships' since 'neither age or experience, social class or intellect, divide them ... Both are provincial meritocrats sprung from the respectable middle classes .... You couldn't put a radicchio leaf between them' (White and MacAskill, 1999, p. 2).

Fourth, Ingham and Campbell are acknowledged to be exemplary and accomplished press secretaries. Ingham's critics conceed his unprecedented ability to orchestrate the government information machine and manage successfully media reporting of government (Harris, 1990, p. 53 and p. 110; Jones 1991b) while Campbell is 'very, very good at his job' which is to 'make the government more effective by controlling its image in the press' (Toolis, 1998, p. 36). Ingham and Campbell also share a reputation as Stakhanovites! Ingham's working day began at 6 a.m. and finished late (Ingham, 1991, pp. 207–23). Campbell likewise began at 6 a.m. and was 'lucky if the last calls come in before midnight' (White and MacAskill, 1999, p. 3): Campbell acknowledges he is a workaholic with 'a massive work ethic' (Hattersley, 1998, p. 3).

Finally, both Ingham and Campbell have expanded the role of the prime minister's press secretary: indeed, Ingham's expansive view of the job was a precondition for Campbell's later consolidation of the power of the post at Number Ten. Ingham kept close control of the lobby (despite the attempted coup by some of its members – see below), used the weekly meetings of information officers to orchestrate the flow of released information about government, became head of the Government Information Service and 'politicised' the post by becoming very closely associated with the policies of prime minister Thatcher. Campbell proved even more vigorous in establishing his supremacy within the lobby, centralised control over government communications at Number Ten, established the Strategic Communications Unit and the Media Monitoring Unit to assist his news management activities, co-ordinated the work of a network of special advisers placed within the various departments of state, enjoyed an unprecedented status (following the 1997 Order in Council) which recognises both his partisan and neutral civil service roles and, since early 2002, became the person to whom the chief executive of the Central Office of Information reports (see Chapters 3 and 4). Less formally, two senior political commentators observed, Campbell 'spends more time with Blair than anyone else, sits in the Cabinet (his predecessors have not), has an overview of government that is denied most ministers and has control over the flow of information'. Perhaps unsurprisingly, some believed him to be 'the second most important man in Britain' (White and MacAskill, 1999, p. 2).

Campbell's resignation on 29 August 2003 evidently created a communication chasm which would be difficult to fill. The red-tops marked his departure with uncritical eulogies. For the *Mirror*, Campbell was 'irreplaceable' (Editorial, 30 August 2003, p. 6), the *Sun* declared him to be 'one of the best cabinet ministers this country never had' (Editorial, 30 August 2003, p. 14), while Stephen Glover writing in the *Daily Mail* asked, 'Can Blair Live Without Him?' (30 August 2003, p. 12). The other question on many commentators' agenda was why Campbell had chosen to resign after giving his own evidence to Hutton, but before the outcome of the inquiry was known. *Mirror* political commentator Paul Routledge suggests Campbell's resignation was 'a perfect piece of timing' intended 'to brilliantly divert attention away from the political tribulations of the Prime Minister' (*Mirror*, 30 August 2003, p. 6). Campbell's close friend and journalist Roy Greenslade demurs from this account. Campbell, he suggests, did not resign because of the 'Kelly affair' or because he had become a 'massive liability' to the government as some newspapers had alleged (Greenslade 2003, p. 2): indeed John Scarlett's evidence to Hutton appeared to clear Campbell of the major allegation of 'sexing up' the dossier to include the '45 minutes' claim. Greenslade offers two reasons for Campbell's departure. First, for the previous year Campbell had become exhausted by the 24/7 demands of his job: he was 'worn down by the treadmill of being the government's presentation guru' (ibid.). But secondly, and significantly, Campbell's resignation dates back to 4 December 2002 and the media feeding frenzy over 'Cheriegate', which delved into Cherie Blair's involvement with 'conman' Peter Foster, the boyfriend of her confidant and 'lifestyle guru' Carol Caplin. Campbell's partner Fiona Millar, Cherie Blair's paid press adviser, was largely ignored during the affair while Mrs Blair preferred the amateur advice offered by Caplin. Millar let it be known she was retiring in September 2003. These events represented a 'breach in the four-way relationship between the Blairs and Campbell/Millar' (Ibid.) and confirmed Campbell's decision to resign. In brief, Greenslade asserts, Campbell's final resignation statement was not spin, nor cliché employed by those politically out of favour, he genuinely wished to spend more time with his family.

Early assessments of Campbell's successor, David Hill, are highly variable. Roy Hattersley describes him as 'tough, blunt, abrasive and scrupulously honest' (*Guardian*, 13 August 2003, p. 26) while the *Mirror's* political correspondent declares Hill to be 'Alastair Campbell Mark 2' (*Mirror*, 30 August 2003, p. 5), the *Independent* prefers the more paradoxical description of Hill as the 'man who can spin with integrity' (*Independent*, 30 August 2003, p. 2). The interim recommendations of the Phillis inquiry into government communications, give him a lesser formal brief than Campbell enjoyed: significantly, Hill will not be allowed the right to direct civil servants, which was unique to Campbell. But Hill remains a powerful figure who is entitled to attend Cabinet meetings and whose wide-ranging and broadly defined brief is to 'provide the political perspective on behalf of the prime minister and assist cabinet ministers with the political context for departmental communications' (*Guardian*, 4 September 2003, p. 4; http://www.gcreview.org.uk).

Hill undoubtedly inherits a troubled legacy and a press office at Number Ten in some disarray following the death of David Kelly and the Hutton inquiry. Godric Smith, one of the prime minister's two official spokespeople, has announced his resignation: the other, Tom Kelly, enjoys a poor reputation after briefing journalists that David Kelly was a 'Walter Mitty figure'. But Hill is highly experienced in political advocacy. While Campbell's background was in political journalism, David Hill is a seasoned public relations specialist who was political adviser and chief of staff to Roy Hattersley from 1971 and Labour's Director of Communications during the leadership of Neil Kinnock and John Smith, leaving the post in 1998 to join Lord (Tim) Bell's PR firm Bell Pottinger Good Relations. It is perhaps too early to assess whether the 'man who can spin with integrity' will prove up to the job of fixing the 'three way breakdown in trust between media, politicians and the public' identified by Phillis (http://www.gcreview.org.uk), but Hill's involvement in fixing 'the Humphrys problem' (see chapter 4) suggests that he is not averse to bullying broadcasters if they become too critical of the ministers he is minding.

THE UNHOLY ALLIANCE: POLITICIANS AND THE LOBBY

The lobby was born in troubled times. In 1884, Fenian bombs were exploding in London, prompting the closure to the general public of that part of the Westminster precinct known as the members' lobby (Foley, 1993; Horgan, 2001, p. 259). Apart from members themselves, access was restricted to political journalists whose names were kept on a special list compiled by the Sergeant-at-Arms. These circumstances of birth explain Kellner's designation of the lobby, borrowed unashamedly from a television advertisement for lager, as those 'political correspondents who are allowed ... to reach the parts of parliamentary buildings that other journalists cannot reach' (Kellner, 1983, p. 275).

In truth the lobby is a cartel for the provision of political information: 'a self-perpetuating elite with written rules, whose members accord government ministers and spokespersons with anonymity in return for privileged access to political information' (Horgan, 2001, p. 259). It is the formal association of the 220 or so newspaper, radio and television journalists based at the Palace of Westminster who constitute the major source of published and broadcast political news (McNair, 2000, pp. 43–4). This 'elite' has expanded considerably in the post-war period. Provincial evening papers joined in the 1940s, the Sundays in the 1960s, the weeklies ten years later and finally the broadcasters (Seymour-Ure, 1991, p. 189). Michael Macdonagh, a gallery reporter in the House at the turn of the century, described the function of the lobby as 'gathering the political gossip of members, the official communications of the government and the opposition' in order to serve them up at breakfast the following day, 'in brief crisp paragraphs, often with spicy personal comments' (Macdonagh, n.d.). Some observers believe that in essence little has changed. Ninety years after Macdonagh, Roy Hattersley offers a similar, if more critical, description. The lobby, the 'unholy alliance' in his preferred phrase, is 'a partnership between politicians and journalists which – since it treats gossip as if it were fact and invention as if it were truth – is profoundly damaging to the democratic process' (Hattersley, 2001, p. 227). But despite these criticisms, the lobby still 'produces practically all the political news we all consume' (Hennessy and Walker, 1987, p. 110; King and Sloman, 1982, p. 174). On a daily basis at 11.30, lobby journalists stroll into the briefing room: 'Tomorrow's news is about to be announced' (Toolis, 1998, p. 29).

The lobby is more stratified than its name implies and in practice constitutes a carefully structured journalistic hierachy (Barnett and Gaber, 2001, pp. 36–7). At the head of this pecking order are the political editors, the very senior journalists with ready access to Number Ten, the office of the leader of the opposition, their editors and the front page of their newspapers. The political editor's seniority is signalled by 'his little slot reserved for him on the front page where his byline goes every day' (cited in ibid., p. 35). The rank below is occupied by the political correspondents who generate the majority of significant political stories, while the bottom layer (typically referred to as 'pond life') are the political reporters sometimes bylined as 'political staff' although this journalistic signature may simply be a ploy to disguise the fact that the story has originated from a news agency (ibid., p. 35).

Since the early 1950s, however, three interconnected processes have led to a considerable change in the character and working routines of the lobby: collectivisation, appropriation and codification. First, the lobby has been transformed from a group of journalists with a disparate set of competitive interests into a collective, ready-made press conference, which is briefed en masse. In the words of one observer 'the old style competitive outsiders were organised into a fraternity of organised insiders' (Margach, 1981, p. 137).

Second, the lobby has been appropriated by government as a conduit for information and, in this process, metamorphosed from an active and critical observer of political affairs into a passive purveyor of government messages. This hungry corps of lobby journalists has a voracious appetite for the political news served up by the government and its official spokespersons. In Ireland this journalistic reliance on government is captured in the colloquial description of the daily 5 p.m. lobby briefings as 'the feed' (Horgan, 2001, p. 269).

Finally, the lobby has witnessed the codification of a set of rules enforcing non-attribution of news sources while simultaneously obliging journalists to rely on a single source, usually the prime minister's press secretary or official spokesperson (Cockerell et al., 1984, p. 36; Hennessy and Walker, 1987, p. 118). In these changed circumstances the lobby has become 'an accomplice of Big government' (Hennessy and Walker, 1987, p. 115): in 'pursuit of an easy life' journalists have 'progressively relegated themselves to the status of mere instruments of government propaganda' (Porter, 1985, p. 87). Before 2001 the lobby was briefed almost exclusively by the Number Ten press secretary and 'what the press secretary says at these briefings is what the prime minister wants the press, radio and television to report' (Cockerell et al., 1984, p. 33). If, for example, the press secretary raises an interesting matter arising from the Cabinet meeting, the likelihood is that it will appear as a news item, replete with the political spin he places on it, in the early evening bulletins on BBC, ITN, Channel 4 and Channel 5 News as well as the evening news bulletins on network radio. The item will probably be developed as a story for the later television news bulletins and feature prominently in the national press the following morning. In this way, the discussion of an item initiated by a government official in an unattributable briefing can structure the political news agendas of the media; in the words of Ian Aitken, a senior political correspondent, the lobby during the 1980s became 'Ingham's hallelujah chorus'. Some commentators have expressed this relationship in more robust terms. *Sun* columnist Richard Littlejohn, for example, claims that in its efforts to manage the news, Number Ten is 'aided and abetted by a bone-idle and corrupt lobby system, littered with journalists who are happy to play the part of spoon-fed stooges' (cited in Jones, 1999, p. 94).

How does the lobby work on a day-to-day basis? The lobby is briefed twice daily about the entire range of government activities and intentions by the prime minister's official spokesperson. Every weekday morning at about 11 o'clock, a group of lobby journalists arrive at the Foreign Press Association for a briefing (before October 2002, briefings were held at Number Ten). A second briefing is conducted in the House of Commons at 4 p.m. in the lobby's own room – its 'secret sanctuary' (Cockerell et al., 1984, p. 43). Access to the 'turret' is via a rather rickety spiral staircase leading off the upper committee corridor of the House of Commons. Typical of the secrecy which surrounds the lobby's affairs, this room does not feature on the building plans of the House (Lawson, 1990, p. 32). But these formal briefings represent a mere fraction of the press secretary's contacts with lobby journalists. Ingham claims that in addition to 5,000 lobby briefings during his residence at Number Ten, he gave 30,000 individual briefings, and that 'it was a quiet working day if I did not brief ten journalists more informally over the phone' (Ingham, 1991, p. 191). Still more informal were the lunches and dinners with journalists. Ingham calculates that 'if these averaged only two a week for eleven years, I chomped my way through 1,000 meals with the fourth estate' (ibid., p. 322).

The main lobby briefing of the week is on Thursdays following the morning Cabinet meeting. A Press Association journalist has described the usual format for meetings: 'The lobby chairman is in charge. He bangs his gavel down on the table whereupon the press secretary from Downing Street gives a run down on the prime minister's working day. He says what statements are likely to take place and he then invites press questions on any topic of the day' (Cockerell et al., 1984, p. 44). The press secretary's Thursday briefing is followed by a briefing from the leader of the house and, at 5.15 p.m. on Thursdays, the lobby is addressed by the leader of the opposition, although this is an on-the-record briefing (Harris, 1990, p. 143; Hennessy and Walker, 1987, p. 126). On Fridays when many MPs are in their constituencies and the House is relatively quiet, a special briefing is held for the Sunday correspondents (Barnett and Gaber, 2001, p. 42), although recently relations between Downing Street and the Sunday lobby have become 'strained' (Rose, 2003, p. 6). Perhaps unsurprisingly, the Lobby has increasingly come under criticism from both journalists and politicians, for the secrecy which characterises its operations. Hattersley acknowledges that

> In any system politicians will speak in confidence to journalists they know well [but by] institutionalising the secrecy – encouraging MPs to sidle up to lobby correspondents and whisper in their ears – we promote the politics of rumour, innuendo and gossip.
>
> (Hattersley, 2001, p. 234)

Three additional criticisms have been levelled at the lobby. First, lobby journalists get 'sucked into the system' (Kellner, 1988, p. 276). They come to feel their task is to promote the interests of the lobby rather than the interests of their readers. Consequently, they fail to challenge government and rarely subject the information, which the government provides the lobby, to the critical scrutiny it deserves. The lobby produces 'lazy journalism undertaken by lazy journalists' (ibid., p. 281): it packages political news and the journalists help to wrap it up. The mutuality of interests on which the lobby is based, makes journalists and politicians collaborators when they should be antagonists. A distinguished political commentator acknowledged this dilemma without resolving it. 'Both government and the media are compelled by the unlimited demands of modern communications to co-operate, yet by all basic tests they are opposing and rival forces' (Margach 1981, p. 129). Indeed the 'guiding principle' acknowledged in journalists' *Notes on the Practice of Lobby Journalism* is a mutual obligation to 'exercise self-discipline to ensure the system works satisfactorily for all concerned' (cited in Jones, 1995, p. 86).

Second, the lobby system is used to fly kites (Gaber, 2000, p. 67; Jones, 1995, p. 84). If ministers are uncertain about a particular policy or its public popularity they can allude to the policy in the lobby, which will guarantee it receives some media coverage. If the subsequent reaction among the public or other politicians is hostile, ministers can deny ever raising the issue and denounce the story as journalistic fabrication. In much the same way, unpopular policy decisions can be released to the lobby and the general public incrementally, thereby removing much of the sting from opposition criticisms by obliging piecemeal discussion of the measure. 'Good news' can be stored up and released at the same time as 'bad news' in the hope of diverting editorial attention and ameliorating the adverse political impact of the latter. Occasionally, bad news can be released when a major story suddenly dominates the news agenda and provides suitable 'cover' which obscures the potential salience of the 'bad news' story and limits damage to government: such occasions can provide 'a good day to bury bad news'. In brief, the lobby encourages government manipulation of news (Franklin, 2003; McKie, 1982, p. 180).

Third, while the lobby system does not typically result in the publication of lies (although this can be the result of lobby briefings), it may promote half-truths and is certainly not the stuff of investigative journalism. Some of the information fed to the lobby, for the reason cited above, turns out to be wrong or only partially true, because the journalists are being used for government news-management purposes. Kellner has an amusing culinary metaphor to hand. 'Lobby information is to real information', he claims, 'roughly what sliced white bread is to real food. It is cheap, conveniently packaged, with most of the goodness and wholesome character taken out of it. It is not wholly without nutritional value but it is not as good as the real thing. But the real thing tends to be more expensive and more demanding on the palate' (Kellner, 1988, p. 278). This of course is the very hub of what journalists find attractive about the lobby. It is an inexpensive way of filling up newspapers with political stories. Investigative political journalism outside the lobby system is very expensive both of money and time; scarce resources indeed!

Any institution which serves such useful functions for both journalists and politicians will inevitably attract supporters. Adam Raphael, the *Observer's* former political editor, rejects the view of the lobby as self-serving and easily manipulated claiming 'this is a ludicrous misunderstanding of how the system actually works. There are about 150 [now 220] members of the lobby representing publications ranging from the far left to the far right. The idea that such a large disparate body can be collectively gulled by being drip fed information from number 10 is inherently implausible' (Raphael, 17 June, 1984, quoted in Ingham, 1991, p. 194). Peter Riddell agrees, recalling Jeremy Tunstall's suggestion that lobby correspondents perform one of three roles: 'tame lapdog, alert watchdog and fierce fighting dog' adding 'often, I would argue on the same day' (Riddell, 1999, p. 26). Criticism, moreover, rests on a misunderstanding about the way in which a journalist develops a story. Journalists may take a feed from the lobby but then consult a much wider network of sources including politicians and advisers from across the political spectrum, before filling out the story with their own and others' ideas about the matter. The lobby briefing may provide the starting point but 'rarely the totality' of a political story (Barnett and Gaber, 2001, p. 41). But, to modify the adage about agenda setting, a briefing which 'tells a journalist what to think about but not what to think' is nonetheless significant. But the political editor of the *Sunday Telegraph* suggests that too much of the criticism of the lobby rests on ignorance peppered with hyperbole: he ends, however, by arguing that the use of codified expression in one branch of journalism renders it legitimate in all journalism specialisms.

> The mystique of the lobby as an organisation that receives secret briefings and all that sort of thing is over-hyped in my view. A lot of nonsense gets written about it ... Its just a lot of journalists talking to a lot of people all in the same place, all at the same time ... When I first joined the lobby I was told by someone who had been there a long time that you weren't ever allowed to put anything that was said in a briefing in direct quotes, and frankly people were already ignoring it and I ignored it. But I wouldn't say 'Bernard Ingham said', I would say 'a senior Whitehall source' – everyone knew what the code was. The code has been simplified now, but there is still a code. Isn't there in all journalism? If you are in business journalism and you talk to the managing director of some company, then you will say 'senior sources at company X' it's just the same thing.
>
> (Cited in Barnett and Gaber, 2001, p. 39)

But many journalists and editors continue to be critical of the lobby (Rusbridger, 2000, p. 20). This scepticism is rooted in the mid-1980s when a group of senior journalists argued that Ingham was abusing his position as a servant of the crown to disparage ministers critical of Thatcher and to manipulate the lobby to help orchestrate their downfall.

The process began with the political demise of Norman St John Stevas in January 1981, continued with the removal of Francis Pym in 1982 and culminated in the destruction of John Biffen's political career in 1986. Biffen was disliked by both Thatcher and Ingham; like Stevas and Pym they considered him too much the 'toff'. But it was his criticism of the prime minister during an interview on *Weekend World* on 11 May 1986, in which he suggested (in what was to prove a farsighted observation) that 'nobody seriously supposes that the prime minister would be prime minister throughout the entire period of the next Parliament', which sealed his fate. The next day, Ingham briefed the lobby against Biffen, denouncing his remarks and questioning his loyalty to the prime minister and support for the government. By Tuesday the ventriloquist national press was expressing the press secretary's view that Biffen was not 'fully integrated' into government. *The Times* claimed 'Mr Biffen was a "semi-detached" member of the Cabinet' (13 May, 1986), while the *Sun* displayed a remarkable lack of originality but at least offered Biffen a modicum of celebrity by describing him as 'a well known semi-detached member of the government' (13 May 1986). Ingham's hallelujah chorus was well-orchestrated and singing as if a single voice!

For her part, the prime minister appeared publicly to support her minister claiming, when questioned in the House about his comments, that she agreed with many of his remarks. But she never spoke to him again. 'Instead', as one observer commented, 'she had him murdered out of the corner of someone else's mouth – quietly, in the dark, away from the public gaze' (Harris, 1990, p. 147).

Some newspapers objected to this political manipulation of the lobby. Between June and September 1986, the *Guardian*, the *Independent* and the *Scotsman* withdrew from the lobby, stating they were no longer willing to comply with its requirement of non-attribution and 'off-the-record' briefings. In future, press reports based on lobby briefing would attribute information to 'Downing Street sources' or the 'prime minister's spokesperson'. Ingham was furious and made it clear he would resist such a change vigorously. *Guardian* journalists were asked by the lobby not to attend briefings until the proposed change could be the subject of a vote by members; on 29 October the lobby decided by 67 votes to 55 not to change the basis on which lobby briefings were conducted (Horgan, 2001, pp. 260–1). Temerity, favourable access to government 'sources' and a predilection for 'lazy journalism' appeared to have carried the day. The *Guardian*, the newly established *Independent* and the *Scotsman* withdrew from the lobby. Correspondents from these newspapers received no information about the prime minister from the press secretary's office. Even the most routine inquiries about the prime minister's whereabouts were unanswered.

Gus O'Donnell, who replaced Ingham when Thatcher resigned in 1990, eschewed the confrontational style of Ingham, volunteered an 'unexpectedly full account of government business' and allowed his briefings to be referred to as 'Downing Street sources' rather than the vaguer 'government sources' which Ingham had always insisted upon (Jones, 1995, p. 86). Within weeks of taking up the post he enticed the 'rebel' papers back into the daily lobby briefings and increased the number of briefings. 'Mr O'Donnell frightens nobody as Mrs Thatcher's Ingham did', *The Economist* claimed, but added, 'he is however liked by everybody – which may prove more useful' (2 November, 1991, p. 42). But, in truth, little had changed in lobby briefings other than the personality of the prime minister's press secretary. Everything else – the secrecy of the organisation, its trivial rituals, the exclusiveness of its membership, the privileged access to government information it enjoys, the ethos of 'lazy' journalism it fosters – remained intact.

Recently, history has repeated itself. Ingham's use of the lobby to brief against ministers critical of Thatcher has found a counterpart in the pejorative and damaging personal comments about members of the Blair Cabinet, which have appeared in the press attributed to a 'senior government source'. In October 1997, for example, 'a Downing Street source' briefed the lobby that David Clark, a forceful advocate of a rigorous Freedom of Information Bill, would lose his Cabinet place in the next reshuffle since he had 'totally lost it' and was the 'despair of his civil servants'. In January 1998 *Observer* columnist Andrew Rawnsley was told at the end of a long informal briefing over the telephone by 'someone who has an extremely good claim to know the mind of the PM [ie Campbell]' that 'you know Gordon, he feels so vulnerable and insecure. He has these psychological flaws' (Rawnsley, 2000, p. 150). By June 1999 Harriet Harman had been declared 'incapable of joined up thinking' while Frank Field was denounced as 'a complete joke'. When Peter Kilfoyle resigned alleging Labour's disdain for its traditional voters, it was claimed 'he's been spending too long in the bars' while a 'senior government aide' suggested that Mo Mowlam's illness had left her 'without the intellectual rigour for her job' with another anonymous 'adviser' claiming to be 'dismayed at her erratic behaviour'. Outside the Cabinet, well-known supporters of Labour such as Ken Follett and Lord Winston have also been briefed against in the lobby. Ironically, when Follett criticised Number Ten for briefing against former friends it was to prove a self-fulfilling prophecy: 'Ken's always been good at fiction, hasn't he?' claimed a Downing Street source, 'serious people will treat his outburst with the derision it deserves' (*Guardian*, 14 February 2001, p. 23).

But this systematic use of lobby briefings to discipline new Labour dissidents – within and without Cabinet – has not prompted the retreat from the lobby which Ingham provoked in the mid-1980s, although it provoked Alan Rusbridger to devise and implement new rules concerning lobby reporting for *Guardian* correspondents. But in the new millennium, the lobby occupies a less significant place in political communications than previously.

THE LOBBY: DEVELOPMENTS AND CHANGE

By the summer of 2002 Labour's use of the parliamentary lobby, as part of a broader strategy of news management, had itself become a severe presentational problem

(Campbell, 2002, pp. 20–21). The continuous opposition chorus which alleged that Labour was strong on spin and presentation but weak on delivery was beginning to be echoed in public concerns about the government and its effectiveness. On 16 July 2002, for the first time since 1938, the British prime minister addressed a select committee of the House. Blair used this exceptional parliamentary occasion to announce his 'Damascene conversion', to repent publicly Labour's reliance on 'spin' and to announce his new intention to 'try to engage in the political debate in a different way' (Blair, 16 July 2002; see Franklin, 2003a). The previous five years had certainly witnessed a number of reforms to the protocols governing the operation of the lobby.

First, in 1997, the prime minister established an inquiry under Robin Mountfield to examine how the Government Information Service might be 'modernised' by incorporating some of the information and communication techniques developed by the Labour Party in opposition at Millbank. The subsequent report had few implications for the lobby except to revoke the principle of non-attribution so jealously guarded by Ingham. On 27 November 1997 the government, acting on Mountfield's recommendation, announced that in future the twice daily briefings of the lobby by the prime minister's press secretary would be on the record. Phrases such as 'sources close to the prime minister' and other journalistic devices to avoid attribution were henceforth redundant. Journalists could now identify the 'prime minister's official spokesman' as the source of much of the political information which informed their political reports (Barnett and Gaber, 2001, p. 38; Hagerty, 2000, p. 10). Campbell finally conceded to journalists the right to identify him by name on 15 March 2000: on the same day a number of broadsheet national news papers also published verbatim reports of the previous day's lobby briefing (*Guardian*, 15 March 2000, p. 12). Perhaps significantly, shortly after, in June 2000, Alastair Campbell handed over the twice-daily task of briefing the lobby to his deputy Godric Smith an experienced information officer and Tom Kelly an ex-BBC political correspondent and former information officer in Northern Ireland. For his part Campbell would no longer be 'fighting over every headline' but adopting a new role as director of strategy and communications (White, 14 June 2000, p. 13; White, 7 January 2002, p. 5). Around the same time, (11 February 2000) the government launched the Number Ten website (http://www.Number-10.gov.UK) containing video footage of the current week's prime minister's question time, a news section highlighting key stories of the week, chat rooms for public feedback but also edited extracts from the previous day's lobby briefing (Barnett and Gaber, 2001, p. 40; Ward, 2000, p. 5).

Second, *Guardian* Political editor Michael White argued that the above changes had been triggered by lobby correspondents' annoyance on learning that BBC documentary film-maker Michael Cockerell had been granted permission to attend and film a number of lobby briefings (White, 15 March 2000, p. 12). When Cockerell's film *News From No 10* was broadcast in July 2000 it certainly shattered the tradition of secrecy concerning the lobby by featuring extensive and unprecedented footage of a lobby briefing including the arrival of Alastair Campbell with half a dozen advisers and supporters from the GICS. It revealed, moreover, Campbell's communications supremacy and the armoury of post-1997 communications organisations he had developed to assist him with his news management ambitions and which empowered him in his relations with the lobby (Cockerell, *News From No 10,* July 2000). Reviews discussing the protrayal of journalists in the programme suggest that their public image might have been better served by keeping the tradition of secrecy intact. One observer could not decide whether the most apt description of lobby journalists was 'malleable sheep' or 'slothful parrots' while A. A. Gill in *The Sunday Times* denounced them as 'a lickspittle-whipped sycophantic bunch of special pleaders snapping and growling over scraps at the kitchen door' (Hagerty, 2000, p. 13). But no matter how unattractive the life forms revealed, Cockerell's film had certainly lifted the stone: the mystique of the lobby was irretrievably lost.

Third, journalists themselves instituted changes. In July 2000, *Guardian* editor Alan Rusbridger argued that the lobby was being used to brief against ministers who were critical of Blair and announced a 'stricter code' on these 'ghostly voices'. Specifically, Rusbridger was unhappy with the anonymous lobby briefings against Lord Winston, Mo Mowlam and Gordon Brown 'or whoever the victim of the moment is deemed to be'. He cited the tabloid headline announcing 'Power crazed and Bonkers' above a picture of Gordon Brown with a story which offered a disparaging attack on the chancellor which was sourced to 'a government colleague'. Rusbridger argued that 'anonymity must not become a cloak for attacking people' and announced that in addition to naming the spokesman at official briefings the *Guardian* would adopt a stricter code for journalists to 'encourage reporters to be as specific as possible about the source of any anonymous quotation' (Morgan, 2000, p. 1; Rusbridger, 2000, p. 20).

Fourth, on 2 May 2002, Alastair Campbell announced that the 11 a.m. lobby briefings were no longer to be confined to the Westminster-based correspondents, but opened to all journalists, including London-based foreign correspondents, to question officials, government experts and sometimes even ministers: occasionally it is televised (Rose, 2002, p. 5; White, 3 May 2002, p. 8). Campbell claimed that voter alienation from politics and falling electoral turnout reflected the continuing 'dialogue of the deaf' between journalists and politicians which had to be resolved. 'We have got to be less buttoned-up' he claimed and 'far more open, far less worried about what you guys are going to write' (cited in *Guardian*, 3 May 2002, p. 1). Journalists responded with suspicion suggesting that the move represented little more than an attempt to 'dilute the lobby's power' (White, 3 May 2002, p. 3). The inclusion of 'countless non-lobby journalists' and 'virtually anyone who cares to turn up', for example, would allow the government to avoid sustained and detailed questioning by political correspondents (Jones, 2002, p. 363; Kavanagh, 2002, p. 17). Moreover, the fact that details of these changes to lobby procedures were leaked from a consultation meeting with broadcasters at Chequers signals, print journalists believe, the government's desire to marginalise troublesome and partisan newspapers in favour of television which has a larger audience reach and is more readily 'managed' by governments via the licence fee (White, 3 May 2002, p. 8).

Labour undoubtedly seems warmer to broadcast than print journalists. In announcing David Hill as Alastair Campbell's successor and accepting the interim report of the Phillis inquiry on the reform of government communications, the Prime Minister effectively invited the cameras into the lobby by asking the Committee to consider whether 'the transparency of government communications would be enhanced by the daily briefings being on camera' (*Guardian*, 4 September 2003, p. 4: http://www.gcreview.gov.uk). Broadcast journalists like Nicholas Jones believe that the limited televising of briefings since autumn 2002 has been valuable in promoting 'wider access' for all journalists, although it is important to note that the long established and on the record Presidential press briefings at the White House have coexisted happily with political communication structures and processes which are characterised by news management and spin (Jones, 2003, p. 49).

The first of the new open briefings was held on 14 October 2002 in the Foreign Press Association in Carlton House Terrace. Journalist Simon Hoggart was unimpressed. The briefing was 'complete chaos'. The room was too small, Westminster based correspondents had to suffer 'the long walk across St James' Park'. Tom Kelly proved evasive in answering questions and only a single foreign journalist managed to ask a question. For Hoggart, proceedings confirmed the old maxim that 'when politicians talk about "openness" what they mean is "concealment". Putting everything on the record in front of anyone possibly including a representative of *al-Qaida newsletter*, gives the perfect excuse for not saying anthing at all, except for a little logistical house-keeping and more of the boasting which always marks this government' (Hoggart, 15 October 2002, p. 10). Lobby chairman Jon Smith claimed 'the quality of information on offer has dwindled noticeably' and the briefings have 'been rendered all but useless for evening newspaper lobby members (Rose, 2003, p. 6).

Amid this flurry of reform and change, but without resort to Trevor Kavanagh's self-serving hyperbole that 'we are being disbanded because we are a thorn in Tony Blair's side' (Kavanagh, 2002, p. 18), it is clear that the lobby is a less significant source of political news than previously. The reasons underlying this decline are evident: many are discussed in greater detail in the following chapter. First, the government's preference for the broadcast media to deliver its message means that political information is increasingly available outside of the official briefings. Ministers make statements in interviews on the early morning Radio 4 *Today* programme and give copious interviews on the College Green, while press officers inform journalists via 'leaks' and by trailing stories. Second, senior members of the lobby will contact the Number Ten press office prior to the lobby – or shortly afterwards – to try to gain additional and private information. Jackie Ashley, political editor of the *New Statesman* claimed that 'more significant than the lobby meetings are the phone calls and briefings which take place outside . . . it's then and in private phone calls, that much of the valuable 'feeding' takes place' (Barnett and Gaber, 2001, p. 130). In brief the corporate character of the lobby is being eroded as the government finds it increasingly convenient to manage and congenial to deal with individual journalists: the collectivisation of the lobby which Hennessey *et al.* observed is being reversed. Third, governments are less and less likely to announce major policy shifts in the House or trail them in the lobby. Modern news management prefers the incremental announcement of policy which maximises coverage: in turn this allows political journalists to intuit the unravelling political agenda without attending the lobby. The government's advisers might mention a new policy in the barest detail in the Friday afternoon briefing for Sunday journalists but will contact journalists directly to follow through with stories for the Sunday and Monday papers. On Tuesday the relevant Minister may well appear on the *Today* programme, so that by the time the lobby is briefed about the issue it is effectively yesterday's news (Barnett and Gaber, 2001, p. 131).

Finally a number of technological developments may have implications for lobby operations. The arrival of satellite, cable and digital delivery systems carrying 24-hour news channels such as BBC News 24, CNN and Sky News means that breaking news is conveyed instantly and live to audiences before correspondents can return to their desks from the lobby briefing. The development of mobile phone and text messaging technology, moreover, means that journalists may now be better briefed – including news which has broken during the lobby and which is conveyed to them via a text message – than the person formally briefing. It also means that politicians, no matter how well briefed, might now be confronted by a difficult question posed by a journalist which they could not possibly have anticipated (Horgan, 2001, p. 270). The implications of the Internet for political journalism are yet to become clear but the expansive electronic access to government and party press releases, Hansard, Select Committee reports, statutes, white papers and government and non-governmental reports, will almost certainly diminish journalists' need to be in close proximity of parliament and to attend lobby briefings.

Chapter Three

☐ NEW LABOUR AND THE END OF SPIN?

In May 2003 Alastair Campbell, then Labour's Director of Communications, unleashed 'shock and awe' on the BBC, alleging partisanship in the Corporation's coverage of the Iraq war and demanding an apology for journalist Andrew Gilligan's use of a single anonymous source for a story alleging that Campbell had 'sexed up' a (dodgy) dossier on Iraq. Subsequently, Campbell invaded *Channel 4 News* (27 June 2003), to make a broad public attack on the quality of journalism at the BBC and again demanded an apology for Gilligan's claim that he had altered intelligence assessments of the threat Iraq posed to the West. Many observers (especially journalists) interpreted Campbell's allegations as a classic 'news management' strategy to shift media attention away from Blair and on to the BBC (Morrison and McSmith 2003; Routledge, 2003 and Tusa, 2003). Murdoch's *Sun* and *Times* began to editorialise against the BBC, while Culture Secretary Tessa Jowell, in a speech to the Royal Television Society in Cambridge, began 'haranguing the BBC with threats about its future independence' (Liddle, 2003, p. 6). The eventual 'naming' of David Kelly as the source by a press adviser at the Department of Defence (9 July 2003), Kelly's televised interrogation by the Select Committee on Foreign Affairs (15 July 2003) and in a private session by the Intelligence and Security Committee (16 July 2003) and his subsequent suicide (17 July 2003) prompted the Hutton inquiry (2 August 2003) and rumours of Campbell's imminent resignation (*Guardian*, 25 July 2003, p. 1) – rumours that were confirmed on 29 August 2003.

The government used Campbell's resignation and the appointment of his successor David Hill, previously a Director of Communications for the Labour party and a Director of the PR company Good Relations, as a platform from which to launch a revised communications structure at Number Ten and to announce the end of spin. But political journalists expressed scepticism about the prospect of the future 'spin-free zone' anticipated by the *Mirror* (30 August 2003, p. 4). In part the scepticism reflected Hill's close resemblance to his predecessor in key respects. A Labour MP and long time colleague declared 'David Hill is Alastair Campbell Mark 2 – tough and competent but with only a passing acquaintance with the concepts of democracy and participation' (*Mirror*, 30 August 2003, p. 5). In part, journalists' scepticism also reflected their understanding that spin and news management were deeply embedded in the structures of governance and delivered electoral benefits to politicians in every party. 'It is a seductive theory to banish media spin and manipulation as if it were an aberration that can be consigned to history' claimed the political editor of the *Financial Times*, 'but spin will not be so easily buried. The reason is that deep in every Labour minister's psyche is the belief that spin works: that without it, Labour would not have achieved two landslide majorities. Senior Conservatives acknowledge privately that they will never get back into power without deploying some of the methods new Labour has deployed' (*Financial Times* 30 August 2003, p. 13). Hugo Young agreed: spin doctors are here to stay because of their central role in contemporary politics and Labour should 'abandon the illusion that the news manager can be dropped as an official functionary. The spun pretence will no doubt emerge that the spinning has stopped. Maybe it will actually become a little subtler. But no British leader, given the media ranged against him, could ever give it up. Or fail to want the equal of Campbell to take on the task' (Young 2003, p. 20).

But journalists' scepticism concerning the end of spin largely reflected the fact that they had heard it all before. The government's announcement of a new transparency in its relations with the press and the public seemed somewhat akin to the boy crying wolf in the children's story. The last occasion on which this tale was related was in July 2002 when Tony Blair addressed the House Liaison Committee.

'SPINOCCHIO', BLAIR AND THE END OF SPIN?

On 29 May 2002, the *Daily Mirror* celebrated the resignation of transport secretary Stephen Byers with a front page splash featuring a mock up of a railway station notice board which announced, 'We apologise for the late departure of Stephen Byers from Platform No 10. This was due to a signal failure to realise he was a useless little fibber who should have buried himself months ago'. The press reporting of Byers during the previous eight months represented the most sustained and vitriolic assault on a politician since the attacks by the Murdoch press on Labour leader Neil Kinnock in the run up to the 1992 general election. Both press campaigns resulted in resignation and confirmed the need for politicians to try to sustain congenial working relationships with the press. Press criticism of Byers illustrated another maxim about press operations. It isn't necessary to formally co-ordinate such attacks: the British press still hunts as a pack.

The chase began on 22 October 2001 when British newspapers published Jo Moore's leaked email with its suggestion that September 11 offered an opportune moment for burying bad news (*Telegraph*, 10 October 2001, p. 2). The collective verdict of many journalists, politicians and members of the public was that Moore should be sacked. For other advisers and spin-doctors however, Moore's email represented little more than 'an unfortunate admission about one of the oldest tricks in the book' (*Guardian*, 16 February 2002). But the press focus on Moore persisted, became an obsession and eventually she 'resigned' on 16 February. Byers' own demise three months later followed a 'catalogue of blunders' including the sale of Rover, the placing of Railtrack in administrative limbo, the highly publicised hostilities in his department between civil servants (Martin Sixsmith) and special advisors (Jo Moore), the continuing crisis for commuters in the rail service, the Potter's Bar crash and growing concerns about rail safety. But many pundits speculated that it was Byers' unwillingness to remove Jo Moore that triggered his own eventual demise. Charlie Whelan, former advisor to Gordon Brown, declared that, 'Byers had to go the minute he refused to sack Jo Moore' (*Daily Mirror*, 29 May 2002, p. 7). Despite the strong support he enjoyed from the prime minister and many back-benchers, the media pressure eventually proved irresistible.

The significance of this sustained press campaign for the Labour government extended beyond the loss of an individual minister: even Stephen Byers who was an early and model recruit to Blair's new Labour army. What was critical here was that Byers seemed to exemplify and symbolise an aspect of new Labour which was prompting growing public concern. Much of the press allegation against Byers was that he was preoccupied with presentation rather than substance, promise rather than delivery, 'spinning' rather than truth telling. On 27 February 2002, the *Daily Mirror* had published another front-page story about Byers. Under the headline 'Spinocchio' a picture of Stephen Byers sported an airbrushed nose extended in the fashion of the original storybook character and betraying a similar tendency to tell lies. Alongside the photomontage the text claimed 'the lie keeps growing and growing until it's as clear as the nose on your face' (*Mirror*, 27 February 2002). An editorial in the *Telegraph* alleged that the word 'spin' had joined with 'sleaze' and 'smear' as one of the 'increasing number of Ss' used to describe 'the downward spiral of the reputation of politics' (*Telegraph*, 7 June 2002, p. 27).

This hostile press coverage represented a substantial reversal of fortunes for the Labour government. The success of the Number Ten and Millbank 'message machine' in managing the news and promoting the government's agenda across the previous five years was legendary. Consequently the Labour government was extremely sensitive to this public mood and promptly announced changes to its communication strategy. Peter Mandelson, who had played a key role in developing Labour's media strategy was an early barometer of this shifting public mood and suggested, in an untypically contrite mood, that 'while the government needs ... a strong team of [media] handlers in the field ... crude clumsy handling of the media by overly controlling and politicised press officers causes more problems than no handling at all because it undermines public trust': a clear reference to Byers and the Jo Moore email. Mandelson also regretted that the image of new Labour had become that of a government 'obsessed by spin' and argued that 'the government must at all times be scrupulous with the facts and what it tells the public'. For their part, ministers must become 'less evasive and "controlling" and more open and directly engaged with the media, and not just those correspondents who work inside the Westminster bubble ... too much of what the government is doing fails to make an impact because its words are dismissed as spin' (Mandelson, 2002, pp. xliv–xlv).

The government appeared to be listening to Mandelson's rebuke. Alastair Campbell, who had already handed over lobby briefings to his deputy Godric Smith, announced changes to the lobby designed to make it a more open and inclusive forum (Rose, 2002, p. 5, *Guardian*, 25 July 2002, p. 11). A month later, in an effort to create a renewed dialogue with the news media, Tony Blair called a press conference at Number Ten and invited senior journalists to pose questions on any area of policy. On 16 July 2002, Blair appeared before the House liaison committee (the first time an incumbent PM had been questioned by a select committee since 1938) to answer questions posed by the backbench chairmen and women of the House select committees and invited the media to help to generate 'a better and more developed debate on policy rather than personalities' that would 'reconnect disaffected voters with politics'. He also acknowledged the government's undue reliance on spin since 1997 – and promised change (Liaison Committee, 16 July 2002).

But some observers remained unconvinced about Labour's rejection of spin suggesting that the government's commitment to openness and its desire to 'relax a little in the battle for the headlines', did not signal the *end* of spin but merely the onset of a new *style* of spin (*Guardian*, 3 May 2002, p. 1). Charlie Whelan, Gordon Brown's ex-spin doctor, claimed, 'there are people predicting this is the death of spin. Nonsense. They're still doing it: and probably with a push from Alastair Campbell' (*Daily Mirror*, 29 May 2002, p. 3). The *Guardian's* political editor announced wryly 'so "no spin is the new spin" has become this years brittle joke' (White, 16 December 2002, pp. 2–3), while a senior lobby correspondent interpreted these developments as little more than 'the latest twist in the game, a tactical ploy of no great merit' (Ashley, 2002, p. 16). Whatever the motives informing these changes in communications policy, it is clear that by mid 2002, the Labour government judged that the growing public perception of the government as predicated on spin and preoccupied with news management was unhelpful – if not electorally damaging. It is undoubtedly a delicious irony that a governing party, which since 1997 had developed a number of new institutional mechanisms and processes to achieve its ambitions for effective news management, was obliged to appear publicly to modify this strategy: in Tony Blair's words 'to try to engage in the public debate in a different way' (Liaison Committee, 16 July 2002). Campbell's preferred phrase was that new Labour and the media must develop 'a more grown up, more honest dialogue that encourages greater accessibility, accountability and interaction' (Campbell, 2002, pp. 20–21). These events provide the context for the most recent declaration of the end of spin and this chapter explores some of the 'less grown up ways' in which the Labour government has engaged in and shaped the public debate since 1997 by using spin and news management.

THE MILLBANKISATION OF GOVERNMENT

Since 1997, the Labour government has tried to replicate in government the highly successful election-winning media operation which it created in opposition throughout the
1980s and 1990s: a process which Gaber described as the 'Millbankisation' of government (Gaber, 1998, p. 10). One year into the new government, Sir Richard Wilson the
Cabinet secretary, in his evidence to the Select Committee on Public Administration
inquiry into the Government Information and Communication Services, argued, 'there
is a more systematic determined effort to co-ordinate in a strategic way, presentation of
government policies and messages in a positive light across the whole of government,
than I can remember since the time I have been in the civil service' (Select Committee
on Public Administration, 1998, p. xii). Cohen's revelation that Labour issued 20,000
press releases in the first two years in government (an 80 per cent increase on the 1992
Major government) helped to quantify this 'systematic determined effort' (Cohen,
1999b, p. 15).

This Millbankisation of government has involved the increasing centralisation of
communications at Number Ten, a more assertive relationship with journalists and
broadcasters and the politicising of the Government Information and Communications
Service (GICS) (Franklin, 1998; Gaber and Barnett, 2001; Jones, 2001; Oborne, 1999).
A very senior officer in the GICS outlined this three-fold strategy along with what he
considered to be its shortcomings.[1]

> New Labour perfected a machine which could do several things. One, it kept
> on top of the media circus. Secondly it was terribly strongly controlled. I
> remember Peter Mandelson saying privately 'The trouble with ministers in
> this government' – and this is going back to the early days of this
> government – 'is that they expected to be told what to say by the centre
> rather than to work it out for themselves'. But they were very, very tightly
> controlled. The joke about the Labour party at the time was that they only
> ever listened to two people: Blair and Blair. They assumed a very aggressive
> stance towards the media, particularly with individual journalists, which is a
> very dangerous thing to do, and I believe that Charlie Whelan, Peter
> Mandelson, Jo Moore and Stephen Byers all reaped that whirlwind. They
> came in with a very strong idea about how to win and how to win was how
> to get the message across. The problem is that getting the message across is
> delivery of nothing more than the message. They also ran up against a civil
> service culture whose main aim in life is to deliver policies and programmes
> with communications as part of the portfolio. And how do you do that? You
> have to reach people to persuade them, make them aware, warn them,
> advise them, whatever. But what the civil service machine is not there to do
> is to persuade people that this policy is right. It must stand on its own

merits. My job is to provide Ministers with the best possible platform from which they can sell their wares, but not to put the best possible gloss on it. The job is to help the government to fulfil its duty to explain and its there to ensure the government secures its right to be heard.

LISTENING TO BLAIR AND BLAIR: THE CENTRAL CONTROL OF COMMUNICATIONS

Centralising communications at Number Ten under the control of the prime minister's press secretary Alastair Campbell (latterly repackaged as director of communications) has been the key priority in Labour's communications strategy. The intention has been to establish the government as the 'primary definer' and shaper of media discussions of policy, to ensure the consistency of the government line and to minimise any media reporting of any dissenting voices within government. Such central control was an early ambition for the government's strategy. A senior member of GICS outlines the context for this centralised control and articulates the extent to which the strategy marked a radical shift in civil servants' relations with the centre.

> Two or three days after they came to power, all heads of information went for a meeting with Mandelson and Campbell at no 10. We were told in a very carefully scripted double act, that they saw our job as being the shock troops of the centre. That they knew that Ministers and their special advisors would become little barons in their own empires if they weren't careful and we were there to help the centre hold it together. I'm not quite sure how they took the sound of our jaws hitting the ground – and I'm not sure they noticed either – because that has never been the job. The job has always been constitutionally to serve the Secretary of State. And, if he is having a row with the centre – and I've worked for a few who have been – then you are on his or her side. You are in the business of keeping the system together, but you don't actually spend your time grassing up the Minister in charge of the department.

> (Interview with the author, July 2002)

The central control established has certainly been strict: but it has also been effective. The Mountfield report on government communications suggested that 'all major interviews and media appearances, both print and broadcast, should be agreed with the Number Ten press office before any commitments are entered into. The policy content of all major speeches, press releases and new policy initiatives should be cleared in good time with the Number Ten private office' and finally, 'the timing and form of announcements should be cleared with the Number Ten Press Office' (Mountfield, 1997, p. 8).

The government's 'communications day' begins with a 9 a.m. meeting attended by senior communications staffs including the director of communications, Jonathan Powell the prime minister's chief of staff, specialist advisers from the Treasury and the deputy prime minister's office as well as representatives from the Cabinet Office and the chief whip's office (MacAskill, 1997, p. 8). The meeting tries to ensure congruence between strategy and presentation and consigns specific individuals to resolve any particular presentation problems arising that day (Mountfield, 1997, p. 8). Labour's determination to stay 'on message', requires that nothing is left to chance. The policy 'message' must be carefully scripted, meticulously rehearsed, universally endorsed by party and government, centrally co-ordinated and favourably presented in the news media (Norton-Taylor and Black, 1997, p. 17).

A number of new (post-1997) institutions are entrusted with key roles in orchestrating relationships between politicians and journalists (Walker, 1998, p. 17). The Media Monitoring Unit, for example, prepares a daily digest of news media content and identifies potentially problematic issues for consideration ('rebuttal') at the morning communications meeting held prior to the 11 a.m. lobby briefing. The establishment of the Strategic Communications Unit (SCU) in January 1998, which includes two special advisors (both previously senior journalists) is responsible for 'pulling together and sharing with departments the government's key policy themes and messages' (Select Committee on Public Administration 1998, para 19): i.e. keeping sources 'on message'. The SCU liaises with the expansive media management organisations in individual departments to co-ordinate government policy messages but also to prevent ministers and special advisers 'forming their own Baronies' (Williams, 2000, p. 10). The SCU also drafts ministerial (including prime ministerial) speeches and inserts common phrases and soundbites to illustrate the consistency of the government's 'message'.

A key task for the SCU is to co-ordinate the media presentation of events and stories for the coming week. The unit prepares a weekly diary of events known as 'the grid' which it presents each Thursday to a meeting of heads of information from the Whitehall departments. The purpose of the diary is to prevent unhelpful clashes between departments' release of news, to ensure that positive developments are not overshadowed by 'bad' news and, on occasion, to 'slip out' any bad news on what is broadly a good news day for the government. The grid is based on the routine returns from departments about their forthcoming news events and includes EU events, political news and 'general events such as the Cup Final and high profile rape trials that might eclipse the latest statistics on hospital waiting lists' (Kavanagh and Seldon, 2000, p. 255–6 and Seymour Ure, 2002, p. 128). Since early 2001, it has been supplemented by a Euro Grid, detailing forthcoming decisions by the European Commission and parliament which might impact on government popularity or policy. A memo from the head of the SCU to heads of information in departments, dated 9 November 1999 outlined the new centralised protocols for developing co-ordinated media coverage. 'From now on' it announced, 'for each major [news] event we will be using a planning document (copy attached) for which the relevant Downing Street press officer will be responsible. As you can see it sets out the key messages that should be communicated by the event, how they link to the government's overall message, and the methods we will be using to get wide coverage in the run up, launch and follow up to the event' (9 November 1999, cited in Williams, 2000, Annex H).

In June 2000, the *Guardian* published a leaked copy of the grid which illustrated the SCU's role in co-ordinating the media presentation of four speeches planned for the third week in May. A memo attached to the grid said the prime minister wished ministers to stress that the government had a 'clear mission and purpose' by 'referring to each other's work'.

> Monday, Chancellor, child poverty: 'no child need grow up in poverty';
> Tuesday, Prime Minister, economy: 'families are protected from boom and
> bust and enjoy rising living standards'; Wednesday, Home Secretary, police
> training and recruitment: 'people need not live in fear': Thursday, Secretary
> of State for Health, medical school expansion: 'we can get an NHS fit for
> the twenty-first century'.
>
> (Cited in Jones, 2001, p. 145.)

The attached memo underscored the overall message 'Big goals. Big arguments. Serious government versus opportunistic opposition' (ibid.). A senior press officer in one Whitehall department claimed the SCU had been a great success in shaping relationships with journalists. 'By organising the diary so strictly', he suggested 'the SCU has played a critical role in the government's efforts to dominate the news agenda' (cited in Williams, 2000, p. 15).

Since February 1998, the SCU's activities have been supported by 'Agenda', a computer system which 'helps to co-ordinate government's publicity activities' by listing 'forthcoming newsworthy events, lines to take, key departmental messages and themes and ministerial speeches' (Select Committee, 1998, xiii and Appendix 12). Since January 2000, however, special advisor Joe McCrea with a team based in the Cabinet Office has developed a new electronic information system known as the Knowledge Network Project (Jones, 2002, p. 348). A leaked document revealed that the aim of the project was to 'explain the government's core messages' by establishing a single database of the government's line to take on every key policy issue across Whitehall. The project also provides the 'best five arguments and the best three facts' in support of every government policy alongside 'key quotes, key facts and rapid reaction to attacks on departmental policy and practice' (cited in *Guardian*, 8 January 2000, p. 5). The project provides government sources with powerful ammunition with which to respond to journalists' critical appraisals of policy. A Cabinet Office memo, leaked to the *Guardian* two weeks after Blair's select committee announcement of the 'end of spin', disclosed government intentions to expand the system to ensure that civil servants 'get a broader feel of wider departmental and government policies, rather than simply their own area or department': the number of civil servants with access to the knowledge network is to be expanded from 54,000 to 300,000 (Travis and Silverman, 2002, p. 2).

This centralised structure regulating relationships between politicians and journalists has prompted perhaps predictable tensions in Labour ranks but also between special advisors and civil servants working in the GICS. In March 1998, for example, Harriet Harman (then secretary of state for health) was chastised by Campbell for giving media interviews without his approval: a leaked fax demanded she explain 'why the interviews with the *Guardian, Women's Hour* and *World At One* were not cleared through this office' (*Guardian*, 30 March 1998, p. 5; Jones, 2001, p. 145). In July 1998, when Frank Field resigned from government, he was denounced in a Number Ten briefing as an 'impractical, abstract theoretician ... incapable of running a department or translating ideas into workable policy' (*Observer*, 2 August 1998, p. 1). Field responded by describing the Number Ten press office as a 'cancer at the heart of government' (*Jimmy Young Programme* BBC Radio 2, 3 July 1998). The 'resignation' of Gordon Brown's communications advisor Charlie Whelan in January 1999, amid allegations that he leaked information about Mandelson's undeclared loan from a Cabinet colleague, aided this process of centralisation at Number Ten. A significant, high profile and potentially oppositional centre of spin within government had been closed down: Campbell had been asking for Whelan's resignation since 2 May 1997 (*Guardian*, 5 January 1999, p. 2). Claims that the sacking of Whelan illustrated the 'mythical' power of spin doctors, however, as well as journalists' tendency to 'overstate' the power of spin doctors, seem unsubstantiated (McNair, 2000, pp. 134–5).

More recently and more spectacularly, special advisor Jo Moore and head of Information Martin Sixsmith, both working in the department of transport, 'resigned' after a 'feud' for communications supremacy flared up between them. Each began to brief journalists against the other, prompting 'mixed' and contradictory 'messages' which in turn caused embarrassment to Number Ten and triggered journalists to question the capacity of 'Downing Street's once fabled spin operation ... to offer consistent explanations' of events: such questions 'sealed the fate' of both and underlined the centralised communications control exercised from Number Ten (*Guardian*, 16 February 2002, p. 13).

SORTING OUT THE AWKWARD SQUAD: LABOUR'S RELATIONSHIPS WITH JOURNALISTS

Relationships between journalists and politicians 'have been transformed over the past ten years' (Barnett and Gaber, 2001, p. 99; Oborne, 2002, p. 33). Labour's uncompromising news management strategy offers journalists and broadcasters 'tough choices'. If they accept the government line, they will be rewarded with the occasional minor 'exclusive' but the 'awkward squad' who are critical will have their bids for interviews denied and will no longer receive telephone tips about 'breaking stories and exclusives' (Gaber, 1998, p. 14). In short, the government is playing an old fashioned game of carrots and sticks (Ingham quoted in *Select Committee on Public Administration*, 1998, pp. 9–14), although some commentators believe that 'with new Labour ... the game is played with an unprecedented degree of nastiness' (Gaber, 1998, p. 14). *Guardian* editor Alan Rusbridger describes how this game was played out in the run up to the 1997 election. Campbell 'used to ring up to cajole, plead, shout and horse-trade' Rusbridger claims. 'Stories would be offered on condition that they went on the front page. I would be told that if I didn't agree they would go to the *Independent*. They would withdraw favours, grant favours, exclude us from stories going elsewhere ... Now we have almost no contact' (cited in Oborne, 1999, p. 184).

A briefing document requested by Campbell and compiled by Carl Shoben and Chris McShane, two special advisers in the Media Monitoring Unit, offered assessments of senior political journalists, their competences, their perceived influence, their political leanings and, most significantly, their support or hostility to the new Labour cause (Milne and Maguire, 2001, pp. 2–3). Twenty-eight journalists are evaluated in the briefing including nine from *The Times*, seven from the *Guardian*, three from the *Telegraph*, three from the *Independent*, two from the *Mail* and one each from the *Mirror* and the *Express*. David Hencke and Hugo Young are both allegedly 'obsessed' with freedom of information while others are mentioned (favourably) for relying more on 'officially placed stories rather than leaks' (ibid., p. 3). Paul Routledge of the *Mirror*, who is widely believed to be out of favour with Number Ten, is described as 'Influential in the sense that his columns appear in prominent placing in the *Mirror* each day. Formally (formerly?) close to Scargill, but now on traditional Old Lab right. Close to Charlie Whelan. Famously an enemy of Mandelson and "new Labour"' (Milne and Maguire 2001, p. 3). No journalists from the *Sun*, not even the well known and influential Trevor Kavanagh, is mentioned. While some journalists might be amused to read official assessments of their professional merits, the leaked briefing document offers testament to Campbell's concern to manage the news.

There is a further reason informing some newspapers' 'friendly' coverage of Labour's performance in government; journalists working for the Murdoch press believe their proprietor has agreed a pact with Tony Blair. It is easy to identify the potential terms of trade. Murdoch's newspapers' support for Labour since the March 1997 election has been handsomely rewarded by the absence of legislation to outlaw the predatory pricing of *The Times* (despite the opportunity provided by the Competition Bill), the unwillingness to regulate the press' continuing invasion of individuals' privacy or Sky's advantageous position in the digital television market as well as the revised provisions on media ownership in the new Communications Act (2003) which allows Murdoch the prospect of buying Channel 5 (Wells, 2002, p. 6). Some journalists argue that Blair is conceding too much policy ground in return for the editorial quiescence of the Murdoch press. Columnist Nick Cohen offers a more ribald metaphor: 'We have a Prime Minister' he argues 'who cannot control his tongue when Rupert Murdoch's posterior passes by' (*New Statesman*, 22 May 1998, p. 20).

But sticks are more commonplace than carrots. In October 1997, Campbell circulated a strident memo to all heads of information in the GICS arguing that 'media handling' (his preferred term for media relations), must become more assertive. 'Decide your headlines' he insisted 'sell your story and if you disagree with what is being written argue your case. If you need support from here [Downing Street] let me know' (Timmins, 1997, p. 1). For journalists writing against the government line, the 'handling' has become rough! Journalists are privately bullied, publicly harangued and excluded from off the record briefings (Kampfner, 2000, pp. 2–3). There are 'very few journalists' whom Campbell 'has not attempted to abuse or humiliate' (Oborne, 1999, p. 181). Labour spin-doctors, moreover, have 'never hesitated to destabilise journalists by going behind their backs to their bosses' (ibid., p. 182). *Observer* columnist Nick Cohen, *Mail* political editor Paul Eastham and the *Independent's* Colin Brown have each been subject to hostile briefings. Given this track record, it is perhaps unsurprising that a biographical article about Campbell observed that 'he performs his onerous tasks with cheerful brutality' (Hattersley, 1998, p. 3; Kavanagh, 2002, p. 14).

Campbell's attitude towards journalists collectively betrays a similar contempt: his first briefing of the parliamentary lobby set the mood. Campbell arrived late after an initial reluctance to attend any meeting with lobby journalists. 'Ok you bastards' he began robustly 'Explain to me just why I should waste my time with a load of wankers like you when you are not going to write anything I tell you anyway': the officials seated behind him reportedly looked 'stupefied' (Oborne, 1999, p. 179). Some journalists suggest that Campbell's bellicose attitude towards journalists, like Ingham before him, reflects his own background in journalism and his sense of being in 'a perpetual state of competition with the political journalists he once worked with' (Jones, 2001, p. 182; Oborne, 1999, p. 179).

Broadcast journalists, especially those at the BBC, fare little better: the 'Humphrys problem' illustrates the claim. In December 1997, David Hill, then the Labour Party's Head of Communications, wrote to BBC Radio 4's *Today* programme threatening to isolate journalists from government sources following a particularly robust interview by John Humphrys with a minister. The letter, which was promptly leaked, is threatening in style, uses military metaphors and subscribes to the belief that it is appropriate for politicians to dictate the style and content of broadcast interviews. 'The John Humphrys problem' Hill began 'has assumed new proportions after this morning's interview with

Harriet Harman. In response we have had a council of war and are seriously considering whether, as a party, we will suspend co-operation when you make bids through us for government ministers ... Frankly none of us feels this can go on' (quoted in the *Guardian*, 13 December 1997, p. 12). Some journalists are thoughtfully ambivalent about both the effectiveness of Labour's news management style and the consequences for their journalistic independence and professional integrity. Adam Boulton, Sky's lobby correspondent acknowledges with admirable honesty, 'the trouble is that the government is operating at a level of news management that is way above the level of British politics. I do not blame Alastair for that. As far as Alastair is concerned, it is all fair in love and war, as long as it's in favour of Tony. On a good day, you can see an intelligent, honest administration at work. On a bad day I feel soiled, when we end up seeing the press conniving in our own manipulation' (quoted in Toolis, 4 April 1998, p. 31). Boulton's final remarks underscore not merely the closeness of journalists' relationships with their political sources but signal the extent of 'cross over' between the two groups in terms of their professional roles and career histories.

Jones neologises the term 'journo-politicos' to describe the new generation of policy advisers who have been at 'the sharp end of the hard sell' which has characterised new Labour's approach to the media. These hybrids – whose background is in 'media, publicity or politics' and whose 'success is judged in terms of their effectiveness in political presentation' – symbolise the degree to which the roles of journalists and politicians have become fused as 'demarcation lines have become blurred' (Jones, 2001, pp. 68–9). For their part, journalists are increasingly being appointed to senior posts in the GICS, or to jobs as special advisors to ministers. The political editor of the *Mirror* alleged that 'Blair's government is stuffed with journalists' (Routledge, 2001, p. 34), while the appointment of a succession of senior BBC producers and broadcasters to government posts has prompted one description of the BBC as 'a regular target for the Downing Street raiding party' (Jones, 2001, p. 79). Similarly, politicians and government sources are increasingly behaving like journalists. The *Independent*, for example, claimed that in the first two years of the Labour government 166 articles were published with Tony Blair's byline: only 13 less than *Sun* columnist Richard Littlejohn across the same period (*Independent*, 8 June 1999). In 1999, the press awards gathering crowned Blair 'Freelance of the Year' for publishing more than 250 articles in 47 publications across the year (Seymour Ure, 2002, p. 130). The great majority of these articles were written, of course, by Campbell and the ex-tabloid journalists who now form the 'pitprops' of the SCU. In these different ways, the roles of politicians and journalists are increasingly overlapping.

THE 'WASHINGTONISATION' OF THE GOVERNMENT INFORMATION AND COMMUNICATIONS SERVICE

In government, Labour has access to the resources and services of the GICS, staffed by 1200 civil servants whose press and public relations activities are governed by a code of conduct (The Whitehall Red Book) designed to guarantee their political impartiality. 'Press officers' according to the Red Book, must 'establish a position with the media whereby it is understood that they stand apart from the party political battle, but are there to assist the media to understand the policies of the government of the day' (Cabinet Office, 1997, para 11).

One consequence of 'assisting the media' in this way, by presenting 'the government's policies in their best light', is that 'some advantage naturally accrues to the party in power': this is 'entirely proper' (Select Committee, 1998, p. xv). For the civil service press officer, however, it is never appropriate to 'justify or defend those policies in party political terms, to use political slogans, expressly to advocate policies as those of a particular political party or directly attack (although it may be necessary to respond to in specific terms) policies and opinions of opposition parties and groups' (Select Committee p. xv). By contrast, special advisors such as the prime minister's press secretary, are not bound by the usual requirements that civil servants should be able to assist governments of 'whatever complexion' and that they should be 'impartial'' (Select Committee, p. xv). The Select Committee on Public Administration, investigating concerns that the Labour government might be politicising the GICS by ignoring these distinctions, concluded there 'is a very fine line between the promotion and defence of government policy and the promotion and defence of the ruling party's policies'; the committee further agreed that the policing of that line was a matter for the prime minister's press secretary's 'own judgement' (Select Committee, p. xv). Since 1997, however, civil servants have expressed growing concerns that this 'line' is too frequently crossed: the 'judgement' of the prime minister's press secretary too frequently exercised injudiciously. Senior information officers have warned about the 'creeping politicisation of the GICS' (Select Committee 1998, p. 80). The government has responded that it is concerned only to 'modernise' the GICS to ensure 'it is equipped to meet the demands of a fast changing media world' (Mountfield, 1997, para 2). But as one observer noted, 'by wrapping up the whole exercise in the language of modernisation and efficiency, Campbell had created a smokescreen which would allow the Blair administration to drive a coach and horses through long-established traditions of civil service neutrality' (Jones, 1999, p. 67). Four developments have triggered civil service concerns.

First, the government has appointed unprecedented numbers of special advisors to promote government policy: Andrew Rawnsley described this expansion as 'an influx of Labour Apparatchiks into posts traditionally occupied by career civil servants' (*Observer*, 1 June 1997). According to the Ministerial code, every Cabinet minister may appoint up to two advisers, 'political' or 'expert'. In practice however, as the Neill committee observed, this restriction has not always been observed. Ministers, moreover, may appoint an unspecified number of unpaid advisers (Select Committee, 2001, para 5). The Major government's 32 advisers were replaced by 60 within the early days of the Labour government at an additional cost of £600,000 (a 44 per cent increase over conservative expenditure) (Franklin, 1998, p. 11). After Labour's first year in office the wages bill for the 70 current advisers stood at £3.5 million (*Guardian*, 17 November 1998, p. 5): a substantial sum, paid from the public purse, to bankroll partisan propaganda distributed from government departments. By January 2001 there were 78 advisors with 26 based at Number Ten, three times as many as under the Major administration: the pay costs are estimated at £4.4 million annually (HC Debs, 22 January 2001, Col 467). Professor Peter Hennessy described the recent growth in special advisers as 'near rampant' (Select Committee, 2001, para 19). A broader historical sweep confirms this tendency towards growth in the appointment of information officers and the acceleration of this trend under new Labour. Between 1979 and 1999 the DHSS, for example, increased the number of information officers it employed by 488 per cent (from 24 in 1979 to 141 in 1997). At MAFF the growth was 77 per cent (22 to 39), at the Department of Transport 185 per cent (13 to 37) and at the DfEE 91 per cent (from 23 to 44) (Davis, 2002, p. 21). But the two years between 1997 and 1999 witnessed a growth of 118 per cent at the DfEE, 53 per cent at the Foreign and Commonwealth Office and 23 per cent at the Department of the Environment (Davis 2002, p. 21).

But the suggestion that GICS has been politicised does not rest simply on the growing *numbers* of special advisers, but reflects senior civil servants' increased training in communications and presentational techniques. A senior GICS officer argued that 'one of the more interesting recent changes is the way in which more and more senior civil servants are being asked to do representational work. The director of the government's regional office for example, has a representational role in the regions of England, in talking to the communities about things like the single regeneration budget. Senior civil servants are appearing more and more on public platforms to explain policy. And one of the reasons we have to look carefully at the training of these people is to make sure that they understand the difference between explanation and crossing the line' (interview, 22 July 2002).

Second, in the first year of the Labour government, 25 heads of information and their deputies, from a total of 44 such senior posts, resigned or were replaced: the Select Committee on the GICS described this as 'an unusual turnover' (Select Committee, 1998, p. xviii). The reasons informing these staff changes were varied but included 'the desire of ministers for information officers to be less neutral than they thought was compatible with their regular civil service terms of employment' (Select Committee, 1998, p. xviii). The retired head of information at the Northern Ireland Office spoke of a 'culling' of heads of information and their replacement 'by 'politically acceptable' temporary bureaucrats': a process he labels the 'Washingtonisation' of the civil service (Select Committee, 1998, p. 86). By 2002 none of the original 44 heads of information remained in post.

Third, this growth of special advisors has created a 'two tier structure of information' in which the advisors have become the dominant partners over civil servants (Select Committee, 1998, p. ix). Advisors are chosen by ministers: they are close and trusted friends, party members who have a long-established professional relationship with the minister. By contrast, heads of information are an inheritance of government and judged to be rule-driven and unduly 'impartial' in their relationships with journalists. Consequently, the significant communications tasks are allocated to the adviser leaving the civil service press officer with more routine day-to-day matters (Lloyd, 1997, p. 12). Jill Rutter who resigned as head of information at the Treasury complained that Charlie Whelan had 'taken over three quarters of her job' (*Telegraph*, 6 December 1997, p. 3). At her leaving party, she claimed that she 'felt like Princess Diana had done – that three in a marriage is one too many' (quoted in Lloyd, 1997, p. 12). Bernard Ingham sympathised with Rutter for refusing to 'waste her time at the Treasury trying to compete with Charlie Whelan the hooligan imported into Whitehall by Gordon Brown' (cited in Jones, 1999, p. 99). GICS officers suggest that the 'enormous increase in the power of the special advisor' is 'widely acknowledged'. In one department, the arrival of the minister's 'workaholic mouthpiece' meant 'every single press release, and there were to be a lot more of them, had to be cleared by a special adviser'. The key task of constructing the weekly grid is also acknowledged to be the adviser's priority. The head of news in one department conceded 'there are no two ways about it, [the special adviser] decides what goes in the diary and when . . . Officials can object, but at the end of the day the decision is his' (Williams, 2000, pp. 27–9).

The consequences for information officers involved in conflict with a special advisor can be dire. When Alan Evans, for example, resisted special advisor John McTernan's requests to draft press releases in a way which Evans judged to be party political and compromising of his civil service neutrality, McTernan described him as 'dead meat'. Evans told a parliamentary committee that 'the drafting of press releases was closely scrutinised to the point of obsession by specialist advisers. They sought to reproduce the tone of the Labour manifesto and repeat its election commitments as emerging news. I would suspect there are a number of senior members of the GICS' he claimed 'who feel they are very much on trial with ministers and who will be concerned that giving unpalatable advice may result in them losing their job. I regard living under pressure of this kind as being politicised' (*Control Freaks*, Channel 5, 28 September 2002). Evans also clashed with Jo Moore at the Department of Transport, Local Government and the Regions (DTLR) when he refused her demands to gather information to undermine Bob Kylie the transport adviser for London, who was opposed to Labour plans to privatise the underground. Evans argued that this was a political task unsuited to a civil servant: he was 'exiled to the foot and mouth inquiry' (*Control Freaks*, Channel 5, 28 September 2002). A senior GICS officer confirmed that 'the key concerns from within the service about special advisers is the lack of leadership or poor leadership by Permanent Secretaries which undermined the ability of the system to resist being bullied and pushed around by advisers

... it goes wrong when special advisers look as is they have become unassailable and when they become gatekeepers to the Minister. It defeats the whole purpose of having a service [GICS]: an objective agency which should advise' (interview, 22 July 2002).

Finally, the most significant change at the GICS has been the need to 'get on message'; i.e. to propagandise for government. In October 1997, Campbell sent a memo to heads of information confirming that the central task of GICS publicity was that the 'government's four key messages' must be 'built in to all areas of our activity'. Labour is 'a modernising government', a government 'for all the people', which is 'delivering on its promises' with 'mainstream policies' which are providing new directions for Britain (*Financial Times*, 9 October 1997, p. 1). Romola Chrispherson, a retired head of information in various Whitehall departments, declared that from the outset 'Campbell and Mandelson [then Minister without Portfolio but with a brief for co-ordinating government communications] were making it very clear what they expected of the government information service'. She described the government's communication strategy as 'Labour's three "Rs"':

> First, rhetoric – getting the message and encapsulating the message in a marketing slogan – new Labour, New Britain, People's Princess – all those soundbites, getting that rhetoric absolutely clear and right and accessible. That's the first 'R'. Second 'R' is repetition, repetition, repetition, repetition. When you're bored with repeating it, it probably means that people are beginning to pick it up. The final 'R' is rebuttal, which is don't let any attack on you go without walloping back at it.
>
> (Cited in *Control Freaks*, Channel 5, 28 September 2002.)

Some information officers have preferred to resign before complying with central dictates which so thoroughly eschew their professional commitments to neutrality. Many senior press officers have:

> privately expressed their uneasiness at being expected to switch to a more aggressive approach where seizing the agenda and occupying the front pages is apparently more important than the content, where events and announcements are relentlessly pushed rather than being left to find their own level according to their news value, and where those media outlets or individuals which did not adhere to the 'on-message' approach are penalised by intimidatory tactics and the threatened withdrawal of access and facilities. In such a climate presentation comes perilously close to propaganda.
>
> (Select Committee, 1998, pp. 1–82.)

These changes at the GICS prompted an inquiry into the service in March 1998. The terms of reference for the inquiry were remarkable by conceding at the outset what the committee was established to decide: namely whether or not the GICS is impartial. Consequently, the terms of reference suggested the committee should try to establish not if the GICS *is* impartial, but 'the extent to which the GICS *should be* politically impartial' and the 'balance between delivering neutral information and giving a political spin' (Select Committee, Press Release, 30 March 1998, emphasis added). Given this starting point, the committee's conclusions were unlikely to be critical of government press operations, but the eventual outcome of the report's inquiries was unpredictably acrimonious.

An early critical report drafted by the clerk was radically modified by the committee's in-built majority of Labour members. The official report, which was eventually published, contained none of the original criticisms of Alastair Campbell and the Government Information and Communications Services nor the many proposals for reform. In the words of one committee member, the report 'could have been written by Alastair himself ... on one side of A4 saying everything in the garden is rosy' (*Guardian*, 5 August 1998, p. 1). The combined opposition members of the committee denounced the redrafted report as 'whitewash' and its supporters as 'the glove puppets of Alastair Campbell' (*Guardian*, 7 August 1998, 4). They also published an alternative report reinstating the criticisms and recommendations for changes in the government information machine: four are significant. First, tapes of lobby briefings should be 'routinely kept for 12 months' (p. xxxii) to check if Campbell has been misleading journalists. Second, advisors who 'undertake significant amounts of party political activity should be paid from party funds and not the taxpayer'. Third, the government should 'consider whether the Strategic Communications Unit gives an undue advantage to the governing party' and, finally, that the House 'examine the concerns expressed by Madam Speaker on the sharp growth in the "pre-briefing" ' [i.e. 'leaking' or 'trailing'] of government policy statements to the press which undermines the authority of Parliament (Select Committee, 1998, pp. xxxii–xxxiii). The major recommendation in the official report was the suggestion for a new code of conduct to define more clearly government's relationships with the media. The code, to be drawn up and policed by Alastair Campbell, 'would make clear the obligations on special advisors and ministers to work closely with press officers in general and the prime minister's official spokesperson in particular' (Select Committee, 1998, p. xx). It seems nothing less than extraordinary, that the principal recommendation of a Select Committee inquiry into the politicising of the government information services, should propose the further centralising of government communications under the control of the prime minister's official spokesperson, especially when that recommendation enjoys the support of only the government members of the committee. Given this political context to the Select Committee's official and alternative reports, it was perhaps unsurprising that the government, in its official response to the inquiry welcomed, 'the Committee's general endorsement of the key role which the GICS plays in carrying out the important task of effectively communicating and explaining the policies, decisions and actions of the government of the day' (Select Committee, 1999, p. iv).

In 2001, as part of its broader inquiry into 'Making Government Work', the Select Committee on Public Administration, published the report *Special Advisers: Boon or Bane*, which concluded that 'All the available evidence suggests that special advisers can make a positive contribution to good government' and that their involvement in government need not 'be threatening to the traditional role of the civil service', but suggested that 'it is time to put the position of special advisers on a firmer footing' (Select Committee, 2001, para 81). The committee endorsed the Neil committee's recommendation for a code of conduct for special advisors, which should offer clear guidance on the relations between advisers and members of the GICS. All adviser posts, moreover, should be advertised with appointments being competitive, consideration should be given to establishing a fund to pay the costs of advisers not recruited under civil service rules, and Parliament should at the 'earliest opportunity' debate a code for regulating the activities of special advisers. (Select Committee, 2001, p. xxv).

A year later, concerns about the politicising of the civil service were still being voiced. Sir Richard Wilson, the outgoing Cabinet secretary, used his retirement speech to warn of the possible dangers. Given civil servants' legendary reputation for understatement and measured language, Wilson's remarks might be judged acerbic. 'It is fundamental to the working of our constitution' he claimed 'that governments should use the resources entrusted to them, including the civil service, for the benefit of the country as a whole and not for the benefit of their political party ... the non-political character of the civil service underpins that convention'. His prescription for change was three-fold: a limit on the number of special advisers should be 'set by Parliament at the beginning of each new Parliament'; special advisers should be banned from managing permanent civil servants, and, in a barely veiled reference to Jo Moore; 'special advisers should not behave illegally or improperly' nor should they 'ask civil servants to do anything improper or illegal ... [and] they should not do anything to undermine the political impartiality of civil servants or the duty of civil servants to give their own best advice to Ministers' (Sherman, 2002, p. 10).

A new and independent review of 'Whitehall's press and spin operations' was announced in January 2003, following the extensive press reporting of 'Cheriegate' and the publication of a bogus 'Intelligence' report on Iraq which was discovered to have been plagiarised and 'pasted together' by an adviser in the Number Ten press office rather than an intelligence officer (*Guardian*, 16 January 2003, p. 2). Chaired by Bob Phillis, chief executive of the Guardian media group, and staffed by journalists, government and party press officers like David Hill, but also including the prime minister's official spokespersons

Godric Smith and Tom Kelly, the committee's brief is to review 'the effectiveness of the government information and communications service ... and the roles played by other civil servants and special advisers who have a responsibility for communications'. Establishing an unambiguous brief, the committee 'should clarify the boundaries between the work that is appropriate to special advisers and work that is not appropriate to them' (*Guardian*, 16 January 2003, p. 2).

The Phillis review was originally scheduled to report in July 2003, but the war in Iraq and the ensuing hostilities between the government and the BBC, the death of the government scientist David Kelly and the Hutton Inquiry, extended their remit and timetable. It was the interim recommendations of the Phillis group that informed the revised Downing Street communication structures announced at the time of Campbell's resignation and Hill's appointment to the post of director of communications. The key intention was to build an unbreachable firewall between civil servants working the GICS and special advisers: between the provision of impartial information and partisan propaganda. Consequently, David Hill will not enjoy any managerial oversight of civil servants but will have a broad responsibility to provide journalists with the 'political perspective' on policy issues. Phillis also recommended the appointment of a new permanent secretary to assume overall responsibility for government communications: a post that Campbell would undoubtedly have labelled 'the Spin Czar'.

At the time of writing, when the reports of Phillis and Hutton are still anticipated, the precise shape of government communications seems uncertain: but there are some indicative straws blowing in the wind. The new director of communications remains an extremely powerful figure at the hub of government communications: certainly the single most significant point of contact between government and media. David Hill's ability to manage the news, by offering or refusing journalists access to exclusives, is undiminished: if Hill chooses to play it, the game of carrots and sticks will continue. Ministers, moreover, continue to work with special advisers whose practice and track record has been to dominate their civil service colleagues in the GICS. The 'message' is likely to remain strongly controlled by the centre: the weekly 'grid' will continue to influence and shape the political news agenda. The continuing, effective operation of the Labour message machine signals that despite Blair's publicly stated commitment 'to look at new and different ways for engaging in serious and proper public debate and to conduct a "spin-free zone"' (Liaison Committee, July 2002), most citizens, as well as members of the Labour party, are still 'listening to two people: Blair and Blair'.

---

1 Personal interview with the author 22 July 2002.

Chapter Four

GOVERNMENT ADVERTISING: ☐ SELLING POLICIES LIKE CORNFLAKES?

Lord Young's seemingly trite observation that 'Government programmes are like cornflakes' and his declaration that 'if they are not marketed, they will not sell' (*PR Week*, 16 March 1988), has proved both precocious and insightful. It marked a watershed in political communications by articulating a new approach to government publicity which addressed voters less as citizens than as consumers. In the late 1980s, the phrase exemplified the minister's and the goverment's growing commitment to the use of advertising and marketing to 'package' policies to win public approval for government measures. Lord Young could certainly not be accused of mistaking the word for the deed: he is typically identified as the driving force behind successive Thatcher governments' enthusiasm for 'selling' policies by his extensive use of advertising. His arrival at the Department of Trade and Industry (DTI) sparked an explosion of advertising and publicity expenditure from £1,785,000 in 1986–87 to £31,276,000 by 1988–89 (*Labour Research*, November 1991, p. 7). This increase was part of a broader but radical shift in government communications' strategy during the 1980s, reflecting successive administrations' concerns to manage political communications by and about government and its activities.

Since 1997, Labour governments have continued and developed these communications concerns. In the month before the 2001 general election, for example, the Labour government spent £3 million on a single advertising campaign about benefit fraud: the same as McDonald's budget for promoting 'Big Macs' (*Panorama*, May 2002). The resonance with Lord Young's earlier claims about cornflakes and policy promotion is evident. What is radical and novel, however, in this longer-term trend is the Labour government's commitment to extending the use of advertising and marketing into the process of policy *making* as well as policy *implementation*. Previously governments' use of marketing techniques have been confined to the presentation of policy. The purpose of advertising and promotional campaigns has been to win public acceptability for policy initiatives and facilitate their implementation. Lord Young's prompt re-badging of the DTI as 'The Department of Enterprise' in 1987, represented a classic example of the use of marketing for policy ends. But recent Labour governments seems to have elevated the presentation of policy to a new significance: one which considers presentation as important, if not more important, than the substantive policy content. Consequently, for new Labour, the facility with which policy options lend themselves to marketing and media presentation is now a crucial ingredient in policy *making*. It was Peter Mandelson, in his role as minister without portfolio, but with a brief to co-ordinate all aspects of government communications, who articulated this new role for political marketing most cogently. Mandelson argued that the government's assessment of whether or not a policy is capable of clear presentation, had become a touchstone of its acceptability to government and its merit as policy. 'There are some who still denigrate the presentation of policy as a diversion from its substance, as a superficial and unnecessary coating to the main product', he argued, 'I take the opposite view ... if a government policy cannot be presented in a simple and attractive way it is more likely than not to contain fundamental flaws and prove to be the wrong policy. Once those flaws surface, the unattractive alternatives are sticking with it or overturning policy in which significant political capital might have been invested. We do not intend to fall into that trap' (Mandelson, 16 September 1997).

This chapter explores successive governments' policies on advertising, marketing and the promotion of policy by considering: the role, function and recent history of the Central Office of Information (COI) which handles government advertising; recent and past advertising campaigns by Conservative and Labour governments, including Labour's highly contentious campaigns in the months prior to the 2001 general election; governments' growing practice of introducing story lines into soap operas to inform the public about particular social policies, as well as the continuing debate about whether in promoting policies in this way, governments are blurring, if not crossing, the very significant line which separates the provision of information about government policy from the use of publicly funded advertising to persuade the public to particular policy choices: in short the line which separates policy *marketing* from *propaganda*. Governments undoubtedly gloss too quickly over the many complexities involved in distinguishing propaganda from the welcome and democratic ambition of 'raising public awareness'. Most notably, politicians seem to shift their positions in this debate reflecting whether they are currently members of the government or Her Majesty's opposition.

THE CENTRAL OFFICE OF INFORMATION: A RUSTING PUBLICITY MACHINE?

The COI is allegedly suffering an identity crisis with some observers querying whether it is 'a source of Big Brotherly propaganda wielding vast and ever growing financial resources to bend our minds?' or merely 'a rusting publicity machine which is gradually grinding to a halt?' (Cobb, 1989a, p. 12). Both descriptions partake of some of the truth of the matter while neither expresses it all. The COI's financial and organisational resources, combined with the expertise and skills of its staff, undoubtedly endow the organisation with substantial propaganda potential (Garner and Short, 1998, p. 181).

Indeed, Carol Fisher in her Chief Executive's *Foreword* to the 2001 Annual Report, declares bullishly that 'with communications taking an increasingly central role in government, our expertise and experience have been in greater demand than ever before' (COI Annual Report and Accounts 2000–2001, p. 3). But a number of organisational reforms, implemented during the mid 1980s, have deprived the COI of much of its traditional influence and demoted the organisation within the broader government information service hierarchy to a degree where, allegedly, it has become 'very much the marginal office of information' (Heaton, 1988, p. 9). Writing in 1990, Harris claimed the reforms had prompted the 'the virtual destruction' of the COI (Harris, 1990, p. 172).

Such pessimism is undermined by the continuing scale of the COI's operations. From its inception, the COI has been, and remains, the major conduit for the greater part of government publicity expenditure. In 2000–2001, for example, the COI achieved its highest ever turnover of £295 million, with advertising income increasing by 70 per cent year on year, while staffing expanded to 399 in April 2001 with a staffing budget of £13.3 million (COI 2001, p. 4 and p. 22). The COI is the very 'heart of the information machine' to use Cockerell's phrase which in a rather confused metaphor, 'houses the technicians of the machine' (Cockerell *et al.*, 1984, p. 57): journalists, press officers, radio producers, editors, web designers and film makers. The prime function of these media professionals/civil servants is to assist the government in communicating information to the public. It is a central agency created to supply publicity materials, services and advice to the government of the day (Garner and Short, 1998, pp. 170–2; Ogilvy-Webb, 1965, p. 44). A central tenet of COI operational philosophy is the requirement for impartiality. The GICS Handbook states that 'Government Information Officers must not be used for image making which is the province of the Party political machine. Ministers must be protected from accusations of using public resources for political purposes, and they in turn have a duty to protect the integrity of civil servants' (GICS Handbook, 1997). In brief, the COI is the bearer, but not the maker, of news: it is important for critics to resist any temptation to 'kill the messenger' (Ingham, 1991). Using a different analogy, Mike Devereau a past director of the service declared 'the COI is the waiter and not the chef' (Cobb, 1989a, p. 12).

A BRIEF HISTORY OF THE COI: BIG BROTHER IN DECLINE?

The COI was established on 1 April 1946 by the Attlee government as a successor to the overtly propagandist, war-time ministry of information (MoI) (Clark, 1970, pp. 28–9; Wildy 1985; Chap. 1, 1986, p. 4). The ministry's propaganda films offered stern warnings to the public advising them to observe the blackout regulations, to dig up their lawns and grow vegetables and not to let slip information which could be seized upon by Nazi spies who lurked around every corner. 'Careless talk', the public was constantly reminded, 'Costs Lives'. In broad terms the propagandist role of the ministry was to teach the public to hate our enemy Hitler and the undoubtedly more difficult task, to love our ally Stalin (West, 1963, p. 31). An official inquiry in 1944, held under the aegis of the coalition government, made recommendations for the future peacetime information services which were largely accepted by the subsequent Labour government (Ogilvy-Webb, 1965, p. 67).

Announcing the impending demise of the MoI in March 1946, Attlee none the less claimed that official information services had become 'an important and permanent part in the machinery of government. It is essential to a good administration under a democratic system', he argued, 'that the public shall be adequately informed about the many matters in which government action directly impinges on their daily lives' (HC Debs., 17 December 1945, Col. 916). The fledgling COI, however, was 'born in an atmosphere of suspicion on the part of the press and the Parliamentary Opposition' (Clarke, 1970, p. 155). The *Daily Express* and the *Daily Mail* denounced the COI as 'propaganda agents for the government in power' – a view given ringing endorsement in more recent times (Franklin 1998, Jones 1999 and 2002) – and a 'direct menace to one of our fundamental freedoms' (cited in Garner and Short, 1998, p. 171).

For their part, the Conservative opposition was hostile to the Attlee government's extensive expenditure on publicity in the early post-war years to win public support for the policy of nationalising the major industries of coal, gas and electricity (Scammell 1995, p. 231). But there was a more general concern that a government publicity machine, born of the explicitly propagandist MoI, might subvert democratic processes (Wildy, 1986, p. 8). The Conservative MP Boyd Carpenter alleged that the COI had become the 'organ of a vast machine of government information which can with difficulty be distinguished from political propaganda' (quoted in Ogilvy-Webb, 1965, p. 77). There were reasonable grounds for concern. The COI had inherited many of the resources and personnel (including the director general) of the old ministry, but Attlee's determination to remove the new organisation from the political arena by making it non-ministerial and non-policy making seemed to persuade most politicians concerning the organisation's legitimacy (HC Debs., 7 March 1946, Cols. 520–21; Clarke, 1970, p. 12). In truth, concerns about the propaganda potential of the COI have never been fully allayed. In the 1980s they re-emerged when the Labour Party, represented by Tony Blair – then opposition spokesperson for trade and industry – alleged the Conservative government was using the advertising and publicity apparatus of the COI for partisan purposes. A decade later, it was the turn of Conservative politicians to allege similar malpractice following Labour's record expenditure on government advertising in the three months prior to the 2001 general election (The *Independent*, 25 May 2002, p. 5. See below for further discussion of these allegations).

A number of financial and organisational changes initiated in the mid-1980s have had important consequences for the operation of the COI and its standing within the Goverment Information and Communication Service. In the mid-1980s, along with the rest of Whitehall, it was subject to the broader Thatcher project which sought to supplant the public service ethos with internal markets as the driving force shaping the operation of government departments. Under the Financial Management Initiative, which set out to streamline the civil service, the COI was 'opened up' to market forces which triggered staff cut backs, while increasing its turnover through work with outside agencies. These changes were introduced in two phased stages.

Initially, the COI was established as the obligatory central organisation for the provision of the great bulk of government publicity and provided services on an 'allied-service basis'. It administered most departmental publicity budgets and made no charge for the work, but drew directly on public funds to meet its budget. In April 1984, however, it became what Whitehall language describes as a 'repayment department', which means that like any other agency it charges its clients for the services it provides. Individual government departments have subsequently assumed direct responsibility for their own publicity budgets and pay the COI for services rendered.

In 1987 further reforms were implemented largely reflecting pressures from Lord Young. Whitehall departments were 'untied' from the COI allowing them the freedom to engage private sector companies to meet their publicity and marketing requirements (Harris, 1990, p. 168; Ingham, 1991, p. 370).[1] The important exception here was, and remains, that departments must channel their advertising expenditure through the COI. This is because the COI's substantial advertising budget – almost £200 million in 2000–1 – gives it leverage to negotiate discounts which, in 1987–8, amounted to £15 million (Cobb, 1989b, p. 14) and for 2001 reached a formidable £91.6 million, with £38.2 million savings on television advertising and £35.7 million on advertising in the press (COI, 2001, p. 23).

The COI's change to a repayment department triggered two consequences. First, it has become 'fitter and leaner' in order to compete for business. Staffing has been reduced substantially from 1,163 in 1979 to 804 in 1987 (HC Debs, 14 January 1988, Cols. 393–94) reaching a nadir of 377 in April 2000 but rising slightly to 399 in April 2001 (COI, 2001, p. 22). Running costs have similarly been reduced (at 1987–88 prices) from £22 million in 1983–84 to just over £18 million in 1987–88 (Cobb, 1989a, p. 12), dipping further to £16.6 million in 1997–98 with a moderate rise to £20.8 million in 2000–1 (COI, 2001, p. 22). But despite the newly arrived competition from the private sector, COI expenditure (at constant 1987–8 prices) more than doubled from £60.5 million in 1982–83 to £141 million in 1987–8 (*Hansard*, 15 January 1988, Col. 404); in April 2001 expenditure had reached £295.4 million (COI, 2001 p. 30). For the early period, the increase is largely explained by the launch of expensive television campaigns to promote privatisation and to combat AIDS and drug abuse: in 2001, the expansive expenditure reflects the unprecedented government advertising spend prior to the May 2001 general election.

The major consequence of the COI's transformation to a repayment department has been that it has lost the ability to control the publicity strategies of individual departments. It has become relatively powerless in comparison with the decentralized press and publicity offices and the special advisors who have achieved a new autonomy. At the time, the COI objected to these developments. Neville Taylor, then director of the COI, protested to the Cabinet Office threatening resignation, but to little effect. The COI's stature had changed irretrievably. On 28 July 1988, the Cabinet Office circulated a letter on the future of government publicity; it had Ingham's footprints all over it. According to the letter, 'the principal source of advice to Ministers and Heads of Department in this field [publicity] is the Departmental Head of Information. Heads of Department should ensure that the Head of Information always has sufficient opportunity to advise on proposals for paid publicity' (quoted in National Audit Office, 1989, p. 54). The heads of information, of course, reported through the Meeting of Information Officers (MIO) to Ingham.

Under new Labour the MIO found less favour with Campbell and its co-ordinating role has diminished: the Strategic Communications Unit (SCU) and the daily communication meetings at Number Ten chaired by the director of communications have assumed some responsibility here. But in February 2002 in a little publicised move Campbell, assumed unprecedented control of government advertising. A quinquennial review of the COI, to which all government agencies are subject, concluded that the chief executive of the COI should report directly to the government's director of communications (then Alistair Campell) when co-ordinating government publicity campaigns. The move triggered some predictable huffing and puffing from opposition politicians. Tim Collins, shadow minister for the Cabinet Office claimed that 'for an unelected hack to be put in charge of the largest publicity budget in the UK is a gross violation of the traditional principles of independence for the civil service and strict neutrality for government advertising' (*Independent*, 25 May 2002, p. 5). Carole Fisher, Chief Executive of the COI resigned in May 2002. The Thatcher government's desire to introduce a competitive market in the provision of publicity services and the ambitions of successive prime ministers' press secretaries, especially Ingham and Campbell, to centralise control of the information services, have combined to bring about a relative decline in the autonomy and influence of the COI in the design and implementation of government publicity and advertising.

THE GOVERNMENT'S PUBLICITY AGENCY?: THE ROLE AND FUNCTION OF THE COI

The COI is a specialist agency created to advise governments about publicity and marketing campaigns, press work, publications and advertising and to supply the necessary staff (journalists, press officers, radio producers, film makers, website designers and editors) and services to implement them (Garner and Short, 1998, p. 171). In brief, its role is that of a publicity agency; its clients are government departments and the royal family. Its output is prolific; its budget, substantial. Some indication of the scale and range of COI activities at the peak of the Thatcher administration's publicity commitments (1987–8) is revealed by a COI expenditure of approximately £150 million on government publicity which purchased some 32,965 advertising spaces on television, placed 9,246 advertisments in printed media and conducted an average of 100 publicity campaigns. It also produced 1,800 publications, more than 140 films, videos and television commercials and took part in 140 exhibitions. The National Audit Office claimed this represented 'an increase in real terms of 55 per cent over 1977–78' (Cobb, 1989a, p. 13).

By 2000–2001, COI activites had expanded considerably expressing new Labour's growing ambitions and expansive budget for government advertising (surpassing even the peak expenditure of the Thatcher governments) as well as changes in communications technology and delivery systems reflected in new web-based service provision. In 2001, COI advertising income increased by 70 per cent on the previous year to reach an unprecedented £192,407,000. In addition to organising promotional advertising and marketing campaigns, for example to reduce teenage pregnancy and increase ethnic minority recruitment to the police[2] and navy, the COI conducted 383 research studies for client departments, completed 2000 jobs with print runs in excess of 20 million, organised 2056 ministerial visits, raised £8 million value-added from private sponsorship, received more than 100 million hits on its news delivery website and achieved discounts on advertising worth in excess of £52 million (COI, 2001, p. 4). The continuing expansion of COI activities in advertising, marketing, publications and film and video making, is detailed in Table 4.1: the Table also signals the sharp increase in income and activity in 1998 following the election of the Labour government.

Table 4.1: **COI income by medium and promotional activity 1996–97 to 2000–2001**

£'000	1996–7	1997–8	1998–9	1999–2000	2000–1
Advertising	69,396	59,039	105,464	113,493	**192,407**
Direct marketing	11,494	8,498	16,959	26,343	**24,168**
Events	1,646	3,573	5,323	4,048	**4,754**
Film and Television	3,207	3,549	2,584	2,212	**1,901**
Publications & Digital Media	21,944	21,366	21,976	25,670	**29,643**
Radio	313	303	159	408	**386**
Regional News Network	5,254	6,037	7,397	9,657	**12,093**
Research	2,975	3,572	4,899	7,103	**10,050**
Sponsorship	296	1,082	4,282	8,782	**10,547**
Other	3,214	3,153	4,359	2,194	**9,429**
Discontinued Services	6,181	517	–	–	**–**
TOTAL	**125,920**	**110,680**	**173,402**	**199,910**	**295,378**

Source: COI Annual reports and Accounts 2000–2001, Stationary Office, p. 4

The aggregate expenditure of more than £192 million on advertising, with an additional £70 million for related promotional films and publications, is a substantial sum but a number of factors make this expenditure even more noteworthy. First, expenditure has expanded despite the considerable shrinking of the state sector. The greater part of the advertising budgets of the Thatcher governments of the 1980s funded the privatising campaigns which no longer feature centrally in government policy. One consequence of the 'privatising' of nationalised industries has been to diminish the state sector but with no visible effect on the size of advertising budgets. Second, bulk purchasing of advertising through the COI, secured 27 per cent on advertising expenditure for government departments and conse-quently the above-cited figures underestimate by approximately one quarter the media value as well as the quantity of advertising actually purchased by government. Third, since April 1984 the COI has been obliged to bid for the publicity work of State Departments in com-petition with private sector agencies such as Saatchi and Saatchi. In 2000–2001, only ten departments purchased publicity and marketing services through the COI signalling an even greater publicity expenditure by government as many departments continue to 'out source' promotional campaigns to private sector marketing and PR agencies.

GOVERNMENT PUBLICITY EXPENDITURE: CHANGING PRIORITIES

The key function of the COI involves the planning and implementation of large-scale, high-expenditure government publicity campaigns. Such campaigns have always formed part of the COI's brief, but traditionally COI publicity and advertising campaigns were concerned to convey public information of an uncontentious and non-party-political character. Prior to the successive Thatcher administrations of the 1980s, most government advertising fell into one of three categories. First, 'recruitment advertising', especially for the armed forces. Second, highly successful 'social persuasion campaigns' which generated unforgettable slogans that became part of British folklore – 'Clunk Click Every Trip', 'Watch Out There's A Thief About' as well as the annual injunction delivered at Christmas, warning partygoers: 'Don't Drink And Drive'. Third, 'public information' advertising typically intended to explain new legislation, or specific concerns such as the introduction of decimal currency or the introduction of metric measures (Clark, 1970, p. 92).

But in the mid-1980s, critics began to perceive radical shifts in the character and composition of government publicity expenditure and campaign advertising: four trends seemed significant and prompted anxieties: more than 100 parliamentary questions were posed on this subject during the 1987–88 session (Blair, 1989, p. 1). First, since 1970, there had been a marked increase in expenditure on advertising, especially advertising on television. Expenditure grew from £60 million in 1982 to £90 million in 1989. Advertising also increased as a proportion of COI publicity spending from 44 per cent in 1970 to 53 per cent by 1987–8. One explanation for this growth, in addition to the costs of the privatisation campaigns, was the increased use of relatively expensive television advertising which accounted for 25 per cent of total government advertising expenditure in 1970 but had risen to 56 per cent by 1988 (Scammell, 1991, p. 314). Second, there was a marked shift from expenditure on overseas to domestic publicity. Overseas expenditure declined from 34 per cent of the COI publicity budget in 1984–5, to 14 per cent in 1987–8. Third, there was an increase in publicity expenditure related to economic and social policy. Much of the increase here was devoted to employment initiatives on which expenditure, as a proportion of COI home spending, rose from 2 per cent in 1978–86 to 26 per cent in 1987; a rise from less than £1 million before 1985 to £37 million in 1986–7. Spending on social security and health also increased from two per cent of home expenditure between 1978 and 1984 to 19 per cent in 1986, reflecting expenditure on unemployment, AIDS and drug abuse campaigns (Scammell, 1991, pp. 315–20).

Finally, there is a pattern of increased publicity expenditure in the year before a general election or in the election year itself. COI data reveal that such increases are evident for every election since 1964 without regard to which party is in office. The increases are notable and significant for the election years 1966, 1970, 1983, 1987 and for the years preceding elections, 1969, 1973, 1978 and 1986 (ibid., p. 325). In the case of the 1992 general election, the increase in expenditure occurs in 1989–90 (£183 million compared to £178 million in the previous year), but it must be remembered that initially the election had been anticipated for June or November 1991. But in the year preceding the May 2001 general election, especially in the three months prior to the election, the increase in government campaigning expenditure was described as 'sensational' (*Panorama*, 26 May 2002 – new Labour expenditure on pre-election advertising is discussed below). All four trends have continued since 1997 following the election of a Labour government: some trends have been exacerbated.

Current expenditure on advertising and marketing campaigns to promote government policy stand at record levels (£192 millions in 2000–2001) reflecting new Labour's renewed emphasis on political marketing campaigns via the COI. Such campaigns, of course, enjoy a substantial pedigree. The Conservative government's marketing of the poll tax offers a classic example of the concerted and co-ordinated effort by government, using the COI and other agencies of the state, to structure media news agendas to win support for a particular policy (Deacon and Golding, 1994). The poll tax campaign illustrated that not all such campaigns can be judged successful, although Golding and Deacon stress that while the government failed to win support for its proposals, it managed to keep certain issues – especially the implications of the new tax for civil liberties as well as for central/local relations – off the news agenda (Golding and Deacon, 1991, p. 16). The poll tax was, of course, a uniquely unpopular issue that generated opposition on all sides of the traditional party divide, considerable public disorder and was eventually influential in the demise of Margaret Thatcher's premiership. Some policies, it seems, are simply too unpopular to be marketed in ways that win popular approval.

More recently in 1998, but with greater success, the COI handled the government's regional campaign to market its 'New Deal' policy designed to reduce long-term unemployment. The campaign involved all aspects of promoting the policy from 'securing media coverage on regional television and in the press' to 'delivery of the New Deal in Job Centres and the development of relevant web site materials' (COI, 1998, p. 3). Other campaigns in 2000 and 2001, many of which specifically targeted local media and some of which were conducted in collaboration with local schools, youth organisations and social and welfare organisations, included campaigns to reduce teenage pregnancy, to promote the working families tax credit and anti smoking campaigns (Shaeffer, 2000, p. 4 and Watt, 2001, p. 13). Extensive national campaigning in 2001 focused on reducing benefit fraud, lone parent benefits and the National Health Service.

A perennial element in the COI's publicity and information campaigns is the prerecorded tapes which are distributed free to local radio stations and television broadcasters and constitute the broadcast equivalent of the news releases issued to local and regional newspapers (Gardner, 1986 and COI, 2001, p. 13). Known as 'fillers' or more familarly in the industry as 'COIs', the format is typically an interview, often with a minister discussing proposed or recent legislation, with the role of the interviewer assumed by a civil servant. The tapes provide local radio with a free 'filler', a publicly funded information subsidy. Such tapes were used extensively when the government targeted local media as part of its promotional campaign for the poll tax (Golding, 1989, p. 6). Take-up rates, as with newspapers, reflect the station's journalistic and financial resources and the COI concedes that 'commercial stations [ie less well staffed news outlets] are more adventurous and less likely to dismiss our output as establishment material' (Gardner, 1986). Some stations are very reluctant to acknowledge that they use the tapes, but one independent station conceded that up to 70 per cent of the tapes it received were broadcast (Cobb, 1989c, p. 12). Given the market-driven pressures under which local radio stations increasingly operate and the consequent resource difficulties they must confront, it is perhaps unsurprising that these 'fillers' have enjoyed growing receptivity and expansive air time (Franklin 1997, pp. 129–30; McManus, 1994). In 1985, the COI distributed more than 400 tapes to local radio stations in the hope of securing free air time (Gardner, 1986): by 2001 the use of such fillers had expanded very strikingly. The COI annual report for 2001 claimed that 'over the past year they [fillers] have been transmitted 708,000 times. That's 11,800 hours of donated airtime – the same as 151 years of episodes of *Eastenders*'. The COI broadcasting of fillers is not restricted to mainstream channels but targets 'ever-wider audiences by broadcasting fillers via a diverse range of media from football clubs and shopping centres to buses and Internet TV' (COI, 2001, p. 13).

This continuous long-term expansion of goverment advertising budgets, combined with the changing composition of government advertising begun in the 1980s, has proved highly contentious, attracting criticism from the public, opposition politicians, academics and even members of the COI and the GICS. The view that successive governments have crossed the line separating public information from party propaganda have been widely expressed across two decades.

PUBLIC INFORMATION VERSUS PARTY PROPAGANDA

Allegations that governments use the COI to disseminate propaganda are difficult to substantiate. Behind the rhetoric of opposition politicians (for it is inevitably – or at least overwhelmingly – opposition politicians who make such claims) lies a very genuine difficulty: and it is a problem for all governments, no matter what their political colour. Expressed broadly, it is the difficulty of how 'public information' might be distinguished from 'party propaganda'. But in the mid-1980s this was a problem which the Conservative government should have recognised only too readily since, in essence, it was the same problem it legislated to resolve in 1986 and 1988 when it tried to establish statutory criteria to distinguish 'legitimate information' about local government affairs from opposition claims concerning 'propaganda on the rates' (see Chapter 5). It is also a problem which Tony Blair should quickly recognise given his trenchant criticisms of Conservative governments in the 1980s for undertaking the kinds of advertising campaigns which – his critics – allege, have characterised new Labour more than any previous government. But the achievement of office, it seems, brings a radically revised vision in which 'propaganda' is transformed into the 'public's right to know' and to be well informed about policy: and routinely! The following two sections focus respectively on Conservative and Labour advertising expenditure and the criticisms which both have attracted.

THE COI IN THE 1980S: THE BEARER OF CONSERVATIVE PARTY NEWS?

Government advertising budgets spiralled massively during the 1980s. By 1988, the government ranked third in the league table of the UK's largest corporate advertisers trailing marginally behind Unilever and Proctor & Gamble (Churchill, 1989, p. 26). By 1989–90 the government had become the nation's largest advertiser as a consequence of its record spend in excess of £98 million (Scammell, 1991, p. 333).

A major component feeding this expansion of government expenditure was the flurry of privatisation campaigns in the mid-1980s beginning with the sale of British Telecom (advertising expenditure for floatation £25 million) in November 1984 followed by British Aerospace (May 1985, £2.3 million), Britoil (August 1985, £3.5 million), TSB (September 1986, £10 million) and the campaign designed to 'Tell Sid' to buy shares in the newly privatised gas industry; the cost of £40 million worked out at £8.75p per share application (Birrell and Hughes, 1989, p. 18). Other privatisation campaigns followed, including British Airways (February 1987, £11 million), Rolls-Royce (May 1987, £4 million), British Airports Authority (July 1987 – interrupted by the June election, £5.7 million), BP (October 1987, £23 million), water (September 1989, £40 million) and electricity

(September 1989, £76 million) (Blair, 1989). Other developments meant the timing was propitious for further expansion of budgets. Growing unemployment in the mid-1980s prompted the government to launch the 'Action for Jobs' campaign while the Department of the Environment mounted a substantial campaign to 'popularise' the Poll Tax to a curiously unreceptive audience in Scotland and later in England and Wales. The emergence of medical and social issues such as AIDS and drug abuse further buttressed government publicity expenditure across the 1980s.

This rapid growth in expenditure on central government campaigns, at, a time when the Conservative government was introducing the Local Government Acts of 1986 and 1988 to limit local government publicity initiatives, seemed bound to stir controversy and invite allegations of double standards, if not hypocrisy (see Chapter 5). Tony Blair, then Labour's shadow spokesperson for trade alleged that government was using public funds to promote party policy rather than simply to inform the public and provide information about new government policy initiatives. 'It is no coincidence', he argued, 'that the areas of the largest increase in [publicity] spending are those of most political sensitivity for the government' (*The Financial Times*, 30 March 1988). A year later his comments were more explicit. 'The government are not just giving the facts, they are promoting the Conservative party view of an area of high political controversy. Now that's not just an abuse of the broadcasting service, that's an abuse of literally hundreds of millions of pounds of tax payers' money'. And again, although by now in more inclusive mode, 'You can see quite clearly that the purpose [of these government advertising campaigns] is not to give us the public the facts, but to sell the government's political message and that's quite wrong' (*Panorama*, 1989).

On 4 September 1989, the BBC's *Panorama* programme explored Blair's allegations by reporting on the design and implementation of the government's 'Action for Jobs' campaign. *Panorama* claimed the primary intention of the campaign, in the run-up to the 1987 general election, was not to provide information about the new scheme for helping unemployed young people back into work but rather to allay voters' fears, especially potentially wavering Conservative voters, about unemployment and convince them of the government's serious intention to tackle this significant issue (*Guardian*, 7 September 1989). The programme commissioned two media specialists (Kevin Baverstock and Kevin Hurdwell) to analyse the government's placing of television advertising slots across a four-month period between January and May 1987. They concluded that the pattern of distribution of advertising across the television regions was more congruent with a campaign targeted at high-income groups in the south east rather than young people in the north east and north west regions which were the uncontested unemployment high spots of the UK. A Department of Employment planning paper leaked to *Panorama* confirmed Baversback and Hurdwell's assessment by identifying the primary target groups as 'influencers', especially senior managers, the City, local government, politicians, community groups, the media and professional advisers, whereas 'the unemployed' were listed only in the secondary target group alongside potential school-leavers and careers advisers (*Panorama*, 4 September 1989). In support of their case, *Panorama* cited Gallup polls illustrating the effectiveness of the campaign in reaching its primary target groups but not necessarily unemployed young people. The polls revealed a 100 per cent improvement in the government's rating by voters on policies relating to unemployment from 15 per cent in July 1986 to 30 per cent by the crucial date of the launch of the 1987 general election campaign.

In the run up to the 1992 general election, a similar press and television campaign costing in excess of £8 million was launched by the Department of Employment to promote Training and Enterprise Councils (TECs). Michael Howard, the then employment secretary, pointed to the information function of the campaign, claiming 'there's no point in having help available if people do not know about it'. Tony Blair, however, suggested that the same motive lay behind the government's urgent promotion of TECs as informed the earlier Action for Jobs campaign: 'Tory Ministers know that the recession, unemployment and training will be important issues at the next general election' (*Labour Research*, November 1991, p. 7). Concerns about the government's growing advertising expenditure combined with changing advertising priorities and the potential which in tandem they offered for propaganda, were not restricted to politicians. Lord Thomson of Monifieth, Chair of the Independent Broadcasting Authority (IBA), alleged the government was 'using the persuasive and visual skills of advertising agencies to a degree which governments did not do in the past' (*The Financial Times*, 9 May 1988).

THE COI IN THE NEW MILLENNIUM: THE BEARER OF LABOUR PARTY NEWS?

Since 1997, but notably since 1999, the Labour government's expenditure on advertising and promotional marketing has spiralled beyond the previously unprecedented levels of Conservative administrations. Labour has undoubtedly been a reforming and innovative government, initiating a good deal of legislative change which in turn suggests a justifiable rationale for the increased expenditure on public information and 'public awareness' advertising. But from the particular perspective which opposition alone seems to engender, conservative politicians, along with political journalists, have expressed concern about the extent and scale of Labour's commitments. But Labour's commitment to advertising has delivered some bouquets as well as brickbats. It is perhaps a deliciously sweet irony that in the spring of 2002 when the government was publicly rejecting its previous commitments to 'spin' and denying opposition claims that it was obsessed with presentation rather than delivery, that *PR Week* (the PR profession's weekly 'trade journal') voted the party number 1 in a list of 20 entrants for the 'most effective PR campaign' for its success in developing a brand which 'sought to shed the image of a spend-thrift, inflationary and union-dominated party and create one that suggested it was in touch with the people' (Jones, 2002a, p. 6).

Advertising began to take off in the early days of the new Labour administration: the commitment has proved costly. During 1997–8, Malcolm Bruce and Margaret Ewing posed a series of parliamentary questions inquiring about levels of 'total expenditure on all forms of publicity and advertising' in each of the major government departments. The replies revealed that costs of publicity and advertising costs were: £15.5 million at the Scottish Office (HC Debs, vol. 313 cols. 266–7); £962,854 for the Lord Chancellor (HC Debs vol. 303, cols. 109–11); £1.3 millions at the Department of International Development (vol. 302 cols. 613–14); £8,109,000 at the Northern Ireland Office (HC Debs (vol. 302 cols. 616–17); £40.97 millions at the Ministry of Defence (HC Debs vol. 302, cols. 441–9); £19,429,000 at Environment, Transport and the Regions (HC Debs vol. 301 cols. 618–19); £436,774 at the Foreign and Commonwealth Office (HC Debs vol. 301 cols. 395–6); £9,216,000 at the Department of Trade and Industry (HC Debs vol. 301 cols. 413–15); £17,724,255 at Social Services (HC Debs vol. 301 col. 443); £22,124,000 at the Treasury (HC Debs vol. 301 cols. 113–4); £16,210,000 at Department of Health (HC Debs vol. 301 col. 14); £609,000 at the Department of Culture, Media and Sport (HC Debs vol. 300 cols. 641–2); £9,080,593 at the Home Office (HC Debs vol. 300 cols. 530–1); £2,015,000 at the Welsh Office (HC Debs vol. 300 col. 520); £17.4 million at the Department for Education and Employment (HC Debs vol. 300 cols. 530–1); £218,700 for the Attorney General (HC Debs vol. 302 col. 578) and £1,518,790 for the Chancellor of the Duchy of Lancaster (HC Debs vol. 302 col. 377). The aggregate expenditure of £165,323,966 represented a substantial sum.

On occasion, the government's enthusiasm for advertising has been striking. In the first three months of 2001, for example, Labour launched 172 new marketing campaigns, spent £97 million on advertising and broke the Thatcherite record of 1989 by becoming the largest purchaser of advertising in the UK. By contrast, Unilever (2nd) spent £34 million while BT trailed in third place with a relatively modest expenditure of £23.8 million: in brief the government spent almost twice as much on advertising as its second and third placed rivals combined (Watts, 2001, p. 13).

The BBC *Panorama* programme entitled 'Tony in Adland' (26 May 2002) analysed Labour's advertising expenditure in the run up to the 2001 election and consciously tried to replicate the earlier *Panorama* programme broadcast in 1989 (see above) in which Tony Blair had been quoted so liberally and critically about the then Conservative government's advertising expenditure. Media analysts Baverstock and Hurdwell were invited again to analyse and comment on three particular adverts which featured prominently in television-based advertising. Each advertisement, paid for from the public purse, focused on 'politically contentious topic' – nurses' pay and the state of the NHS, benefit 'cheats' and benefits for lone parents – which the programme argued was inapropriate given the election context.

The programme levelled three criticisms. First, expenditure of this magnitude was inappropriate and difficult to defend given the context of the imminent election. From April 2000 to March 2001, government advertising expenditure increased 70 per cent on the previous year eventually totalling £192 million. 54 per cent of this budget was crammed into the last 3 months of the year: £29 million in January, £19 million in February and £49 million in March, an all time record for a single month (the week before the election campaign was expected to start but eventually postponed because of the foot and mouth epidemic). Hurdwell claimed that 'to spend a quarter of your budget in the last month of the financial year suggests bad financial management or a significant plan to spend the money in that month'. This suspicion of possible electioneering was endorsed by Neville Taylor, director general of the COI between 1985–1988. 'To concentrate expenditure and impact and message . . . in the run up to an election' he argued 'has got to smell. It has to indicate another motive for doing it' (Taylor quoted in *Panorama*, 26 May 2002).

Second, much of the advertising targeted the wrong audience and was thereby an inefficient use of public funding. One advertisement, for example, focused on nursing recruitment but, *Panorama* alleged, it was more concerned to boost the image of the NHS. The advertisment which ran in February and March 2001 related the story of a young boy who was injured in a road traffic accident: the advert listed the 22 specialist nurses 'who saved Joe's life'. But the media analysts suggested that at a cost of £3 million (which 'put them in the same league as B&Q') the advert nonetheless targeted the wrong audience. Lord Bell (previously of Saatchi and Saatchi and a former advisor on advertising to the Conservative government) suggested that 'these advertisment were occupying a lot of airtime to communicate the values of the NHS but they are nothing to do with recruitment . . .'. Bell also suggested that television advertising is an ineffective way of recruiting nurses. 'TV is a mass market, a blunt instrument that costs a great deal of money. It is not an efficient means of identifying a target audience and getting them to apply for a job' he argued: 'You don't see any other recruitment advertising on TV' (Bell quoted in *Panorama*, 26 May 2002). Bell's view was confirmed by the government's own research which concluded that 'disappointingly, interest in finding out more about nursing declined' across the period of broadcasting the advertisements. But *Panorama* alleged the 'campaign may have been just what the doctor ordered for new Labour – a soft sell for the NHS' (*Panorama*, 26 May 2002).

Third, the timing of the advertisements so close to the election might signal government ambitions to cross the line between 'general government advertising and tax-payer-funded "puffs" to promote the Labour cause' (Waugh 2002, p. 5; White 2002, p. 9). Certainly this was the view of a number of distinguished civil servants such as Sir Michael Partridge Permanent Secretary at the DSS (1989–95) who claimed the advertisment about nurse recruitment 'only really had nurse recruitment tacked on the end. The rest of it you could mistake for a "party political" saying, now we've got a good NHS'. He denounced an advertisement about benefits for lone parents as 'an improper use of taxpayers' money' since it was insufficiently factual and amounted 'to a general puff for government policy ... It seemed to me to be crossing the line' (Partridge in *Panorama*, 26 May 2002). If the three criticisms above can be sustained they suggest that government, by its use of pre-election advertising, might be able to subvert newly imposed limits on election expenditure. Lord Armstrong, head of the home civil service between 1981 and 1987, argued, 'there are very strict rules about election expenses and this could be a way in which ... the party in government could be spending more on purposes related to the campaign than the law allows ... If I were the opposition I think I would be asking a good many questions about this' (Armstong in *Panorama*, 26 May 2002). But despite these loudly mooted concerns, critics believe there is little effective control of government's marketing and public relations expenditure and activities.

CONVENTIONAL WISDOM: REGULATING GOVERNMENT COMMUNICATIONS

Central government publicity activities are not constrained by statute but, as in many other areas of their operations, by unwritten conventions. The major convention regarding government publicity, funded from the public purse, is that promotional advertising campaigns should not be launched until the relevant policy has been discussed and approved by Parliament. Sir Fife Clark, a former director general of the COI, established the line between government information (factual presentation by the government services about public policy) and party propaganda (advocacy of party policy which is a matter for ministers and party organisations) at the point at which a bill becomes an Act. 'A basic convention ... governing COI production', he claimed, was that 'while legislation is in progress no money from public funds is spent on publicity ... nevertheless as soon as a new scheme has been passed by Parliament, the government has a duty to make its details known' (Clark, 1970, p. 14).

But in truth, certainly in central government, this convention has often been breached by both Labour and Conservative administrations. The 1945 Attlee government, for example, produced 'popular' versions of some white papers, including its proposals for the NHS, while the Conservative government in 1971 printed 5 million copies of an abbreviated version of the white paper on Britain's application to join the [then] EEC. More contentious, and quite without precedent, was the publication by the COI in January 1986 of 100,000 copies of the leaflet *Paying for Local Government: the Need for Change* at the same time that the government's proposals for the Poll Tax were published in the green paper *Paying for Local Government*. Five years later the story was much the same. The shadow Cabinet accused the government of spending taxpayers' money to advertise a white paper outlining the Conservative proposal for a *Citizen's Charter*. In the run-up to the 1992 election, Neil Kinnock the leader of the Labour party claimed the charter was 'launched with £8 million of taxpayers money as undisclosed Tory Party election expenditure' (*Guardian*, 24 July 1991). In 2001, a Labour pre-election advert concerning benfit fraud did not fall foul of the convention by claiming that 'People who commit benefit fraud are getting away with millions of pounds of your money' (a factual statement) but drove a coach and horses through the convention when it added the tag line 'We aim to put a stop to it' (a future policy commitment of the Labour party).

A note from the Cabinet Office submitted to the Widdicombe committee in 1985, entitled 'Central government conventions on publicity and advertising', attempted to formalise these unwritten conventions for the first time. The major conventions were that publicity should be relevant to government responsibilities: content, tone and presentation should not be party political; the treatment of issues should be objective, should not be personalised, employ political slogans or directly attack the opinions and policies of opposition parties; material on controversial subjects should not be distributed unsolicited except where the information directly affects the recipients' interests and costs should be justifiable (Ingham, 1991, p. 368). Interestingly, these conventions bear a striking similarity to the guidelines embodied in the various codes of practice issued in the wake of the Local Government Acts 1986 and 1988, intended to regulate local government public relations activities (Franklin, 1988b, pp. 26–32); indeed Widdicombe's ambition was consistency and he intended that 'basically the rules for both should be the same or similar' (Heaton, 1988, p. 9). But they are also similarly flawed.

The main difficulty is that the conventions lack sufficient precision to allow discrimination between acceptable and unacceptable publicity. Consequently, while it might be acceptable to proscribe local government publicity supporting unilateral disarmament (defence policy) or a homeland for the Palestinians (foreign policy), as inappropriate to a local authority's brief, it is less clear what might not be 'relevant to government responsibilities' in the context of central government. Similar difficulties arise when trying to define what is 'party political' or 'unsolicited' and 'in the recipients' interests' (Franklin 1988b, pp. 26–32). Again, the requirement that publicity costs should 'be justifiable' is inadequate unless the criteria for assessing costs and the identity of those who will formulate them are stated.

On 28 July 1988, the Cabinet Office, prompted (Ingham alleged) by criticism of Lord Young's DTI campaigns, issued a supplementary set of guidelines for publicity along with other changes. The Cabinet Office, rather than the COI, would in future rule on the propriety of campaign publicity, while the Treasury would be final arbiter on matters relating to the value for money of publicity (Harris, 1990, p. 169; Ingham, 1991, p. 375).

The new conventions were broadly understood to constitute a 'tightening' of the rules (*UK Press Gazette*, 15 May 1989, p. 14; *The Financial Times*, 17 May 1989). They also warned ministers and heads of departments that ' "image building" whether explicit or implied and whether of government or minister, is not acceptable' (Ingham, 1991, p. 375). The revised convention also stated that 'it would be counter productive if the level of spending on a campaign impeded the communication of the message it is intended to convey by itself becoming a controversial issue' (ibid.). Both prohibitions have clearly proved risibly inadequate to quell concerns about government advertising: especially Labour's recent advertising expenditure and its commitment to the media presentation and packaging of policy and its leading personalities. The conventions governing publicity are so loosely framed that it requires an almost Olympian leap of the imagination to envisage the sort of 'malpractice' which might constitute a breach of their intentions. Moreover, even when such a breach is identified, as is evidently the case with Labour advertising in 2001, it is uncertain which institutions might operate as a brake on government ambitions. The requirement, since February 2002, that the chief executive of the COI should report directly to the director of communications, David Hill, does not seem to offer any greater prospect for regulation of these conventions. By contrast, the restrictions on local government publicity are much less equivocal. Section 2 of the Local Government Act 1988 outlaws any publicity material which 'promotes or opposes a point of view on a question of political controversy which is identifiable as the view of one political party and not another'. Such admirable lucidity would have rendered the Conservative's privatisation campaigns and much of the promotion of the Poll Tax, along with Labour's campaigns against benefit frauds and promoting benefits for lone parents, wholly unacceptable. The division between information and propaganda, which is notoriously difficult to define, has been drawn by successive Conservative and Labour governments in what seemed to be a partisan or at least an inconsistent and idiosyncratic manner.

SOFT SOAP OR HARD SELL? NEW LABOUR, NEW MESSAGES, NEW MARKETING STRATEGIES

The National Year of Reading (NYR) was launched amid considerable media razzmatazz by the Department for Education and Employment (DfEE) on 16 September 1998. The public relations consultancy Hill Knowlton had been appointed a year earlier to be responsible for the planning and day to day implementation of the campaign. The government's aims were ambitious: the campaign intended 'nothing less than a sea change in the nation's attitude to reading' (DfEE, 1998a, p. 2). More specifically, the objective was to 'ensure that by the year 2002, 80 per cent of all 11-year-olds will reach the standards expected of their age in English' (ibid., p. 3). For David Blunkett, then secretary of state for education, to launch such a campaign seems uncontentious, if not highly desirable, given these objectives. But what sparked political controversy was the marketing strategy employed by the government: especially the commitment to using *Coronation Street* and other soap operas 'as useful conduits for policy messages' (Henderson, 2002, p. 23).

This marketing strategy was not new. Conservative home secretary Ken Baker, for example, used *Brookside* to promote anti-drug policies in the early 1990s, the BBC radio soap the *Archers* was initially broadcast as a public information service for farmers and featured story lines initiated by the Ministry of Agriculture (Carroll, 1998, p. 4), while a report commissioned by Barnados revealed that 70 per cent of children cited soap operas as their major source of information about HIV/AIDS (Barnardos, 1993). But what seemed new was the Labour government's enthusiasm and determination to use soap operas to sell policy as well as soap. Under the headline 'Big Brother Blunkett is accused', the *Daily Mail* quoted a Conservative spokesperson who denounced 'this government intervention into the world of television soap operas' as an 'Orwellian nightmare' which the 'licence payer would reject as propaganda on the telly' (*Daily Mail*, 17 September 1998). The government promptly dismissed the allegation claiming the purpose of the campaign was to 'raise public awareness' about literacy problems.

The *Guardian* reported the official launch of NYR by carrying a picture of David Blunkett enjoying a pint of beer, ensconced behind the bar of the Queen Vic on the set of BBC's popular soap opera *EastEnders*. Soap stars Patsy Palmer (Bianca) and Sid Owen (Ricky) were pictured with the politician. The actors were sporting T-shirts emblazoned with the NYR logo and posed very carefully to ensure that the jacket covers of Bill Bryson's *Notes from a Small Island* and John Gray's *Men are from Mars, Women are from Venus*, which they were holding, were clearly visible and would provide the photographer with a good shot. The photo opportunity at the Queen Vic was a particularly apposite location for the campaign launch because the soap opera was introducing a new story line which involved the character Grant Mitchell reading to his baby daughter, Courtney.

Government press officers working on the campaign managed to persuade scriptwriters and directors of peak time soap operas, including *Brookside, Coronation Street, EastEnders, Hollyoaks* and *Grange Hill*, to feature story lines in these popular dramas which promoted the key ambitions of the campaign. *EastEnders* and *Coronation Street*, for example, agreed to feature stories about adult literacy problems while 'children's television favourites such as *Hollyoaks, Grange Hill* and *Brookside* will carry plotlines promoting reading as "fun" and "cool" pastimes to dispel the myth among youngsters that only boffins enjoy books' (Lepkowska, 1998). Television producer Phil Redmond gave the scheme his enthusiastic backing (*Guardian*, 17 September 1998, p. 4). When literacy-related stories were featured in *Brookside*, programmes were 'followed up with a helpline, *Brookside* learning materials and a *Brookside* video. When viewers phone the helpline they will be referred on to their local Brookie Basics Centre where they can improve their literacy in a relaxed setting' (*The National Year of Reading Update*, October 1998, p. 4).

While soap operas are currently among the most favoured programmes to access for promotional purposes, by ministers and press officers, NYR was also promised coverage 'in a wide range of popular programmes such as *Ready Steady Cook* and *Esther*', in Channel 4's *Big Breakfast* and in BBC television and radio programming for schools such as *Look and Read* and *Words and Pictures* (DfEE, 1998b pp. 6–7). This 'free' access to prime time audiences was supplemented by paid advertising with a budget of £1.8 million. The first in a series of television advertisements, part of a campaign entitled *A Little Reading Goes A Long Way* and designed to encourage fathers to read to their children, was broadcast the evening before Blunkett's photo opportunity at the Queen Vic and carefully timed to coincide with Manchester United's game with Barcelona in the European Champion's League: a scheduling which guaranteed maximum target audience reach.

The NYR launch on the *EastEnders* set was promptly followed by a press conference attended by Ken Follett, Estelle Morris and Phil Redmond: other celebrity backers included the Spice Girls, Chris Evans, John Cleese, Olympic champion Linford Christie and jockey Richard Dunwoody. Such celebrity firepower guarantees press interest but in the spirit of a 'belt and braces' approach, the DfEE distributed 5,000 'press packs' 'containing highlights of the events that will be taking place around the country'. Perhaps unsurprisingly, the *National Year of Reading Update* was able to confirm that 'media coverage has been incredible and we are delighted with the enthusiastic way in which the press has greeted the launch of the year' (September 1998, p. 1). This flurry of promotional activity was funded largely from the public purse with the DfEE meeting the £1.8 million bill for television advertising with a further expenditure of £750,000 to help fund local initiatives.

The purpose of outlining these details of the NYR campaign is to illustrate the extent of the government's commitment to fund advertising and public relations activities to promote even relatively 'low key' policy issues such as literacy. But the campaign to promote NYR raises significant concerns about whether the government is marketing policy in a way which risks moving too closely in the direction of propaganda. The NYR was evidently not a politically contentious policy unlike the earlier campaign during the 1980s to privatise the water, gas and electricity industries. Nor is it necessary to endorse the self-serving criticisms of the Conservative MP who accused 'Big Brother Blunkett' of holding views 'straight out of 1984', to feel a degree of unease about the extent to which government and the GICS seem eager to incorporate policy messages into soap opera and other popular television light entertainment programmes (*Daily Mail*, 17 September 1998). The deployment of such a public relations strategy is increasingly commonplace. A report by the think tank Demos, for example, recommended the further use of television soap operas to promote socially desirable practices such as 'good parenting' (Straw 1998), while in 2001 a campaign to prevent teenage pregnancy, with £60 million funding, nonetheless intended that the inclusion of story lines about teenage pregnancy in soaps would form a key element in the marketing mix (Shaeffer, 2000, p. 4).

But the NYR and similar campaigns raise a number of significant concerns. The first is the extent of public knowledge about the costs of these campaigns. It is uncertain, for example, whether the public is aware that during 1997–98 the government spent in excess of £165 million on advertising and promoting its policies, rising to more than £200 million in 2001. Second, it is at the very least a point for debate to assess whether these substantial sums of public money are most effectively and properly spent in the publicising, rather than the provision, of particular services: £165 million would fund a good number of school buildings and new teaching jobs. The campaign to promote NYR, moreover, presents a particular irony: namely, at the same time that central government was spending money on advertising campaigns to encourage reading, local government – in the teeth of local opposition – was closing libraries to meet spending targets imposed by central government! Third, there is a concern about the opacity of these arrangements and the extent of public awareness of the involvement of governments and their advertising specialists in developing the plots and storylines which unravel in viewers' sitting rooms. A 'health warning' at the end of each programme emphasising the ambitions of ministers to introduce campaigning social policy messages into soaps might surprise many viewers of these popular programmes. But it would at least guarantee that members of the public understand that the sudden proliferation of characters in *Coronation Street, Hollyoaks, Brookside, EastEnders* and *Grange Hill* who seem preoccupied with problems such as teenage sexuality and pregnancy, HIV, adult literacy or drug abuse, is more than mere coincidence. Fourth, what is significant here is not the particular *content* but the *practice*. The concern is not whether the government's messages are socially worthy and might achieve desirable ends, but rather the knowledge that partisan messages are being inserted into popular programming and that these messages may be accepted by viewers with little criticism or even awareness that these are government-sponsored messages. Indeed, the fact that these messages seem socially desirable may even accelerate their transmission through society. The legitimacy achieved by this use of television for propaganda, moreover, is troubling: it hardly seems to occasion critical comment. The *Guardian*, reporting Blunkett's photo opportunity at the Old Vic, expressed few misgivings about the government's plans to 'mobilise all the propaganda weapons of popular culture to improve the nation's reading skills' (*Guardian*, 17 September 1998).

This use of the highly popular soap opera genre for the promotion of social issue messages is gaining currency globally. In South Africa, for example, *Soul City* has been broadcast in prime time on Saturday evenings since 1992, by SABC-1, the popular broadcasting channel. The programme is part of the government's 'edutainment' campaign and routinely carries messages about health issues such as HIV/AIDS, tuberculosis and anti smoking messages (evaluation of specific story lines is available at www.soulcity.org.za). In Mexico, soaps perform a similar function with key messages focusing on family planning, child abuse and drugs campaigns (Henderson, 2002; Nariman, 1993).

In the US, the government's commitment to weave social policy messages into the narratives of soap operas has developed a step further and perhaps presages future developments in the UK. It has certainly prompted criticisms concerning propaganda from both academics (Brennen, 2000) and journalists (Farhi, 1997; Forbes, 2000; Lacey, 2000).

In January 2001, the on-line magazine *Salon* published a story about 'a hidden government effort to shoehorn anti-drug messages into . . . network television programming' (Forbes, 2000). Forbes reported that government officials preview, edit and approve scripts and advance footage of prime-time television shows and popular soaps including *ER*, *Beverley Hills 90210*, *Chicago Hope*, *The Crosby Show*, *The Drew Carey Show*, *Sabrina the Teenage Witch* and *Seventh Heaven*. Five networks, NBC, ABC, CBS, WB and Fox (and since 1999 UPN), he alleges, have included anti-drugs messages into more than 100 episodes of their programmes in order to receive a lucrative but 'complex' government advertising subsidies (Brennen, 2000, p. 5; Forbes, 2000). In October 1997, Congress approved a $1 billion anti-drug advertising campaign, rolled out across five years, that required the media to match advertising slots bought by the government with an equivalent number of public service announcements (PSAs): essentially a two for one deal. The White House Office of National Drug Control Policy (ONDCP) headed by the drug czar Barry McCaffrey, declared the arrangement to be 'the largest and most complex social-marketing campaign ever undertaken' (Forbes, 2000).

Negotiated at a time of advertising 'doldrums' the broadcasting networks became increasingly critical of the arrangement as the demand for advertising slots expanding during the late 1990s reflecting an economic upturn and the expansion of dot.com companies. McCaffrey offered the networks a solution which allowed them to reduce the number of PSAs they had initially promised in return for allowing the government access to prime time programming for its anti-drug messages. McCaffrey also constructed a labyrinthine formula for discounting the PSAs against programme inserts. 'An on-strategy storyline that is the main plot of a half hour show' he claimed 'can be valued at three 30 second ads. If there is an end tag with an 800 number for more information . . . it is valued at an additional 15-second ad. A main storyline in an hour long prime time show is valued at five 30-second ads, while such a storyline in a one hour daytime show is valued at four 30-second ads' (cited in Lacey, 2000, 1A; and Brennen, 2000). Forbes illustrates the formula with the example of Murdoch's News Corporation which owns the Fox television network and sold the Clinton government $20 millions of advertising. Fox submitted a two-part *Beverley Hills 90210* programme to the ONDCP in which the central character was on 'a downward spiral into addiction' in order to recoup some of matching advertising which Fox had agreed to provide. The ONDCP eventually conceded that the programmes should be valued at between $500,000 and $750,000 toward the repayment of matched advertising (Forbes, 2000).

This renegotiated arrangement provides opportunities for government information officials to preview programmes and approve them or argue for script changes. Some scripts are reviewed more than once. Some government plot lines were 'as subtle as a brick through a window'. One episode of *Chicago Hope*, for example, was rewritten to include graphic accounts of 'the tragedies afflicting young post-rave revelers' which included 'drug-induced death, rape, psychosis, a nasty two-car wreck, a broken nose and a doctor's threat to skip life-saving surgery unless the patient agreed to an incriminating urine test' (Forbes, 2000). Such examples make clear the impact of the agreement on the creative output of the networks, but while the network executives brokered this agreement with the government, the great majority of the programmes writers, producers and other creative workers knew nothing of the arrangements. John Tinker, executive producer of *Chicago Hope* said that he knew nothing about the government incentives to include certain story lines in the script nor of the government's complicity in shaping character and plot developments (Brennen, 2000).

For their part, government officials declare themselves content with the outcome of the campaign and cite a 15 per cent reduction in drug use across the year 1999–2000. The official discourse is less about propaganda than mutual commitment to the promotion of information which is socially beneficial. An official of the ONDCP claimed 'I guess we plead guilty to using every lawful means of saving America's children' (Brennen, 2000, p. 13). As in the UK with the National Year of Reading and other social persuasion campaigns conducted via soap operas, the US government distinguishes between 'positive pro-social information and the seemingly dangerous messages of propaganda and espouses an ideological position that finds the idea of pro-social manipulation an oxymoron' (Brennen, 2000, p. 15).

---

1   There have been other organisational changes. On 22 June 1992 ministerial responsibility for the COI transferred to the minister for the Cabinet Office from the chancellor of the exchequer. Since that date the COI has been a Department of the Minister for the Cabinet Office, who is accountable to Parliament and its Select Committees for all COI activities. Taking into account the advice of the chief executive, the minister determines the overall policy and financial framework within which the COI operates but does not typically become involved in day-to-day management.

2   The scale of COI campaigning is considerable in terms of expenditure and target audience reach. The campaign to recruit ethnic minority applicants into the police force, for example, involved commercials in 'Bollywood' cinemas, and advertisements in the ethnic minority press, women's magazines, local radio stations, as well as the design of a dedicated website and television based advertising. The campaign was highly effective judged by target audience response. The campaign generated 44,243 telephone calls which converted to 16,121 expressions of interest and 91,000 hits on the website which generated a further 12,172 expressions of interest which, in tandem, triggered the largest rise in the number of police recruits for more than a decade: 990 new officers. The COI television commercials won a bronze award at the British TV Advertising Awards and the website won a gold award at the Cannes International Advertising Festival.

Chapter Five

☐ LOCAL GOVERNMENT PUBLIC RELATIONS: SPINNING THE LOCAL AGENDA

Given the traditional hostility which characterises relationships between journalists and public relations officers (PROs), a recent review of local government public relations concluded paradoxically by nominating the 'Town hall' as 'the last bastion of good municipal journalism'. Paradox gave way to contention in the explanatory suggestion that 'without the carefully prepared material provided by professional local government PROs, local newspapers are unlikely to be able to perform their role as principal institutions of the public sphere' (Harrison, 1998, p. 168). This conclusion reflects a growing body of research which reveals that local government, through its public relations offices, is assuming an increasing prominence in setting the local news agenda by providing resource-hungry local newspapers with what Gandy describes as 'information subsidies' (Franklin, 1988; Gandy, 1982). Another study confirms the acceleration of this trend and suggests 'an increased media dependency on the information subsidies provided by PR' (Davis, 2002, p. 17).

Successive governments throughout the 1980s and 1990s reached a similar conclusion although they preferred to describe local government's growing campaigning and public relations activities as 'propaganda'. In the mid-1980s, central government concluded that the expansive publicity ambitions of local government were hindering the achievement of its own policy objectives: 'propaganda on the rates' distributed by 'local spin doctors' had to be stopped. Interestingly the phrase 'spin doctor' has rarely been applied to the activities of local government public relations specialists even though it offers an apt description for much of their media relations work. A senior PR practitioner argues that avoiding the opprobrium associated with the term spin has been among the major achievements of PR in the local setting, establishing its superiority over the news management activities of national government spin doctors.

> I do consider myself a spin doctor but I think in local government we are actually better at it. Being good at spin doctoring or media management is like being a good theatre director in that when you go to see a play, you don't notice the bits of direction, you just get what the play's about. You get the emotions, you get the power and you get the story. But you don't see the

director's hand on anything and you certainly don't call the director on stage at the end of the play and say let's give him a big clap for putting this play together. You should never see the director. And the best PR, the best image management, is when you don't see it, when you don't notice it. I think the fact that on the national stage spin doctors have become the story, is a huge, huge error on their part . . . what happened when Labour got into power is that you had individual spin doctors going around showing off about how clever they were at manipulating the media – the media don't like that and quite rightly so. They don't like being shown up as having been manipulated . . . So you should never show off and I think in local government there have been some brilliant practitioners who know precisely the image they want for their council, but have done it in a way which does not attract labels of spin doctoring and manipulation. And that is the greatest bit of spin doctoring and manipulation of all.

(Interview, 27 September 2002.)

But local government public relations has not always been so successful at 'covert operations'. The very public tensions between central and local government first arose in the 1980s when the radical aspirations of Thatcherism were restructuring many aspects of economy, society and polity. In the Commons, the Conservative government confronted little opposition reflecting its substantial parliamentary majority as well as the weakness of the Labour Party at the national level. But at the local level, the Labour Party enjoyed control of the then Greater London Council and the great majority of the larger authorities in the industrialised, urban regions, especially in the north of England. It was from these strongholds in local government that the party began to use its public relations resources to launch attacks on the policies of the then Conservative administration. Central government responded promptly to silence the oppositional voices emanating from the local state. A battle for communications supremacy developed between central and local government: the prize for each of the protagonists was control of political communications within the local setting. Eventually, the government enacted legislation which placed severe restrictions on local government's public relations activities. Opposition criticism of the Local Government Act 1986 denounced its censorial character claiming the legislation represented 'nothing less than an attempt to gag local government, to silence opposition, to censor debate and seriously to reduce the free flow of information and ideas' (*Local Government Chronicle*, November 1985, p. 1317).

While this degree of controversy and conflict has undoubtedly proved inconvenient and troublesome to government, it articulated one aspect of the pluralism 'built into' British political structures. This potential for conflict across different 'levels' of government represents one of the legendary 'checks and balances' on which representative and responsible government is founded. But the arrival of the era of 'postmodern elections', characterised by continuous campaigning and the emergence of political parties such as new Labour which are highly disciplined, centrally controlled and in which communications with citizens and supporters enjoy a new priority, means that where conflict occurs the battle cries are more muted (Norris, 1997, p. 2). Twenty years on, new Labour's preoccupation with the centralised control of political communications ensures the potential for continuing conflict between central and local government public relations as each attempts to influence local news agendas in their favour, but the communications prominence of central government, which previous administrations legislated to guarantee, generates a less public encounter between spin doctors and public relations specialists in distinctive sectors of government.

This chapter explores three aspects of public relations in the local government setting: first, the development and functions of local government public relations since 1945; second, the historical roots of government hostility to local government public relations and, finally; central government's statutory response to local public relations activities, articulated in the Local Government Acts 1986 and 1988. But access to local media is highly contested: local government public relations officers are among the most effective, but not the only, players in the news management game. In the local setting a wide range of organisations harbour communication ambitions and seek to secure favourable coverage or promote particular policy messages. Local and regional political parties (Franklin and Richardson, 2001, p. 211), for example, along with trades unions and a host of voluntary and charitable organisations (Deacon, 1999, pp. 59, Fletcher, 1995) all vie for access to local news media. But equally significant are the *national* organisations which make routine forays and excursions into local political communication networks, providing information and serving as a source for local news media while attempting to set the local news agenda. The Central Office of Information (COI) and the newly formed Government News Network (GNN) are crucial here (see Chapters 3 and 4). The chapter begins by offering a brief overview of the role of these national organisations in local political communications.

NATIONAL INFLUENCES ON LOCAL NEWS: THE COI AND THE GOVERNMENT NEWS NETWORK

There are a number of national political agencies which are routinely influential in local, as well as national, political communications: the parliamentary lobby, is an obvious example (Franklin, 2003; Ingham, 1991). The prime ministers official spokesperson briefs journalists from the regional press at 11 a.m. each weekday. These meetings are highly influential in shaping the political news agenda of the regional press. The press secretary can also command the services of the 1200 press officers and public relations staff in the Government Information and Communication Service (GICS) which has in recent times adopted a more assertive posture towards journalists: especially local journalists. (Franklin, 2000; Jones, 1999).

But it is the network of regional offices of the COI, known as the Regional News Network (RNN) but renamed the Government News Network and co-opted into the GICS in April 2002, which is the most effective 'national' organisation for shaping local news. The RNN was always an anomoly within the broader COI structure given its focus on news management rather than publicity campaigning. The GNN is comprised of a number of regional offices based in Birmingham, Cambridge, Cardiff, Edinburgh, Leeds and other major cities in the UK. These regional centres are much more akin to press offices than COI headquarters, originating material on behalf of their clients and feeding it into regional, local and national media networks, liaising with local media, providing audio-visual feeds for radio and television journalists at press conferences, making information and campaigning materials available online and facilitating press and other arrangements when ministers, members of the royal family or other digniatries make local visits (Clark, 1970, pp. 104–7; Cobb, 1989b, p. 14; COI, 2002, p. 45).

Michael Heseltine at the Cabinet Office in 1996 funded 11 senior press officers (SPOs), within the (then) COI regional network, to provide a cross-departmental monitoring service and feedback on media issues in the region. The broad purpose of this relatively new 'network within a network' was to help co-ordinate and improve the presentation of government policies in the regions (Hammond, 2000, p. 41). An early task for Peter Mandelson when he was minister without portfolio, but carrying a brief for the co-ordination of government communications, was to conduct a communications audit of the COI with a particular focus on the regional network: he concluded that it was 'well placed for providing a very extensive network to reinforce key government messages' (Baird, 1997, p. 13). The period since 1997 has witnessed a renewed emphasis on the regional and local co-ordination of news management and political marketing campaigns via the COI and its regional network (Garner and Short, 1998, pp. 172–3; Hammond, 2000, Ch. 3). In 1998, for example, the COI handled the government's regional campaign to market its 'New Deal' policy designed to reduce long-term unemployment. The campaign was wide-ranging and included 'securing media coverage on regional television and in the press' to 'delivery of the New Deal in Job Centres and the development of relevant web site materials' (COI, 1998, p. 3). The prime minister and the then secretary of state for education, David Blunkett, briefed regional media directly and in person with the resulting coverage in the regional media being a 'significant increase' compared to the 'small piece' on the same subject in the *Financial Times* (Watson, 1999, p. 20).

Since February 1999, moreover, local and regional newspapers – along with women's magazines and the ethnic minority press – have been identified, in the government's media strategy, as specific targets for the government's news management ambitions (Hammond,

2000, Ch. 3). The emphasis on regional newspapers in this revised news management strategy was described by one journalist as 'an aggressive gear change' reflecting a desire to try to marginalise troublesome mainstream national media preferring to focus on the 'less relentlessly sceptical arms of the media such as regional newspapers' (White, 1999, pp. 2–3).

The government's primary strategy for influencing local news is to issue press or news releases. These releases containing information about government activities, written and packaged as 'newsy' stories by information officers are distributed daily by the GNN; they constitute a potent influence structuring the news agendas of the leading newspapers and broadcasting organisations. A previous director general of the COI claimed that journalists are 'free' to use them 'as much as they want in any form they choose' (Clarke, 1970, p. 14), but Hillyard and Percy-Smith suggest that 'Departmental press releases are often treated uncritically as 'fact' by journalists who do not challenge the official version of events and are therefore used as channels for state propaganda' (Hillyard and Percy-Smith, 1988, p. 125). Regional and local newspapers provide particularly 'accessible' sites for the placing of articles which feature prominent national politicians' byline (although ghosted by press officers and special advisers). Journalist Peter Oborne, for example, recalls the 'spectacular stunt' in 1998 when Alastair Campbell 'managed to foist an identical exclusive by Tony Blair on more than a hundred regionals, each distinguished only by an individual paragraph which acknowledged the local audience' (Oborne, 1999: 199). When there is no countervailing or oppositional perspective to the government's line, or when pressures of deadlines or shortage of editorial resources prevails, journalists may simply publish press releases verbatim. In this way the government's view can become prominant and persuasive.

The operation of the press section of the Northern Ireland Office (NIO), based at Stormont Castle throughout the 1980s and 1990s, illustrates the point well (Miller, 1994, p. 124; Spencer, 2000, p. 17). The press office delivers:

> press releases to news desks in Belfast three times a day and in 1991–2 employed fifty eight staff in its Belfast and London offices ... it spent £7.2 million on press and PR administering a population of 1.5 million ... in the same year by comparison the Scottish Office which administers 5 million people spent £1.1 million.
>
> (Miller 1996, p. 208.)

Some journalists in the six counties believed they were unduly reliant on the press section of the Northern Ireland Office as a source of news, but the NIO was difficult to ignore despite their belief that it served up an unhealthily partisan diet of news designed to promote the offical line of the British government. The editor of Belfast's Unionist news-paper *The Ulster Newsletter*, for example, alleged it was 'essentially a political office . . . in the business of selling policies. Policies decided by Westminster which have no popular mandate here in Northern Ireland' (Channel Four, *The Media Show*, September 1989). Journalists also suggest that newspapers which printed articles critical of government policy were 'punished' by the NIO and denied access to the detailed background briefing papers, press conferences and insider receptions, which form the basis for reporting politi-cal events in the province. The Editor of the *Ulster Newsletter* claimed that 'If you're not one of its [the NIOs] friends you don't get access to basic information' (ibid.). Consequently, journalists were doubly damned. They could choose to receive NIO press releases which they knew to be partial, but which offered a good deal of contextualising information in the 'Notes to the Editor' which accompanied each release. Alternatively they could 'go it alone' but risk exclusion from the very heart of political news in the province.

Research studies suggested that journalists typically chose the former option and that the NIO was highly successful in getting the government's message across. A survey of Belfast journalists' uses of NIO press releases across a three month period revealed that all newspapers relied, albeit to varying degrees, on the NIO as a news source: one newspaper published 77 per cent of the 140 releases issued across the survey period. But more significant than the quantity of NIO press releases published by local newspapers is the quality of what might be termed the 'transformation process' to which they are subject: there is little editing of press releases, with many being published 'virtually verbatim' (Hardy, 1983).

In June 2000 when executive powers formally devolved to the Northern Ireland Assembly and its Executive, most government information officers were transferred into the new Executive Information Service (EIS) which in summer 2001 had a staff of 38 press officers and a budget of £1.3 million. A survey of 19 senior journalists drawn from television, radio and print, conducted between October 2000 and March 2001, revealed many journalists were 'concerned about the number of press releases put out by the EIS' (Fawcett, 2001, p.8). During the final four months of 2000, the Northern Ireland Executive issued 900 press releases compared to the 597 issued by the considerably larger Scottish Executive. The new EIS, moreover, was substantially outpacing its predecessor Northern Ireland Information Service (NIIS) which produced just 421 press releases during the last four months of 1997 (Fawcett, 2001, p. 9). The journalists' concern is that since the old NIIS was too influential in shaping news agendas, the greatly increased number of press releases issued by the EIS will serve to undermine further the independence of local news media in Northern Ireland.

In this respect Belfast journalists differ little from local journalists in other settings where reliance on government news sources is evident. An upublished survey of regional editors conducted by the COI in 1999, revealed that 50 per cent of responding local and regional editors (from a sample of 202) identified their local COI office as their most useful and frequent point of contact for government information. The local office of the GNN ranked more highly than MPs, other news media, lobby correspondents and the Press Association (PA). (Hammond, 2000, pp. 42–3).

LOCAL INFLUENCES ON LOCAL NEWS: LOCAL GOVERNMENT PUBLIC RELATIONS

A BRIEF HISTORY OF LOCAL GOVERNMENT PUBLIC RELATIONS: THE MODERN TOWN CRIER

Local government public relations can boast a considerable lineage which can be traced back to the medieval town crier who rang a bell inviting local citizens into the town square to hear current news and government proclamations. The more recent growth of public relations dates from the end of the Second World War (Franklin and Turk, 1988, p. 32). In March 1945, the National Association of Local Government Officers (NALGO) published a *Report on Relations Between Local Government and the Community*, which argued that a prerequisite for greater involvement by local people in their community was a better appreciation of the nature of services provided by local government (Hill, 1966, p. 34). Central government thinking was moving in a similar direction. In 1947 the minister of health established a consultative committee on publicity for local government, which suggested that publicity would not only enrich local democracy but also help in recruiting the officers and elected members necessary to staff local government. In the following year, in response to the committee report, the Local Government Act gave authorities the statutory power to establish information centres and provide courses on municipal affairs.

There were few initiatives during the 1950s and by the early 1960s public relations professionals were in post in only seven of the 62 counties, seven of the 29 metropolitan boroughs and 25 of the 4,000 borough and county borough councils (Hill, 1966, p. 175; West, 1963, p. 31). In May 1962 a report by the Association of Municipal Corporations (AMC) entitled *Local Government Publicity* recommended the appointment of a local government information officer to be funded jointly by the four local authority associations: the AMC, the County Councils Association (CCA), the Urban District Councils Association (UDCA) and the Rural District Councils Association (RDCA). The officer would undertake four major tasks. A first priority was to establish working relationships with the media and serve as a contact for press enquiries. The officer was also to publish articles and information about local government to raise public awareness, establish links between the various public relations officers working in local government and, finally, to provide an advice and assistance service to local authorities.

The Local Government Information Office was disbanded in the early 1970s anticipating that the reorganisation of local government in 1974 would prompt a major expansion of public relations (Sobol, 1980, p. 136); the expectation proved correct. The newly created authorities, especially the larger metropolitan counties, were eager to establish their identity with their respective publics by providing information about the authority and its activities. There was also a widespread desire to improve the public image of local authorities which were too frequently perceived as 'boring, remote, expensive, unfriendly and bureaucratic' (Society of County and Regional Public Relations Officers, 1985, p. 310). Finally, at the time of local government reorganisation, a number of reports including those of Wheatley (1969), Bains (1972), Redcliffe-Maud (1974) and Skeffington (1975), were stressing the importance of placing local government communications in the hands of professionals (Smith, 1986, p 32). A government circular captured this mood with its claim that 'if the democratic process is to flourish, there must be ready access to full information about a local authority's activities' (Department of Environment, 1975, paras. 9–10).

In 1974, for the first time, substantial resources were set aside for public relations provision. In its first year of operation the West Yorkshire Metropolitan County Council appointed five specialist staff and allocated a budget of £106,440 for public relations (*Halifax Courier*, 8 February 1974). Sheffield City Council in 1974 had a full time staff of ten and one of the largest public relations budgets set at £161,000 (*Yorkshire Evening Post*, 2 February 1974).

PUBLIC RELATIONS: STAFFING AND BUDGETS

By the late 1980s, public relations departments were well established within the larger county (92 per cent), metropolitan district (93 per cent), London boroughs (87 per cent) and Scottish regional (88 per cent) authorities. In the smaller authorities the commitment to public relations was less clear, with only 35 per cent of English and Welsh district councils, 28 per cent of Scottish island and district councils and a mere 25 per cent of Irish district councils having a public relations department (Franklin, 1988b, pp. 40–1). These figures represented a rapid and substantial growth in personnel. Research revealed, for example, that 50 per cent of PROs had been in post for less than three years (ibid., p. 48).

By the mid 1990s, there had been a further if steadier increase in the local government public relations sector with 'all but the smallest authorities employing or retaining some kind of public relations support' (Harrison, 1995, p. 150, Audit Commission 1995, p. 9). The Audit Commission report, *Have We Got News For You*, moreover, envisaged an expansive future despite the restrictions of the 1986 and 1988 Local Government Acts (cited in Davis, 2002, p. 19, 24; Mackey, 1994: Chs 5 and 6). In 1994, the IPR Local Government Group's report *Beyond The Horizons* claimed that 'a thousand public relations professionals work in local government, producing 60,000 items of publicity a year and spending £250 million: they generate over 100,000 news releases annually with coverage running into miles of print' (cited in Harrison, 1995, p. 151).

The 1990s witnessed considerable changes in local government organisation with the emergence of 46 new unitary authorities between 1995 and 1998, alongside proposals for regional government and the devolution of powers to a Scottish parliament and a Welsh assembly (Wilson and Game, 2002, pp. 67–8): these organisational shifts had implications for public relations. A survey of all 410 local authorities in England and Wales, conducted by the Local Government Association (LGA) in March 2001 revealed a continuing trend in the expansion of public relations' staffs especially in the larger and more populous authorities (Vanston and Sykes, 2001). Eighty-five per cent of local authorities now employ at least one public relations specialist, while 38 per cent employ between one and two staff, 21 per cent between three and five staff and a further 26 per cent have more than five staff (See table 5.1). County councils are most likely to have more than five full time equivalent staff (74 per cent) and district councils least likely (8 per cent). The *Talk Back* report published by the Audit Commission suggested that the largest public relations departments may number 20 or more staff (Audit Commission 1995, p. 11), while another data set recording staffing levels which varied between one and fifty PROs: in the larger authorities the average staff size is 13.[1] Table 5.2 signals that in the larger authorities, the number of staff devoted to public relations can be substantial.

Partisanship correlates significantly with numbers of PR staff employed with 19 of the 20 largest public relations departments being sited in Labour authorities (Franklin, 1988b, p. 44). It should be noted however that these public relations resources are very modest given the size, range and contentious character of some local government activities such as Social Services which include responsibilities for child protection.

Table 5.1: **Numbers of public relations staff employed by local authority type (%)**

	MB	LB	UA	CC	DC	WU	Total
Less than one	9	0	3	0	22	9	15
One	4	0	12	0	26	18	19
Two	9	0	22	11	24	27	19
Three	9	8	9	4	12	27	11
Four	4	11	9	11	4	0	6
Five	0	15	3	0	4	10	4
More than five	65	66	42	74	8	9	26

Base: 301
Code: MB Metropolitan; LB London Borough; UA Unitary Authority; CC County Council; DC District Council; WU Welsh Unitary

Table 5.2: **Largest, smallest and average size of pr staffs by local authority type**

Type (Number of respondents)	Lowest number of staff	Highest number of staff	Average number of staff	Median number of staff
County Councils (13)	2.5	18.5	9.9	9.7
London Boroughs (10)	9	46	20	16
Metropolitans (14)	3	40	18	11
Unitaries (26)	1	50	7	4

Information concerning public relations budgets is difficult to establish. In part this reflects a genuine diversity in size of department and funding practice across different authorities. But it also reflects the fact that the Local Government Act 1986 required local authorities to keep an account of their public relations expenditure and those who judged this to be unnecessary created a complex range of 'creative accountancy' techniques which render precise assessment of budgets problematic. The figures below should consequently be considered indicative rather than definitive. Three general conclusions are evident (Franklin, 1988b).

First, there is substantial variation in the size of budgets; in 1988 the range was between £3,500 and £1,500,000. Widdicombe reported annual expenditure in the counties ranging from £80,000 to £1.6 million; in the Metropolitan districts and London Boroughs budgets varied between £50,000 and £200,000 (Widdicombe, 1985, para. 40). Generally the sums allocated for public relations are modest with only 35 per cent of PROs controlling a budget in excess of £100,000, less than 15 per cent spend more than £250,000 while 7 per cent are allocated budgets over £500,000 (Franklin, 1988b, p. 50). In 2001–2002, across 142 local authorities, the budgets for PR varied between £17,000 to £3,945,500 in a large London Borough. Table 5.3 reveals that the largest average budgets are expended in the London Boroughs and metropolitan districts.

Table 5.3: **Lowest, highest, and average budgets for pr by local authority type**

Authority Type	Lowest budget	Highest budget	Average budget	Median budget
County Council (13)	£86,000	£800,000	£449,262	£400,000
London Borough (10)	£354,000	£3,945,000	£1,162,3000	£713,250
Metropolitan Borough (14)	£85,000	£3,300,000	£879,515	£467,750
Unitaries (26)	£30,000	£1,949,000	£348,157	£229,000

Second, Labour authorities spend more on public relations than their Conservative counterparts. In 1988, 22 (88 per cent) of the 25 largest budgets for public relations were in Labour controlled authorities. Expressed slightly differently, 2.7 per cent of Conservative authorities spent over £150,000 on public relations, while the equivalent figure for Labour authorities was 22 per cent – eight times greater. Third, budgets generally were increasing, perhaps reflecting little more than the increase in staffing levels noted above. But in 25 per cent of authorities, in 1988, budgets had increased significantly while only 9 per cent of authorities reported any decline in funding. By 2001, 50 per cent of local authorities were anticipating an increase in their communications budget for 2001–2002 (see Table 5.4), with only 19 per cent expecting a budget decrease. Welsh unitaries are most likely to envisage an increase in budget (72 per cent) with unitary authorities least likely to anticipate a budget hike (30 per cent). It is important to remember that the sums spent on public relations is typically a very small proportion of an authority's total budget. The Widdicombe interim report, for example, suggested that expenditure was less than 0.1 per cent of total budget in more than 50 per cent of authorities (Widdicombe, 1985, para. 40). The Audit Commission's report *Talk Back* confirms this variation in the size of budgets and their relative modesty but also suggests that while establishing patterns of expenditure on public relations activities is diffcult, in part reflecting the lack of clarity in defining what constitutes publicity, most expenditure estimates are 'likely to understate the true position' (Audit Commission, 1995, p. 25).

Table 5.4: **Is the communications budget planned to increase/decrease in 2001–2002?**

	MB	LB	UA	CC	DC	WU	Total
Budget will increase by more than inflation	16	31	10	25	15	45	18
Budget will increase by inflation	26	19	20	43	36	27	32
Budget will stay the same	26	19	37	25	36	9	31
Budget will decrease by up to 2%	16	19	7	0	6	9	9
Budget will decrease by more than 2%	16	12	26	7	7	10	10

Base: 301
Source: Vanston and Sykes, 2001, p. 13

PUBLIC RELATIONS: THE FIFTH ESTATE?

The Institute of Public Relations (IPR) identifies a broad brief for local government public relations including press and media relations, customer relations, publicity, campaigns and promotions and communications within the authority (IPR, 1986, para. 2.2). For their part, public relations officers prioritise press and media relations. Invited to rank order the five activities according to the amount of time they allocated to each, 67 per cent cited press and media relations as their first working priority with almost 90 per cent citing media work as their first or second priority (Franklin, 1988b, p. 59, see also Fedorcio,

Heaton and Madden, 1991, p. 33; Theaker, 2001, p. 176). Typically, media relations occupies at least 40 per cent of senior PRO's working time (Audit Commission, 1995, p.16): a priority confirmed by one senior practitioner. 'I'd say that media relations is still absolutely the flagship of the PR service' he claimed,

> It's the thing that everybody notices. It's probably the most important thing certainly in the minds of the councillors, who have an unhealthy obsession with the local media ... But it is absolutely the flagship service. If you are not getting your media relations right, if you are not getting a pretty high proportion of your stories covered in the local press and in a positive way then forget about anything else, your service will just not survive and you as an individual will not survive.

> (Interview, 27 September 2002.)

The LGA study identified the different elements which compose media relations work: the study findings signal that *all* local authorities value and actively engage in the various aspects of media relations (see Table 5.5). One outcome of this media relations aspect to public relations is that most local authorities (92 per cent) report 'fairly good' (42 per cent) or 'very good' (50 per cent) relationships with local newspapers, while 91 per cent report 'Fairly good' (41 per cent) or 'very good' (50 per cent) relations with local radio and 68 per cent report 'fairly good' (45 per cent) or 'very good' (23 per cent) relations with local/regional television. Working relations with national newspapers seem markedly much less well developed with 31 per cent of authorities reporting that no effective relationship exists, but where there is contact only 17 per cent describe this as 'fairly good' (14 per cent) or 'very good' (3 per cent). (Vanston and Sykes 2001, pp. 16–17).

Table 5.5: **What aspects of media relations does your council conduct? (%)**

	MB	LB	UA	CC	DC	WU	Total
Issuing news releases	95	100	100	100	99	100	99
Answering media inquiries	95	100	100	100	98	100	99
Press cuttings service	67	88	79	89	82	91	82
Media briefing events	80	92	97	89	70	82	78
Developing media strategies	76	92	94	96	68	73	77
Placing features	71	92	73	93	75	64	77
Developing media crisis plan	76	92	82	89	54	82	66
Monitoring and evaluating media coverage	65	69	64	71	54	59	59
Implementing media crisis plan	48	69	76	71	37	54	48

Base: 313
Source: Vanston and Sykes, 2001, p. 20)

The main purpose of this media work is to try to structure the news agendas of local media in favour of the authority. If news media are important in structuring public news agendas by selecting and prioritising issues for their readers, PROs are similarly crucial in setting the media agenda. PROs are clearly influential players here. If the media constitute a fourth estate, public relations professionals, to adopt Baistow's phrase, undoubtedly form a fifth (Baistow, 1985, Ch. 7; Gandy, 1982, p. 7).

An explanation of PROs' success in influencing the content of local media requires a brief discussion of the news-gathering techniques and resources of the local press. Expressed bluntly, local newspapers are profit-seeking business enterprises. The need to minimise news-gathering costs prompts some papers to fill their editorial columns by 'buying in' editorial copy at a lower cost than it could be produced by an in-house journalistic team. It is common practice for local papers to buy copy from the Press Association or a local press agency to supplement the work of staff journalists. But some local newspapers' requirements for cheap copy have prompted a related development. Free newspapers, in particular, have become reliant on the news output (press releases, press conferences and handouts) emanating from non-news organisations especially the public relations departments of the local authority (Franklin and Murphy, 1991, pp. 22–4). Again the factors shaping this reliance are economic and organisational. Local journalists are poorly paid, de-unionised and increasingly hard pressed for time (Franklin and Murphy, 1998, p. 9). New entrants to journalism, moreover, display little of the enthusiasm for local politics which characterised an earlier generation. The editor of a local newspaper group complained that;

> We don't have a specialist writer for politics in local papers these days, which is a deep concern to me. We always had people who came into journalism because they were interested in politics . . . but these days I can get a young reporter in and it can be a year and they still don't know who their local Councillors are. They've shown no interest in interviewing them or meeting them . . . the reporters are simply not specialist enough to write about politics. And sadly we don't cover Council meetings now, and we don't cover Committee meetings – we ain't got the staff.

> (Interview, June 2001.)

Journalists' indifference to local politics, combined with newspapers' growing preoccupation with the 'bottom line' along with continuous cost cutting and staff reductions to achieve profitability in ever more competitive local markets, means that newspapers' reliance on PR materials has become commonplace (Franklin and Murphy, 1998, p. 9). Consequently, local government PR departments have become prolific in their output of press releases. While virtually all (99 per cent, see Table 5.3 above) local authorities issue press or news releases, the larger metropolitan authorities, unitary authorities and county councils distribute the greatest number of these information subsidies (See Table 5.6). The development of Internet communications has added to this press dependency with one PR specialist arguing that, 'the Internet has had an enormous impact because all councils have websites and journalists can now download their press releases straight from the website, go into the archives, and search out their stories in that way. So there is a lot more given to the local media on a plate' (Interview 20 September 2002). A PRO claimed 'it's clear that many frees rely heavily on handouts from the public services to fill editorial columns' (Heathcote, 1986, p. 9; see also Baistow, 1985, p. 67) while another offered a stark choice to anyone seeking coverage in the local press: 'it is a case of "no press release, no coverage"' (Cowley, 1996, p. 8).

Table 5.6: **News releases distributed by authority type in 2000–2001**

	MB	LB	UA	CC	DC	WU	Total
Up to 250	12	52	11	27	85	50	61
251–500	41	29	67	38	14	17	27
501–750	29	19	15	23	1	17	8
751 and above	18	0	7	12	0	16	4

Base: 259
Source: Vanston and Sykes, 2001, p. 21

For their part, local government PROs have come to regard free local newspapers as ready outlets for stories which, predictably, are uncritical and tend to stress the positive aspects of local government administration. PROs feel confident that their press releases will be reproduced more or less verbatim, because some local, especially free, newspapers are editorially understaffed (Franklin, 1986b, p. 26; Richardson 1988, p. 102). The logic of competition between papers in the local market, moreover, obliges paid weeklies and, to some extent, even daily papers to resort to these low-cost news-gathering strategies typical of free newspapers (Williams, 1996, p. 10). As the news editor of the *Sheffield Telegraph* lamented:

> As staff numbers have diminished there is less time to spend on stories. For example, twenty years ago each reporter was allocated an area of the city and he would spend one day a week out of the office, knocking on doors in his patch, then filing reports. Now no one has the luxury of a day out of the office looking for material – you have to do it over the phone. You lose something if you haven't been there – taking it down the phone is no substitute. And its easier to use a press release, more convenient if the relevant information is summarised than if you have to go out and find it out yourself.

> (Cited in Harrison, 1998, p. 167.)

The importance of press releases for the editorial content of local newspapers has been assessed by examining PROs' ability to 'place' stories in the local press. Press releases issued by the public relations department of Northumberland County Council were compared with local press coverage of local politics to establish the take-up rate of stories and assess the extent of any journalistic editing of the press release to enhance the story. Of the press releases issued across the two months of the study, 96 per cent generated stories in the local press. This was a very high strike-rate especially when compared to similar studies abroad (Franklin and Turk, 1988). But analysis of the newspapers revealed that many other local government stories featured in the papers had probably originated from public relations departments in the neighbouring County and Metropolitan District Councils.

Most press releases stimulated stories in more than one paper with publication in three or four papers being commonplace. Only 11 of the 44 releases published in the press made a single appearance, while 19 were published in three or more newspapers. The local press seems to be recycling the same news around the local area. The two daily papers, *The Journal* and the *Newcastle Evening Chronicle*, were much less reliant on the press releases as news sources, although 22 of the 44 releases did prompt stories in the two papers. But when press releases were used they were always substantially edited. This editing of the release contrasted sharply with journalistic practice on the free weeklies where editing was rare. Weeklies either reproduced the press release verbatim and in full or simply removed whole paragraphs or changed their order. What is significant is that none of the published stories contained any additional information to the original release; the bulk of these releases were swallowed whole and uncritically by a copy-hungry free press. These local findings have subsequently received a more generalised confirmation. In a nationwide survey of local government PROs, 82 per cent of respondents claimed that more than three-quarters of press releases issued resulted in stories in the local press (Franklin, 1988b, p. 81).

The willingness of local newspapers to accept these information subsidies reflects the professional skills of local government PROs but, more importantly, it reflects newspapers' lack of journalistic resources. Most daily papers, for example, employ a 'municipal', a journalist specialising in local government affairs, whereas on weekly paid papers local government is merely one aspect of a broader journalistic brief, perhaps including courts, industrial affairs and business. The logic of these varying newspapers staffing levels suggests that daily, weekly paid and weekly free newspapers might form a descending hierarchy of dependence on information subsidies. This pattern of reliance is confirmed by the available research findings. When asked which local newspaper is 'most likely to use a press release' 42 per cent of PROs identified free newspapers compared with 30 per cent paid weekly, 22 per cent evening paper and 5 per cent daily (ibid., p. 82). Consequently Davis concludes that 'public relations has increased its influence [in local agenda setting] not as a result of powerful spin doctor pressure ... but because working news journalists have become increasingly stretched as a result of rising competition. Public relations professionals with their rapidly increased resources, have thus been ideally placed to make good the short fall in news-producing industries' (Davis, 2002, p. 17).

The importance of information subsidies to the local press is occasionally illustrated quite dramatically. The abolition of the Greater London Council, for example, with the consequent closure of its 30-strong press department which had been handling 200 press inquiries daily and issuing 1,200 press releases annually, created great difficulties for local media. A meeting of London media staff, convened to discuss this 'information vacuum', concluded that the demise of the GLC press office meant 'there was likely to be a shortage of London news stories' (*UK Press Gazette*, 31 March 1986, p. 17). It was this ability of local government PROs, especially at the highly publicity-conscious GLC and the larger Labour controlled local authorities, to 'manage' press agendas and thereby public knowledge and opinion, which began to prompt anxieties in some Conservative politicians about local government public relations in the early 1980s.

LOCAL VERSUS CENTRAL GOVERNMENT 'SPIN DOCTORING'

Government's initial anxieties about public relations were triggered by local government's media-based campaign against proposals to abolish the Greater London Council (GLC) and the six metropolitan county councils in the mid 1980s. But government concerns also reflected Conservative allegations that some Labour authorities were misusing their legitimate powers to issue information for partisan purposes and thereby crossing the line between information and propaganda. Specifically, the suggestion was that certain Labour authorities were distributing municipal newspapers, free to local residents, which were highly critical of central government: a practice which the tabloid press, with its love of the trite phrase, dubbed 'propaganda on the rates'. These very public spats between central and local government represent an early manifestation of the continuing controversy about spin doctors and their role in political communication.

THE CAMPAIGN AGAINST ABOLITION: DAVID VERSUS GOLIATH?

In May 1983 the Conservative manifesto announced the party's intention to abolish the GLC and the six metropolitan county councils. The government case for abolition was based on arguments about 'anti-bureaucracy'. Expressed broadly, these councils were expensive, inefficient and without any distinctive service provision to justify their existence. Government critics alleged a covert, political motive behind abolition. Each of the six metropolitan councils was controlled by the Labour Party and enjoyed a politically radical image in the media. The press, for example, typically referred to South Yorkshire Metropolitan County, as the 'Socialist Republic of South Yorkshire'. GLC leader Ken Livingstone, a highly effective media performer, was severely censured by the tabloid press for his political radicalism; the *Sunday Express* described him as 'the IRA-loving, poof-loving, Marxist leader of the GLC' (27 September 1987). Livingstone used the GLC's public relations department to criticise government's domestic policies. Thatcher was allegedly furious to gaze over the Thames from Westminster to see a large banner draped across the GLC headquarters displaying the monthly unemployment figures for Greater London. It all proved too much. The GLC and the 'Met Counties had to go' (Harris, 1986, p. 494).

The Local Government Act 1985, which made provision for their abolition in April 1986, prompted the GLC and metropolitan counties to initiate a very public two-year campaign against abolition which was unprecedented in mobilising resources to stage a carefully orchestrated campaign against the government's proposals. At different stages in the campaign, the councils deployed a range of strategies including lobbying MPs and peers, generating favourable media coverage through the activities of their public relations departments, as well as the mass persuasion techniques of poster campaigning and advertising in the national press (Myers, 1986, pp. 109–18). The campaign was ultimately unsuccessful but it served to illustrate the potential for such campaigns to embarrass government by taking local government's case directly to the public. It also provided an inspiration to other local authorities.

The GLC employed the advertising agency Boas Massimi Pollit (BMP) to produce a series of posters and press advertisements highlighting the threat which abolition posed to local democracy. The posters were highly acclaimed within the advertising industry but also proved effective in realigning public opinion behind the GLC. The posters promptly became collectors' items. An early poster featured a very earnest Ken Livingstone under the caption 'If You Want Me Out You Should Have The Right To Vote Me Out'. Another announced in bold white letters on a black background – a simplicity designed to underscore the gravity of the message – 'From Now On You Have No Say In Who Runs London' (Myers, 1986, p. 111). A second phase in the poster campaign featured more 'humorous' messages. One celebrated press poster featured the local government minister in a court-jester's outfit, while another pictured members of the Cabinet with bananas sticking out of their ears.

Nationally, the metropolitan counties campaign was built around three groups comprising the six leaders, their chief executives and a group of liaison officers. This basic three-group structure was expanded to meet particular needs by the addition of an advertising and publicity group, the appointment of a freelance public relations specialist, lobby correspondents and parliamentary lobbyists (Franklin, 1987b, p. 44). The lobby correspondent, who was referred, to as 'the man with no name', was used to secure information from Ingham's morning briefings at Number Ten and other ministerial briefings, while the parliamentary lobbyists worked in Parliament to create a favourable climate of opinion towards the local government case. The freelance public relations specialist was to generate sympathetic national media interest in the campaign.

The central government counterblast came late in 1983 when Thatcher accepted a proposal from Bernard Ingham – contained in a seven page memo dated 30 December – for an official Whitehall committee to design and implement a public relations campaign supporting government policy on abolition; the scheme was endorsed by a meeting of Patrick Jenkin (the Minister with responsibility for overseeing abolition) and other Cabinet Ministers on 18 January 1984 (Hollingsworth, 1986, p. 98). The Ingham plan made 20 public relations suggestions including 'remedial action with troublesome journalists' and the 'placing' of 'special articles in the *Sunday Express, News of the World* and regional press'. Articles by Jenkin began to appear in the national press throughout January, although *The Sunday Times* refused to publish. Ingham also advised ministerial appearances on 'phone-ins or discussion programmes including the JY Prog [the Jimmy Young Programme]' and proposed 'a comprehensive diary to which all Departments contribute relevant dates, events and Ministerial engagements which might be turned to good account' (Harris, 1990, p. 117). He also advised the government to organise pressure groups like the Aims of Industry to launch their own propaganda campaign against the GLC.

Set against the combined propaganda fire-power of the tabloid press, Bernard Ingham, Conservative Central Office and a motley crew of rightwing pressure groups, the efforts of local public relations officers in the various authorities were like David confronting Goliath. The eventual outcome, however, ran counter to the biblical story. Within weeks of the end of the campaign the government invited the Widdicombe Committee, previously established to examine the conduct of local authority business, to 'consider as a matter of urgency the use made by some local authorities of their discretionary powers to engage in publicity exercises' (Widdicombe, 1985, Introduction). The government claimed that the public was increasingly concerned about the political nature of some publicity and therefore Widdicombe's recommendations should form the basis for new legislation intended to bring together the existing 'hotch potch' of law in this area. From the outset, PROs were suspicious about the underlying purposes of Widdicombe, claiming that 'a cynic might suggest that the inquiry was an expensive but expeditious way of attempting to get some form of moral backing to curtail anti-abolitionist activities' (Society of County and Regional Public Relations Officers, 1985). But if this was the government's intention they were to be disappointed by Widdicombe's report published on 31 July 1985. The committee made a number of recommendations. Certain aspects of local government public relations, especially the personalised attacks on Mrs Thatcher and other leading Conservative politicians, required amendment. Widdicombe also recommended making explicit the prohibition on party-political publicity and proposed that local authorities keep a separate account of their publicity and advertising expenditure. But significantly, Widdicombe concluded that 'there is much positive good to be gained from local authority publicity' (Widdicombe, 1985, para. 162). Moreover, it is not 'wrong in principle for local authorities to issue materials dealing with matters of political controversy, nor to express a view on such matters' (ibid., paras. 122–3). This last judgement is clearly important in its implications for local government publicity since it asserts local authorities' rights to discuss and publicise precisely such issues as abolition. In its final form, however, the Local Government Act 1986, although claiming an inspiration in Widdcombe's recommendations, went beyond the committee's recommendations to restrict local government public relations in significant respects (Theaker, 2001, p. 176).

IMPOSING A STATUTORY SILENCE: THE LOCAL GOVERNMENT ACTS OF 1986 AND 1988 AND A CODE OF PRACTICE FOR PUBLIC RELATIONS

The Local Government Act 1986 enjoyed an eventful passage through Parliament during which the government's original intentions were modified substantially by the House of Lords. The Act had two major consequences for local government public relations. It prohibited local authorities from issuing publicity of a party political nature and empowered the minister to issue a code of practice governing local authority publicity.

BANNING PARTY PUBLICITY

Section 2 was designed to prohibit party publicity. The qualifying adjective 'party' is significant since it acknowledges, following Widdicombe, that publicity may still legitimately deal with matters of political controversy (Gutch and Percival, 1986, p. 3). The Act prohibits the publication of material which 'appears to be designed to affect public support for a political party'. This formulation is problematic. The concern seems to be with the *appearance* of the publicity rather than the *intention* of the authority which produces it. What is to be established in law, therefore, is, does the publicity *appear* to have been designed to affect political support, not *was it designed* with this intention in mind. The inadequacy of such a clause to assess the party political nature of publicity is evident. The crucial elements in such an assessment – the nature of the publicity itself and the intentions of those who produced it – are both missing from the government's criteria (Franklin, 1988d, p. 17).

Help is at hand. Section 2–2(a) offers guidelines. In assessing whether publicity is party political, 'regard shall be had to whether the material refers to a political party or to persons identified with a political party'. The problem here of course is that virtually every local councillor is a member of a political party and presumably therefore 'identified' with it (Franklin, 1988c, p. 18). Literal interpretation of the law would place comprehensive strictures on local government publicity, be quite impractical and lead to absurdities. Would it prohibit council leaders, for example, from signing their names on the council's annual report? In response, government claimed the concern was to prohibit only publicity which personalised issues as much of the poster advertising in the campaign against abolition had portrayed Thatcher and her Cabinet prominently and in unflattering ways. 'It is emphatically not the case', claimed Lord Elton, 'that clause 2 is intended to ban local authorities from referring to a council member by name or from explaining his party political affiliations' (HC Debs, 18 February 1986, Col. 561). But local councillors may have found ministers' protestations of innocence less than credible. Laws which are vague and general in their wording typically have the small print written by a process of judicial interpretation in test cases.

There was a second difficulty with the 1986 Act and it proved to be fundamental. The major intention of the Act was to outlaw party political publicity but there was no definition of a political party within the Act. Denning confessed his ignorance: 'I think it's impossible to define the words 'party political'. he claimed. It's like an elephant; you can tell it when you see it but you cannot define it' (HC Debs, 18 February 1986, col. 586).

Government's awareness of the shortcomings of the 1986 legislation combined with their determination to control local government publicity and political communications, resulted in a new Local Government Act in 1988. The Act, which achieved a ready press notoriety for its clause 28 which prohibited local authorities from 'promoting homosexuality', was a curious amalgam of diverse but very significant provisions for various aspects of local government administration. Clause 27 dealt specifically with publicity and public relations and 'beefed-up' the loopholes in Section 2 of the 1986 Act by proscribing any publicity material which 'promotes or opposes a point of view on a question of political controversy which is identifiable as the view of one political party and not another'.

Clause 27 was promptly denounced by journalists, public relations organisations and the local authority associations as nothing less than censorial: Clause 27 proposed other restrictions. Before issuing any publicity, local authorities should have regard to 'content and style', the 'time and circumstances of publication' and the 'likely effects' on those to whom it is directed. All these prescriptions were imprecise, impractical and censorial, and offered no advice on how to measure these 'likely effects'.

A CODE OF PRACTICE FOR PUBLIC RELATIONS

Section 4 of the 1986 Act empowered the minister to 'issue one or more codes of recommended practice as regards the content, style distribution and cost of local authority publicity'. The Local Government Act 1988 required mandatory compliance with the code. Clause 27 suggested that 'a local authority proposing to issue publicity will be under a duty to take into account all the relevant provisions of a code. *Failure to do so will render their decision unlawful*' (my emphasis).

The first code introduced in January 1986, along with its successors, was rigorously opposed by local politicians from all parties, as well as journalists, MPs, peers and lawyers. The Society of County and Regional Public Relations Officers[2] (SOCPRO) detailed three objections. First, the code rendered many aspects of the public relations task unworkable. The requirement that local government publicity should not be 'personalised', for example, was unrealistic. A press release which begins 'Cllr. Joe Bloggs, Chair of the Education Committee said ...' has already become personalised. There was also a question of double standards here since central government press releases invariably begin with the appropriate minister's name. Second, the code would probably result in a decline in press reporting of local government and, where such coverage did occur, press releases which could not be enlivened with personal information would undoubtedly further the image of local government as a faceless, nameless bureaucratic machine. Third, the code's prohibition of publicity which 'directly attacks policies and opinions of other political parties or groups' was denounced as censorial. Press releases and media interviews cannot avoid 'attacks' on policies since disagreement and conflict are the very stuff of politics, local or otherwise. The code was withdrawn in February 1986; a successor introduced in May 1986 met a similar opposition and fate. A third code was issued for discussion by local government on 9 January 1987.

SOCPRO again objected to a number of the latest code's 15 clauses, describing them as 'dangerously undemocratic' (*PR Week*, 27 February 1987). Particularly problematic was the clause which suggests that local authority publicity should not 'attack, nor appear to undermine, generally accepted moral standards'. But the question of what constitutes 'generally acceptable moral standards' is no less contentious than the issue of whether or not it is desirable, as John Stuart Mill claimed it was in the nineteenth century, to 'attack' them. From certain perspectives, a local authority which produces materials for a counselling service on abortion or a helpline for AIDS, may be considered to be 'undermining' or at least 'appearing to undermine' these unspecified and ill-defined but 'generally accepted moral standards'.

In addition to these provisions, the code prohibits local authorities from placing advertisements in party-political publications, places severe restrictions on television, radio and billboard advertising, warns against the use of slogans in local authority publicity and limits the scope of local government publicity to 'promoting the *facilities* rather than enhancing the public *image* of the council'. In the words of one local government public relations specialist, the code is 'a verbose and patronising weapon against an authority' (Peshchek, 1987, p. 17).

The Local Government Acts of 1986 and 1988 place in sharp focus a more general struggle between central and local government for control of local political communications. Opponents of the Acts argue that in wording, if not intention, they are vague and indeterminate, creating a 'catch-all' category of prohibitions which effectively outlaw most types of publicity (Allen, 1986, p. 1). In this mood of uncertainty, the need to scrutinise publicity to ensure its conformity with the provisions of the Acts militates against effective public relations in the local government context. Symptomatic of these anxieties is the decision of some local authorities to cease publication of their municipal newspapers.

For their part, practitioners certainly believe that the Code has been highly effective in restraining public relations activities in the local context. One PR specialist suggested that 'the local government acts and the code they established have, within the PR community, become very much a code of practice. The code is very effective. People call it 'the code' and we know what they are talking about. And part of the induction of local government PR practitioners is to make them aware of it, that it sets very clear parameters to their role and that they should never step outside of them' (interview, 20 September 2002). The code was revised during 2000 with local government public relations organisations such as SCUPRO (the successor to SOCPRO) arguing that any new code must take account of the role of the Internet in local communications and the need to modernise a code which currently 'is outdated and handicaps the modernisation of local councils' (press release, 24 September 2002 www.scupro.org.uk/news/code_11_12.htm). The new code, issued in April 2001, continues to require local authorities to 'have regard to the provisions of the code' in coming to any decision on publicity where publicity is defined as 'any communication in whatever form, addressed to the public at large or to a section of the public'. A shorthand expression here might simply say 'all communications'! (press release LGA/SCUPRO 10 July 2001 at www.scupro.org.uk/news/code_11_12.htm).

Central government dismisses claims of censorship as an over reaction and argues that the Acts have merely systematised existing law in this area in line with Widdicombe's recommendations. The law allegedly remains necessary to curtail the excesses of a minority of local councils leaving the vast majority to continue their publicity activities without hindrance. But when these legal restrictions are placed in the context of successive central governments' growing enthusiasm to package and promote their own policies, combined with an eagerness to silence oppositional voices in the media and elsewhere, it is difficult to believe that governments intend that local government public relations should carry on with 'business as usual'. Government's announced intentions, however, are perhaps less significant than the actual effects of the legislation and the code. Law, so the adage runs, works according to a spirit as well as a letter, but where the letter of the law is unclear the reliance upon spirit is enhanced. Central and local government are mutually suspicious in this area and, in the absence of authoritative, judicial decisions, local authorities have assumed that the Acts will be interpreted strictly and implement their publicity strategies accordingly. The autonomy and vitality of the local government PR, which characterised the campaign against abolition, has been replaced by a deathly hush discreetly orchestrated from the centre. All too rarely is the public given an opportunity to applaud the conductor.

---

1   The author is indebted to Liza Greaves for providing anonymous and non-specific data from a database established across the four years prior to 2001–2002 and drawing on returns from 142 local authorities including 74 boroughs/districts, 14 county councils, 11 London boroughs, 14 metropolitan districts, 27 unitary authorities and two 'others'.

2   SOCPRO became SCUPRO – the Society of County and Unitary Public Relations Officers and later LG Communications in September 2002 reflecting changes in local government organisational structures especially the introduction of unitary authorities.

Chapter Six

PACKAGING THE POSTMODERN ELECTION ▢

On 15 October 1924, Ramsay MacDonald delivered 22 speeches on the road from Glasgow to Newcastle. The next day he addressed 6,000 people in Leeds, 10,000 in Cleckheaton and 20,000 in Huddersfield, before attending an evening rally in Manchester. Nationwide electioneering based on large scale public meetings without the campaign advisers and speech writers who support the modem politician, must have been a hard slog, but to little purpose; without a sophisticated sound system only a handful of those in the crowd would have heard his rhetoric above the heckling of others. MacDonald exemplified 'premodern' campaigning which found its counterpart in the US in the 1948 Trueman versus Dewey contest. Such campaigns were characterised by 'traditional face-to-face retail politics for getting out the message, with whistle stop railway tours across the country, meetings with party notables and ticker tape parades in major cities and keynote speeches before packed crowds' (Norris, 1997, p. 3). In those days, the key media were newspapers and radio, but the advent of television gave politicians instant access to audiences of a size which MacDonald could barely imagine. From its inception, however, some politicians were wary of television, suggesting that the new medium might corrupt, as well as convey, party communications. Critics argued that television images of the party and the packaging of politicians might become more electorally consequential than the party's commitment to its manifesto policies (Franklin, 1994; Rosenbawm, 1997).

The 1980s proved to be a decade of political communication change which witnessed the 'professionalising' of campaigning (Kavanagh, 1995) with parties becoming increasingly reliant on mass media to communicate their messages to the electorate. Parties recruited small armies of marketing, advertising and public relations specialists to develop strategies for promoting positive media images of their leaders, senior politicians and key policies. By the mid-1990s, the transition to postmodern political communications was evident. Its defining and emerging features included 'the fragmentation of audiences and outlets ... the tabloidization of news due to fierce commercial pressures' but significantly 'the move towards the *permanent campaign* with the continuous feedback provided by polls, focus groups and electronic town meetings to inform routine decision making and not just campaigns' (Norris, 1997, p. 6). Few demur from this notion of continuous campaigning. Even Alastair Campbell announced on the eve of poll 2001 that 'campaigns are won throughout the Parliament, not just the final weeks of the election campaign' (*Telegraph*, 7 June 2001). Under the conditions of postmodern elections, parties have been transformed by this 'permanent campaign in which the techniques of spin doctors, opinion polls and professional media management are increasingly applied to routine everyday politics' (Norris, 2000, p. 173; see also Farrell, Kolodny and Medvic, 2001). Expressing similar sentiments in a different phrase, Blumler and Kavanagh suggest that parties have entered the 'third age of political communication' (Blumler and Kavanagh, 1999, p. 209).

By the 2001 general election, television had long since become the major political battleground for parties to contest, their most important point of access to voters and voters' most trusted source of political information (Worcester and Mortimore, 2001, p. 147): Parties' uses of the Internet for campaigning, along with voters' access to the web for information, were expansive, even portentous (Coleman, 2001) but not yet significant in disseminating party messages (Downey, 2001): the 'premodern' media of newspapers continued to offer a highly contested site for news management. By 2001, politicians in every party, the general public, political journalists, academic observers and pundits of every kind, had come to believe that media reporting of the campaign in tandem with parties' ability to incorporate their messages into media coverage was crucial to the outcome of the election: notwithstanding the conceptual complexities of establishing the effects of media messages on their audiences and readers (see Chapter 9). In turn, the influence of news media, especially television, on the style and substance of the campaign has become so central that 'to say 'television is the campaign' is no longer novel, let alone shocking, but a truism' (Seymour-Ure, 1991, p. 174). Some observers continue to express concern that in this process of modernising party communications, the 'soundbite' and the promotion of the party leaders via suitably presidential 'photo opportunities' have acquired an overblown significance which is perhaps more central to parties' electoral success than the informed advocacy of policy (Franklin, 1999; Jones, 2001a; Kurtz, 1998). Despite these reservations about postmodern campaigning, MacDonald would undoubtedly have approved whole heartedly of a technology and campaigning style which allowed him to address voters in Glasgow and Huddersfield simultaneously without leaving the comfort of his study in London. MacDonald was an innovator: in 1930, he installed a prototype television set in Number Ten (Cockerell, 1988b, p. 341).

This chapter explores party communications in the context of general elections by addressing two broad questions. First, in what ways and with what success do parties try to use mass media as part of their overall campaign strategy to communicate their political message to voters? Second, how do the various media report the different parties' policies and the politicians contesting the election? Local party communications in the constituency setting are examined in the following chapter by posing the same questions.

PARTY COMMUNICATION STRATEGIES

Parties employ two broad strategies to communicate messages to the public: propaganda and news management. Parties buy advertising space in newspapers and on billboards or are allocated free broadcast time on radio and television, in order to present their policies. In such circumstances, parties control the content of the political message directly and access to the audience is unmediated by journalists or broadcasters. Second, but judged to be more significant in campaign terms, parties attempt to influence or 'manage' the way in which newspapers and broadcasting organisations report the issues and progress of the parties during the campaign.

PARTY PROPAGANDA: SPREADING THE GOOD MESSAGE

PARTY ELECTION BROADCASTS

Party election broadcasts (PEBs) have their origins in a brief *aide-memoire* agreed between the Labour government, the Conservative opposition and the BBC in 1947. The document, which was in essence a set of rules formalising and regulating politicians' access to television, constitutes a significant landmark in the history of political broadcasting (Goldie, 1977, pp. 341–4).

Political broadcasts were allocated to one of four categories. First, there were uncontroversial ministerial broadcasts which explained government policy in a factual and uncontentious way. The second category embraced controversial ministerial broadcasts, where the opposition party might seek the right of reply. Thirdly, there were party-political broadcasts (PPBs) and, during election periods, party election broadcasts which would be allocated by agreement between the two parties and the BBC. The BBC would offer the parties free broadcast time and facilities. The content of the broadcasts was to be determined by the parties without any editorial control by the BBC. The final category was for controversial discussions in which two or more parliamentarians from the different parties participated (Semetko, 1991, pp. 15–16; Seymour-Ure, 1991, pp. 164–5). Parties' access to television was now formalised; the party election broadcast (PEB) was born.

Their role has always been to allow parties to present their policies and politicians to the voters, to rally the faithful and, parties hope, to convert some of the doubters, to offer ideological ammunition to the politically committed but, increasingly and significantly their role has become to place issues on news and election campaign agendas (Scammell and Semetko, 1995, p. 28). The recent Electoral Commission report on *Party Political Broadcasting* confirmed that they provide 'the one opportunity available to ... parties to present a message directly to the electorate through the broadcast media ... The principle that political parties should be able freely to publicise their platforms and policies to voters, and that voters should be able to receive such information, is a vital one' (Electoral Commission, 2003, p. 3). Audiences remain high, 'at about 13 millions [in 1992] much higher than the main evening news' (Scammel and Semetko, 1995, p. 39), while in 2001, 63 per cent of respondents to a MORI poll conducted for the ITC thought it was 'very important' or 'quite important' for election broadcasts to be shown on television (ITC,

2001). In the US, where candidates are obliged to purchase airtime for advertising political messages, this constitutes by far their largest campaigning expenditure (Kaid and Holtz Bacha, 1995, p. 1): during the 2000 Presidential election year, more than $1billion was spent on the election with a total of $400 million devoted to advertising (Powell, 2001, p. 4)

The first televised PEB featuring Liberal former home secretary Lord Samuel was transmitted live at 8 p.m. on 15 October 1951 (Rosenbawm, 1997, p. 46). Each of the three main parties broadcast PEBs during the election but this constituted television's only contribution to the campaign since the BBC, at that time the only broadcaster, believed that election coverage risked embroiling the Corporation in political controversy. In 1955, each of the parties broadcast three PEBs prompting the press, rather precociously, to dub the campaign 'the first TV election' (Cockerell, 1992, p. 33). The absence of video recorders and the need to transmit studio broadcasts live, meant that PEBs were a high risk strategy. A Labour PEB, entitled *Your Money's Worth*, was designed to show how dramatically prices had risen under the Conservative government. The studio set presented an ordinary living-room with a table on which were placed, side by side, identical portions of butter, cheese and other goods. Dr Edith Summerskill, who chaired the party's National Executive Committee, played the role of the housewife; her small-screen husband was Harold Wilson. Summerskill spoke about the cost of living and illustrated her points by sticking a Labour price label into one portion of food, followed by the inflated Conservative price into the other. Lady Falkender, then Marcia Williams, recalls the rehearsals:

> Edith would say, 'now here we have cheese that has gone up so much' and she would plonk the marker straight into the butter, and then she would put the marker for the butter straight into the cheese. And by the time they had said to her, Edith, start again, under the studio lights the butter was melting, the cheese was sort of dribbling and the whole thing was a scene of utter chaos.
>
> (Quoted in Cockerell, 1988b, p. 34.)

Each rehearsal over-ran by six minutes as Summerskill and Wilson vied theatrically for prominence. The Labour Party's producer, Tony Benn, recalls that 'it was with sinking hearts and Edith full of gin that we approached transmission' (ibid.). The eventual broadcast proved as chaotic as the rehearsals: it had to be faded off the air. We realised then, claimed Falkender, 'that we had to come to terms with television' (ibid., p. 35). Following the 1955 election, Wilfred Pickles, the popular radio broadcaster and Labour's early 'special adviser' suggested that the best formats for television PPBs were firstly 'straight talk', secondly 'straight interview', thirdly 'straight talk with simple visuals' and finally 'press conferences especially with apparently hostile questions' (Rosenbawm, 1997, p. 49).

Modern-day PEBs are radically different in both form and content from their 1950s precursors. The 1980s witnessed the ending of the fixed transmission time for the four terrestrial channels (usually 9 p.m.); the shortening of the length of many broadcasts to five or ten minutes which allegedly represents the viewers' maximum attention span (Bell, 1982, p. 15); a lower profile for politicians in broadcasts and their replacement by actors; the use of voice-over techniques; a focus on personalities rather than policy; a greater appeal to emotion above reason: and the introduction of a wider range of shots and sequences familiar to viewers from their everyday television watching – faster editing, location sequences, the use of music, collage sequences and the use of graphics (Rosenbawm, 1997, pp. 59–69; Scammell and Semetko, 1995, pp. 20–1).

In the 1987 election, one of the Labour Party broadcasts seemed to signal a renewed significance for PEBs in the communications campaign. Directed by Hugh Hudson, written by Colin Welland, scored by Michael Kramer incorporating music by Brahms and Beethoven and produced by John Gau Productions, the broadcast promptly became dubbed 'Kinnock – The Movie'. The nickname reflected the unashamedly presidential style of the broadcast which created a precedent by its inclusion of a closing shot which superimposed the word 'KINNOCK' and the Labour rose over the palace of Westminster; the Labour Party was not credited. The 'movie' established a trend with John Schlesinger (*Midnight Cowboy*), Mike Newell (*Four Weddings and a Funeral*) and Stephen Frears (*My Beautiful Laundrette*) subsequently offering their services as PEB producers to the various political parties.

The most significant PEB of the 1992 campaign was undoubtedly the Labour broadcast made by Mike Newell broadcast on 23 March, which featured the case of a young child's wait for minor surgery to her ear, to illustrate the wider argument about hospital waiting lists; the PEB became known as 'Jennifer's Ear'. The broadcast prompted an outcry but, many reporters suggested, brought the election to life. The tabloids alleged that the Labour Party was unprincipled to exploit a child's personal suffering for political gain (Harrop and Scammell, 1992, p. 203). The Conservative Party made similar claims adding that the affair exposed Kinnock as an unsuitable person to be prime minister. The debate quickly moved on from health issues to a row about who had leaked the identity of the child to the newspapers. Both the major parties pronounced the other guilty (Harrison, 1992, p. 164). The issue dominated press, radio and television election coverage for days, with one analysis of the television election agenda suggesting that 'the war of Jennifer's ear came in fifth' (Hanna, 1992b, p. 16). If the function of PEBs is not merely as 'message vehicles but also as potential news stories and important tools for influencing the new agenda' (Scammell and Semetko, 1995, p. 21), then the broadcast must be judged a success. But, given the unsavoury allegations and acrimony which followed the broadcast and the public distate they engendered, it is uncertain whether or not Labour benefitted electorally from the broadcast.

In 1997 a number of single issue and minority parties including James Goldsmith's Referendum Party, the UK Independence Party, the Pro Life Alliance, Sinn Fein, the British National Party, Arthur Scargill's Socialist Labour, the Green Party and the Natural Law Party each enjoyed a single broadcast. What characterised PEBs in the 1997 campaign, however, was their unrelentingly negative character. Labour's apocalyptic vision of 'what would happen if the Conservatives got another five years' was a montage of 'sightbites' (Harrison, 1997, p. 152) which illustrated cuts in the NHS, an explosion of street crime, the closure of homes for older people, tax hikes and the Conservatives split even further over Europe. Other Labour PEBs featured Fitz the new Labour bull dog and symbol of British patriotism and pride who in the early shots appears dejected and gloomy but is quickly restored by the broadcast's exegesis of Labour policies in time to trot off set to the caption 'Give Tony Blair your mandate'. Biopics were also popular. Labour featured 'Tony: the home video', Molly Dineen's fly-on-the-wall film which portrayed Blair, the young family man, playing football with his children and cooking them an evening meal while talking to camera about his political ideals and ambitions (Harrison, 1997, pp. 151–3).

In 2001, the negative character of the PEBs was exemplified by the Conservative broadcasts produced by the Yellow M agency under the supervision of Tim Collins (Golding and Deacon, 2001, p. 5; Harrison, 2002, pp. 151–2; Wring, 2002, p. 98). The party's first PEB, reminiscent of Bush's 1988 allegation against the Democrats that they were responsible for the crimes committed by black rapist Willie Norton, blamed Labour for two rapes committed by two prisoners released early under a government scheme. The broadcast presented a group of prisoners gloating and smiling as they left jail while the voiceover announced 'Labour have let out 35,000 convicted criminals under their early release scheme'. After scenes showing a burglary, street theft of a mobile phone, a woman about to be mugged and dealers selling drugs to young people, the PEB presented a list of further crimes and adds '. . . and two rapes' (Pipkin, 2001, p. 4; Watt, 2001, p. 13). The film moved on to present 'the mute misery of people, captive in their homes, unable to afford petrol at £6 a gallon which 'could' be the price under Labour' (Harrison, 2002, p. 151).

On 24 May the Conservatives aired their broadcast on education: the theme for the PEB was 'What are your children *really* learning under new Labour?'. Amid dark images and menacing music the broadcast runs through a typical school day to reveal how Labour has abandoned children. Schools are running on a four day week because of staff shortages ('10,000 teacher vacancies in secondary schools'), while students truant in order to shop lift, steal cars, sell or buy drugs and spray graffiiti on every railway bridge in town. The broadcast ends with the lights being switched off at 4 p.m. as the school is closed: the voice over claims 'Conservatives will offer parents discipline, standards and choice in schools' (Watt, 2001a, p. 15). As Harrison notes, negative advertising is paradoxically the most effective, if unpopular, but when 'even the *Daily Mail* says a Tory broadcast is in the gutter and a *Daily Telegraph* focus group finds it 'too extreme' it seems a fair bet it has gone too far' (Harrison, 2002, p. 151).

By contrast, Labour PEBs were more upbeat in 2001. The party repeated the 1997 successful biopic of Blair, but also relied on the well tried and tested formula of including cameo celebrity appearances in the early ads. The first broadcast reviewed the achievements of Labour's four years in office, with a voice over by actor Kevin Whately to the accompaniment of the Lighthouse Family's hit record *Lifted*. Blair's Britain was an undoubtedly happy place exemplified in images of smiling children, happy and prosperous workers and thriving NHS patients. The coup for the PEB was the much trailed appearance of then Spice Girl Geri Halliwell who appeared for no more than a couple of seconds serving tea to a group of extremely happy pensioners: the party's final ad of the campaign similarly featured two stars from the youth soap *Hollyoaks* (Pipkin, 2001, p. 3). But these celebrity cameos backfired badly when the *Sun* declared in a front page article on the eve of poll that Halliwell was not registered to vote (allegedly on security grounds) while Terri Dwyer of *Hollyoaks*' fame was simply too busy to vote (*Sun*, 6 June 2001).

Perhaps unsurprisingly, the 1990s, witnessed a rumbling dissatisfaction with the system of party election broadcasts, alongside growing support for the suggestion that they should be replaced by political advertisements, similar to the American system of paid advertising (Bell, 1982; Brignull, 1992; Scammell, 1990). Three reasons inform and favour the transition.

First, the system of PEBs which developed in the 1950s when the BBC enjoyed a broadcasting monopoly has become outmoded in the context of a modern, competitive, market-driven, multi-channel, digital, cable and satellite broadcasting system. (Scammell, 1990). Second, PEBs are ineffective. Viewers seem easily bored and enthusiastic only to switch off: in 2001, 57 per cent of viewers changed channels or turned off when the PEB began (ITC, 2001). In a similar study the proportion of voters claiming to have watched a PEB dropped from 78 per cent in 1979 to 58 per cent in 2001 (Worcester and Mortimore, 2001, p. 166). Those who continue watching are more politically knowledgeable, interested in politics and committed in their support for a particular party. PEBs, it seems, preach to the converted (Scammell, 1990, p. 207; Brignull, 1992, p. 8). Finally, there is a growing body of research from the USA to suggest that short 30 or 60-second advertising slots have a number of beneficial consequences for the campaign (Bell, 1982, p. 15). Political advertising devotes greater attention to the issues than the television news media, provides political information to the electorate, offers accurate precis of party and candidate platforms, helps to set the election agenda and offset any bias in news media, generates interest in the campaign, raises money for the parties, increases turnout and offers the most appropriate means by which parties can legitimately influence and persuade voters (Hall-Jamieson, 1984, p. 452; Scammell, 1990, pp. 205–6).

In the British context advocacy of political advertising has tended to prompt opposition on the grounds that it might subvert the quality of the election debate (Electoral Commission 2002, p. 12). Opponents find five arguments persuasive; much of their firepower draws upon what they consider to be the shortcomings of political advertising in America. First, it is alleged that short 30-second commercials would necessarily result in the oversimplification and trivialising of complex political issues. Parties would offer slogans and soundbites as a substitute for sustained political discussion. Second, advertising personalises the campaign. The image, appearance and media skills of party leaders would become more important in determining electoral outcomes than party policy. Third, advertisements can be persuasive and manipulative, as well as informative. Skilful editing can create visual images which make covert appeals to emotions rather than inviting viewers to engage rationally in debate with the issues. Fourth, political advertising might favour negative campaigning and tempt parties to emphasise opponents' weaknesses rather than talking to their own strengths. Finally, the cost of political advertising would give a substantial but unfair advantage to the party with the greatest financial resources. The outcome of elections might reflect little more than who has the deepest pockets (Electoral Commission, 2003, p. 16; Scammell, 1990, p. 208). In the US, following the 1988 election, newspapers developed 'Adwatch' features designed to educate and warn readers about advertising campaigns which attempted to mislead and misinform voters as well as campaigns which risked confusing 'issue ads' (policy based) with 'image ads' (emotionally based) (Milburn and Brown, 1997, p. 166). Any move to emulate this American-style paid political advertising would take Britain a step further down the undesirable road which Blumler has called 'the modern publicity process' (Blumler, 1990, p. 10).

To hear these arguments is to feel their force, but many of the misgivings expressed have already become features of British election campaigns. Parties do simplify their messages to make them attractive, they hire advertising agencies to devise effective electioneering slogans, advertising is largely negative and party leaders make great efforts to speak in snappy soundbites. Party leaders' average speaking time in television news reduced from 37.3 seconds in 1992 to 24.8 seconds in 2001 on BBC news and from 32 seconds to 21.2 seconds on ITN (Golding and Deacon, 2001, p. 5). Ordinary politicans fare less well: their broadcast time reduced from 26.5 seconds in 1992 to 20.3 seconds in 2001 on the BBC with equivalent ITN figures reducing from 22.3 seconds in 1992 to 17.6 in 2001 (Golding and Billig, 2002, p. 109). Soundbite culture is well embedded. PEBs for the three major parties, moreover, are unequivocally presidential in style and deploy all the editing and production techniques devised by human kind to reinforce their messages (Harrison, 1997, pp. 152–3; Harrison, 2002, p. 149).

Recent reviews of PPBs roundly reject paid advertising with the Electoral Commission claiming 'overwhelming support among political parties and broadcasters ... for maintaining the ban on political advertising'. Paid advertising would restrict television access to those with 'sufficient financial resources', might trigger a 'spending race between larger parties which they could ill afford' and would create problems for 'maintenance of political balance by broadcasters' (Electoral Commission, 2003, pp. 25–6). The debate concerning the desirability of paid advertising has been superseded by two more pressing concerns: first, whether PEBs should be shorter; second, whether parties should be allowed more flexibility in selecting different 'packages' of PEBs (Electoral Commission, 2003, pp. 31–2; BBC/ITC, 1998, p. 11).

The amount of time allocated to party broadcasts has reduced substantially from the initial PEBs in the 1950s which typically aired for 15 minutes. In part this reduced role for PEBs reflected parties' perceptions of their diminishing campaign signficance which, even a decade ago, one observer believed was 'approaching near vestigial proportions' (Harrison, 1992, p. 174). As long ago as 1979, the Saatchis wished to replace the allocated ten minute slots with five of two minutes, although broadcasters believed this would make them too similar to commercial product advertising and confuse viewers (Rosenbawm, 1997, p. 62). During the 1997 election parties were still offered either 5 or 10 minute slots for PEBS, but in 1998 the BBC, ITC, SC4 and the Radio Authority launched an extensive consultation about the possible reform of party political broadcasting and proposed that 'the ten minute option [for broadcasts] be removed and that parties should be offered the alternative of a three or four minute slot' (BBC/ITC 1998, p. 4). Parties did not dissent from this change, indeed they broadly welcomed it with William Hague, then Conservative leader, describing the reform as 'sensible' suggesting that shorter broadcasts would prove 'more interesting for the viewer and probably more useful for the political parties' (Ahmed, 1998, p. 8). Consequently in advance of the 2001 election, the BBC offered parties three options for PEB length: 4 minutes 40, 3 minutes 40 and the shortest yet of 2 minutes 40 seconds. The three main parties each opted for broadcasts of the shortest length except for one Labour PEB which ran for 4 minutes 40 seconds (Pipkin, 2001, p. 3).

In 2002, the Electoral Commission, triggered by the low turnout in the general election of the previous year, issued a consultation paper inviting views about reforms of party broadcasts which might increase voters', especially young voters', engagement in politics (Electoral Commission, 2002). The Commission's report concluded that there 'is a strong case for reducing the length of party broadcasts ... to a minimum length set at 1 minute

30 seconds' (Electoral Commission, 2003, pp. 31–2). Perhaps more innovatory was the Commission's suggestion that 'if communication with the electorate is to be effective, not only should broadcasts be short but they should be repeated several times'. Consequently the Commission proposed a series of 'packages' for parties which allow them to create a balance between the length of broadcasts and the frequency with which they are shown involving 'a choice between fewer, longer broadcasts or more, shorter broadcasts' (Electoral Commission, 2003, p. 32).

In truth these changes simply formalised party practice which has increasingly favoured shorter PEBs which are judged to be more effective and persuasive: between the 1992 and 1997 elections, the Conservative party failed to use some of their allocated slots (Harrison, 1997, p. 149). Table 1 clearly illustrates the retreat from party broadcasting since 1959.

Table 6.1: **Decline in Party Broadcast Time 1951 to 2001 (in minutes)**

Year	Lab and Cons Total	Three Party Total	Grand Total
1951	30	45	45
1955	120	135	135
1959	190	215	215
1964	150	195	195
1966	120	155	160
1970	100	130	135
1974 Feb	100	130	135
1974 Oct	100	140	145
1979	100	130	145
1983	75	115	130
1987	95	145	150
1992	87	127	142
1997	50	70	110
2001	29	39	58

Source: Pipkin, 2001, p. 3

Table 6.1 illustrates that by the 2001 election, the amount of time devoted to PEBs had declined to about one fifth of the 1959 peak with the three main parties opting to use less than 40 minutes airtime for their broadcasts. But given the flexibility of schedule packages proposed by the Electoral Commission, future elections may witness fewer and shorter PEBs broadcast repeatedly: commercial marketing and political advertising in the US reveal that repetition is highly effective in increasing viewer recall of the message. If PEBs *were* reduced to 30 seconds and parties were allocated the same amount of time they enjoyed in 1959, then short PEBs could be repeated 430 times across the election campaign (Pipkin, 2001, p. 5).

POLITICAL ADVERTISING: POSTERS AND NEWSPAPERS

Political posters are one of the oldest surviving forms of political communications. The most memorable of their terse, snappy, messages have become a permanent memory in the public's collective consciousness – from Lloyd George's 1918 poster demanding 'A Land Fit for Heroes' ('A Fit Country For Heroes to Live In' were his actual words) to the Saatchis' celebrated pun above a snaking dole queue in 1979 that 'Labour Isn't Working'. A common early style for posters was to feature a picture of the party leader above a slogan such as 'You Can Trust Him'; Baldwin and Churchill were both marketed in this way. But the poster format became increasingly redundant as the age of publicity innocence gave way to television (Lawson, 1992, p. 27), although it remains more significant than campaign advertising in the press (Scammel and Harrop, 1997, p. 183).

Posters continue to fulfil important communications functions for parties. They convey political ideas about their own or their opponents' policies. Driving or walking home past the same roadside hoarding each evening guarantees the repetitive exposure which imprints the political slogan and visual image on the mind (Armstrong, 2000, p. 8; Powell, 2001, p. 4). Posters, moreover boost the morale of local party workers by creating a party presence in the community. Their purpose is less to win over converts than to 'hearten established supporters and reassure wobblers' (Fletcher, 2000, p. 23). But increasingly the function and communications significance of posters, as with PEBs, is to create news and gain television coverage for the party. In 1992, posters were printed in a smaller number than might be imagined. The unveiling of a party's latest poster was less significant for the message and image it contained than the photo opportunity it provided for the leading politicians in the party (Harrison, 1992, p. 156): posters 'are more likely to be seen on *News at Ten* than on poster sites' (Sambrook, 1992, p. 17).

Posters, although increasingly technically slick and glossy, still try to capture attention and convey their message by employing some form of linguistic device and word play or by a visual pun. In 1935, for example, Labour pledged itself to wage 'Not Wanton War but War on Want'. In 1987, the Saatchis' caption above the picture of a British soldier with his arms raised in surrender, announced 'Labour's Policy on Arms', while in 1992, the image of a black bomb with the word 'Tax' printed on it in white letters was captioned 'Labour's Tax Bombshell'. More recently, in 2001, a Conservative poster exemplified the visual pun by featuring a pregnant Tony Blair above the caption 'Four Years of Labour and He Still Hasn't Delivered' (Wring, 2002, p. 97). The 'Tax Bombshell' campaign in January 1992 was judged successful in preventing Labour from opening an early lead, but other Conservative posters were criticised. The political thrust of 'You Can't Trust Labour', for example, was easily reversed by spray can deletions of the 't' in 'Can't', while the caption 'Labour's Double Whammy' above two large red boxing-gloves symbolising increased taxes and increased prices required the interpretative skills of a seasoned semiologist to decode its meaning. But assessments of the efficacy of poster advertising are subject to fluctuation. 'If you win everything you did was brilliant', an advertiser claimed, but 'if you lose, everything you did was bloody disastrous' (Katz, 1992, p. 23).

Three final points about posters are important. First, their messages are invariably negative and critical of opponents. This seems to be an inherent feature of the poster format which does not lend itself to promoting policies: 'In three words on a poster you can knock the hell out of the opposition but it is much harder to put a positive case' (ibid.). The ideological and policy differences between modern parties, moreover, are modest and tend to stress *means* rather than *ends*: but, as one senior advertising executive noted 'differences of means are difficult to dramatise in a few words on a billboard . . . it is easier just to rubbish opponents' (Fletcher, 2000, p. 23). This adversarial style is not new. The Saatchi's 1997 poster featuring a masked Tony Blair with red 'demon eyes' under the slogan 'New Labour, New Danger', can trace its ancestry to a poster from the 1929 election which warned: 'Socialist Schemes Mean £250,000 More in Taxes' and portrayed Ramsay MacDonald as a highwayman complete with mask. The strap-line of the poster read, 'It Will Come out of Your Pocket'. Interestingly, this attempt literally to demonise Blair and new Labour generated the opposite effect to that intended: voters objected to the poster and moved away from the Conservatives. The poster failed to acknowledge the important difference between 'a slagging campaign and a reasoned attack': even where the latter is critical (Cozens, 2001, p. 6). Consequently, 'ads like Demon Eyes don't work because there is no substance to them. But the Tories' Tax Bombshell ads in the 1992 election had real impact because they provided new information' (ibid.). Nonetheless the 2001 campaign posters remained highly negative and many targeted party leaders. The TBWA agency produced 'Just William' which featured the precocious teenager William Hague hectoring the Conservative party during his first and now infamous, conference speech, while a second Labour poster featured Thatcher's hair superimposed onto the 'follically challenged' Hague to signal that politically he was little more than his mentor's apprentice (Wring, 2002, p. 97). Politically, the effect was devastating: aesthetically, it was more than a little alarming! The Yellow M agency appointed by the Conservatives in May 2000, produced some effective but highly negative advertising, although none matched the impact of the poster for the Scottish Parliamentary campaign which featured Tony Blair's face against a blue background with the single word 'BLIAR' emblazoned in yellow (Butler and Kavanagh, 2002, p. 58).

Second, political advertising remains a unique exemption from the Advertising Standards Authority's code of practice requirement that advertisement should be 'truthful'. The exemption provoked controversy in 1991, when the authority received 108 complaints about Saatchis' poster for the Conservative Party, 'Labour's Going for Broke Again'. Some complainants objected to the strap-line 'Government Warning', which threatened to confuse government advertising with party-political advertising. Others objected that claims about high Labour expenditure were exaggerated and untrue. The authority argued that its code of conduct meant it was unable to consider the complaints. In a democratic society, the authority suggested, 'political parties and others wishing to make controversial statements should be free to make out their own case and to use advertising for that purpose' (Henry, 1991c). The matter is clearly contentious, but decision-making in any society, democratic or otherwise, requires accurate and truthful information.

Finally, the impact of poster advertising appears to be diminishing: in 2001 only 50 per cent of voters recalled having seen them compared to 70 per cent in 1997. The decline affects both major contenders equally. In 2001, 31 per cent recalled seeing a Conservative poster (53 per cent in 1997) and 35 per cent a Labour poster (55 per cent in 1997). More significantly, only 2 per cent of respondents to a MORI survey reported that posters had influenced their voting intentions: in 1997 the figure was 4 per cent (Worcester and Mortimore, 2001, pp. 170–1).

The most effective poster designs are typically reprinted as advertisements in the national press although since 1987 press advertising has played a diminishing role in the campaign. The 1987 campaign marked a record expenditure on newspaper advertising, including the £3 million spent by the Conservative Party in the last week of the campaign: 'wobbly Thursday' proved a lucrative day for newspaper proprietors. Subsequently, the 'advertising battle has moved away from newspapers and towards poster sites' (Scammel and Harrop, 1997, p. 183). The 1987 'peak' reflected the 336 pages of political advertising in the national daily and Sunday papers, which reduced to 288 in 1992, 99 in 1997 and a mere 30 pages in 2001 (ibid., p. 182; Scammell and Harrop 2002, p. 179). Interestingly in 2001, Labour was the only major party to buy newspaper advertising (7 pages) but was 'out gunned' by Unison (8.5) and almost matched by Charter 88 (6.7): minority parties (UK Independence Party, 5) and groups (British Democracy Campaign, 3) also bought space in the national press to promote their electoral message (ibid.).

The impact of press advertising and posters on voters' electoral preferences is difficult to assess (see Chapter 9), especially given the relative campaign expenditures of the three major parties in 2001 and their subsequent electoral fortunes. The Conservative spend of £12.7 million outstripped the combined expenditure of Labour (£10.9 million) and the Liberal Democrats (£1.3 million). Figures for minority parties revealed the campaign expenditure 'gap' despite the new Electoral Commission rules which for the first time placed a cap of £15.4 million on all parties: Green Party (£43,087), Plaid Cymru (£87,121), Scottish National Party (£226,203) and the UK Independence Party (£693,274) (Watt and Tempest, 2001, p. 14). But in Scotland the Conservatives spent

£972,967 to win a single seat while Labour spent £1.1 million but secured 56 victories: in brief Labour spent just under £20,000 for each seat while Conservative's single seat cost the party just under £1 million. Given this uncertainty of outcome, it is perhaps unsurprising that parties are increasingly persuaded that the propaganda weapons of posters, newspaper adverts and PEBs are of secondary significance in their campaign armoury. The big guns remain the various techniques the parties employ to influence and shape media reporting of the campaign, the party leaders and the topics selected as the key election issues. News management lies at the heart of parties' communications campaigns.

NEWS MANAGEMENT: GETTING THE MESSAGE ACROSS

Parties try to influence media campaign coverage in four ways. First, they try to set the election news agenda so that media attention is focused on issues which are favourable to them. Second, parties try to structure their contacts with broadcasters to allow them some control over politicians' media appearances: i.e. parties negotiate 'rules of engagement'. Third, parties coach politicians in media presentation skills to guarantee political messages are communicated as effectively as possible. Fourth, if all the above fail and parties believe that a particular broadcast presents them in an unfavourable light, they complain.

SETTING THE NEWS AGENDA

The daily party press conference was 'invented' by the Labour Party in 1959 and designed to catch the attention of broadcasters who were reporting the election for the first time; it was promptly emulated by the Conservatives (Seymour-Ure, 1991, p. 162). Its significance reflects the fact that British elections campaigns have become in effect a succession of 'discrete single day units' in which parties try to place specific issues on the news agenda (Blumler, et al., 1986, p. 104). Many months before the election, the communications team designs the campaign schedule which designates particular issues to be the focus of media attention on particular days. During each day the theme or issue is presented to the media via 'news conferences, campaign visits, photo opportunities and a selection of key speakers and subjects ... with, on occasion, publication of a leaflet and a party political broadcast' (Hewitt and Mandelson, 1989, p. 52). Parties believe that persistent repetition of the message across the news day will maximise its impact on the audience and place electorally favourable issues on the news agenda: alternatively a party may wish to establish a news agenda which highlights electorally difficult issues for the opposition and obliges them to confront journalistic questioning on those policy areas.

One of the earliest, well documented and most notorious examples of party manipulation of news agendas was the case of Mark Burgess in June 1987. In the previous November, Peter Mandelson (then director of communications for the Labour Party) and Patricia Hewitt (the leader's press secretary) convened a meeting at her own house to organise the campaign schedule for the forthcoming election. Mandelson decided that on 4 June, 'minus 7 in the campaign', the party should devote the day to the health service (Hewitt and Mandelson, 1989, p. 52). But to make the health story work in television terms, the party needed to find a poignant example to illustrate its arguments. A young boy called Mark Burgess, who had been waiting many months for a heart operation, seemed tailor-made for Labour Party purposes. A television news story, however, requires suitable pictures. On 3 June, the party arranged a photo opportunity involving Neil Kinnock talking to nurses coming off duty at St Thomas's Hospital. On 4 June when the Burgess case was detailed in the early morning press conference, the television producers already had suitable pictures to accompany the story in news bulletins across the day. On the BBC's *Six o'Clock News*, as if in line with a Labour Party cue, the headline story by John Sargent gave viewers details of 'the case of Mark Burgess from Gravesend who needs open heart surgery'. The agenda setting plan, hatched in Hewitt's front parlour some eight months previously, had finally come to fruition (Gould, *et al.*, 1989, p. 83).

The Labour Party had manufactured a news event and, with the complicity of the news media, had rocketed health issues on to the campaign agenda. Journalist Robert Harris claimed the incident was 'blatant news manipulation by party spin doctors', but Channel 4 political correspondent Elinor Goodman resisted the charge. The Burgess story was, she claimed, 'a genuine story which in news terms would be hard to resist' (*Dispatches*, Channel 4, 18 March 1992). She acknowledged, however, that competition between broadcasting organisations served parties' news management purposes. 'If the BBC come up with this story about this boy Mark that's going to look like perfectly legitimate free standing research', she argued, 'my news desk is going to come back and say, "well why didn't we have that – that was a great story". It's all very well to be holier than thou and saying – "Thou should not have done it". Thou try not doing it' (ibid.).

Subsequent elections have come to be seen as a battle between journalists and politicians for control of the news agenda (Blumler and Gurevitch, 1998, p. 177). It is a battle which politicians, given careful election planning, the expertise of campaign managers and the extensive use of press conferences, briefings and private polling, are well resourced to win. During the 2001 election, moreover, there was substantive agreement between the parties about the key issues on which the contest should be fought. This was matched by the high degree of similarity with which the major television channels (BBC, ITV, Channel 4 and Channel 5) ranked campaign issues, with Europe, taxation, health and public services constituting the first four items for most stations. Alluding to the agenda setting competences of the parties, one observer noted that 'this high measure of convergence might appear reassuring, but might it not also be just a shade disquieting' (Harrison, 2002, p. 138). Parties also seemed successful in keeping certain issues off the agenda. The pre-election media focus on 'rail chaos ... the foot and mouth epidemic and major controversies over welfare benefit cuts' was 'swept to the margins of media attention in the campaign itself' (Deacon, *et al.*, 2001, p. 106). There was seemingly a 'consensus on non-issues as well as issues' (Harrison, 2002, p. 139).

But the 2001 election also revealed that parties' carefully constructed news agendas can be disrupted by unforeseen events. On 16 May two meetings between senior politicians and members of the public undermined Labour's plans to place its manifesto launch at the head of the election agenda. First, Blair was confronted by Sharon Storrer, the partner of a patient seriously ill with cancer, who complained eloquently, forcefully and very publicly, about the failures of the NHS under new Labour: Blair looked noticeably shaken by the confrontation which enjoyed wide coverage on the early evening news bulletins (Ingham, 2001, p. 587). Worse was to come. On a visit to North Wales John Prescott met Countryside Alliance supporter Craig Evans: Evans threw an egg at the deputy prime minister who responded with a punch. The subsequent scuffle 'Brought the election to life' and received predictably high news salience. As the *Guardian* headlined the following day, 'Protester Throws an Egg, Prescott Throws a Punch and Labour's Big Day Is in Turmoil' (*Guardian*, 17 May 2001, p. 1). The tabloids had a field day. The *Mirror* front page featured a photomontage of Prescott as a boxer under the headline 'ManiFISTo', the *Sun* headlined 'Two Jabs: Prescott Punch Up', while the *Daily Mail* preferred 'Two Jags Floor Show': by contrast only *The Times* and the *Guardian* featured the Labour manifesto launch on the front page. The 'Prescott punch' was by far the most widely covered front page story across the campaign: (Worcester and Mortimore, 2001, p. 154). But towards the end of the 2001 campaign, public *ennui* began to take its toll. Party press conferences became 'tired affairs and by the end of the four weeks both Labour and Tories weren't bothering to hold them every day' (Damon, 2001, p. 599).

BENDING THE RULES OF ENGAGEMENT?

A second news management strategy involves parties negotiating with broadcasters about the format of programmes, the style which political interviews will assume or the content they will explore. Politicians want television coverage, but on their own terms. There is a constant haggling over what are known as 'the rules of engagement'.

Some politicians, for example, simply refuse to appear on programmes with rival politicians. Others are reluctant to appear with professionals such as teachers or doctors. If a politician refuses to engage in debate or to participate in a panel discussion, broadcasters must decide whether they really want an interview with a particular politician and the implications of such a decision for the overall political balance of the programme. Where politicians consent to appear with others, they may try to insist on a running order of appearances which guarantees them the last word. Alternatively they may refuse to have their interview sandwiched between two others. Many politicians will appear only on live programmes denying broadcasters any possibility of editing their remarks. Some politicians will only appear in programmes to be broadcast at peak viewing times (Fox, 1990,

p. 19; Jones, 1992, p. 64). Parties, moreover, act as gatekeepers deciding which politicians will appear on particular programmes (See Chapter 3). If the night editor of the *Today* programme tells the Downing Street press officer 'No, we don't want Margaret Beckett for the third day running', for example, the reply might well be 'Then we won't put anyone up' at which point 'it becomes a game of brinkmanship' (Kampfner, 2000, p. 3).

The political interview is the most focused meeting between politicians and broadcasters and consequently it is the point at which the rules of engagement have become most fiercely contested. During elections the setpiece interviews with party leaders, conducted by Messrs Dimbleby, Paxman, Humphrys or Frost, have become one of the most celebrated rituals of television campaign reporting. The significance of the interview, according to Robin Day, used to reflect its ability to unwrap much of the party packaging allowing viewers to see the politician behind the image. 'It is the viewer's one defence', Day alleged, 'against the image maker, the ad-man, the teleprompter . . . the viewer has a chance to see the political leader' (Day, 1989, p. 129). But this is precisely what makes live interviews potentially so hazardous for the politician and consequently the focus of parties' news-management activities. A gaffe by the leader can reputedly cost the campaign. But the politicians arguably have won. The 'big interview' has been 'hi-jacked' by politicians to the extent where it is 'virtually a dead letter' (ibid., p. 127*).*

Politicians have developed a range of strategies for coping with even the most probing and unrelenting inquisitor. First, politicians, but especially senior figures in each party, receive training in how to handle media interviews: how to answer questions or, if necessary, how to evade answering them. If politicians are suitably briefed, 'they should be able to take control' (Fox, 1990, p. 19). A research study analysing a number of television interviews by Thatcher and Kinnock concluded that both evaded more than half of the questions asked, by ignoring the question, offering invective against the opposition party, giving an incomplete answer or claiming to have dealt with the issue already (Bull and Mayer, 1988, p. 45). When an intransigent interviewer meets a skilled media performer the resulting interview can be bizarre. The edition of *Newsnight* when Jeremy Paxman posed the same question ('Did you threaten to overrule him?') fourteen times to then home secretary Michael Howard is one such occasion (*Twenty Years of Newsnight*, Channel 4): John Humphrys' quizzing of Harriet Harman by posing a question about cuts in benefits for lone parents 11 times, is another (Radio 4, *Today*, 12 December 1997). But Humphrys believes a vicious circle operates. 'Politicians want to control the agenda, perfectly understandably' says Humphrys, 'so they get taught how to deal with people like us. We then respond to that – possibly by interrupting a little bit – and I have sometimes got a bit stroppy' (cited in Cockerell, 2003, p. 7).

Second, politicians anticipate questions and commit answers to memory. Worse still, they arrive at the interview with a prepared agenda determined to stay 'on message' and deliver carefully rehearsed policy statements with little regard for there relevance to the questions. When politicians have 'their manifestos all canned in their minds' there is little prospect of 'dialogue or having questions answered in a reasonably direct way' (Day, 1989, p. 129). Third, politicians routinely imply impartiality against the interviewer. Thatcher deployed a succession of phrases to suggest the interviewer was interrupting her unfairly: 'no, please let me go on . . . may I just finish . . . I must beg of you . . . Yes, but one moment . . . no, don't stop me . . . yes, but if I might have my reply'. In brief she was adept at 'continually wrong footing interviewers' and making them 'feel obliged to justify or even apologise for their role as interviewers' (Bull and Mayer, 1988, p. 44).

Fourth, politicians may simply refuse to answer certain questions. During the 2001 election campaign, Jeremy Paxman became increasingly frustrated by Blair's unwillingness to answer a particular question and his attempts to move onto a different subject. Eventually Paxman, asserted 'I assume you want to be prime minister, I just want to be an interviewer, so can we stick to that arrangement?' (cited in Deacon, Golding and Billig, 2001, p. 102). Occasionally, the refusal may involve an attempt to intimidate the interviewer. 'There are politicians', Paxman recalls, 'who say "If you ask me that question you will regret it. . . . If you ask me that question I will take it up with the Director General. . . . If you ask me that question I will walk out." Now clearly it does concentrate the mind when you are on the air in twenty seconds and a politician is saying that to you'. Paxman's response to such challenges may be untypically brave: 'My personal view is that . . . you absolutely have to ask it. You can't possibly agree to these attempts at blackmail and bullying' (*The Media Programme*, 29 October 1989).

Fifth, politicians may try to avoid difficult interviewers. In 1979 Gordon Reece, Thatcher's media adviser, drew up an 'enemies list' of interviewers who were potentially hostile to Thatcher or who brought out her worst features in interview: Campbell drew up a similar list for Blair (Milne and Maguire, 2001, pp. 2–3). Thatcher's marketing strategy led her to refuse interviews on major news and current affairs programmes preferring softer programmes like BBC Radio 2's *Jimmy Young Show*: a bonus here was the largely female C1 and C2 audience which she wished to target. Blair has proved similarly keen to select popular programes, sometimes in the daytime schedules, which deliver large and demographically desirable audiences but which also offer 'easy' questions and opportunities to develop the politician's personal image. During Blair's appearance on ITV's *Richard and Judy Show*, for example, he found it easier to address issues such as Cherie's new bathing costume, his relationship with his father-in-law (well-known actor and left-wing activist Tony Booth) and to suggest that Glenn Hoddle should resign as manager of the English football team following ill-advised remarks about disabled people, than he might have done if he was being interrogated by John Humphrys or David Dimbleby. There are other ways to avoid difficult interviews. A senior journalist on the *Today* programme claims that a minister 'who usually took part from remote studios, boasted to me that when he didn't like the way an interview was going, he pressed the "hang up" button' (Kampfner, 2000, p. 3).

Finally, politicians may completely reject the interview and seek other forms of media coverage. A predictable American import rather than a home grown product, the photo opportunity was introduced into British political communications by Gordon Reece. Before 1979, no previous aspirant to Number Ten had conducted a press conference in the middle of a field in John Gummer's constituency, clutching a two-day-old calf. Political correspondent John Sargent recalled that 'it did seem as if that was the moment when British politics changed quite significantly' (*Dispatches*, 18 March 1992). In a cliche which is often attributed to Conservative director of communications Harvey Thomas, 'a good picture can say more than a thousand words'. Conveniently, moreover, photo opportunities do not require politicians to respond to journalists' questions with the attendant dangers of offering hostages to electoral fortune. Subsequently, the photo opportunity has become a marketing staple with politicians preferring to pose before a camera and force feed their daughters beefburgers during a beef scare, or to playfully head a football with Kevin Keegan, rather than address substantive policy questions by a skilled and forceful interviewer (Franklin, 1999).

Politicians' use of these evasive techniques in interviews has certainly restricted the ability of interviewers to get beyond the packaging to the politician, but some interviewers believe that Robin Day's regret at 'the passing of the political interview' may be precocious. Interviews can still present a challenge to politicans although increasingly it is one they have been trained to meet. David Frost's interview with Neil Kinnock in 1987, for example, revealed the electoral weakness of Labour's defence policy. Interviews can prove especially danger-ous for politicians when they are conducted by members of the public, who are ignorant about the agreed rules of engagement (McNair, Hibberd and Schlesinger 2002, pp. 410–11). Pensioner Mrs Gould's persistent questioning of Thatcher about the sinking of the Belgrano on *Nationwide's* live phone-in evidently threw the prime minister off balance. In the 1992 elec-tion, Kinnock's prevarication and waffle concerning Labour's position on proportional rep-resentation during the *Granada's 500* programme was very damaging. On 10 March 2003, Tony Blair was subjected to sustained and critical questioning, about his policy on war with Iraq, by a female audience on *Tonight with Trevor MacDonald*: at the programme's conclusion the audience slow hand clapped through the credits.

GROOMED FOR THE PART!
Harold Wilson once remarked cynically, 'most of politics is presentation and what isn't is timing' (Jones, 1992, p. 63). Politicians and parties have certainly taken his message to heart. Senior politicians are endlessly groomed for the leading role they play in the television drama which politics has become. Politicians must master the techniques necessary for the successful television presentation of policy and themselves. This may

require changes to even the smallest details of a politician's appearance to make them more 'telegenic'. Successful marketing demands the right product image if the consumers' brand loyalty is to be guaranteed.

Every aspect of a politician's appearance must be geared up to the demands of television and may be modified until it conforms to the media adviser's perception of the 'right image'. The significance of politicians' appearance was first realised when audience responses to the debate between Kennedy and Nixon prior to the 1960 presidential election were analysed. A majority of those who heard the speeches on radio believed Nixon had won, whereas a majority of television viewers pronounced Kennedy the victor. Radio listeners heard only the persuasive rhetoric of the erudite lawyer, but didn't see the dark shadow on Nixon's apparently unshaven face nor the sweat on his forehead. Kennedy had shaved immediately prior to the interview and looked fresh, less sinister and more trustworthy. Media advisers believed Nixon's appearance contributed to the demise of his campaign (Atkinson, 1984, p. 174).

Gordon Reece worked closely with Thatcher from 1975 and transformed her television image. Reece commissioned private polls which revealed the public's dislike of Thatcher's voice which seemed too shrill and upper class, her style too hectoring and her appearance too school marmish. Thatcher's metamorphosis into an ordinary housewife began with the conversion of her adversarial screeching into a more mellifluous discourse. Reece appointed playwright Ronald Millar to help write Thatcher's speeches and employed a voice tutor from the National Theatre who recommended humming exercises which reduced the pitch of Thatcher's voice by 46 Hz. This reduction had other beneficial consequences. It slowed her speech delivery and made her sound more statesmanlike (Atkinson, 1984, p. 174). Reece advised her to wear simple, less fussy clothes on television, to wear less make-up, to soften her hair style, never to wear a hat and to keep her jewellery simple. Reece's advice to emphasise her natural attractiveness prompted the regular tinting of her blonde hair and the capping of her teeth to get rid of a gap (Atkinson, 1984, p. 117). John Major argued he would never succumb to the machinations of the image makers, but media revelations that he tucked his shirt into his underpants led to a series of subtle changes in his appearance during the summer of 1991. His hair, his spectacles and his suit all went in for an overhaul. For his part, William Hague suffered presentational difficulties from the outset, exemplified by the opening lines of Simon Hoggart's parliamentary sketch the day after Hague's first appearance in the House as leader of the opposition: 'The foetus has landed' Hoggart announced (Hoggart, 2002a, p. 50). Labour MP Tony Banks preferred to describe Hague as 'the Mekon'. Hague's haircut, his new (shaven) haircut, his baseball cap, his northern accent and his self-proclaimed capacity to drink beer, all contributed to the challenging brief he presented to party image advisers. Hague's successor, Iain Duncan Smith has suffered similar 'image difficulties'. In August 2003, newspapers carried reports of the efforts by Conservative central office and Paul

Baverstock, the new director of communications, to help Iain Duncan Smith to 'master his gestures, control the frog in his throat and learn how to speak effectively in public' (*Daily Telegraph*, 14 August 2003, p. 6; *The Times*, 15 August 2003, p. 8). At a cost of more than £100,000, he has been 'taught to breathe from his stomach like an opera singer' and has enjoyed 'one-to-one tuition in "power walking"' to teach him to 'stride purposefully, how to pause and wave to the audience, and how to climb the stage' (*Daily Telegraph*, 14 August 2003, p. 6).

Labour leaders were similarly reconstructed for public consumption, while their shadow cabinet were colour co-ordinated and coiffured by image stylist Barbara Follett *(Guardian,* 3 February 1993): a new verb 'to Follett' captured this preoccupation with politicians' appearance. Kinnock's balding, but combed over, hair style was cut short and tidied to avoid comparisons with Arthur Scargill. Dark-grey double-breasted suits replaced his casual clothes and added an element of gravitas to his impression of a British prime minister. The party was eager to avoid the media recriminations of Michael Foot's donkey-jacketed appearance at the Cenotaph. Kinnock, moreover, was not allowed to smoke his pipe in interviews for fear of evoking, at least in the public's mind, the ghost of Harold Wilson.

Blair's premiership has also been characterised by press comment about his appearance and attempts to package Blair by emphasising his youthful appearance and style: he was also presented as a family man, especially following the birth of his fourth child Leo in 2000. But increasingly, press speculation focused on whether he tinted his hair to remove the greying at the temples, while his first appearance at a press conference wearing reading glasses occasioned comment on the BBC's flagship news programme. His choice of suits, especially a purple suit attracted particular press attention. There is clearly a belief among media advisers that the suit is at least as important in the battle for the hearts and minds of voters as the policies of the politician who wears it.

BESIEGING THE BROADCASTERS

Complaining has long since become an institutionalised strategy through which parties try to influence the reporting of election news. At the 1991 Conservative conference, Chris Patten urged party members to 'jam the switch boards' of broadcasting organisations to protest about any anti-Tory bias. In the run-up to the 1992 general election, there were daily running battles between the party spin doctors and broadcasters about campaign coverage (Harrison, 1992, p. 156). The pressure on broadcasters to yield to party demands was unprecedentedly high. A BBC news reporter claimed:

> It's relentless and coming at us from all sides ... They're all trying either to kill a story or spin us a line. They'll phone up before the news and say 'We think your top line should be this'. Or they'll phone after a bulletin and say,

'We want you to change your piece to camera, because the party doesn't accept your concept'.

(Phillips, 1992, p. 27.)

A barrage of complaints from both major parties similarly characterised the run up to the 1997 election. Then Conservative defence secretary Malcolm Rifkind claimed on Radio 4's *Today* programme that 'the BBC are becoming a real menace' because of their 'shabby journalism' (McNair, 2000, p. 157), while Labour's Brian Wilson, in a *Daily Telegraph* article, accused John Humphrys of abandoning 'even handedness' in his interviews with Labour politicians and suggested that Humphrys had subjected John Prescott to 'rudeness and constant interuption' (Wilson, 1996).

For the 2001 election, the BBC established a central unit to deal with complaints: they anticipated complaints from the Conservatives who for many years had dubbed the BBC the 'Blair Broadcasting Corporation' (Harrison, 2002, p. 147). But Labour also seemed determined to 'get their retalliation in first' with press articles before the election, while Campbell complained that the *Today* programme was pursuing the *Daily Mail's* agenda (*Observer*, 15 April 2001, *Sunday Telegraph*, 6 May 2001). During the campaign, Margaret McDonagh, General Secretary of the Labour party, accused broadcasters of colluding with anti-government protesters to generate 'good copy' (Macintyre, 2001, p. 594). Her comments were widely derided as a rather crude attempt to bully and intimidate journalists but they were also widely reported and discussed: 'TV To Blame For Protests Says Labour' (*Daily Telegraph*, 22 May 2003) and 'Labour Fury at TV "Setting Up" Protests' (*The Times*, 22 May 2003). Two weeks after the election, the BBC's deputy director of news claimed that relations between the Labour government and the Corporation reached 'an all time low during the election . . . they are opposed to anything but the most pasteurised form of coverage' (Damazer, cited in Tomlin, 2001, p. 7).

With the advent of permanent campaigning the pressure on broadcasters from politicians, and party spin doctors, armed with computer software such as excalibur designed to effect 'rapid rebuttal', is persistent (see Chapter 3). One political journalist working on the BBC's *Today* programme recalled the constant telephone complaints from party officials that began as soon as the programme went on air at 6.30 a.m. and continued until the close at 9 a.m.: there were constant demands for corrections ('they even faxed me a statement, setting out the words I should use for my "correction" '), apologies, requests to 'stop talking off the top of your head' or Alastair Campbell declaring he is 'fed up with the garbage you've been putting out'. Such pressures are persistent and daily but 'the larger the election looms, the more the spinners of all parties will try to bludgeon programmes into submission. After all the tactic has so often worked in the past' (Kampfner, 2000, pp. 2–3).

MEDIA COVERAGE OF GENERAL ELECTION CAMPAIGNS

On 8 May 2001, moderniser Tony Blair eschewed the traditional statement to Parliament and in rather pious fashion, announced the coming general election from the stage of a girls' school in London. Matthew Parris, then sketch writer for *The Times* captured the occasion.

> With a cross behind him, sacred stained glass above him, the upturned faces of 500 school girls in pink-and-blue gingham before him, and to the strains of a choir singing 'I who make the skies of light / I will make the darkness bright / Here I am', Mr Blair launched his campaign at the St Olave's and St Saviour's church school in Southwark ... Alastair Campbell clapped caringly ... Something amiss with the chapel sound-amplification caused Mr Blair's voice to sound as if he had just inhaled from a helium tap. Listening to it made us feel as though we had. But the speech was for television.
>
> (Parris, 2002, pp. 436–7.)

Fellow sketch writer Simon Hoggart confirmed that 'the whole event stank of spin doctors' sweat' (*Guardian*, 9 May 2001, p. 2) despite pundits' claims that 2001 would be a 'post spin' election (Deacon, *et al.*, 2001, p. 103). Other journalists were less measured and less kind. Peter Riddell described the event as 'nauseatingly exploitative', Andrew Marr believed it was 'a hideous cringe-making example of soft propaganda (Marr, 2001, p. 11), while Parris denounced the photo opportunity as 'breathtakingly, toe-curlingly, hog-whimperingly tasteless [and] unbelievably ill-judged' (Parris 2002, p. 437): 'child abuse' concluded Frank Johnson in the *Telegraph* (Ingham, 2001, p. 590). The public seemed similarly unimpressed by the campaign launch.

Voter apathy was undoubtedly the common enemy all parties needed to confront in 2001. The challenge for politicians and journalists alike was to persuade voters, readers and viewers to engage with the political debate. The reasons for this apathy were endlessly rehearsed in newspaper columns and on television. The public was sceptical about the need for an election, disagreed with its timing in the wake of an epidemic of foot and mouth disease, criticised Labour's emphasis on spin and presidentialism rather than policy: polls persistently predicted a Labour landslide, while a healthy economy sat uneasily alongside growing desenchantment with the political process. In brief, 'the 2001 election was a big yawn, as massive a turn-off as it was a foregone conclusion ... it was a desperate show' (Ingham, 2001, p. 586). BBC journalist Nicholas Jones wished to 'add another factor. A sense that the level of engagement among journalists was lower than in previous elections and this transmitted itself to the electorate' (Jones, 2001, p. 600). Whether journalists and their election coverage were cause or consequence of voter apathy remains a moot point, but media audiences for election coverage plummetted: consequently newspaper circulations crashed along with viewing figures for broadcast news programmes.

During the campaign, audiences for BBC's *News at Ten* dropped from 4.9 million to 4.2 million while ITV's *News At Ten* was down 21 per cent on 1997 audience figures: shares for Sky News and News 24 dropped by almost a half compared to figures for stories such as floods (Tomlin and Morgan, 2001, p. 1). As part of its election coverage, Channel 5 News conducted an experiment in which volunteers were wired to establish which was more exciting, watching the election or watching paint dry: perhaps predictably the paint won (Harrison, 2002, p. 135). As newspaper circulations dropped, the *Sun's* editor claimed 'It's always like this in a general election, but in this one it's worse' (Tomlin and Morgan, 2001, p. 1). During election week the front page of the *Mirror* pictured the three party leaders asleep or yawning under the headline 'P.S. Exciting Isn't It?' (*Mirror*, 5 June 2001).

FROM THE TORY PRESS TO THE TONY PRESS: PRESS PARTISANSHIP AND DE-ALIGNMENT 1992 TO 2001

The most striking feature of press coverage of the 1992, 1997 and 2001 general elections has been the shifting partisan allegiances of newspapers across the period (Deacon, Golding and Billig, 2001, p. 103). A shift described by journalist Peter Hitchens as a move from a 'Tory' press to a 'Tony' press: from newspapers offering overwhelmingly support to the Conservative Party in 1987 and 1992 to newspapers supporting Tony Blair and in some cases the Labour Party in 1997 and 2001. In 1992 the *Sun* famously and arrogantly pronounced that 'It Was the Sun Wot Won it' for the Conservatives, while in 1997, Murdoch's disenchantment with Major generated the significant front page headline 'The Sun Backs Blair: Give Change A Chance' (17 March 1997). Almost exactly four years later, on the day after Gordon Brown's 'astounding budget', the *Sun* offered further enthusiastic endorsement of Blair: 'It's In The Bag Tony: You might as well call the election now' ... 'Blair gets our support for a second term' (8 March 2001 – see also Toynbee, 2001, p. 17; Wintour, 2001, p. 12).

This coincidence of shifting press and voter electoral preferences prompted some political communication scholars to suggest that newspapers' election coverage had been influential in shaping readers' electoral choices (Linton, 1995), while others spoke forcefully against such influence (Curtice and Semetko, 1994; McKie, 1998, p. 129) arguing that Murdoch had simply followed where his readers and market interests led: adding that Murdoch's maxim is 'always join the winning side, don't be seen dead with losers' (Toynbee, 2001, p. 17). It seems reasonable to assume, however, that both Blair and Campbell subscribed, at least to some degree, to the 'tabloid effect' school of media influence since Campbell's priority for his media strategy, following his appointment as Blair's press officer in 1994, was to at least 'silence' the *Sun* if not metamorphose it into a new Labour cheerleader

(Franklin, 1996, p. 18). Blair's trip to a Newscorp leadership conference in the Hayman Islands in July 1995 seemed similarly motivated.

The shift in newspapers' support between 1992 and 1997 was certainly dramatic. In 1987, the circulation gap between papers supporting Conservative and Labour peaked at 48 per cent: it fell slightly in 1992, but remained robust at 43 per cent. By 1997 however a sharp reversal was noticable with 11 of the 19 national newspapers supporting Labour (Deacon, Golding and Billig, 2002, p. 109). In 1997, 8.1 million voters (62.2 per cent) were reading a Labour supporting newspaper with only 4.5 milllion (32.5 per cent) reading a Conservative leaning paper (Wring, 2002, p. 93): the 1992 press allegiances had been almost exactly reversed. Significantly the shift expressed a collapse of support for Conservatism rather than any Damascene conversion to Labour. David McKie, identified four positions of partisanship which 'adopting tabloidspeak' he titled 'the "clingers", the "swingers", the "waverers" and the "quaverers" ' (McKie, 1998, p. 116). The clingers were the Labour supporting tabloids (*Mirror*, *Sunday Mirror* and *People*) which had stuck with the party in hard times and had no cause to desert them in more favourable times, while the swingers were the papers which previously supported the Conservatives (the *Sun*). The waverer was the *Daily Mail* which began and ended pro-Conservative but wavered reflecting the shifting allegiance of its proprietor Lord Rothermere. The quaverer was the *Daily Express* whose joint owners Lord Stevens (Conservative) and Lord Hollick (Labour) subscribed to distinctive political beliefs: the *Express* kept to its Conservative faith, but 'its trumpet through the campaign gave forth an uncertain sound' (McKie, 1998, p. 116).

The decisive shift in press partisanship occurred after the 1997 election. By 2001, seven of the ten national papers and six of the Sunday papers supported Labour: only three declared for the Conservatives. In circulation terms, 72 per cent of voters were reading a pro-Labour paper compared to just 7.8 per cent who were reading a newspaper which supported the Conservatives (Wring, 2002, p. 93): a remarkable shift from 1992. But three qualifications are necessary here. First, as noted above, the shift in allegiance represents a press 'de-alignment rather than re-alignment' (Scammell and Harrop, 2002, p. 154): a collapse of support for the Tories as much as any eulogy for Labour. Newspapers revealed highly variable degrees of commitment to the pro-Labour cause. The *Mirror*, for example, supported Labour strongly compared to recent convert *The Times* which offered only modest endorsement of the party. But the *Mirror's* support for Labour was itself qualified by a sense of resentment stemming from Labour's recent more ardent courtship of the *Sun*. In brief, press partisanship in 2001 was complex (Deacon, Golding and Billig, 2001, pp. 109–11). Second, by 2001 most broadsheets no longer articulated a single homogenous editorial voice reflecting the development of op-ed pages during the 1980s and 1990s, in which differing positions on particular issues were contested in intra-newspaper debates. (Seymour Ure, 2002, p. 121). Third, in 2001 many of the newspapers which supported Labour were purchased by readers who were moving away from the party, a trend most notable at the pro-Labour *Guardian* where 13.5 per cent of readers switched to Liberal Democrat: at the *Independent*, the figure was 11.5 per cent (Wring, 2002, p. 96).

A comparison of election reporting in the *Sun* in 1992 with coverage in 2001, however, exemplifies the marked difference in support which Labour achieved across the decade. In 1992, every lead election story, with the exception of a eulogy for John Major, allegedly 'A Man for All Reasons' (3 April 1992), was a personalised, highly negative attack on then Labour leader Neil Kinnock. The onslaught began on 16 March 1992 with 'I was wrong, wrong, wrong, Kinnock owns up', which was followed by a front-page picture of Jennifer Bennett who had featured in the 'Jennifer's Ear' PEB, with the headline, 'If Kinnock Tells Lies about a Sick Little Girl, Will he Ever Tell the Truth about Anything?' (26 March 1992). Later in the campaign, the *Sun* suggested some Kinnock-free zones if Labour won: the Australian Outback, the Arctic Circle and the space shuttle. The eve-of-poll edition carried the headline 'Nightmare on Kinnock Street' and explored a favourite theme of Conservative propaganda in a front-page editorial 'A Question of Trust'. The following eight pages were devoted to rubbishing the Labour Party in a series of articles which ranged from the offensive to the bizarre. Barbara Castle recalled that her 'stomach turned' as she read the *Sun's* assertions that all planning applications would have to be approved by gay and lesbian groups 'as well as ethnic groups' if Labour was elected *(Guardian,* 19 April 1992, p. 19). Subsequent pages offered a more humorous, less pernicious, election coverage, including exclusive revelations by the *Sun's* psychic that Mao and Trotsky vote Labour, Queen Victoria and Elvis Presley vote Conservative, Hitler votes Loony while Genghis Khan doesn't know (Harrop and Scammell, 1992, p. 184). The *Sun's* 'Election Day Special' featured the now infamous picture of Kinnock's head inside a light bulb. The headline asked simply, 'If Kinnock Wins Today, Will the last Person to Leave Britain Please Turn Out the Lights'. The text announced with no apparent sense of contradiction, 'You know our views on the subject but we don't want to influence you in your final judgement on who will be Prime Minister! But if it's a bald bloke with wispy red hair and two Ks in his surname, we'll see you at the airport'. The paper's valedictory commented, in a style reminiscent of American comedian George Burns, 'Goodnight and thank you for everything' (9 April 1992, p. 1): a brilliant and politically devastating tabloid front page.

In 2001, the style and message was radically different. As in 1997, the *Sun* declared its support for Labour prior to the campaign although its editorial support was notably ambiguous throughout. On the day after the election was called, for example, the *Sun* published its own manifesto which, with its emphasis on tax cuts, hard line policies on crime and asylum, the demand for more teachers and nurses and its insistence on saving the pound, was closer to a Conservative than Labour agenda. (Scammell and Harrop, 2002, p. 162). But the *Sun's* proximity to new Labour was underscored by the ability of

Trevor Kavanagh, its political editor, to deliver exclusives on the likely date of the election, the rescheduling of the election to June and the composition of the post-election cabinet (David Blunkett would be the next home secretary who would 'Blitz Asylum Cheats' 16 May 2003): Campbell seemed to be leaking exclusives to Kavanagh in return for the *Sun's* political backing (Leapman, 2001, p. 18). But the paper's support could never be taken for granted. Many of its election editorials spoke warmly of William Hague while the *Sun's* unequivocal anti-European stance, which triggered the famous headline alleging Blair was 'the most dangerous man in Britain', was evident in an editorial of 28 May which insisted that if Blair called a referendum on Europe, 'our opposition wouldn't just be unprecedentedly ferocious – it would be deeply, even mortally damaging to Tony, Gordon and everyone connected with the project. Don't make us do it Prime Minister' (*Sun*, 28 May 2001). But in 2001, the *Sun's* evident but equivocal endorsement of Labour was captured in its polling day headline: 'Don't Let Us Down Tony' (Scammell and Harrop, 2002, p. 171): undoubtedly less gushing, if slightly more deferential, than 1997, but politically some distance from the 1992 ravaging of Kinnock.

The other tabloids, the *Mirror*, *Sunday Mirror*, *Sunday People* and *Star*, similarly supported Labour in 2001 while the *Mail*, although highly critical of Labour failed to offer explicit endorsement of the Conservative cause. For the broadsheets, the *Guardian*, *The Times*, *The Financial Times*, the *Observer*, *The Sunday Times* along with the *Express* and *Sunday Express*, newly purchased from Hollick's MAI media group by Richard Desmond, all offered varying degrees of support to new Labour. Only the *Telegraph*, the *Sunday Telegraph* and the *Mail on Sunday* endorsed the Conservatives: the *Independent* and the *Independent on Sunday* remained eponymously that!

Certain significant patterns or features of coverage were evident in 2001. First, there was a close correlation between the size of a newspaper's readership and the presence of election coverage. Consequently, while the *Guardian* (18 per cent), *Daily Telegraph* (17 per cent), *Independent* (16 per cent), *The Times* (15 per cent) and *The Financial Times* (10 per cent) in aggregate accounted for 76 per cent of all election articles published in the press, these papers enjoyed only 20 per cent of circulation. By contrast, the *Sun* (16 per cent) and the *Mirror* (15 per cent) attracted 31 per cent of all newspaper readers but published only 12 per cent of total election related articles (Worcester and Mortimore, 2001, p. 153): expressed differently, tabloid newspapers attribute a lower news salience to election stories than their sister broadsheet titles. In weeks 3 and 4 of the campaign broadsheets published approximately three times as much coverage as tabloids while in the final week tabloids (2164 square centimetres) closed the gap on broadsheets (3887 square centimetres) (Deacon, Golding and Billig, 2001, p. 104).

Second, it is not only the quantity of coverage in the tabloids and broadsheets which differs. The *Daily Star's* front page coverage, for example, when the two stories devoted to the Prescott punch are discounted, consisted of four stories: 'Geri [Halliwell] Goes Into Labour' (14 May), 'Britney [Spears] Backs Labour' (16 May), 'Jordan [a topless model] Stands As An MP' (23 May), and 'Jordan: I've Got 'em By The Ballots' (24 May). Each front page story was accompanied by a photograph of a scantily clad Geri, Britney or Jordan (Worcester and Mortimore, 2001, p. 154). As if to prove that the intense competition in the tabloid market generates convergence not diversity of editorial style and content, the *Sun* mounted a 'Get 'em Out to Vote' Campaign which employed all the seductive talents of the three finalists from the paper's National Cleavage Week (Deacon, Golding and Billig, 2001, p. 104).

Third, the themes ranked in the election agenda reflected the different techniques employed to measure them. Scammell and Harrop, for example, counted front page lead stories and editorials. On this calculus the agenda was Europe (21 [18 per cent] stories and 33 [12 per cent] editorials), Party strategies (16 [14 per cent] stories and 18 [7 per cent] editorials), Prescott (16 [14] stories and 11 [4 per cent] editorials) and opinion polls (11 [9 per cent] stories and 3 [1 per cent] editorials). They noted the absence of Northern Ireland, sleaze and manifestoes, which won a place in the 1997 'top 10' and the emergence of Prescott, asylum and public services in the top 10 issues in 2001. But foot and mouth which delayed both local and national elections was 'conspicuous by its absence' (Scammell and Harrop, 2002, p. 168). By contrast, the Communications Research Centre at Loughborough University, counted themes mentioned across all election coverage and, by this measure, the election process (45 per cent of all issues coded) topped the election agenda followed by Europe (9 per cent), the health service (6 per cent), taxation (5 per cent), crime (4 per cent), education (4 per cent), public services (3 per cent), social security (3 per cent) the economy (2 per cent) and constitutional issues (2 per cent) (Deacon, Golding and Billig, 2001, pp. 106–7).

Fourth, the Loughborough researchers also quantified the degree of presidentialism in press coverage of the 2001 election. Blair dominated and appeared in 18 per cent of all press coverage, followed by Hague (12 per cent) and the Liberal Democrat leader Charles Kennedy (4 per cent). The entire Labour party (excluding Blair) enjoyed only 33 per cent of coverage, the Conservatives 22 per cent and the Liberals a mere 3 per cent; less than the coverage enjoyed by their leader alone (Deacon, Golding and Billig, 2001, p. 105).

'LESS OF THE SAME': TELEVISION COVERAGE OF THE 2001 GENERAL ELECTION

Television coverage of the 2001 general election was characterised by Martin Harrison as delivering 'less of the same' (Harrison 2002, p. 134). Three indicators substantiate Harrison's claim. First, the main terrestrial television channels did not extend their flagship news programmes to offer the fuller election coverage they delivered in 1997. Second, the extent of election coverage was reduced on all channels. In 1997, for example, election reporting in the BBC lunchtime, evening and main news represented 62 per cent, 54 per cent and 67 per cent of the news programme: by 2001 those figures were reduced to 57 per cent, 50 per cent and 56 per cent. At ITV the equivalent 1997 figures for election coverage were 60 per cent, 48 per cent and 57 per cent compared with only 45 per cent, 46 per cent and 49 per cent in 2001. Finally, editors were more willing to lead with non-election stories than previously. At the BBC, five of the 30 main bulletins across the election headlined non-election stories, compared with one in 1997: ITV featured non-election leads on 10 occasions compared with seven in 1997. Channel 4 dropped from 28 election leads (out of 30) in 1997 to 18 in 2001 (Harrison, 2002, pp. 135–7). But broadcast coverage remained considerable with aggregate output on BBC1's *10pm News*, ITV *News at Ten*, *Channel 4 News*, *Sky News* and BBC2 *Newsnight* amounting to 5842 seconds in the opening week of the campaign and rising to 6276 seconds in the final week (Deacon, Golding and Billig, 2001, p. 104). Broadcast journalists were as conscious of public apathy as their print colleagues: 38 per cent of voters believed that there was 'much too much' or 'a little too much' coverage, with a bare majority (51 per cent) stating coverage was about right and only 4 per cent believing there was too little television reporting of the election (Worcester and Mortimore 2001, p. 150).

In contrast to press reporting of the election, television coverage of the campaign is obliged to be fair and even-handed, reflecting broadcasters' statutory obligations as well as their professional commitments. The tradition of public service broadcasting has always stressed the need for broadcasters to 'educate, inform and entertain', but it has laid equal emphasis on the requirement for television to be an unbiased and impartial arbiter, especially in the realm of political broadcasting. In addition, the charters and franchises which grant organisations permission to broadcast are awarded on conditions which stress the need for impartiality in broadcasting (Franklin, 2001, p. 132). Legal constraints, such as the Representation of the People Acts, further consolidate balance in election coverage (Negrine, 1989, p. 192). But finally, balance in election broadcasting is guaranteed by politicians' diligence in monitoring programmes. As Golding observed, 'a mildly paranoic regard for the click of stopwatches and the whirring of videos at party headquarters, conspire to produce equity' *(Guardian,* 16 March 1992, p. 13). In 2001, journalists' concern to achieve balanced programming generated remarkable outcomes. An analysis of the total number of broadcast quotes by the leaders of the three main parties used in election programming on BBC1, ITV, Channel 4, Channel 5 and Radio 4, for example, revealed that Blair's 344 citations were matched closely by 359 for Hague and 349 for Kennedy: the figures for BBC (Blair 101, Hague 103, Kennedy 93) and ITV (Blair 89, Hague 87, Kennedy 92) illustrate the very striking degree of balance in election broadcasting (Harrison, 2002, p. 140).

Seven features of television coverage of the 2001 election are notable: some reflect continuity, others change, in broadcast election reporting. First, journalists and programme makers presented the 2001 election using a wide range of programme formats. The flagship news programmes, such as BBC's and ITV's *News at Ten*, *Newsnight*, Channel 4 and Channel 5 News and Sky News, as well as BBC and ITV regional news programmes, were joined by current affairs programmes (*Panorama*) and the regular political programmes (*On The Record*) to provide up to date coverage of election events. The 'access' programmes presented studio-based discussions, or phone-ins, with a live audience posing questions to a single politician. On BBC, David Dimbleby hosted a series of *Question Time* specials devoted to the party leaders, while Jonathan Dimbleby hosted *Ask The Leader* for ITV. The election stalwart, *Election Call* provided radio and television audiences (although relegated to BBC2 from BBC1 in 2001) with opportunities to quiz politicians. Journalists' emphasis on presenting the views of ordinary voters to counteract party spin triggered a number of innovations. BBC *Breakfast Time* carried recorded comment from undecided voters who had been loaned video equipment to make their own 'mini packages', *Channel 4 News* commissioned its own battle bus and visited marginal constituencies, while *Newsnight's* Jeremy Vine set off on a tour of the UK in an old van to gather public opinion nationwide (Harrison, 2002, pp. 142–5; Wring, 2002, pp. 88–9). In 2001, moreover, the Internet provided radio journalists with opportunities to dabble with pictures. Nick Clarke hosted webcam discussions with politicians which could be downloaded from the *World at One* website (Damon, 2001, p. 597).

Second, a good deal of television news coverage focused on party orchestrated photo opportunities, constituency visits and walkabouts. In truth, there is no 'real' story to report, merely a 'pseudo event' manufactured by party media advisers to attract television coverage. But journalists seem to find them irresistible – or perhaps parties control election news opportunities so closely that this is all that is available (Jones, 2001a, p. 601) – and report them at the expense of 'real' news. Worse, broadcasters' commitments to parity exacerbate the problem by obliging them to balance the un-newsworthy photo opportunity of one party 'with the opposing political party's un-newsworthy walkabout' (Negrine, 1989, p. 196). Andrew Marr described these 'mutually cancelling soundbites' as 'ping-pong packages' (Harrison, 2002, p. 142) . Journalists evidently became frustrated with such party news management strategies. Having reported Blair's visit to a construction site near Inverness to see 'the biggest hole in Scotland', followed by a visit to Microsoft that regressed into a product launch, afternoon tea with a young couple to discuss the congenially low level of mortgage rates and a visit to the Happy Haddock Chip Shop, Jon Snow reported in some despair from the set of *Brookside*, 'Has it really come to this?' (Harrison, 2002, p. 141).

Third, Campbell's allegation early in the campaign that journalists were interested in 'process rather than policy' was substantiated by television's preoccupation with the conduct of the election which dominated the news agenda. Almost half (45 per cent) of the broadcast items analysed by the researchers at Loughborough focused on the 'process' of the election: the policy issues of Europe (9 per cent), the health service (6 per cent), taxation (5 per cent) crime (4 per cent) and education (4 per cent) lagged a good way behind (Deacon, Golding and Billig, 2001, p. 107). Television coverage of one aspect of the election process, however, has plummetted. Since 1992 when, for only the second time since polling began, polls failed to predict the result accurately, they 'met their Waterloo' (Crewe, 2001, p. 86). Polls remain a focus for television reporting of the campaign but in 1992, 57 national polls were conducted and poll findings ranked in first or second place in the election agenda, accounted for 12 per cent of radio and television election news and featured on 21 per cent of tabloid front pages (*Guardian*, 11 April 1992, p. 8). By 2001 there were 21 polls (Butler and Kavanagh, 2002, p. 124) but no television news programme led with poll findings (Harrison, 2002, pp. 136–7), despite the fact that the 2001 polls were the most accurate since 1987 with the final four exit polls average error being 1.6 per cent: well within the 3 per cent acceptable margin of error (Worcester and Mortimore, 2001, p. 246).

Fourth, television coverage reflected the predominantly negative character of the campaign. The Conservatives inclination to fight the campaign as an opposition party rather than a government in waiting, was reflected in television coverage which reported the party as twice as likely as Labour to be attacking their opponents (15.9 per cent of appearances critical compared with 9.6 per cent for Labour), but only half as likely to be presenting their own policies (13.5 per cent Conservative and 24.5 per cent Labour). The Conservatives (3.3 per cent) were also twice as likely as Labour (1.8 per cent) to be reported in the context of internal dispute (Golding and Deacon, 2001, p. 5).

Fifth, the election coverage was highly presidential: again, almost certainly reflecting party news management. Blair (35.6 per cent) and Hague (26.4 per cent) appeared in 62 per cent of all broadcast news items: when Kennedy (11.9 per cent) and Brown (11.8 per cent) are included, these four senior politicans appear in nearly 86 per cent of all coverage. Senior Labour politicians like Chris Smith, Clare Short, Mo Mowlam and Ann Taylor were virtually invisible: women had a poor election with only Ann Widdicombe appearing in 3.2 per cent of television news items (Golding and Deacon, 2001, p. 5). The absence of women politicians at the morning press conferences became a focus of journalists' criticism of Labour.

Sixth, in 2001 there was considerably greater journalistic mediation between politicians and viewers. Journalists were more than usually evident in campaign reports. The phenomenon of journalists preferring to talk to other journalists, for example, rather than politicians or an acknowledged expert, was increasingly apparent: the seeking of 'in house' opinions during what is increasingly dubbed 'conversational journalism' guaranteed that Andrew Marr became 'one of the campaign's stars' (Harrison, 2002, p. 143). Journalists, moreover, are taking a greater part of any given interview with a politician. In the

Newsnight interviews with party leaders, for example, Paxman colonised 30 per cent of broadcast time and 33 per cent during the Blair interview (Golding and Deacon, 2001, p. 5).

Finally, but perhaps in part related to the point above, politicians' contributions to election programming was briefer than previously as soundbite culture became consolidated. The average speaking time for party leaders per election item reduced from 37.3 seconds in 1992 to 24.8 seconds in 2001 on BBC news with equivalent figures for ITN being 32 to 21.2 seconds (ibid.)

Television reporting of the 2001 election displayed many of the features which characterised earlier campaigns, although coverage was reduced across most channels. Coverage seemed scrupulously fair in terms of the allocation of broadcast time between the major parties, but the idea that balance can be measured by a stopwatch is coming under increasing challenge both from broadcasters and politicians. Television presented the key issues to viewers in an election agenda which was subject to influence and manipulation by the parties. Significant issues such as agriculture, transport, defence, Northern Ireland and the environment were marginalised even though their significance immediately prior, or subsequent, to the election were evident. The negative character of the party campaigns was faithfully captured and reflected in television coverage. The tendency of television reports to focus on leaders at the cost of excluding many other politicians' voices from the election debate was more evident in 2001 than previously. At best, television reporting of the campaign must be judged only a qualified success. The ability of politicians to influence *who* will appear and *what* will be discussed, in election coverage, seems increasingly apparent.

THE E-LECTION: REPORTING THE CAMPAIGN IN CYBERSPACE

In 2001, pundits claimed that the forthcoming election might prove to be the 'first net election' in much the same way that 1959 had subsequently come to be acknowleged as the 'first television election': they were to be profoundly disappointed. Some cyber enthusiasts had portentously crowned the 1997 election with the same title: the *Independent* heralded 'Britain Online For First Election On The Internet' (25 June 1997, p.9). But with only 2 per cent of the population online (Coleman, 2001), such announcements seemed precocious while more sober assessments declared 'the impact of the new medium . . . was minimal' while 'the attention devoted to it [the Internet] in the media was similarly disproportionate' (Ward and Gibson, 1998, p. 93). But the failure of early sightings of the first net election did little to dampen enthusiasm for cyber politics.

In 2001 the Internet was undoubtedly the most exciting potential innovation of the campaign (Coleman 2001a). The major and minor parties, all had websites targeted at party members, journalists and the wider public (Ballinger, 2002, p. 225): journalists cannibalised them. But they also constructed them: and effectively! The BBC News Online and the *Guardian* sites were praised by the Hansard Society and, on the day after the election, Aunty had a staggering 15.75 million callers: 25,000 people downloaded the SNP manifesto compared to the usual hard copy print run of 5,000 (Gaber, 2001, p. 38). But as in 1997, the conclusion of most observers was one of 'disappointment' (Coleman, 2001a, p. 115): it seems clear that once again the Internet 'played a bit part' in the drama of the 2001 election (Downey, 2001, p. 605). Even cyber enthusiasts like Gaber acknowledged that the Internet's 'influence was at best only marginal' (Gaber, 2001, p. 38).

But if not the first net election, the Internet played a substantially increased role in the 2001 election. Coleman identifies four potentially expansive online activities in 2001. First, the net was deployed for the 'e-marketing' of parties and candidates: 'little more than e-commerce applied to politics' (Coleman, 2001a, p. 115). The Labour Party recognised young people as high net users and floating voters and targeted this niche market with their site ruup4it.org.uk which contained lively graphics, celebrity messages, competitions and tips on who to vote for (Downey, 2001, p. 605). Estimates signal that less than 1 in 5 candidates established sites even though the Labour Party offered local parties an off-the-shelf web template, although incumbents and challengers in marginal contests were more likely to create sites (Gibson and Ward, 2001). Second, the Internet provided innovative online resources for voters such as websites for debate or simply poking fun at politicians (or even for throwing eggs at them – specifically at John Prescott at www.spinon.co.uk the site attracted a peak 600 hits a second). Third, some of the traditional news media expanded their print or broadcast capacity to deliver election information, by providing much greater as well as more readily accessible and interesting information and debate online (Damon, 2001, p. 597). Finally, it was anticipated that the interactivity of the Internet could facilitate a new, more participatory style of politics in 2001 although 'this approach was mainly conspicuous by its absence' (Coleman, 2001a, p. 115). This third function of the Internet in the campaign setting was developed considerably in 2001 and allowed news media to expand election coverage substantially. So how extensive was online provision in 2001 and how widely was it accessed by voters?

Online election 'coverage' was dominated by news media organisations with existing reputations for public service commitments: BBC News Online and the *Guardian* were prolific, but the *Daily Telegraph*, *The Financial Times*, *The Times*, the *Independent* and Channel 4 each produced a wealth of in depth electoral information online. Coleman details the extent to which BBC television and radio coverage was supplemented and expanded by an extraordinary wealth of online information and debate.

> BBC News Online provided detailed accounts of the main policy issues and the parties' perspectives on them; a guide to marginal constituencies;

analyses of opinion polls as they were released; an 'online 1000' panel who were surveyed on various issues throughout the campaign; a 'persuade me to vote' feature in which the public tried to urge intended non-voters to participate in the election; a 'virtual vote' feature allowing voters to play with their own online swingometer; an archive of BBC election coverage since 1945; guides to the electoral system and the local elections; a link to the Newsround site and an 'If U were PrimeMinister' feature in which several thousand pre-voters stated their political policies; regular webcasts with leading politicians; and several online discussion fora. Moreover, all the main news and current affairs programmes from radio and television were available live or recorded via RealAudio.

(Coleman, 2001a, p. 119.)

The *Guardian's Election 2001* site was similarly impressive with a daily email newsletter, downloadable election posters from across the twentieth century, discussion forum and a search engine called Aristotle which could answer intriguing questions about candidates and elections and deliver the names of all candidates who were married, Oxbridge educated or from Scotland (Coleman, 2001a, p. 120).

This extraordinary archive of readily accessible and downloadable materials provided by online extensions of 'old media' news organisations attracted unprecedented usage. A MORI poll established that 33 per cent of respondents enjoyed Internet access and of that group 18 per cent used the net for an election-related activity. 11 per cent visited a media website, 7 per cent used email or websites to seek out information about the election of a particular candidate, 5 per cent sent or received emails about the election, 4 per cent visited websites that featured 'humorous' election materials, 2 per cent responded to a web-based opinion poll, while 1 per cent volunteered to work for a party online (Gaber, 2001, p. 38). The BBC site enjoyed half a million page views each day throught the election (Coleman, 2001a, p. 119). Gaber concludes enthusiastically that these data signal that 'in the course of a dull and uninspired election campaign almost three million people used email or the internet to participate in, and find out about the election' (Gaber, 2001, p. 38). But these audiences remain small and relatively insignificant compared to the 'old media' of print and broadcast news. The 18 per cent of the 33 per cent of the population polled by MORI which form the basis of Coleman and Gaber's studies and which enjoyed Internet access, constitute only 5.9 per cent of the wider population: by contrast 9 million watched the flagship news on two television channels (BBC1 and ITN) alone, while the 30 million readers of the national press learned about the election from newspapers.

The limited role of the Internet in the 2001 election is explained by two features of new media. First, television and newspapers predominate because they embody 'push' technology rather than the 'pull' technology of the web. Pull technology requires greater effort by users to seek out information: the push technology of television delivers information on a plate (Ballinger, 2002, p. 238; Downey, 2001, p. 606). Second, access to the Internet is limited: the reach of television is comprehensive. In 2001 only a third of the population enjoyed web access. There is moreover evidence of a growing digital divide with class, gender and age mediating Internet access. Sixty-two per cent of the top 10 per cent of households measured by income have access to the web compared to only 7 per cent of the lowest 10 per cent of households by income. Men (57 per cent) are more likely than women (45 per cent) to access the web and 85 per cent of 16–24 year olds compared to only 6 per cent of those aged 75 or over use the Internet (ibid., p. 605). There is a real problem for parties who might seek to use the web to win votes, since 'relatively wealthy, male, urban internet users are the most unlikely people to be floating voters' and it follows that parties wil be unlikely to consider 'the internet as a cost effective vote winner' (ibid.). The role of the Internet in elections has been the subject of punditry, hyperbole and speculation about a new age of postmodern electioneering. But the evidence from 2001, suggests that even today Ramsay Macdonald would be well-advised to stick with newspapers, radio and, if the prototype television set he had installed at Number Ten in 1930 works, to contemplate the prospects of campaigning via television which remains most voters key source of information about their polity. Some cyber-sceptics place the significant communications revolutions further back in history. Chomsky, for example, suggests we should be more 'modest' in our claims for the Internet. 'The major advances in speed of communication and ability to interact took place more than a century ago. The shift from sailing ships to telegraph was far more radical than that from telephone to email. The Internet could be a very positive step towards education, organisation and participation in a meaningful society. But if you look at the latest figures for Internet use, things such as pornography and e-shopping overwhelm everything else' (Chomsky in the *Guardian*, 17 October 2002, p. 4). Ramsay Mac would undoubtedly have disapproved!

Chapter Seven

☐ LOCAL NEWSPAPERS, LOCAL PARTIES AND REPORTING THE CONSTITUENCY CAMPAIGN

Recent academic studies of local political communications are relatively scarce (Carty and Eagles, 2000; Denver and Hands, 1997 and 1998; Franklin, 2003; Franklin and Murphy, 1991; Franklin and Parry, 1998; Franklin and Richardson, 2002; Larsson, 2002; Neveu, 2002). This mere handful of published studies of *local* political communications provides a rather asymmetrical counterpoint to the burgeoning literature documenting the extensive reporting of general elections in the national news media and the 'packaging of politics' by parties at the national level (Bartle and Griffiths, 2001; Blumler and Gurevitch, 1996; Franklin, 1994; Jones, 2001; Kavanagh, 1995; McNair, 2000; Negrine, 1996; Norris, 2000; Norris *et al.*, 1999; Scammell, 1995; Stanyer, 2001; Street, 2001). With rare exceptions, studies of local campaigning have largely become an anachronism (Carty and Eagles, 2000). Typically published during the 1980s, earlier studies tended to focus on the impact of campaign expenditure on electoral outcomes (Johnston, 1987); case studies of particular campaigns by academics (Holt and Turner, 1968) or individual, usually successful, protagonists (Mitchell, 1982); comparative studies of the local campaign in other democratic polities (Goldenberg and Traugott, 1984); a particular party's approach to the constituency campaign (Janosik, 1968); the likely impact of new technology on the local campaign (Waddle, 1989; Gibson and Ward, 2001); the analysis of issues promoted by candidates in their election addresses (Butler and Kavanagh, 1984) or the awareness of political issues among local party activists

The overall conclusion of this handful of studies is that the local campaign is broadly irrelevant to the eventual result of the general election. Indeed most political communications scholars consider the local campaign to be well and truly dead. The frenetic activities of election agents, candidates and party activists are judged to constitute little more than a bizarre quinquennial ritual enacted to virtually no electoral effect. This precocious obituary constitutes part of a more general scholarly neglect of local news media. Local newspapers remain poorly researched, even less well understood and mistakenly assumed to be uncommitted to political reporting. Most studies of the local press are not academic but autobiographical, typically reflecting the early professional life of the journalist author (Keane, 1996), or disdaining accounts alleging local journalists' failure to report issues of consequence for their communities (Fisk, 4 August 2001). In political communications research, local newspapers typically attract little more attention than it takes to dismiss them as the 'local rag' (Franklin and Murphy, 1998, Ch. 1).

This neglect is unfortunate for a number of reasons. First, the 1300 local newspapers published in the UK enjoy a substantial readership: circulation and distribution figures continue to rival sales of national newspapers (national newspapers 91,282,065, local and regional newspapers 71,873,716). The existence of local press monopolies, moreover, means that in most settings the local newspaper enjoys an even greater readership than a popular national tabloid (Franklin and Murphy, 1991: 7). A study in Leicester, for example revealed that 83 per cent of households read the local *Leicester Mercury*, but only 56 per cent read the UK's most popular newspaper the *Sun* and a mere 25 per cent the *Daily Mirror* (Golding, 1989). Consequently local newspapers may prove highly influential in defining news and setting the local agenda for their readerships (Franklin, 1989b).

Second, previous research suggests that local newspapers are notably less partisan in their election coverage than their national newspaper counterparts, they explore a wider electoral agenda, provide readers with detailed information about candidates and issues and constitute, via the letter's page, an easily accessible local forum for readers to debate the merits of candidates, policies and local issues. Measured according to these criteria, local newspapers undoubtedly provide a better journalistic account of elections than their sister national papers (Franklin and Parry, 1998, pp 226–7).

Third, it is commonplace for politicians and political communications scholars to argue that the extent to which a party enjoys the support of national newspapers during the campaign is crucial to the election outcome. Following the 1992 election, the *Sun* famously claimed 'It was the Sun Wot Won It' (*Sun*, 11 April 1992). Consequently, winning the editorial support of the *Sun* remained a crucial ambition for new Labour in 2001 (Toynbee, 2001, p. 17). Given the priority which politicians evidently ascribe to winning supportive coverage in the national press, political communications scholars' indifference to the possible impact of local press coverage on constituency level electoral outcomes, seems curious.

This chapter seeks to identify the complexities, as well as to restore the significance, of the local campaign and local media reporting of that campaign, by reporting the findings of a unique longitudinal analysis of local journalists' coverage of the constituency campaign in selected constituencies in the West Yorkshire region of England during the 1987, 1992, 1997 and 2001 UK General Elections.[1]

LOCAL PARTY, LOCAL MEDIA RELATIONS: 'NEGOTIATING' ELECTION COVERAGE

Studies of local party campaigning in these West Yorkshire constituencies across four general elections revealed that parties' media strategies varied widely across constituencies reflecting the different political situations they confronted, their enthusiasm for the enterprise and their highly variable access to financial and human resources. Two trends however were clear. First, a commitment to political marketing and media based campaigning was discernibly greater in all constituencies in 2001 than 15 years earlier.[2] Second, enthusiasm for media campaigning was more evident among Labour than Conservative or Liberal Democrat local parties: and always had been! The various studies, moreover, support Ericson's suggestion, that the relationship between local politicians and local news media is best understood as essentially collaborative rather than conflictual. By typically stressing the potential for conflict in journalist/politician relationships, however, (exemplified by the popular perception of the journalist as 'watchdog') this mutual reliance between the two groups can be overlooked. Locally, politicians and journalists seem to be locked into an exchange relationship in which 'insider' political information is traded for access to editorial space to disseminate messages congenial to a particular candidate, policy or ideology (Ericson *et al.*, 1989). Each side gains from this exchange and has a clear interest in sustaining collaborative rather than conflictual ways of working. In this sense, news becomes a negotiated outcome of this carefully structured exchange between politicians and journalists.

PARTY NEWS MANAGEMENT STRATEGIES

The effectiveness of local parties' news management activities is a significant factor shaping the extent and character of local newspapers' coverage of the constituency campaign in UK General Elections (Franklin 1989, 1992 and 1998). The period since 1987 has witnessed a growing concern to 'professionalise' the local campaign, with parties displaying an increasing enthusiasm and facility for using local news media as part of their broader campaigning strategies. In 1987, both the Conservative and Labour parties were aware of the campaigning potential which local media offered, but within each party it was possible to identify distinctive attitudes to local media and to characterise party election agents as either 'traditionalists' or 'modernists': the former predominated in the Conservative Party (Franklin, 1989, p. 217).

Traditionalists tended to dismiss the campaigning significance of the local press. They knew little about the organisation, ownership and readerships of local newspapers, attributed little influence to their political coverage and were professionally ill-equipped to orchestrate a media-based campaign. Perhaps unsurprisingly, traditionalists preferred the well-tested direct communication strategies of leafleting, canvassing and public meetings where they were more able to direct and control the content of political communications. Modernists, by contrast, were knowledgeable about local newspapers, understood their working regimes and the significance of deadlines across the news day. They were experienced in drafting press releases, convening press conferences and significantly, modernists perceived election news as a negotiated outcome of contacts between journalists and party personnel.

By 1992, there were no traditionalists in the Labour Party: a few remained among the Conservative ranks. The 1992 election marked a watershed for local party campaigning. Local media, especially local newspapers, assumed a central significance in parties' local campaigning strategies. The press officer became elevated to a central role in the campaign team.

Throughout the campaign parties issue press releases to local newspapers and radio stations informing them about specific events involving their candidate for that day. The time and location of events, as well as the details of possible photo opportunities are clearly specified. Press releases are written in a journalistic style and constructed in the form of a news story, but they also incorporate the particular 'spin' which the party wishes to place on the event. Parties claim that local journalists, who are typically under resourced and hard pressed to meet editorial deadlines, will often accept these well crafted press releases which, with the minimum of revision, can be published under the by-line of a local journalist or 'Political Correspondent'.

This political marketing activity typically begins well ahead of the actual campaign and constitutes a continuous and on-going party function between elections. A press officer interviewed after the 2001 election claimed:

> We began about six years ago, about two years before the 1997 election.
> The candidate had just been selected and wasn't well known in the
> constituency. So the priority was to get coverage every week in the run up to
> the election. So we would meet up and decide on story lines and most weeks
> we would get 3 or 4 stories in the local paper. During the recent election
> [2001] we had a good story in every day of the campaign showing our
> candidate as a local person serving the local community.

The purpose of this sustained marketing activity by parties seems unambitious but all party agents believe it achieves a crucial function: candidate recognition – to establish their candidate's identity with local voters. 'Local press coverage of your candidate is vital' a regional press officer claimed:

> You can't do anything without it. You really can't. You can't get your
> candidate into national media because they are not interested. Most people
> don't read the leaflets we put out and it is very hard to get one candidate to
> meet 75,000 people personally. So as many photographs as you can get over
> the four year period of your candidate or MP doing things that people will
> recognise, or at places that people will recognise. That is the number one
> task ... So we worked very very hard to get her in the local paper. And she
> was in more or less every day for about 18 months before the election,

sometimes with a photograph. And people started coming up to her in the
street and talked to her about local issues. And there was no other way of
getting her in front of people at that time.

Research studies from previous elections reveal that issuing press releases or 'information
subsidies' as Gandy described them (Gandy, 1982) is a highly effective marketing tool for
securing the coverage which party agents identify as central to a successful campaign. A
comparison of the press releases issued by the Labour Party in one constituency during
the 1992 general election, with the local newspaper's election coverage, revealed that 29
press releases generated 28 stories in the newspaper. The paper published at least one
story based on a press release each day of the campaign: on three days all coverage of the
Labour Party derived from party sources. Journalistic revision of press releases was
minimal. A third of the stories simply replicated the release verbatim: a further fifth made
modest revisions and published between 50 per cent and 75 per cent of the original text
of the press release. Local journalists were sceptical about press releases claiming that they
usually 'spiked them' but one local journalist conceded that 'the Labour Party was well
geared up, they had some good press releases, some good copy, so they got a decent share
of the coverage' (Franklin, 1994, pp. 166–72).

Given this success, it is perhaps unsurprising that press officers have come to enjoy a
considerably enhanced status in the local campaign team. Establishing a press office and
waging a concerted campaign via local media has become increasingly recognised as a
strategic necessity. A party official claimed:

> A campaign is about selling as much as anything: it's about promotion. So it
> means using all kinds of media to try and promote the candidate and the
> party. I think we are all getting a lot more aware of the power of local
> media and I think local media must be feeling that. I'm not sure that in
> 1983 we would have been putting out press releases. I think back to earlier
> times in the Labour Party and I'm not sure we would have said straightaway
> 'Who is the Press Officer' and 'You sort out your campaign team'. I think in
> those days we were a bit more blind about the importance of local media.

PRESS/PARTY RITUAL COLLABORATIONS

For their part, journalists and editors readily acknowledge that election reporting has
become a collaborative exercise between parties and journalists: a series of elaborate joint
rituals, protocols and pre-election meetings define the nature of the collaboration. The
collaboration, moreover, is routinised and highly regulated. When the election is called,
local newspaper editors arrange a meeting with candidates and party agents and establish
the conventions which will dictate coverage. But they also specify the role which they have
come to expect parties will play in coverage. This includes identifying the kinds of stories

they wish the parties to 'deliver' as well as the extent of coverage the paper will provide. These working arrangements between the local paper and political actors reflect the well-established protocols which govern the paper's 'peacetime' political coverage. The news editor on a local evening paper explained the very clear exchange basis on which the relationship between journalists and politicians rests: editorial space in exchange for news and information:

> We write to them [the parties] and set out what we hope to achieve, what our aims are, *what we are promising them and what we expect from them* [my emphasis]. Just basics really: then we speak to them. Me and the Editor have been here now for a couple of elections and two of the MPs were sitting MPs so in the past we've had the meeting in the office here. We asked them if they wanted to come in this time and they said 'Are you doing the same routine, because we know it so that's ok'. We talk to them regularly enough so there isn't a need to sit down and have a formal meeting. But there's always some candidates chosen about 6 months before the election, who are new to the area, so we have them in at that stage.

Editors expect parties to bring news stories to the paper and specify precisely the kind of stories they will publish. In previous years election news had enjoyed a special place in the editorial priorities of the local press. An election story was worthy of publication simply because it was an election story: this journalistic attitude shifted markedly with the 1997 election. From that date, election news was judged by the same news values as other stories. This 'deregulation' has 'opened up' the newspapers to potentially greater party influence and has created highly variable prospects for election coverage reflecting parties' access to marketing resources. Parties viewed these editorial changes differently: it placed the onus on them to deliver newsworthy stories if they wished to secure election coverage. These changed news priorities and their implications for parties were articulated clearly at pre election meetings. 'Years and years ago' an editor claimed:

> We used to have guidelines. 'You can have two picture stories this week' or 'you can have three stories' or whatever. This time we said to every candidate 'Tell us what you are doing and we will decide if we are going to report it and how we are going to report it' ... We give them advice. We tell them that their policy on private schools or this or that is interesting and we tell them that just reiterating what Blair or Hague said the night before won't get into our paper because it won't interest our readers. A story's got to prove its newsworthiness.

LEADING THE TANGO: THE DOMINANCE OF THE LOCAL PRESS

What is extremely significant here is the undisputed dominance of the local press in these ritualised press-party relationships: and by both parties to that relationship. Parties enjoy some considerable success in shaping election news, especially in the context of under resourced local newspapers, but most journalists and all politicians believed that newspapers remained dominant in this relationship of mutual complementarity, reversing Gans' celebrated dance metaphor that 'although it takes two to tango ... sources do the leading' (Gans, 1979, p. 116). Parties may, in certain circumstances and in certain settings, be successful in securing coverage of their candidates and policies. But such success is always achieved in the context of local newspapers setting the broader agenda, deciding and telling parties in advance of the election about the kinds of issue they wish parties to emphasise in press releases, as well as dictating the extent of coverage to be devoted to electoral concerns and its allocation between the various contesting parties. Party officials are in little doubt about who is dominant in this relationship. 'It is definitely a relationship with two sides' a party official acknowledged:

> The newspaper doesn't want to have nothing to report, but equally the MP wants good coverage. Neither side wants to fall out with the other too much but MPs certainly need newspapers more than the other way round ... I think newspapers are in the driving seat. It might be just the way I feel but it has always seemed to me that we are at their mercy: completely at their mercy. It doesn't matter whether you come up with the best story and the best picture in the world. If they don't feel like covering it, then they won't ... They have the upper hand. If you want to have news reported in a local paper then you have got to work with the people that are there. They can be as horrible as they like. And you just have to let them be.

This phenomenon of local media dominance is in stark contrast with the power relationships which characterise interactions between politicians and media nationally. The new Labour government, highly committed to marketing its policies and well equipped with marketing resources, increasingly deploys what has been described as a strategy of 'carrots and sticks' to exploit rivalries between national media outlets for 'scoops' to secure favourable coverage (Ingham in Select Committee on Public Administration, 1998, pp. 9–14). The relationship between the two groups is characterised less by collaboration than a government ambition to achieve compliance. But in a setting where local newspapers enjoy circulation monopoly, the power relationships between the two groups are reversed. Asked about pressures from party spin doctors a local journalist commented, 'there was one Conservative candidate in a Bradford constituency and he was used to bullying journalists and I could tell he was trying to lead me into a certain direction. You have got to be careful. But what have we got to lose? What have we got to lose by not following their agenda? Nothing!'

THE OUTCOME OF LOCAL NEGOTIATIONS: NEWSPAPER COVERAGE OF UK GENERAL ELECTIONS

The local press provided extensive and detailed coverage of the 2001 General Election. The 24 newspapers analysed published 1250 election related items (934 [74.7 per cent] articles, 64 [5.1 per cent] editorials and 252 [20.2 per cent] readers' letters) across the four weeks of the campaign and devoted 69,350 square centimetres of their columns to election news. Although remaining substantial, election coverage in 2001 was considerably less than in previous elections and represented a 15 per cent reduction on 1997 (81,542 square centimetres) and a striking 39 per cent reduction in overall reporting compared to the 1992 election (113,030 square centimetres). The mean size of articles in 2001 (55.5 square centimetres) was also down on the 1997 figure (65.5) but was virtually equivalent to the 1992 average of 54.8 column cms.

There were particular reasons to explain the reduced 'square footage' in 2001: in interviews journalists and editors recited them endlessly. Public apathy, the delayed election date, the absence of any political crisis or urgency, the narrowness of party differences, the alienation of the public from politics and politicians and an anticipated low turn out, signalled that 2001 would be a difficult election for journalists to sell to readers. But it was the sense of certainty about the eventual outcome which journalists cited most frequently: one journalist observed, 'It was almost a case of Man United playing Colchester'. Whether or not to cover the election at all and, if so, how much coverage to allocate, had been a topic for serious discussion at many papers. One editor acknowledged, 'In 1997 we sat down and asked "Is the election really worth the space we give it?" We decided yes. But this time the debate took longer. We knew turn out would be well down judging by the Euro and local election results, but we decided that the election is the one time when people do take some interest in politics'. Employing a different football metaphor, he suggested that 'from the news side of things, it's a bit like the cup final'.

But despite this decline in the overall *volume* of reporting of the 2001 election, local newspapers' coverage allocated to the distinctive editorial formats of articles, editorials and letters is broadly consistent across the four most recent General Elections: the exception here is the 1992 election (See Table 7.1).

The total number of published items in 2001 (1250) is very similar to the overall figures for election coverage in 1997 (1248) and 1987 (1194). Again there may be particular reasons which offer some explanation of the untypical blip in the 1992 coverage. First, reflecting trends in the national press, local newspapers experienced an unprecedented expansion in titles during the late 1980s: the sustained recession of the early 1990s, however, prompted closures. Consequently, the 13 free weekly newspapers in 1992 had reduced to 7 by 2001: by contrast the 9 paid weekly papers in the 1987 study had mushroomed to 15 by 1992. Second, by 1997 many local newspapers had adopted a

Table 7.1: **Local newspapers' election coverage in 1987, 1992, 1997 and 2001**

Year of election	Article	Editorial	Letter	Total
1987	921 (77.1%)	35 (2.9%)	238 (19.9%)	1194 (100%)
1992	1544 (74.9%)	42 (2.0%)	475 (23.0%)	2061 (100%)
1997	858 (68.8%)	86 (6.9%)	304 (24.4%)	1248 (100%)
2001	934 (74.7%)	64 (5.1%)	252 (20.2%)	1250 (100%)

changed approach to election reporting which emphasised the news value of a particular story rather than judging stories worthy of publication simply because they were *election* stories. These revised and more demanding editorial priorities might be anticipated to generate a lower story count.

Election reports in local newspapers in 2001, as in previous elections were accorded a highly variable news priority. The daily regional, the daily evening, the paid weeklies and the free weeklies formed a highly differentiated hierarchy of enthusiasm for election news (See Table 7.2).

Free weekly newspapers' reporting of the 2001 election displayed the indifference which characterised their previous election coverage. The seven free newspapers published only 23 election related items (21 articles and 2 letters) across the entire campaign. Free newspapers failed to publish a single editorial about the election and only two readers letters: the two letters, published on the same page in the *Aire Valley Target* on 31 May 2001, were identical. The *Calderdale News* with a free distribution in excess of 36,000 copies weekly carried no election reporting in 2001. But these aggregate data understate the extent to which the free press neglected election news because of the tendency for coverage to be focused in a single paper: the *Wharfe Valley Times* published 13 election stories or 56.5 per cent of free newspaper overall coverage. Journalists offered three reasons for lack of coverage. Free newspapers subscribe to a distinctive editorial style. An editor claimed 'they're meant to be entertaining: bright positive news that drops through your letterbox once a week to cheer you up, brighten you up. The election doesn't really fit into that agenda'. Limited space moreover means, 'you might run into problems with balance. You might get a bright story from the Liberals and another the next week, but then the election comes and that's all you've covered. If you want coverage that doesn't have holes you leave the election alone'. Finally, free newspapers recycle old news. Editorial is cannibalised from the paid weekly papers in the newspaper group: 'the Subs put them together very quickly but by the time the free paper comes out all the stories are a week old because they've already been in the paid paper'.

Table 7.2: **Items of election coverage by newspaper title**

Paper Title	Paper Type	Circulation	Article	Editorial	Letter	Row Total
Aire Valley Target	Free	49,630	2	–	2	4 (0.3%)
Bradford Star	Free	56,000	2	–	–	2 (0.2%)
Calderdale News	Free	36,000	–	–	–	–
Huddersfield Weekly News	Free	70,000	1	–	–	1 (0.1%)
Leeds Skyrack Express	Free	53,824	2	–	–	2 (0.2%)
Weekly Advertiser (Dewsbury)	Free	42,846	1	–	–	1 (0.1%)
Wharfe Valley Times	Free	45,732	13	–	–	13 (1.0%)
Batley News	Weekly	8,833	28	3	13	44 (3.5%)
Brighouse Echo	Weekly	6,450	45	2	3	50 (4.0%)
Colne Valley Chronicle	Weekly		17		8	25 (2.0%)
Dewsbury Reporter	Weekly	12,776	35	4	24	63 (5.0%)
Hebden Bridge Times	Weekly	3,788	15		5	20 (1.6%)
Heckmondwike Herald	Weekly	8,397	52	3	12	67 (5.4%)
Holme Valley Express	Weekly		17	–	8	25 (2.0%)
Huddersfield District Chronicle	Weekly		14	–	8	22 (1.8%)
Mirfield Reporter	Weekly	12,776	33	3	15	51 (4.1%)
Morley Advertiser	Weekly	3,556	11	–	6	17 (1.4%)
Morley Observer	Weekly	4,389	27	2	2	31 (2.5%)
Pudsey Times	Weekly	27,357	6	–	–	6 (0.5%)
Spenborough Guardian	Weekly	8,397	52	4	10	66 (5.3%)
Todmorden News	Weekly	4,977	14	–	2	16 (1.3%)
Wakefield Express	Weekly	31,937	22	–	3	25 (2.0%)
Halifax Courier	Daily evening	27,590	244	16	77	337 (27.0%)
Yorkshire Post	Daily regional	71,632	281	27	54	362 (29.0%)
Total			934 (74.7%)	64 (5.1%)	252 (20.2%)	1250 (100.0%)

By contrast, election reporting in the sampled paid weekly newspapers was vibrant and plentiful, but again journalists' commitment to coverage varied across the different newspapers. Coverage ranged between the 6 items published in the *Pudsey Times* to the more typical 67 items reported in the *Heckmondwike Herald*. Even newspapers with modest circulations like the *Spenborough Guardian* (8,397) and the *Brighouse Echo* (6,450) devoted considerable editorial attention to the election publishing 66 and 50 items respectively. The daily papers, the *Halifax Courier* (337) and the *Yorkshire Post* (362) published, on each day of the campaign, an average of more than 15 articles, readers' letters and editorials informing and involving readers in the unravelling election story.

Certain longitudinal trends concerning the extent of election coverage by the different types of newspaper across the four elections, are illustrated by Table 7.3.

First, election coverage in free newspapers peaked in 1992 (in common with many other aspects of local newspapers' election reporting) but slumped in 2001: and across all categories of election coverage. In 1987, free newspapers' election news represented 5.7 per cent of all newspaper coverage: equivalent figures for 1992 and 1997 were steady at 6.0 per cent and 5.9 per cent respectively. In 2001 however, the 23 election

Table 7.3: **Number of election items by newspaper type across 4 general elections**

Newspaper type	Item type	Year			
		1987	1992	1997	2001
Free	Article	50 (73.5%)	103 (83.7%)	54 (71.6%)	21 (91%)
	Editorial	0 (–)	3 (2.4%)	3 (4.1%)	0 (–)
	Letter	18 (26.5%)	17 (13.8%)	16 (23%)	2 (9%)
	Total	68 (100%)	123 (100%)	73 (100%)	23 (100%)
Weekly	Article	251 (71.1%)	595 (67.5%)	329 (73.8%)	388 (73.9%)
	Editorial	11 (3.1%)	12 (1.4%)	32 (7.4%)	21 (4%)
	Letter	86 (25.8%	274 (31.1%)	83 (18.8%)	119 (22.1%)
	Total	348 (100%)	881 (100%)	444 (100%)	528 (100%)
Daily	Article	231 (73.8%)	359 (68.6%)	167 (47.2%)	244 (72.4%)
	Editorial	4 (1.3%)	12 (2.3%)	25 (6.8%)	16 (4.7%)
	Letter	78 (24.9%)	152 (29.1%)	162 (46%)	77 (22.8%)
	Total	313 (100%)	523 (100%)	356 (100%)	337 (100%)
Regional	Article	389 (83.7%)	476 (91%)	308 (82.4)	281 (77.1%)
	Editorial	20 (4.3%)	15 (2.9%)	26 (7%)	27 (7.5%)
	Letter	56 (12%)	32 (6.1%)	41 (10.6%)	54 (15.5%)
	Total	465 (100%)	523 (100%)	375 (100%)	362 (100%)

stories in free newspapers accounted for a mere 1.8 per cent of coverage across all types of newspaper.

Second, paid weekly newspapers have broadly increased their election reporting across the 14 years of the study. In the main this trend reflects the increased publication of articles (from 251 in 1987 to 388 in 2001) although some modest increase in editorials offset by a slight decline in published letters is also evident across the study period.

Third, while daily evening newspaper coverage has remained largely constant, certain aspects of regional morning coverage has shifted. The article count, for example is substantially lower in 2001 (281) than in 1987 (389). The number of published letters has climbed steadily across the last three elections to match a similar sustained increase in published editorials. Overall what is striking is the general constancy of coverage across the newspapers which comprise the West Yorkshire press.

More significant than the *extent* of the election coverage is the *character* of the press reporting, especially the papers' ambition to articulate a *local* news agenda, their attempts to 'lighten' the electoral news agenda and make the election news entertaining and finally the degree of partisanship evident in coverage.

CONSTRUCTING AND REPORTING A LOCAL ELECTION AGENDA?

Local journalists' believe that a *good* election story is a *local* story. Such sentiments were expressed repeatedly in interviews. A senior editor claimed that a good election story is 'something that affects local people: a local issue. We had lots of Conservatives writing us letters about "stealth taxes" but to be honest I don't think people locally are interested'. Another editor confirmed that in pre-election meetings with candidates he advised them to deliver local stories if they wanted coverage. 'We tell them that we like local issues being addressed' he claimed 'and they tend to follow that as past practice shows ... So most of the stories we're carrying are actually local stories: all the issues of the town with the politicians getting involved. So it's not all tax and NHS. It's actually addressing local issues'.

Journalists' preoccupation with local stories received strong endorsement from political parties in 2001. Parties have always identified local issues as being attractive to journalists, but in 2001 local parties made special efforts to target local concerns and to stress the local nature of their candidates. These ambitions to 'go on the local issues especially in volatile seats' was a national party strategy. 'There was a determined effort by the national party' a press officer claimed 'to stress local issues. In the 246 seats that we won for the first time in 1997, we were all following the same plot: stressing the local. The candidate had to be a local person, who understood the constituency, the people and their problems and issues. It was definitely something that we were trying to emphasise, that over the last four years this candidate has got stuck in to tasks that people around here wanted to be done'.

The results of this substantial agitprop effort, was a flurry of newspaper stories, clearly based around parties' press releases, emphasising the local nature of candidates. A newspaper profile of one candidate, for example, quoted her confessing that 'I couldn't think of living anywhere else. I've lived here all my life (she can just about see the house in New Bond Street where she was born, from her office window), and I can't see me leaving . . . There's no place like Halifax'. An article on the opposite page announced that the same incumbent 'met up with a couple of ladies who she had worked with at Northowram Hospital many moons ago. (Does she know everyone in Halifax? It sometimes seems she does)' (*Halifax Courier*, 17 May 2001, pp. 4–5). As the campaign intensified candidates accused their opponents of being 'outsiders' or, using a disparaging local word, 'incomers'. In one Yorkshire constituency a candidate was denounced as being from Lancashire (an unforgivable trait) while another story alleged that if the Conservative candidate won he would be an 'alien MP for Halifax' (*Halifax Courier*, 6 June 2001, p. 6).

Analysis of newspapers' coverage established the prominence of a 'local' (733 – 58.6 per cent) focus in election reporting above items displaying an emphasis on 'national' (517 – 41.4 per cent) concerns. Indeed election coverage in 2001 was notably more locally oriented than in 1997 (49.7 per cent local), 1992 (47.7 per cent local) or 1987 (44.7 per cent local). But the issue of local and national coverage proved considerably more complex than these bald figures might suggest with different newspapers displaying distinctive commitments to local news (See Table 7.4).[3]

Table 7.4 illustrates the gently descending hierarchy constituted by the various local newspapers' divergent concerns with local issues. At one end of the scale, 86.4 per cent of free weekly papers editorial is devoted to local matters while the regional morning paper

Table 7.4: **Local and national emphases in different types of newspaper**

| | *Type of Issue Reported in Item* | | | | *Total* | |
| | *Local* | | *National* | | | |
	Count	*Row %*	*Count*	*Row %*	*Count*	*Row %*
Weekly paid	19	86.4%	3	13.6%	22	100.0%
Daily	421	79.6%	108	20.4%	529	100.0%
Free Weekly	204	60.5%	133	39.5%	337	100.0%
Regional	89	24.6%	273	75.4%	362	100.0%
Total	733	58.6%	517	41.4%	1259	100.0%

the *Yorkshire Post* offers only scant account of local concerns (24.6 per cent of items) and is predictably more focused in its columns on the national and international dimensions to election stories (75.4 per cent).

The complexity of local press coverage does not end here. Table 7.5 illustrates not merely the extent to which different editorial formats correlate with different emphases on the 'local' or the 'national' in election coverage, but a more significant and interesting phenomenon. Since articles can be considered an expression of journalists' issue agenda, while letters articulate readers' preferred concerns, Table 7.5 reveals nothing less than the highly divergent appetites of journalists and readers for local and national news and the degree to which these two communities pursue distinctive issue agendas. This divergence is curious on at least two counts. First, these two groups seem to be talking past each other with little if any shared interest in the particular focus of election concerns. Second, while journalists perennially claim to be market led, providing their readers with the local stories they demand and which allegedly constitute the 'bread and butter' of local journalism, for their part readers express little interest in local concerns and seem to be obsessed with national issues.

Table 7.5: **Local and national emphases in election coverage by editorial format**

Format	Type of issue reported		Total
	Local	National	
Article	646 (69.2%)	288 (30.8%)	934 (100%)
Editorial	22 (34.4%)	42 (65.6%)	64 (100%)
Letter	65 (25.8%)	187 (74.2%)	252 (100%)
Total	733 (58.6%)	517 (41.4%)	1250 (100%)

Two findings are striking. First, while almost 70 per cent of articles are locally oriented expressing journalists' ambitions to provide readers with election stories with a focus on local issues, only 25.8 per cent of readers letters share this local concern. By contrast, 74 per cent of readers' letters concentrate on national matters. Local journalists, at least so far as election coverage is concerned, seem to be talking past, rather than to, their readerships. But if journalists have wrongly attributed an interest in local issues to their readers, they are not alone, given parties' declared preoccupation with local matters and local candidates in their media campaigning strategies. Second, Table 7.5 illustrates the disjuncture between journalists' approaches to election coverage within the same newspapers. The journalistic focus on the local, so evident in articles (69.2 per cent), finds no equivalent among the senior group of journalists who write the editorials where the preferred predominant focus (65.6 per cent) is on national policies and issues. Some journalists appear to be closer to their readers' interests and concerns than others. The distinctive electoral agendas of journalists and readers are revealed when the thematic priorities expressed in articles and letters are compared (See Table 7.6).[4]

Table 7.6: **Comparison of the thematic priorities of articles and letters**

Rank	Article focus	Percentage	Letter	Percentage
1	Candidate	52.7%	Europe	17.0%
2	'Horse Race'/Poll results	8.5%	Taxation	13.5%
3	Europe	7.7%	Candidate	12.9%
4	Education	4.3%	Welfare/Social Services	9.9%
5	Crime/Juvenile Crime	3.8%	Religion	8.8%
6	Health/NHS	3.7%	Health/NHS	7.0%
7	Taxation	3.6%	Regional Policy	4.7%
8	Welfare/Social Services	2.8%	Apathy/Alienation	4.7%
9	Industry	2.4%	Economic Management	3.5%
10	Agriculture/Foot & Mouth	2.3%	Public Expenditure	3.5%
11	Race/Immigration/Asylum	2.1%	Race/Immigration/Asylum	3.5%
12	Economic Management	1.6%	Education	2.9%
13	Regional Policy	1.6%	Crime/Juvenile Crime	2.9%
14	John Prescott and the egg protest	1.6%	John Prescott and the egg protest	2.9%
15	Transport	1.4%	Industry	2.3%
Total		100%		100%

For readers, the two key issues in their wide ranging electoral agenda are Europe (17 per cent) and taxation (13.5 per cent), but these topics figure much less prominently in journalists' concerns (Europe 3rd – 7.7 per cent and taxation 7th – 3.6 per cent). In pole position for journalists, in a much narrower agenda, is 'candidate' (52.7 per cent) reflecting their ambition (a constant theme in interviews) to present readers with information about candidates and to stress candidates' 'localness'. This theme does overlap journalists' and readers' five most frequently cited items, but occurs in third place in readers' priorities (12.9 per cent). Even this limited concern with candidates requires qualification, however, since parties are both legendary and effective in orchestrating letter writing campaigns to the local press during elections: especially 'knocking' letters about opponents. One journalist commented that 'we get to know the same typewriter – some very boring letters especially about the pound'. Consequently, a good number of these letters about candidates might therefore reflect party, rather than reader interests.

There are many other divergences between readers' and journalists' priorities expressed in Table 7.6. Education and Crime, which rank 4th and 5th respectively in journalists' agenda are well down the listings at 12th and 13th for readers. Similarly, journalist preoccupation with polls and the horse race element of the election (ranked 2nd) and the significant issue of agriculture and the foot and mouth outbreak (10th) find no resonance in the readership agenda.

In summary, local newspaper reporting during the 2001 General Election remained predominantly local: in truth coverage was more local in 2001 than in previous elections. But the local flavour of coverage varied radically across different newspapers in the local press and, within the same type of newspaper, across distinctive editorial formats. These findings challenge journalists' claims to be addressing readers' concerns in their election coverage. For their part, readers' preoccupation with a national election agenda may simply reflect the fact that for the first time in 2000, regional television surpassed local newspapers as the prominent source of news for a mjority of people. Regionally based television tends more than local newspapers to foreground national above local concerns.

BOOZE, BEARDS AND BACKSIDES! DUMBING DOWN THE ELECTORAL AGENDA?

Reporting of the 2001 general election was conducted in a nadir of public apathy about politics and politicians: at 59 per cent of the voting population, the eventual turnout was the lowest since 1918. Politicians and journalists anticipated that this would be a difficult election to sell to their respective audiences; citizens and readers.

Journalists responded in two ways. First, most confirmed that they were 'happy to lighten it to keep the readers interested'. One time-tested editorial strategy is to report quirky, amusing stories which nonetheless retain a link with the political or electoral mood. In 1997, for example a number of newspapers reported the outcome of children's elections conducted at local schools: other papers carried the story about a local butcher who was selling red (Labour), blue (Conservative) and Yellow (Liberal Democrat) sausages on election day (Franklin and Parry, 1998, p. 217).

Analysis of newspaper contents confirmed the increased emphasis on such gimmicky and quirky stories in the recent election. In 2001, nearly a quarter (295 – 24 per cent) of all published items were coded as quirky or amusing compared to 230 (19 per cent) in 1987. The increase here is modest but clear. 'Pick Up Your Party' for example, an article on

'Election Ales', replaced sausages with beer and announced that a local supermarket was selling Red Flag Bitter, True Blue Bitter, Alliance Bitter and Nationalist Brew (*Halifax Courier*, 25 May 2001, p. 13). The more sober *Yorkshire Post*, reported a poll of 999 members of the public to assess their reaction to the leaders of the three main parties growing facial hair: the headline announced 'Growing Beards Would Shave Votes off Voters, Party Leaders Warned' (4 June 2001). The overwhelming majority of respondents disapproved, but the paper evidently believed the poll results justified the airbrushing of beards on photographs of the party leaders. The visual effect was not as crude as a marker pen on an election poster, but the flamboyance of the facial hair inscribed on politician's' portraits made clear the newspapers' intention to 'keep the readers interested'.

A final example. On 31 May the *Morley Observer* carried an editorial headed 'Bottoms Up For A Politician Free Week' in celebration of 'National Bottoms Week': an almost identical editorial was published in the *Dewsbury Reporter* (a sister paper within the same newspaper group) on 25 May 2001 entitled 'Getting To The Bottom Of Things – Away From Politics'. Ultimately this turned out to be another poll story! 'We can't help thinking that most people will be more than happy if we give politicians and the General Election a wide berth this week' the Editor suggested, as he reported the findings of a national poll which revealed 'that Tony Blair is generally regarded as having the best rear of the party leaders with William Hague, well, bottom. Charles Kennedy, as you would expect, occupies the middle ground'. A journalist on the same newspaper who was asked about this particular editorial argued, 'We were really worried about overkill. So I think he tried to lighten it ... It's been hard work. We've all been walking on treacle for the last four weeks. And we felt that people had just about had enough'.

A second editorial strategy for engaging readers with the election was more significant and seemed to have been adopted almost universally by local newspapers. It involved devoting coverage in the early stages of the election to highly personalised candidate profiles which sought to engage readers' interest through a human interest focus rather than any discussion of candidates' policy commitments: a substantial proportion of local election news was refracted through the prism of human interest. A senior editor explained:

> We decided for the poor readers' sake that we were going to make the
> election as interesting as we could. So my suggestion was that we interview
> the candidates as people as well as politicians – get pictures of them at
> home with their family – and try to find out why they came into politics and
> what they hoped to achieve: rather than go on their policies.

Such a strategy reinforced local journalists' enthusiasm for focusing on political celebrities. One local paper profiled Ann Taylor a well-known and senior member of the Labour Party. The editorial emphasis was on 'her high profile job, how she could do it as a mother and the small things like her clothes and how she's started wearing make up because she's going on television. It might seem rather banal but it does grab the reader seeing the person and how she has had her haircut'. These profiles also allowed journalists to stress candidates local credentials. The Conservative candidate, for example, was a barrister:

> But he was born in a one up and one down council house with an outside toilet and his grandma was a single mum. So I went on that and said in my introduction that he isn't your typical 'pin stripe' Barrister parachuted in from down south: he's a local lad and he's standing on that. Oh, and his granddad was the local preacher at the Heckmondwike upper Chapel.

This strategy of writing personalised candidate profiles to promote readers' interest in the election resulted in a considerable increase in election stories focused on candidates rather than policies. In previous elections parties had expressed precisely these concerns that journalists might pay insufficient attention to explorations of policy. In 2001 a striking 552 (44.2 per cent) items of election coverage focused on candidates at the expense of policy (698 – 55.8 per cent): in 1987 the equivalent figures were 394 (33 per cent) and 798 (66.8 per cent).

Many journalists denied that this approach representing any 'dumbing down' of the election coverage, but some were undoubtedly uncomfortable, if not defensive, about this editorial approach. 'I hope it doesn't come across as tacky' a journalist commented 'because it wasn't done in a sensational way and it always seemed to swing around to politics anyway because politicians didn't want to talk about their private lives'. Some journalists, moreover, genuinely believed that it was equally important to provide readers with an insight into candidates, their personalities and their personal histories, as much as their policies. 'We wanted to show that these were real flesh and blood human people with foibles' one seasoned journalist remarked 'with things to be proud of but foibles as well'. There was also an opportunity towards the end of the campaign for candidates to draft a personalised policy statement which the paper agreed to publish because, as a journalist commented 'we knew they were itching to get their policies into print. So we said to them, the week before the election we will give you 450 words to write how you would run the country and to put your national policies forward. And they were happy with that'. Local journalists' endeavours to engage their readers with an election which was widely judged to be unnecessary and uninteresting involved them in some professional compromises.

DISRUPTING A 'BALANCE OF PARTISANSHIP': NEWSPAPERS, POLITICS AND THE 2001 ELECTION

Party allegations of press partisanship in election coverage are routine and keenly felt: journalists' protestations of innocence are similarly forceful. One regional press officer complained vehemently about what she believed to be the biased reporting of her candidate. She also made some unequivocal statements about the perceived importance of the local newspaper to the outcome of the campaign. 'I would go so far as to say that the local paper is a Kingmaker' she argued. 'I spent a long time fighting that campaign and worrying about why it was so hard, why it was so awful. And I came to the conclusion that it was in large part due to the local newspaper. So that is how important they are. They actually have the ability to potentially win and lose elections, if they are that biased.' Press partisanship is evidently contentious. Newspaper editors typically assign a junior reporter to count column inches, measure photographs and monitor coverage.

This study employed a number of indicators to measure partisanship, but the most decisive is the comparison of the number of positive and negative appraisals each political party receives in press coverage.[5] On this account, previous studies revealed a 'balance of partisanship'. This seemingly paradoxical phrase implied that the overall balance in press coverage, achieved across the West Yorkshire region, did not result from aggregating the 'balanced' reporting of a number of individual newspapers but, on the contrary, reflected the partisan sentiments expressed in one newspaper being counterbalanced or neutralised by the differing political commitments of a different newspaper. In 1997, for example, the Conservative Party received 889 press appraisals of which 308 (34.6 per cent) were positive compared to 789 appraisals for the Labour Party of which 287 (36.4 per cent) were positive. Journalists would be hard pressed to produce a more equitable balance between parties in their election coverage: especially across 1248 items of coverage reported in 25 different newspapers. But the partisan sentiments of the press became apparent when the appraisals of parties in particular newspapers' coverage was analysed. In 1997, for example, The *Yorkshire Post* was strongly supportive of the Conservatives: the *Halifax Courier* was less critical of the Labour Party. This 'balance of partisanship' has not been sustained in press reporting of the 2001 election disrupting a pattern of election coverage evident since 1987(see Table 7.7).

Three findings emerge from Table 7.7. First, the overall balance of partisanship which characterised press coverage of previous elections has been disrupted. In 2001, the West Yorkshire press reported the Conservative Party more favourably than the Labour Party with coverage including a higher percentage of negative than positive appraisals of the Labour Party. The Conservative Party received an aggregate 751 appraisals of which 345 (45.9 per cent) were positive compared to Labour's overall 1245 appraisals of which 462 (37.1 per cent) were positive. The Labour Party received considerably more press attention than the Conservatives (494 appraisals) but a substantial proportion of these (377 or 76.3 per cent) were critical. 2001, of course, was the only occasion across the four studies when the Labour Party entered the election following a period in government: journalists as well as challenger politicians enjoy criticising governments. But, the Conservative Party risked similar journalistic opprobrium in 1987, 1992 and 1997 and on those occasions the balance of partisanship was sustained. The erosion of this balance is illustrated neatly in Table 7.8.

Table 7.7: **Positive and negative appraisals of parties in local newspapers**

Paper Title	Paper Type	Conservative		Labour		Liberal Democrat	
		Positive	Negative	Positive	Negative	Positive	Negative
Aire Valley Target	Free	0	0	0	0	0	0
Bradford Star	Free	1	0	1	0	1	0
Calderdale News	Free	0	0	0	0	0	0
Huddersfield Weekly News	Free	0	0	0	0	0	0
Leeds Skyrack Express	Free	0	0	0	0	0	0
Weekly Advertiser (Dewsbury)	Free	0	0	1	1	0	0
Wharfe Valley Times	Free	6	3	7	8	5	0
Batley News	Weekly	15	15	16	15	5	2
Brighouse Echo	Weekly	6	11	23	14	9	0
Colne Valley Chronicle	Weekly	10	10	8	8	3	1
Dewsbury Reporter	Weekly	21	13	22	56	10	4
Hebden Bridge Times	Weekly	9	10	10	16	9	3
Heckmondwike Herald	Weekly	23	26	29	41	16	2
Holme Valley Express	Weekly	10	11	8	9	2	1
Huddersfield District Chronicle	Weekly	8	10	7	7	1	0
Mirfield Reporter	Weekly	8	7	8	30	7	4
Morley Advertiser	Weekly	2	4	4	8	0	0
Morley Observer	Weekly	7	18	18	16	6	1
Pudsey Times	Weekly	6	2	7	3	2	0
Spenborough Guardian	Weekly	23	23	29	40	16	2
Todmorden News	Weekly	8	10	9	16	9	3
Wakefield Express	Weekly	6	7	14	20	10	0
Halifax Courier	Daily evening	68	86	124	166	46	12
Yorkshire Post	Daily regional	108	140	117	309	34	40
Total		345	406	462	783	191	75
		(45.9%)	(54.1%)	(37.1%)	(62.9%)	(71.8%)	(28.2%)

Second, the Liberal Democrats are the only party to enjoy a positive overall appraisal by the local press. The party received 266 appraisals of which 191 (71.8 per cent) were positive. This tendency was evident in all previous studies. This supportive coverage seems to reflect little more than the extent to which the party was marginalised in the perceptions of rival parties and journalists. In the context of negative campaigning, the Liberal Democrats were rarely judged to be the main oppositions by the two major parties

Table 7.8: **Local newspapers' appraisals of parties**

Year of Election	Conservative		Labour		Liberal Democrat	
	Positive	Negative	Positive	Negative	Positive	Negative
1987	513	839	420	721	276	205
	(37.9%)	(62.1%)	(36.8%)	(63.2%)	(57.4%)	(42.6%)
1992	889	1524	977	1750	601	373
	(36.8%)	(63.2%)	(35.8%)	(64.2%)	(61.7%)	(38.3%)
1997	308	581	287	502	122	107
	(34.6%)	(65.4%)	(36.4%)	(63.6%)	(53.3%)	(46.7%)
2001	345	406	462	783	191	75
	(45.9%)	(54.1%)	(37.1%)	(62.9%)	(71.8%)	(28.2%)
Total	2055	3350	2146	3756	1190	760
	(38.0%)	(62.0%)	(36.4%)	(63.6%)	(61.0%)	(39.0%)

and consequently failed to draw their fire: strategically, the party was considered unworthy of disdaining. Most journalists, likewise, did not view the Liberal Democrats as potential winners in many constituencies and, given journalists' interests in the 'horse race' the party received only approximately one fifth and one third of the coverage allocated to the Labour and Conservative parties.

Third, the partisan commitments of particular newspapers are evident in their election coverage as in previous studies. While the *Batley News* remained strikingly balanced in its coverage, The *Yorkshire Post* published 248 appraisals of the Conservative Party of which 108 (43.6 per cent) were positive, but only 117 (25.5 per cent) of the paper's 426 appraisals of the Labour Party were similarly positive. At the *Dewsbury Reporter*, 21 (61.8 per cent) of the 34 published appraisals of the Conservative Party were positive whereas only 22 (28.2 per cent) of the 78 published appraisals of Labour were positive. Across the paid weekly newspapers, only the *Brighouse Echo* reported the Labour Party more favourably than the Conservatives.

Two other features of press partisanship during the 2001 election are noteworthy. First, newspapers' expressed attitudes to the various political parties differ markedly across distinctive editorial formats (see Table 7.9).

Table 7.9 reveals that journalists are more evenhanded in their reporting of both major parties than editors and readers. The Conservative Party, for example, enjoys 49.4 per cent positive commentary in articles compared to the overall coverage (45.9 per cent positive) while journalists also strike a more balanced note in their reports of the Labour

Table 7.9: **Local newspapers' appraisals of parties by editorial format**

Item type	Conservative		Labour		Liberal Democrat	
	Positive	Negative	Positive	Negative	Positive	Negative
Article	259	265	384	478	184	54
	(49.4%)	(50.6%)	(44.5%)	(55.5%)	(77.3%)	(22.7%)
Editorial	20	17	19	68	0	8
	(54.1%)	(45.9%)	(21.8)	(78.2%)	(0%)	(100%)
Letter	66	124	59	237	7	13
	(34.7%)	(65.3%)	(19.9%)	(80.1%)	(35.0%)	(65.0%)
Total	345	406	462	783	191	75
	(45.9%)	(54.1%)	(37.1%)	(62.9%)	(71.8%)	(28.2%)

Party (44.5 per cent positive) than is evident in the overall coverage (37.1 per cent positive). Journalists continue, however, to report Conservatives slightly more favourably (49.4 per cent positive) than Labour (44.5 per cent positive). But significantly Labour is ravaged in editorials. Almost four-fifths (78.2 per cent) of the commentary on the Labour Party is critical in editorials, whereas the Conservative Party basks in a surplus of positive (54.1 per cent) appraisals. Readers' letters are, perhaps predictably more critical of both parties than journalists and notably more critical of Labour (80.1 per cent negative) than Conservatives (65.3 per cent negative).[6]

Second, local press coverage became more hostile towards the Conservative Party as the campaign progressed but warmed in its response to Labour's campaigning initiatives (see Table 7.10).

Table 7.10 reveals that when the percentage of positive comments about each party published each week is analysed, the Conservative Party enjoyed supportive coverage (59.30 per cent) in the local press during the week in which the election was called (but before parliament was dissolved) and during the first week of the campaign (53.6 per cent): but thereafter positive press commentary declined until by the final week of the campaign only 33.1 per cent of reported commentary was positive. By contrast, the reporting of the Labour Party remained predominantly negative across the campaign but grew more supportive: from 34.8 per cent positive in the pre-dissolution week to 41.5 per cent in the final week of the campaign. It is possible that local press reports simply reflected the increasingly pessimistic prognoses in national media about the likelihood of a Conservative victory: alternatively it might have been a response to the more vigorous media based campaign conducted by the Labour Party in these local constituencies. Labour Party officials offered a pragmatic explanation.

Table 7.10: **Local newspapers' appraisals of parties during the election**

Week of Campaign	Conservative		Labour		Liberal Democrat	
	Positive	Negative	Positive	Negative	Positive	Negative
Pre-dissolution	54	37	48	90	6	5
	(59.3%)	(40.7%)	(34.8%)	(65.2%)	(54.5%)	(45.5%)
1	52	45	70	113	33	19
	(53.6%)	(46.4%)	(38.3%)	(61.7%)	(63.5%)	(36.5%)
2	81	96	85	178	48	11
	(45.7%)	(54.3%)	(32.3%)	(67.7%)	(81.4%)	(18.6%)
3	117	145	173	281	88	29
	(44.7%)	(55.3%)	(38.1%)	(61.9%)	(75.2%)	(24.8%)
4	41	83	86	121	16	11
	(33.1%)	(66.9%)	(41.5%)	(58.5%)	(59.3%)	(40.7%)
Total	345	406	462	783	191	75
	(45.9%)	(54.1%)	(37.1%)	(62.9%)	(71.8%)	(28.2%)

Our people were in Westminster and theirs were all in the constituencies. Blair made the announcement at about two in the afternoon. Within ten minutes the Tory candidate had her four-wheel vehicle with Tory posters plastered all over it, driving up and down the middle of the town centre. Within ten minutes she was there with her blue rosette meeting people. We couldn't do anything like that because our candidate was the MP and stuck in London ... We had the advantage in 1997 because our people were in the constituencies and theirs were in Westminster. But this time it was noticeable that they had the first week to rush about, organising events and having their photographs taken: our people were in London thinking 'how am I going to get this fax machine home on the train'.

CONCLUSIONS

Local newspapers' reporting of the general election represents what has been termed a 'negotiated outcome' reflecting the distinctive relations between journalists and local parties in particular settings. Both sides of this relationship derive benefits from working collaboratively rather than in ways which generate conflict. The relationship is essentially a trading relationship in which newspapers offer parties editorial space and opportunities to convey messages to voters in return for insider information about political events and activities. These relationships vary widely reflecting the resources, skills and energy which each side can muster. A senior national politician with a coterie of press officers and special advisors is more likely to win favourable coverage in a small circulation local newspaper, with few journalists or financial resources, than when dealing with a large circulation regional newspaper with a specialist political correspondent. These power and resource relationships between press and party display a considerable diversity across different constituencies and, along with the party preferences of readers and newspapers, help to shape the eventual character of the election coverage.

There is a crucial difference, however, between press/politician relationships in the national and local setting. In the local setting the press is dominant: politicians and journalists concur in this judgement. A local party with an effective media strategy can undoubtedly use local news media to 'get its message across', but the local party always operates within parameters established by the local press. Local newspapers dictate very clearly the extent and character of coverage which they are prepared to offer to local parties across the election period. Moreover, a growing editorial indifference to election news, in tandem with an editorial preference for 'lighter' stories, means that newspapers increasingly place the onus on local parties to deliver election stories for publication. Journalists have become more passive, while retaining their dominance, in press/party relationships. Parties fully understand the limits which local newspapers impose on their news management aspirations but also believe that there are nonetheless considerable electoral advantages to be gained from planning and operationalising a media-based campaign at constituency level. Small gatherings of the party faithful in draughty village halls are a campaign anachronism. The sight of party zealots canvassing reluctant residents, aggrieved by the interruption to their evening meal or their favourite soap opera, have become much rarer. Parties increasingly subscribe to the view that their political messages are best communicated, and the hearts and minds of voters most effectively won, not in poorly attended meetings or in acrimonious doorstep encounters, but most subtly and persuasively in the columns of the local 'rag'.

1   Two methodological techniques have been deployed to generate data for these election studies. First, semi-structured interviews have been conducted with journalists and editors of local newspapers as well as political candidates, their agents and press officers for the three major political parties (Conservative, Labour and Liberal Democrat) in 10 West Yorkshire constituencies located in central England: Batley and Spen; Bradford North; Bradford South; Colne Valley; Halifax; Leeds East; Leeds North; Leeds West; Pudsey and Wakefield. Second, each item of election coverage (article, editorial or reader's letter) in a comprehensive sample of free weekly, paid weekly newspapers and daily evening and regional morning newspapers, circulating in the ten constituencies, was coded for 38 variables (including, for example, partisanship in coverage, incumbency status of candidate, the type of newspaper, the use of photographs and headlines, etc) across the campaign period and analysed using SPSSx. The author is grateful to the Nuffield Foundation for its financial support for the studies conducted in 1992, 1997 and most recently in 2001.

2   There have been significant developments in local newspapers and local electoral politics across the study period. The number of local newspapers, for example, has shifted radically expressing the launch of new titles and the closure of others. The 21 newspapers reporting the elections in 1987, had grown markedly to 31 by 1992, but declined to 25 by 1997 and reduced further to 24 by 2001. Circulations also dipped, reflecting more general trends to declining number of titles and circulations throughout the UK local press. Sales of the daily

Yorkshire Post reduced from 87000 in 1987 to 77,535 in 1997; by 2001 it had declined markedly to 71,632. Circulation figures for the *Batley News* reveal a similar pattern with the 1987 readership of 12,843 dipping to 9,156 in 1997 and 8,833 in 2001. These changes have been accompanied by significant shifts in patterns of newspaper ownership. Half the newspapers in the 1987 study were independently (often family) owned by small local companies: by 1997 all newspapers had been incorporated into large media conglomerates.

Political change has also been evident. In 1987 the ten constituencies in the study were represented by 4 Conservative, 4 Labour and 2 Liberal Democrat MPs: political balance had been a crucial criterion informing the selection of constituencies for study. Following the 1997 election all constituencies had elected a Labour member: Ten Labour incumbents entered the 2001 contest.

3   All items of election reporting were assigned to one of four categories reflecting their focus on national or local concerns: 'local'; 'predominantly local with national'; 'predominantly national with local'; 'national'. In 2001 the great majority of items were distinctly 'local' or 'national' and consequently the categories were conflated.

4   The thematic contents of articles and letters were coded for 29 issues/themes. Table 7.6 lists the 15 most frequently occurring themes.

5   The other three indicators include: party prominence (measured quantitatively) in press coverage; the number of published quotations by party spokespeople, and; the number of photographs of party members. But while these indicators measure which party has been the beneficiary of press coverage they do not indicate the political direction of the press coverage. The Conservative Party, for example, might enjoy substantial but highly critical coverage. Consequently it is the assessment of the number of positive and critical appraisals which each party receives which offers the definitive judgement.

6   It is important to note that readers' letters are subject to editorial selection which may favour vociferous, opinionated and critical letters above more measured letters which may get spiked. In brief letters which are published may not be representative of the letters which a paper receives. Parties, moreover, typically make great efforts to 'fix' the letters' page by submitting letters which are highly critical of their political opponents.

Chapter Eight

PARLIAMENTARY ☐ COMMUNICATIONS: 'THE BEST SHOW IN TOWN?'

Bernard Weatherill, the Speaker of the House in 1989 when cameras first began to broadcast from the Commons, described the resulting parliamentary programmes as 'the best show in town' (Franklin, 1992, p. 3). The theatrical metaphor was appropriate since one of the most persistent objections of opponents of the cameras was that television would trivialise the Commons' proceedings by incorporating Parliament into the entertainment industry. Conservative MP Roger Gale alleged that MP-TV might become mere 'info-tainment' (Gale, 1992, p. 106). A similar attitude and reluctance characterised politicians' approach to press reporting of parliamentary affairs: an attitude described by one observer as 'conservative and cack-handed' (Sparrow, 2003, p. 5). When journalists were initially allowed into the chamber, they were not permitted to take their pens with them which made a good memory a prerequisite for a career in journalism. The parliamentary reporters on *The Times* were legendary for their powers of recall. Sketch writers have always been less popular with members than the gallery reporters. From Charles Dickens who published *Sketches by Boz* in the *Morning Chronicle* during the 1830s (Parris, 2002, p. 368) to contemporary observers such as Quentin Letts and Simon Hoggart, sketch writers have declared themselves, 'not interested in straight Parliamentary coverage' but only interested 'in cheap jokes, unfair barbs and a slanted version of the day's events'. Simon Hoggart concedes that 'some MPs hate it. Tony Benn ... curled his lip with contempt when he told me he never read what I wrote' (Hoggart, 2002a, p. ii). But even sketch writers allegedly 'no longer take the proceedings as seriously as they did' (McKie, 1999, p. 8). Given this scepticism and, on occasion, hostility by politicians towards media, it is perhaps unsurprising that television should have been excluded from the House of Commons until as recently as 1989.

The argument here is that while critics were undoubtedly correct to suggest that televising Parliament risked trivialising proceedings in the House, by focusing on highly newsworthy events such as Prime Ministers Questions to the neglect of more sober and reflective events such as those on the committee corridor, the arrival and consequences of cameras in the Commons has been more complex. Two significant developments characterise the decade or more since television broadcasting began.

First, contra these early claims about trivialising the Commons, the major concern expressed by journalists and academic observers during the 1990s, has been the evident marginalising of parliament in news reports. The decade has witnessed a marked decline in television coverage of Parliament (Coleman, 1999; McKie, 1998; Negrine, 1998): similarly in newspapers, the absence of parliamentary coverage is notable (Franklin 1996, 1996a, 1997; Riddell 1998; Straw, 1993 and 1999). The reasons for this decline in reporting are complex, but I would argue that parliamentary coverage has become a victim of successive governments' preoccupation with news management and policy promotion. One concrete example of this preoccupation is the increasing tendency for politicians, especially Ministers and senior politicians, to prioritise appearances on television and radio to announce policy initiatives, above making statements in the House.

There is a second significant trend. The current but much diminished coverage of parliament focuses overwhelmingly on ministers and the front benches to the exclusion of other parliamentary players. Journalists' news values, which favour celebrity, conflict and a focus on powerful, authoritative politicians, resonate closely with government's news management strategies intended to promote senior politicians. The 'best show in town' now offers star billing to the government of the day and a handful of senior politicians. The prime minister 'tops the bill' and delivers a carefully rehearsed and professionally crafted script of soundbites: in the prevailing presidentialism, the parliamentary agenda is lost. Back-benchers are typically ignored by journalists and cast in the role of audience for this ever more insignificant drama. Parliament has become merely another forum where policy is packaged for citizens' consumption but, paradoxically, a significant consequence of this growing news management has been to re-cast a key player into a minor role. This marginalising of Parliament has been resisted. In April 1998, Speaker Boothroyd condemned the government's practice of 'trailing' policy announcements in news media and warned the prime minister and senior ministers to 'rein in their apparatchiks and media spin doctors' (*Guardian*, 9 April 1998, p. 5). Five years later, Speaker Martin felt obliged to rebuke a senior minister for detailing changes to education policy on BBC's *Breakfast With Frost* before announcing them to the House (*Guardian*, 31 January 2003, p. 6).

This chapter explores the relationship between Parliament and the media by addressing four key questions. First, why have MPs been so wary of the media until recently and, more specifically, what objections did they raise to televising the House? Second, have members' misgivings about the media been confirmed or confounded by the experience of television broadcasting? Third, why has newspaper reporting of the House declined so dramatically across the 1990s? Finally, what political or electoral advantages, if any, might the different political parties try to achieve as a result of cameras in the Commons?[1]

PARLIAMENT AND NEWS MEDIA: THE DEBATE ABOUT TELEVISING THE COMMONS

The parliamentary use of the term 'Strangers' betrays a great deal about the House of Commons' traditional attitude towards towards the public: but especially the media. Historically, Parliament's relationship with the media has been characterised by a certain coyness, if not suspicion, combined with a good deal of concern that too close a relationship with the media might pervert the traditions and procedures of the place. Consequently, progress towards the broadcasting of Parliament has proved tardy.

For their part, broadcasters have always been enthusiasts of parliamentary broadcasting: the first issue of the *Radio Times* (28 September 1923) published a front page article by Arthur Burrows, director of programmes, who argued that broadcasting from the House was 'bound to happen' (Hill, 1993, p. 39). But in 1923, the House refused John Reith permission to broadcast the King's 'gracious speech' opening the new parliamentary session, while in 1942, even Winston Churchill's suggestion that his wartime speeches could be recorded for later broadcasting was unacceptable to a majority of MPs who believed that such a precedent might have propagandist implications in peacetime (Seymour-Ure, 1974, p. 139). In 1949, The Beveridge Committee rejected the idea of televising Parliament, arguing that it would have 'probable effects which most people in Britain would think harmful' (Beveridge, 1949, para 264). The 'fourteen day rule', moreover, a censorial mechanism which prohibited television discussion of any topic likely to be raised in Parliament during the subsequent fortnight, was not abandoned until 1956 and proved a formidable barrier to journalists' ambitions for parliamantery broadcasting (Cockerell, 1988b, p. 41).

But in October 1958, television cameras were eventually allowed into the Lords to record the State Opening of Parliament (Coleman, 1999, p. 6). Events seemed to be moving in broadcasters' favour when the 1959 general election was reported extensively in news bulletins and the BBC produced programmes such as *Hustings*, while Granada television broadcast *Election Marathon*: both programmes featured unprecedented pictures of parliamentary candidates being questioned by members of the public (Blumler, 1967, p. 52). In June 1975 the House agreed to an experiment in sound broadcasting which lead to the radio broadcasting of Parliament from 3 April 1978. The televising of the proceedings of the House of Lords began in January 1986 and was declared a success with the permanent televising of the House beginning in 1986. The cameras entered the Commons, again on an experimental basis, on 21 November 1989: the experiment was judged a success and permanent televising from the House began in 1990 (Franklin, 1992, p. 10). Since November 1998, BBC Parliament has broadcast live, 'gavel-to-gavel' coverage of the Commons and the Lords (recorded) as well as 26 hours of Committee coverage: the BBC estimates audiences ranging between 30,000 to 50,000 at any given time (Coleman, 1999, pp. 21–2).

Since May 1965 there had been no less than 12 debates proposing the televising of the House: it would certainly not prove possible to accuse members of rushing to judgement. The debate in November 1985, moved by Janet Fookes was only narrowly defeated by 275 to 263 (Franklin, 1986, p. 286) with Labour MP Austin Mitchell alleging that Prime Minister Thatcher's 'last minute' change of heart prompted several conservative MPs to shift their original decision and follow her into the 'no' lobby: Mitchell claimed that 'Thatcher's influence was clearly crucial' (Mitchell, 1995, p. 2). On 9 February 1988, however, the televising of parliament was secured with a majority of 54. This debate, like all the previous occasions since 1965, had been decided on a free vote (Nelson, 1988, p. 148) but it illustrated clearly the extent to which the televising of parliament had become a partisan issue. The Labour Party strongly supported the motion with 176 (86.3 per cent) voting in favour and only 28 (13.7 per cent) against. For their part, Conservatives were less favourably disposed to admit the cameras with 116 (33.4 per cent) voting in favour and 231 (66.6 per cent) against. Of the 264 members voting against the proposal, some 88 per cent were Conservative but only 11 per cent Labour (Franklin, 1989b, p. 486).

ARGUMENTS FOR TELEVISING THE HOUSE: 'FILLING THE PUBLIC GALLERY FOR 1,333 YEARS'

The substantive arguments in favour of televising the Commons have tended to stress the democratic benefits which would accrue from broadcasting proceedings (Nelson, 1988, p. 148). Advocates suggested that televising the House would make it more accountable to the public and enhance participation in the political process. During the experiment in televising the proceedings of the Lords in 1985, ITN compared television to an electronic extension of the public gallery and calculated that if the gallery seated 65 people for the 140 days of the parliamentary session, *News at Ten* on 3 April 1985 with 12,136,000 viewers watching the debate on unemployment was equivalent to filling the public gallery for 1,333 years (ITN, 1985, p. 1). Such figures represent an unrealistic extrapolation, of course, but they indicate the possibilities for television to enhance accountability and participation. Television, it was argued, might also perform an important educational function revealing to the public the procedures and conventions of the House and, by reporting debates, the key policy issues of the day.

Yet grander claims suggested that television might serve to halt the twentieth-century decline of Parliament by publicising, and thereby bolstering, its effectiveness as a checking mechanism on the executive during a period when it has become commonplace for governments to enjoy a large majority in the House. Charles Kennedy expressed the matter succinctly: 'As a party firmly committed to the principle of open government, we believe that the public have a right to see their elected representatives at work' (Kennedy and Culey, 1992, p. 117).

ARGUMENTS AGAINST TELEVISING THE HOUSE: 'AN UNHAPPY MIX OF FACT AND FARCE'

Four broad strands of argument against televising the Commons can be identified in a review of the 12 debates since 1965: they can be labelled technical, reputational, party political and procedural (Franklin, 1986a, p. 287).

Technical objections emphasised the difficulties arising from the introduction of the cameras, lighting and sound equipment necessary to broadcast from the House. Cameras, it was alleged, might be bulky and intrusive and would certainly require powerful lighting generating a degree of heat which would be unacceptable (HC Debs., 20 November 1985, col. 280), while cameras sited in the gallery would show only the top of members' heads. In brief the installation of cameras 'would create chaos' (ibid., col. 296). Dull and unimaginative camera shots resulting from restrictive rules of coverage continue to be a major complaint (Franks and Vandermark, 1995, p. 61; Snow, 1999, p. 6).

Some politicians believed that television would damage the reputation of the House and exacerbate the disrespect which they argued radio broadcasting had prompted. Edited television coverage would emphasise the more sensational and newsworthy, if less typical, aspects of the Commons' activities, giving viewers a distorted picture of parliamentary proceedings. MP-TV would become 'info-tainment', an unhappy mix of fact and farce (Gale, 1992, p. 107). The serious business of Parliament would be neglected in favour of the dramatic. Joe Ashton, MP, queried, 'If the cameras had been there when Lincoln was shot, does anyone believe they would have remained focused on the play?' (HC Debs., 20 November 1986, col. 287).

A third set of objections suggested that cameras might promote the interests of political parties inequitably by focusing on the prime minister and the leader of the opposition and thereby 'squeezing out' minority parties. Television, moreover, might disadvantage smaller parties by reinforcing public perceptions of an adversarial two-party contest in the House. Consequently, the Liberal Democrats' enthusiastic support for the principle of televising has been 'tinged with concern that as the 'third party' televising the House's proceedings would in practice prove to be to our disadvantage' (Kennedy and Culey, 1992, p. 117).

Procedural objections have ranged from the relatively minor to the highly significant. Debates have generated routine predictions that some members would behave more theatrically and that television would prompt the 'cult of the personality' (HC Debs, 20 November 1985, col. 298). Members would speak more, interrupt more, put down more questions, raise more points of order and address their constituents rather than other members in the chamber (ibid., col. 353). The front bench would monopolise in debate and the back bench would 'end up something like Cecil B. de Mille's chorus from Samson and Delilah' (ibid., col. 307). Television would exacerbate the already-gladiatorial style of Prime Minister's Questions and might lead to the organisation and manipulation of debate (ibid., col. 346).

The major procedural objection has been that television would pose a serious threat to the essential character of the House. The late Quintin Hogg (Lord Hailsham) claimed, 'Parliament is a wonderful and unique institution and I want to keep it as it is ... it is different in character after television is brought in. That is what I am afraid of' (HC Debs, 28 May 1965, col. 1665). David Amess, in the debate following the experiment in broadcasting, echoed Hogg's sentiments closely: We have allowed ourselves to be seduced by the media', he claimed. 'Increasingly the House seems to be more media driven than the other way round and I regret that ... We have trivialised our proceedings and Members of future Parliaments will never know how this place used to be' (HC Debs, 19 July 1990, cols. 1268–1269).

TELEVISING THE COMMONS: A DECADE OF DECLINE?

To what extent has the experience of Parliamentary broadcasting across the last decade resolved the problems which members anticipated? Initial assessments by parliamentarians, academics and journalists were highly favourable with one study querying 'what was the fuss all about?' since 'cameras are now seen as so much part of the furniture' (Franks and Vandermark, 1995, p. 57): by the end of the 1990s, however, each of these groups held serious reservations about the consequences and operation of parliamentary television.

EARLY EVALUATIONS: A 'FULL, BALANCED, FAIR AND ACCURATE ACCOUNT OF PROCEEDINGS?'

The First Report of the Select Committee on Televising recommended that programmes should 'give a full, balanced, fair and accurate account of proceedings with the aim of informing viewers about the work of the House' (First Report, 1989–90, para. 37). Research commissioned by the Committee and conducted by the Parliamentary Research Group at the University of Leeds, revealed that broadcasters broadly met these objectives (ibid., p. 35). Seven findings of the research were noteworthy and addressed members' misgivings.

First, broadcasters made generous provision for parliamentary footage in programmes ensuring that 'Westminster appeared remarkably frequently and prominently in both national and regional news services' (First Report 1989–90). The BBC's *Nine O'Clock News* reported an average 3.4 parliamentary stories each programme compared with 2.9 on ITN's *News At Ten*, 2.5 on *Channel 4 News*, 1.5 on *Newsnight* and 2.2 on *Sky News* (Tutt, 1992, p. 130). Second, coverage of Commons' committees was considerable with the BBC's *Nine O'Clock News* and ITN's *News at Ten*, devoting between 8 and 12 per cent of their total parliamentary broadcast time to committee coverage: parliamentary review programmes such as Channel 4's *Parliament Programme* allocated a generous 31 per cent of coverage to committees. But even at this early stage, the report noted that coverage of committees often reflected journalists' news values with parliamentary footage used to supplement news coverage of political stories. Third, Prime Minister's Questions did not dominate anywhere although it was the single most-frequently reported aspect of Commons' proceedings in national news programmes forming 23 and 38 per cent of all parliamentary coverage in the *Nine O'Clock News* and *News at Ten* respectively (First Report 1999–90, p. 41). Fourth, coverage included a wide range of members in their various parliamentary roles with back-benchers constituting between a quarter and a third of MPs featured in national news programmes, rising to three-fifths (60 per cent) in the BBC's weekly regional output (First Report, 1989–90, pp. 42–43). Fifth, Parliamentary television was markedly bi-partisan, paying relatively little attention to Liberal Democrat members and members of the other seven parliamentary parties (First Report, 1989–90, p. 14). While Conservatives made 3,873 contributions during televised programmes compared to Labour's 2,274, other parties such as the Liberal Democrats (395), Plaid Cymru (24) and Ulster Unionists (19) enjoyed substantially fewer opportunities to contribute to programming (Tutt, 1992, pp. 135–8).

Sixth, the evidence concerning the impact of televising on members' behaviour was mixed. Parties seemed increasingly conscious that the appearance and performance of their members was a significant matter. Consequently, Harvey Thomas, then Conservative Party public relations adviser, coached more than 100 Conservative MPs on how to appear 'concise, interesting and sincere' in their contributions in the chamber (*PR Week*, 26 October 1989). But research by the Aston University Group suggested that changes in members behaviour were few and, significantly, where changes were observed they were judged to have led to an improvement (Cumberbatch *et al.*, 1992, p. 207).

Finally, both advocates and opponents of the cameras claimed changes in House procedures as a consequence of televising. Conservative Roger Gale notes the growing practice of 'doughnutting' (i.e. surrounding a speaking MP with attentive acolytes) (Gale, 1992, p. 104), while Liberal Democrats argued that televising had prompted four changes to House procedures, each with significant implications for the Liberal Democrats, all minority parties and all back-benchers (*First Report*, 1989–90, pp. 76–79): an increase in the length of front-bench speeches; the Speaker's increased use of the ten-minute rule which limits the length of back-bench contributions to debate; the increase in opposition spokespeople's responses to government statements and, finally, a much greater pressure on question time – especially Prime Minister's Questions – which tends to 'squeeze out' the smaller parties (First Report 1989–90, pp 76–79; Hetherington *et al.*, 1990, p. 2).

PARLIAMENTARY TELEVISION AT THE MILLENNIUM: THE MYSTERIOUS CASE OF THE VANISHING MPS

The conclusion of the report of the Select Committee on Televising Parliament that 'British television has responded impressively to the challenge presented by its long-awaited entry to the House of Commons' has been contested at the end of the millenium by academics (Coleman, 1999; Franklin, 1996 and 1997) broadcasters (Snow, 1999) and journalists (McKie, 1999; Wintour, 1999) who voice a growing concern about the virtual disappearance of television reporting of the House. But there is little consensus here. McNair, for example, argues that the alleged decline in television coverage is little more than a 'myth': the reality is that reporting from Parliament is greater than in 1989 because of the 'gavel-to-gavel' coverage provided by the BBC Parliament channel since 1998. (McNair, 1999, pp. 36–7). But a simple increase in programming does not generate greater audience reach if, as Coleman claims, 'most of this [parliamentary coverage] is scheduled outside prime time or on less accessible channels (Coleman, 1999, p. 8): a point confirmed by the ITC/BSC report on audiences which revealed that audience figures for 24 hour news channels are surprisingly modest (Hargreaves and Thomas, 2002, pp. 37).

A Hansard Society study of Parliamentary broadcasting conducted in 1999 identified 'a major reduction in the coverage of Parliamentary stories over the decade since the cameras entered the Commons' (Coleman, 1999, p. 7): responding to the report, broadcaster Jon Snow claimed, 'MPs are vanishing from our screens' (Snow, 1999, p. 6). Three key findings are persuasive. First, across the 63 days of the study period which sampled 252 news broadcasts on BBC and ITN between January and March 1999, Parliament appeared in only 0.7 per cent of news items compared to 3.5 per cent in the Leeds study in 1989. There is no longer any regular scheduled national coverage of Parliament on ITV while the BBC concentrates coverage in BBC Parliament giving rise to accusations that 'the BBC is meeting its formal obligation to "show the green benches" of the House of Commons rather than seeking to promote such coverage to a mass audience' (Coleman, 1999, p.8). A dumbed down news agenda which prioritises coverage of crime and celebrities above the spartan reporting of politicians, moreover, means that MPs are 'ten times less likely than celebrities to appear on early evening news bulletins and six times less likely than criminals' (Wintour, 1999, p. 1).

Second, by 1999, front-benchers 'overwhelmingly' dominated coverage (Coleman 1999, p. 8). A decade earlier, appearances by Prime Minister Thatcher accounted for 268 actuality excerpts, more than any other member, but considerbly less than government back-benchers (770 contributions) and back-benchers from the two main parties (1,392). But in 1999 front-benchers 'stole the show' with Tony Blair featuring in 53 stories: more appearances than all the back-benchers combined (Wintour, 1999, p. 1). The report concluded that Parliament is 'frequently used more as a scenic backdrop for the coverage of the executive than as a means of reporting the legislature' (Coleman, 1999, p. 9). As

Peter Riddell confirms, 'New Labour strategists have regarded appearances by Mr Blair and other ministers in the Commons as merely one part of a communications strategey rather than a central aspect of democratic accountability' (Riddell, 1998, p. 8). Third, there is not only less Commons coverage on terrestrial channels, but less people are watching Parliamentary programming than a decade ago: in 1989 *A Week In Politics* enjoyed an audience of 600,000, while in 1999 Channel 4's *Powerhouse* attracted approximately 100,000 (Coleman, 1999, p. 8).

On radio the same decline in programming and audiences for parliamentary broadcasting is evident. Radio 5 Live continues to broadcast 120 minutes of live parliamentary coverage weekly, including Prime Minister's Question Time and ministerial statements but, in 1998 following three House debates on radio broadcasting, the BBC dropped *In Committee*, shifted *The Week in Westminster* to a graveyard slot in the Thursday evening schedule and, while slightly increasing the broadcast time of *Yesterday in Parliament* to 23 minutes, consigned it to long wave transmission (previously it was broadcast on long wave and FM) which was guaranteed to reduce audiences radically since only 80 per cent of listeners can receive long wave transmissions (Hill, 1999, pp. 18–19; Riddell, 1998, p. 13). Paradoxically, the BBC 'spin doctors' presented these changes as 'BBC news to strengthen its Parliamentary coverage' and 'Coverage Significantly Enhanced' although one ex-BBC parliamentary broadcaster believed the 'net effect of these changes' would be 'to bring about a massive reduction in the listening figures for the BBC's parliamentary programmes' (Hill, 1999, p. 19).

NEWSPAPER REPORTING OF THE COMMONS: PARLIAMENT ON THE SPIKE?

In Conan Doyle's detective novel *The Cardboard Box* Dr Watson, relaxing in his chair on a sunny August day, complains that he is bored; 'there is nothing in the newspapers' he observes. Holmes responds, with his usual combination of patronising pedagogy and impatience, by offering his companion what strikes him as the rather obvious explanation; 'Of course not Watson. Parliament is not sitting'. Victorian middle class gentlemen like Holmes and Watson expected newspapers of record to publish full and extensive accounts of Parliamentary proceedings. The belief that gallery and sketch reports from the House were desirable and essential ingredients in the broader editorial diet of a serious newspaper, was no more contested than similarly widespread beliefs concerning the civilising mission of the British Empire, the supremacy of English cricket or the popularity of Liberal governments. Much has changed across the last hundred years.

Between 1988 and 1993, the gallery tradition of reporting Parliament suffered a serious decline and precocious death, although it is notable how few obituaries mourned the passing of this significant and, once vigorous, tradition of political journalism. Some journalists unashamedly spoke ill of the dead and even of their complicity in the demise.

Simon Jenkins, ex-editor of *The Times*, for example, confirmed that it had been his decision 'to stop parliamentary reporting' since he 'couldn't find anyone who read it except MPs': Jack Straw doubts Jenkins' claim alleging that it 'is one that was never put seriously to the test' (Straw, 1999, p. 31). The 'sharp and universal' (Riddell, 1999, p. 29) decline in coverage, however, is uncontested and reflected in the jibe that 'if you want to keep a secret make a speech about it in the House' (John Cole quoted in Franklin, 1996a, p. 13). Journalistic staffs have declined accordingly. Simon Hoggart recalls:

> When I began reporting from the Commons in 1973, *The Times* had a total of sixteen parliamentary correspondents, based in one vast room, whose sole job it was to provide digests of debates, statements and question times, generally spread over two full pages of the paper ... now they have just us, the sketch writers.
>
> (Hoggart 2002, p. 11.)

But it is not only the amount of coverage that has changed. Newspapers' parliamentary reports no longer explore a distinctive parliamentary agenda preferring to subsume the coverage of parliament under the broader terrain of politics; in the words of a senior political journalist 'everything is "lobbyised" these days'.[2]

THE DECLINE, THEN 'COLLAPSE,' OF PARLIAMENTARY REPORTING

Seymour-Ure's 1977 study of the provincial press, which sampled coverage on ten days in each Parliamentary session, provided early evidence of a decline in the reporting of parliament in the 1920s and 1930s which is considerably earlier than most studies date any decline (Seymour Ure 1997, See Table 8.1). McQuail's content study conducted for the 1977 Royal Commission on the Press also noted the very modest coverage of parliamentary debates in local and regional newspapers (McQuail, 1977, p. 29).

More recently, evidence illustrating declining coverage was provided by Jack Straw's 1993 report which found that while coverage of parliamentary debates had been remarkably constant between 1933 and 1988 averaging between 400 and 800 lines in *The Times* and between 300 and 700 lines in the *Guardian*, there was a 'sudden decline' to less than 100 lines in each paper by 1992. The much lower coverage in the *Mirror* remained steady (Straw, 1993, p. 47; Straw, 1999, p. 29). McKie conducted a similar study of reporting in *The Times*, *Daily Telegraph*, *Guardian* and *The Financial Times* for sampled periods during 1946, 1966, 1986 and 1996 and concluded that coverage had not so much declined as 'collapsed' (McKie, 1999, p. 19). The number of lines of parliamentary coverage carried by *The Times* declined from 4148 lines in 1946 to a mere 290 in 1996, despite a growth in pagination across the period from 48 pages in 1946 to 228 by 1996. The other papers

Table 8.1: Coverage of parliament in three regional dailies

	Yorkshire Post		Manchester Guardian/ Guardian		The Scotsman	
	Parliamentary Coverage as a % of					
	Total space	Total editorial	Total space	Total editorial	Total space	Total editorial
1900	–	–	7.6	11.4	6.3	9.6
1912	5.3	6.9	8.4	12.0	6.7	10.2
1924	5.5	7.6	5.8	8.0	5.9	9.8
1936	3.8	4.7	4.1	5.2	6.2	8.0
1948	1.7	2.1	8.3	12.0	6.7	10.6
1960	2.0	3.4	3.3	5.3	3.6	5.8
1972	1.6	2.9	3.0	4.3	3.9	4.8

Source: Seymour Ure, 1977, cited in Negrine, 1998, p. 9.

revealed a similar retreat from parliamentary coverage: *Daily Telegraph* (3424 to 527); *The Financial Times* (1120 to 74) while only the *Guardian* sustained the quantity of coverage (2751 to 2331) although the paper increased in size from 32 pages in 1946 to 204 in 1996 (McKie, 1999, p. 24).

The findings of a study, conducted at the University of Sheffield, which analysed 820 parliamentary reports in a selected sample of the *Guardian*, (362 items) *Mirror* (112 items) and *The Times* (346 items) between 1990 and 1994, offer further confirmation for Straw's conclusions but, significantly, noted other consequences for parliamentary reporting following its detachment from a designated parliamentary page (Franklin, 1996a and 1996b).

First, the focus of parliamentary news had shifted. Stories concerning scandal or alleged misconduct by individual MPs emerged as the third most popular subject from a list of 40 identified subject categories for parliamentary reports. Scandal, moreover, enjoyed higher editorial salience than significant policy concerns such as education, local government or race/immigration issues: education reports and coverage of local government had declined four fold and six fold respectively across the period (Franklin, 1996a, p. 15, 1996b, p. 60). 'Scandal stories' had grown five hundred per cent since 1990, and across all newspapers: they accounted for 11 per cent of parliamentary reports in the *Guardian* but only 10 per cent in the *Mirror*. Some aspects of tabloid journalism seem not to be restricted to the 'red tops'.

A second trend is the growing preoccupation with the activities of government ministers and other senior politicians to the relative neglect of the back-benches and the virtual exclusion of minority parties. Ministers were quoted in 26 per cent and Shadows in 18 per cent of parliamentary reports, while figures for Conservative and Labour back-benches were as low as 8 per cent and 5 per cent respectively. Where a political party was the prominent focus of a report, in 98 per cent of cases it was the Labour or Conservative Party; in only 1 per cent of such reports did the Liberal Democrats enjoy prominence.

Third, journalists tended to report Parliament with an increasingly critical edge; more measured and balanced accounts of proceedings were less evident than previously. Across the study period, 48 per cent of reports were critical, 20 per cent were laudatory, 2 per cent were both and 28 per cent were neither one nor the other. A trend is discernible. The *Guardian* increased its critical coverage by 50 per cent, the *Mirror* by 350 per cent between 1990 and 1994, while the balanced coverage of *The Times* was striking with 104 critical reports balanced almost perfectly with 102 laudatory items of coverage.

Finally, Members enjoyed few opportunities in newspaper reports to voice their opinions directly through quoted comment. Nearly half (47 per cent) the newspaper coverage analysed reported no politicians' quotations. The phenomenon of journalists preferring to talk to other journalists, rather than interviewing politicians or others with specialist subject knowledge, became pervasive across the 1990s. Journalists are increasingly mediating between politicians and readers in their parliamentary reports. Soundbite culture, moreover, has invaded parliamentary reporting. Politicians' longer quotations are in decline; almost halved since 1990. Reinforcing this trend to report soundbite, shorter quotations have increased by 50 per cent over the same period.

In summary, the extent and character of parliamentary reporting has fundamentally changed during the 1990s. There is a good deal less coverage in both quality and tabloid newspapers than a decade earlier; what coverage remains is increasingly driven by news values rather than projecting a distinctly parliamentary agenda. Journalists' commentary on parliamentary affairs has, moreover, departed from its traditionally balanced character to become increasingly disdaining.

EXPLANATIONS OF DECLINING PARLIAMENTARY COVERAGE

Political journalists, sketch writers and parliamentary broadcasters identify very different causes of these changes. Many regret the decline in coverage; few anticipate a return to the more comprehensive gallery reporting of the 1980s.

Some journalists interpret the decline in parliamentary coverage as a symptom of a more general malaise afflicting journalistic standards triggered by deregulation and an increasingly competitive media market (McKie, 1999, p. 10; Negrine, 1998, p. 41). Cost cutting, bottom line journalism and targeting niche audiences is considered incompatible with reflective and considered parliamentary reporting as news editors decide 'whether a crucial debate on the Maastricht treaty . . . is given a higher priority than a story about the antics of the Royal Family or Michael Jackson' (Straw, 1993, p. 45). Reduced parliamentary coverage is simply part of what one political editor described as 'a gravitational decline in journalism . . . which I place at the feet of Rupert Murdoch and the standards he propagated so successfully . . . *The Times* parliamentary page got crushed. It was the last thing to get crushed and many other things got crushed on the way'. The impact of these changing news values and journalistic standards also impacts on political programming more generally (Perkins, 2003, p. 6; Rose, 2003, p. 4). The *Politics Show* which replaced the long running *On The Record* and launched on 2 February 2003, features 'a South Park style animated cartoon, has gag-writers on the staff' and has 'abandoned the set piece extended interview with a senior politician' (Perkins, 2003, p. 6). Gerald Kaufman, chair of the select committee on media and culture, described the launch edition of the BBC's 'new viewer-friendly, youth-oriented *Politics Show*' as 'unpromising' and concluded he would not be watching next week (Kaufman, 2003, p. 8).

Others argue that the decline in parliamentary reporting in newspapers is simply one consequence of the burgeoning coverage in other media, especially television (Straw, 1993, 1999; White, 2003). The arrival of cameras in the Commons, the expansion of cable, satellite and digital delivery systems and the increased airtime devoted to political programming, especially on Sundays, have made a considerable impact on parliamentary coverage. The argument here is not simply that television has 'sidelined' newspaper coverage but that it has influenced in damaging ways the broader culture of journalistic coverage. Riddell argues that increasingly, 'the snappy and the catchy are preferred over the reflective and considered. Pictures are better than words: personalities than scandals' (Riddell, 1998, p. 13). Television coverage of the Canadian Parliament (Taras, 1996, p. 7) and the German Bundestag (Schatz, 1992, pp. 246–7) is judged to have created a similar journalistic focus on conflict, sensationalism and politicians' gaffes. The resulting programming is often shallow with little time or prospect for detailed analysis: a poor surrogate for the press coverage which is the opportunity cost. Roy Hattersley makes the point:

> What happens on College Green? The television reporter asks the politician
> to explain the policy as briefly as possible. The politician responds to the
> request and is told that his statement is admirable in every way, but slightly
> too long. He tries again but still exceeds his ten seconds. Arguments about
> the problems of compression are met with the invincible but infuriating
> explanation that the news bulletin is barely twenty minutes long, only five
> minutes will be devoted to politics, two political subjects must be covered,
> other parties must have their say, and each participant has to be identified.
> 'So when we've done the recording will you walk towards the camera for an

identifying shot?' Do not tell me that television makes up for the inadequacy of newspaper coverage of serious politics.

(Hattersley, 2001, p. 241.)

This connects to journalists' third explanation: they commonly blame MPs and their ambitions for news management for the reduced coverage of the House (Franklin, 1997, p. 244; Negrine, 1998, p. 40). George Jones, political editor of the *Daily Telegraph* alleges that 'sometimes there are more MPs queuing on Abingdon Green or in the Millbank studios to give their soundbites to the cameras than are waiting to catch the Speaker's eye in the chamber' (cited in Franks and Vandermark, 1995, p. 67). But it is *parties'* increasing reliance on packaging politics, along with their determination to set the news agenda, which is crucially damaging to parliamentary coverage. Peter Riddell explains:

> Parties know they have a better chance of influencing the political agenda by launching initiatives outside the Commons, rather than inside the House, where the other parties have the right of reply ... all Gordon Brown's main policy proposals in opposition were made outside the commons, usually carefully leaked just before the formal announcement to one or two favoured journalists to stimulate interest among the broadcasters ... Labour has behaved in largely the same way in government, with rare exceptions. Mr Blair is far more likely to give a radio or television interview or to appear on the pages of a tabloid or broadsheet paper with an article written by him, or in his name, than he is to speak in the Commons.

(Riddell, 1998, pp. 10–11.)

So parliament is bypassed in the search for publicity and personal or policy promotion. Journalists increasingly regret the way that soundbites have become 'the main medium of political exchange'. Significant procedures of the House are now devalued with Prime Minister's Question Time reduced to 'a rabble of soundbites designed to capture the bulletins'.

Nearly all journalists identified changes in the character of the House as crucial to the decline in press coverage (Negrine, 1998, p. 39): it is in many ways a downgraded, less attractive forum, described by some observers as little more than 'Blair's lapdog' (Cowley, 2001, p. 815; Roth, 1999, pp. 21–2). The floor of the House of Commons 'is no longer the central arena of politics' (Riddell, 1999, p. 29) but only one among a number of political arenas which engage journalistic interest: one journalist claimed that 'power has dribbled away from the chamber'. Journalists also claimed that the quality of debate had declined reflecting the reduced quality of increasingly disciplined, quiescent and career-conscious back-benchers. Add to this mix the substantial government majorities which guarantee largely predictable outcomes, the debasing of certain proceedings such as PMQs with planted questions and propagandist answers, along with the public's growing disenchantment with politicians and many journalists believe the declining coverage of parliament is adequately explained.

Finally, journalists explained the decline by suggesting that readers are not interested in parliamentary coverage. Competition and shortage of space prompt sharp editorial judgements: journalism is demand-led and audience demand for parliamentary reporting is modest. But there has always been an argument for reporting Parliament which extends beyond any market driven rationale: the need for parliamentary broadcasting springs from the democratic requirement to inform citizens not the market need to provide consumers with popular programming. Some journalists concede the case, but argue that 'the public service view has all but disappeared'.

These five accounts by journalists which stress the increasingly competitive media market, the expansion of broadcast media, MPs and parties' growing publicity consciousness, the changing character of the House and the presumed lack of interest in political and parliamentary affairs by readers and viewers, do not represent distinctive explanations but may connect, reflecting more deeply rooted changes in Britain's system of political communications. Such systemic shifts may prove increasingly resilient to change.

NEW MEDIA NOT NEWS MEDIA: WEBCASTING AND A 'COMMONS IN CYBERSPACE'

Towards the conclusion of his Hansard Society study bemoaning the 'collapse' of newspaper and television reporting of the Commons, David McKie identifies a possible 'saviour . . . a new champion of parliamentary coverage, likely in time to transcend all that has gone before it'. The saviour is 'electronic' and is 'now racing to the rescue of under-reported MPs'. McKie identifies this saviour as the rather broadly defined 'information revolution' which, using Internet technology, is spreading rapidly to deliver widely based public access to information (McKie, 1999, p. 19). Coleman concludes his report for Hansard in similar fashion. Rejecting 'far-fetched visions of push button democracy', he argues nonetheless that the interactive character of new media, combined with their capacity to connect the public directly with their representatives, suggests that 'the new media environment could have significant implications for political communication' (Coleman, 1999, pp. 25–6). The possibility that new media might create opportunities for continuous, unedited and direct coverage of Parliament and its committees is an obvious and desirable ambition for such a revolution.

But MPs initially distrustful attitudes to new communications technologies, exemplified by their early reluctance to admit print and broadcast media into the House, are likely to slow down the adoption of electronic and digital communications. As the new technology is accepted, members attempt to regulate it strictly but, eventually, the new technology becomes an integral part of parliamentary life and members come to believe that they cannot work effectively without it. Writing in 1999, Coleman argued that the new Internet-based technologies 'hover somewhere between the first and second stage of this process' (Coleman, 1999a, p. 372). But other scholars report less traditional attitudes and a greater take up by back-bench MPs who 'make extensive use of personal computers, internet connections and websites to help them with their work. Their offices are filled with computers. They could not work without word processors, spreadsheets, electronic diaries, databases and emails . . . information and communications are everywhere' (Campbell, *et al.*, 1999, p. 388; see also Stanyer, 2001, p. 349). But in what ways might the House's embrace of new media technologies assist public access to the proceedings of parliament, perhaps via the reporting of events in the House? There is undoubtedly some initial evidence here. Since 23 October 1996, for example, Hansard – 'that most venerable and respected of custodians of the record' – has been publicly available in electronic format on the web: previously the electronic version was only available to MPs (McKie, 1999, pp. 18–19). During the 1950s, sales of the hard copy Commons Hansard used to reach 20,000 copies each day, but by the 1990s this figure had reduced substantially to 5000 (ibid).

A more striking example of McKie's 'electronic saviour' was the launch of www.parliamentlive.tv on 8 January 2002. The site broadcasts continuous streaming audio visual coverage of the Houses of Commons and Lords, along with audio coverage of Select Committees. The site is designed and maintained by TwoFourTV.com and is funded jointly by Lords and Commons. Future plans for the site include the incorporation of government sites into the streamed coverage so that viewers are able to call up additional materials, documents and information to put debates into context. But for the moment the advantage of the site is that it offers the public gavel-to-gavel coverage of both houses and all committees unmediated by the selective editing and interpretive commentary of journalists. David Lepper who currently Chairs the Select Committee on Broadcasting claims the key ambition is 'to widen the choice of what people are able to see, allowing them to choose for themselves rather than being dictated to by news editors' (Gibson, 2001, p. 42). New media, moreover, appear to imitate their predecessors in certain respects. When the Commons was first televised in 1989, PMQs proved remarkably and unexpectedly popular with American audiences. www.Parliamentlive.tv attracts as many overseas visitors as it does UK residents.

Undoubtedly the most ambitious and engaging proposal for developing the political communications potential of new media has been Blumler and Coleman's suggestion for a 'civic commons in cyberspace' (Blumler and Coleman, 2001). The idea draws inspiration from early remarks by new Labour architect Philip Gould who suggested that Internet and interactive communications technology required that 'new forms of dialogue must be created' between politicians and citizens. Focus groups and market research are 'an essential part of this dialogue. So too are the interactive party broadcasts and "Town Hall" meetings at which politicians can be questioned and held to account' (Gould, 1998, pp. 297–8). The civic commons would be an 'entirely new kind of public agency'. It would be publicly funded, independent of government and essentially a deliberative assembly responsible for 'eliciting, gathering, and co-ordinating citizens' deliberations upon and reactions to problems faced and proposals issued by public bodies (ranging from councils to parliaments and government departments) which would then be expected to react formally to whatever emerges from the public discussions'. The civic commons must be acountable to a range of stakeholders including 'communities (local and of interest), local authorities, public service broadcasters, organisations promoting citizenship and democracy as well as the parliaments and assemblies of the UK. The key functions of the new civic commons would be to promote, publicise, regulate, moderate, summarise and evaluate the 'broadest and most inclusive range of online deliberation via various new media platforms including the web, e-mail, newsgroups and digital TV' (Blumler and Coleman, 2001, pp. 16–17).

The new media technologies, through which such a deliberative body would be accessed and would operate, have significant if more generalised civic potential. First, new media require more active users than previous media of communications: the Internet, moreover, is uniquely an interactive medium facilitating participation in unprecedented ways. Second, the Internet provides a forum in which there is the prospect for greater numbers of citizens to share experiences and information. Third, the Internet is not so readily prone to censorship as other media. Fourth, the Internet provides citizens with access to large data stores which can be used in different ways and allow citizens to tailor their uses of data to particular needs. Fifth, ease and low cost of Internet access, reduce any potential 'influence of social status on political involvement'. Consequently, poor communities, groups and citizens 'can undertake acts of communication and monitoring that previously were the domain mainly of resource rich organisations and individuals' (ibid., p. 13).

But Blumler and Coleman also acknowledge a number of 'downsides to online civic engagement' (ibid., p. 15). First, online communications risks offering politicians the prospect of 'disintermediation', namely the ability to address targeted audiences without the critical intervention of journalists and media: and hence the prospect of steering the political agenda and public debate in a particular direction. Second, the limits of public influence need to be clarifed at the outset of consultations: 'excessive expectations can lead to public disappointment' (ibid.). Requirements for democratic participation are not met by Internet chat. Third, the civic commons should avoid populist claims to empower citizens or promise participants an unrealistic degree of political influence. Finally, some policy discussions may be highly complex, require supportive explanatory documentation and the involvement of expert contributions: discussions of this kind risk lapsing into prejudicial exchanges: but 'the purpose of online consultation should not be to seek "obvious" answers of devising better policy' (ibid., p. 16).

In the short term, at least, the major problem with such a civic commons is the modest number of socially, ethnically skewed and gendered citizens who might participate in its deliberations: given the most recent evidence illustrating patterns of use of online news sources (Hargreaves and Thomas, 2002). For the moment, television coverage in news bulletins and regional parliamentary programmes, broadcast on mainstream terrestrial channels, provides the majority of people with their knowledge and information about parliamentary affairs. The arrival of cameras in the Commons has created new opportunities for news management: many observers, including two recent Speakers of the House, believe that such opportunities have been seized with alacrity.

TELEVISING THE COMMONS AND POLITICAL MARKETING

Since the arrival of cameras in the Commons in 1989, proceedings in the House are no longer consigned to the relative obscurity which even an electronic Hansard affords. Events in the Commons are potentially an item for a flagship news programme conveyed directly into 16 million voters' homes with an immediacy, vitality and credibility which cannot be matched by even the most able of newspaper sketch or gallery reporters. For the public, Commons television provides a potentially significant additional source of information about political, as well as parliamentary, affairs. For the parties, but especially the government, it offers new opportunities to package their policies and present senior politicians to the public: especially in the run up to a general election. We are now in the 'info-tainment-business', Roger Gale announced with evident regret. 'Watch us perform with increasing desperation as any general election draws near. The cameras are in, the gloves are off. The only victim will be democracy' (Gale, 1992, p. 107).

But while Commons' television may provide opportunities for promoting parties, politicians and policies, the watchful eye of the camera can also prove politically damaging: it can also heighten the political salience of issues and events and even help to shape their course. Margaret Thatcher may have been a early victim of this process. Few people who watched Geoffrey Howe's resignation speech in 1990, for example, could believe that the corrosiveness of the speech on Thatcher's leadership was not intensified many times for being televised live and replayed on numerous news programmes during the following two weeks. Throughout key sections of the speech, the television director in the Commons' control room held a 'mid-range' camera shot which just captured Howe in the top left of the television screen with Thatcher in the bottom right; in effect a reaction shot and against all the rules of coverage. But televisually and politically, the effect was devastating. Viewers could watch every moment of Thatcher's evident discomfort and grimaces as Howe set out his incisive and vengeful accusations about her style of leadership. Similarly, Robin Cook's resignation speech on 20 March 2003, reflecting his opposition to the war with Iraq, was all the more effective politically because viewers could watch the reaction on the faces of politicians on the front bench of the Labour Party who were obliged to listen to the unrelenting eloquence of his argument.

PROCEDURAL MEDIA OUTCOMES: BEING SEEN IN THE PARLIAMENTARY DRIVING SEAT

Any discussion of the political marketing potential of parliamentary television is necessarily speculative since party managers do not wish to disclose tactics or appear disrespectful to the procedures of the House. It is important, however, to distinguish between *procedural media outcomes* and *political media opportunities*. The former are the unconscious, unplanned advantages which any party might enjoy as a consequence of the procedures of the House; the latter reflect the conscious strategies designed by politicians to secure political advantage from the presence of the cameras. The distinction is not water tight and politicians may try to secure additional political media opportunities by building on the advantages which House procedures offer: politicians attempts to manage PMQs offer an obvious example of such 'overlap' and are discussed below. A number of procedural media outcomes can be identified.

First, parliamentary television gives prominence to the party of government and the official opposition reflecting their prominent roles in the House's activities. But this broadcast focus undoubtedly serves to reinforce public perceptions of an adversarial two party battle in the House to the relative disadvantage of minority parties. The party of government also benefits from being presented as the authoritative definer and initiator of political events in the chamber. Thursday's business questions in which the leader of the House sets out the programme for the House's work for the coming week adds to this aura of authority and initiative. The viewer can be in little doubt about who is in the parliamentary driving-seat. By contrast, the opposition parties risk being seen as merely reactive or worse, perhaps wholly negative and overly critical.

Second, Prime Minister's Questions (PMQs) offer a further parliamentary event from which the party of government can expect to score 'PR points'. The prime minister appears highly knowledgeable about all aspects of government policy: the authoritative source, to whom all others in the House address questions. The leader of the opposition can also appear informed and challenging. Currently, Ian Duncan Smith is allocated procedural opportunities to confront the prime minister across the table of the House and consequently enjoys an authority denied to the leaders of other parties. But after the three questions which the procedures allow, speaker Martin calls other questioners; the prime minister appears to have 'seen him off'. The Liberal Democrats confront particular presentational difficulties with PMQs. Charles Kennedy is lucky to get called once a week, enjoys a smaller quota of questions than the leader of the opposition and it may appear as if he is being constantly slapped down. On the days he is not called, viewers might assume that he simply does not have a question to ask. Worse still, if the cameras show Kennedy rising in his place but not called, his credibility and that of the Liberal Democrats might be seriously undermined.

Third, but perhaps the most substantive procedural media outcome of parliamentary television, is the possible effect on the electoral success of incumbents in an parties. Studies of local parties' media campaign strategies in 1997 and again in 2001, revealed that election agents were eager to secure media coverage for their candidates in the two years prior to the election; television appearances were particularly prized. The purpose of such media appearances were simply to acquaint electors with the name of the candidate for their particular party (Franklin and Parry, 1998, p. 211; Franklin and Richardson, 2002, p. 37). But if this modest media exposure is considered electorally significant, then the regular weekly appearances by incumbent MPs on regional television news and parliamentary programmes across their five year period of office might provide a considerable advantage over opponents.

The procedures of the House are not even-handed in the opportunities for media coverage they offer political parties. But procedural media outcomes may be exacerbated by the operation of political media opportunities.

POLITICAL MEDIA OPPORTUNITIES: PLANTING QUESTIONS AND MAKING STATEMENTS

Since 1989, politicians, parties and governments have undoubtedly made conscious efforts to use the cameras in the Commons to their advantage. In the run up to elections, journalists' enthusiasm for election coverage makes them politicians' willing accomplices as the latter attempt to hijack parliamentary programmes to supplement election coverage in television news bulletins. In the run-up to the 1992, 1997 and 2001 elections, MP-TV was dominated by election concerns.

PMQs provide a key forum for parties seeking political media opportunities. Since many voters believe elections are a choice between personalities as much as policies, PMQs offers a perfect shop-window in which parties can display their leaders. The opposition undoubtedly try to strike the prime minister with a parliamentary 'exocet', while promoting the qualities of their own leader and front-bench team, but it is the governing party which seems potentially to enjoy the most political media opportunities at question time.

The whips can plant 'soft' questions with friendly back-benchers allowing the prime minister to respond assuredly and show a calm confidence despite the pressures of such a high-profile parliamentary occasion. Whips can also plant questions probing areas of policy success for the government, which provide the prime minister with 'agitprop' opportunities to make statements detailing favourable aspects of the government's record. Alternatively, whips may try to give air time to back-benchers who have not been 'overly active' in their constituencies and need to make a parliamentary showing. Members with seats in very marginal constituencies might similarly receive a publicity fillip by being seen questioning the prime minister.

Following the 1997 general election, the new Labour government made an early 'modernising' reform of House procedures by reducing the twice weekly PMQs to a single session on Wednesdays. Questions had become discredited during the Major years and often regressed to a twice weekly shouting match. Blair promised a new, responsible, informative but non-confrontational PMQs, although the government generated some hostility among back-benchers by introducing the reform without consulting the speaker of parliament. The first session was stashed with planted, polite questions and reminded one journalist of 'those political interviews before the arrival of Robin Day which often went something like this:

> Prime Minister, thank you for coming to the studio. I believe you have a bill connected with unemployment.
> Yes, I do.
> Could you describe it?
> Certainly. It is our intention to abolish unemployment insofar as that proves practicable.
> I am sure the country will be delighted to hear that Prime Minister. Thank you for coming here tonight.
> Tony Blair was slightly more forthcoming.
> Jean Corston (Lab Bristol E.) inquired whether there would be measures to combat crime?
> 'The Home Secretary is announcing a series of beneficial measures which we hope will have an effect on cutting crime'.
> Stephen Twigg ... inquired what plans the government had to combat drug-related crime. It turned out there were many such plans.
> Stuart Bell (Lab Middlesborough) told us how excited the whole country was by the 26 Bills in the Queen's speech. 'What will you do for an encore?'
> An awful truth dawned: there are going to be as many Labour greasers as there were Tories. It's just that their style will be different consisting of theatrical, luvvie-type flattery.
>
> (Hoggart, *Guardian*, 22 May 1997, p. 1.)

New Labour with its 'control freak reputation' has exacerbated these tendencies making 'new Labour MPs adoring of their ministers in public'. Those who want 'to keep their seat or perhaps even be promoted should restrict themselves to adoring stooge questions' (Roth, 1999, p. 23).

Ministerial statements, including prime ministerial statements, provide further political media opportunities. Speaker Bernard Weatherill noted, quite soon after the arrival of the cameras, the increase in ministerial statements, 'often on subjects whose importance or

199

urgency has not been immediately apparent' (Weatherill, 1992, p. xiv). Ministers may try to manage the news by storing up 'good news' to retrieve party popularity on an occasion when the government's record is under fire in the House and beyond. In the run-up to the 1992 general election, Chris Pattern, then party chair distributed a memo to all ministers instructing them to prioritise the work of their departments in a way which allowed them to make favourable comments in the House to maximise political advantage. More recently, the the Strategic Communications Unit, under the control of Blair's director of communications constructs a weekly 'grid' which schedules and co-ordinates the release of government news both within and without Parliament and works closely with the Leader of the House to secure maximum publicity advantage for the government (See Chapter 3). Prime ministerial statements may serve similar ends. Tony Blair's statement to the House on 25th February 2003 detailing the 'moral' case for a war against Iraq was evidently intended to secure maximum publicity for the occasion and present the prime minister as the nation's leader, at a time of international crisis, credentialised by the authority which only his position at the dispatch box can deliver. But increasingly, important policy statements are made outside the House on the *Today* programme or *Newsnight* following extensive briefing and trailing by special advisers. The later statement in the Commons is 'usually an anticlimax, thinly attended and thinly reported' (Riddell, 1998, p. 30).

Points of order, broadcast live after question time, assumed a new significance with the televising of proceedings. The number of points of order raised with the Speaker increased substantially from 44 in November and December 1988, the year before broadcasting began, to 88 by November/December 1989 to 149 by February/March 1990 (Cumberbatch, *et al.*, 1992, p. 208). Points of order raised after question time are more or less guaranteed live coverage on BBC television. Members' intentions seem to be to secure coverage in the regional news or parliamentary programme broadcast in their constituency.

Back-benchers are, to say the least, enthusiastic to appear on regional television especially in the run-up to an election. Some show great tenacity for the enterprise. The producer of a regional parliamentary programme claimed that during the first month of broadcasting he was approached by four local MPs who were willing to ask any question in the House, which the producer thought would be of interest, if they would be guaranteed television coverage. Broadcasters were intended to report events in the House, not participate in them. This seems a paradigmatic case of the tail wagging the dog, but such behaviour is not exceptional. Politicians, locally and nationally, have increasingly shown themselves eager to issue press releases and make statement to the press to gain coverage for themselves or their cause. Cameras in the Commons have simply provided another medium through which to communicate with voters.

Some commentators even suggest that the revised sitting times for the House, introduced on 7 January 2003, reflect at least in part, Members' desire to win back media attention: morning sittings were a 'response to the media agenda . . . By bringing forward their most interesting procedures to earlier in the day they hope to get more media coverage and thereby impress the voters' (White, 2003, p. 6). This represents an attempt to secure political media opportunities on a grand scale.

Television might, in these various ways, prove influential in shaping political outcomes by offering distinctive but highly variable media opportunities to different political parties. Television has certainly changed the Commons, but that was inevitable. The House was one of the last, but arguably one of the most significant, arenas of political activity to be televised. Since 1989, broadcast proceedings have offered the public a new source of political information to use, among other things, to inform their electoral choices. But in Britain's media democracy where the packaging of politics is increasingly rife, it was perhaps inevitable that politicians would seek to use this new channel of political communication to their particular advantage. Paradoxically, Parliament is less likely to feature on television in the new millennium than a decade ago, reflecting the ambitions of individual politicians who increasingly bypass Parliament believing that the best way to promote their political careers and favoured causes is by making statements which will be reported on television, rather than participating in House debates. It also reflects the ambitions of successive executives to manage not only events and debates in the House but also their representation on screen. But despite this marginalising of Parliament in reality and representation, the House retains a significance which means it cannot be wholly excluded from the media democracy that the British polity has become.

---

1   In discussing this relationship between Parliament and the media, it is important to acknowledge the significant constitutional changes since 1989 when television broadcasting from the House began and the only Parliament was based at Westminster. In recent times, power has devolved to Brussels and Strasbourg. Since 1999, power has devolved to a Scottish Parliament (Schlesinger, Miller and Dinan, 2001) and the Welsh and Northern Ireland Assemblies (Fawcett, 2001). There is an elected Mayor and Assembly for London with continuing discussion of further regional assemblies. As power shifts, so will the focus of news and parliamentary reporting (Riddell, 1998, p. 14). Since November 1998 BBC Parliament accordingly broadcasts not only live and unedited coverage from the Commons and Lords, but daily and weekly reports on the European Parliament, alongside weekly reports on the Scottish Parliament and the Welsh Assembly.

2   Much of the citation material here derives from interviews conducted with senior political correspondents and journalists working in print and broadcast journalism. Many thanks to Kim Fletcher, Simon Heffer, Simon Hoggart, Nicholas Jones, Brian MacArthur, Chris Moncrieff, Robin Oakley, Matthew Parris, Peter Riddell and Michael White for sharing their views about the causes and consequences of the changing patterns of Parliamentary reporting across the 1990s.

Part 3
The audience and political communication

Chapter Nine

POLITICAL COMMUNICATION ☐
AND AUDIENCES: INFORMING OR
PERSUADING THE PUBLIC?

Three activities, rather than two, now dominate many people's lives: working, sleeping and watching television. In Britain, the length of the 'working week' and the 'viewing week' are drawing ever closer. Before leaving for work, many people read a national newspaper and, on their return home, they relax with the 'local rag'; during their lunch-break they may read a workmate's newspaper, magazine or book. Radio fills the gaps in the media day. Radio 4's *Today* programme, the *Radio Five Live* phone-in, local radio news about road works and local traffic jams, or pop music offered by *Radio 1* or an ILR station, accompanies the journey to and from work by car. For those travelling by train, bus, tube or bike, a Walkman or MP3 player seems to have become an indispensable companion. During the course of the day, the average person will devote almost seven hours to watching television, listening to radio, reading a newspaper or scanning the web for news, information or entertainment (Grant, 2002, pp. 116–17; Hargreaves and Thomas, 2002; Hart, 1991, pp. 46 7; Seymour-Ure, 1991, pp. 145–6): reading news is the fourth most popular Internet activity for the Web's 407 million global population (Sussman, 2001, p. 1). By the turn of the millennium, television viewers in the UK were able to choose from more than 40,000 hours of programming every week (DTI and DCMS, 2000, para 1.1.2) while the contents of the Worldwide Web increased by more than 3.2 million pages and more than 715,000 images every 24 hours (UCLA Centre for Communication Policy, 2000, pp. 4–5). The public appetite for media seems insatiable; most people are avid consumers of their products. But few will ever find themselves in front of a television camera or microphone cast in the role of 'performer'. The great majority 'remain anonymous members of the audience, of "the public"' (Hood, 1980, p. 15).

Characterising the audience as 'anonymous' is perhaps among the least offensive and disparaging descriptions used by some researchers. Jane Root, for example, in her book *Open the Box*, offers the image of the television viewer as a zombie, often 'slouched' in front of the television, indiscriminately consuming the message of every programme and advertisement with an uncritical relish (Root, 1986). In America, the term 'couch potato' expresses the presumed essential passivity of television viewers who enjoy 'spudding out' in front of 'the box' (Ehrenreich, 1991, pp. 15–18). In the late 1990s, the BBC television programme *The Royle Family* parodied this alleged obsession with television by offering voyeuristic insights into the Royle family's hearth and home, filmed from the perspective of the television screen, which assumed the (literal) focus of all household activities and uniquely inspired and informed household conversations and family beliefs. Such passivity is carefully nurtured. Raymond Williams argues that programme planners consciously create a 'flow' of programmes designed to ensure that viewers absorb a continuum of interwoven messages of sound and vision, rather than watching discrete programmes. Programmes merge into adverts and previews of other programmes in what he calls an 'endless amorphous collage'. This is why, Williams observes, people tend to say I watched '*television*' rather than saying 'I watched a *specific programme*' (Williams, 1974, p. 94). But value judgement, if not prejudice, can be encoded in the very language used to describe an activity. The words 'watching' and 'viewing', for example, imply passivity. There is no word to describe the *activity* of attending to television. By contrast, 'reading' a newspaper is active, signalling a process of 'doing' rather than merely 'receiving'.

A second description of television audiences is hardly more flattering and uses the metaphor of addiction. Television is judged to be a drug on which audiences are hooked. The viewer is presented as helpless to television's persuasive and pervasive influences. Children and young viewers are presumed to be especially vulnerable to the addictive and powerful messages emanating from the screen: hence the title of Marie Winn's 1977 book *The Plug in Drug; Television, Children and the Family*. The allegedly compulsive character of television may even be explicitly recognised as in the programme title of the popular 1990s television quiz show called *Telly Addicts*. Such accounts of media influence are replete with words like 'indoctrination' and 'propaganda'.

But the presumed influence of media on audiences may be more apparent than real, for two reasons. First, people view or read media messages with varying degrees of concentration, commitment and engagement with the broadcast and published materials. Viewers, for example, are certainly not 'glued to the box'. Research studies reveal that 'half the time the television is on the audience is doing something else' (Cumberbatch and Howitt, 1989, p. 9; Gunter and Svennevig, 1987; Taylor and Mullan, 1986, p. 205); activities may range from ironing, or playing the cello to having sex (Collett and Lamb, 1960; Root, 1986). Another study confirmed that 'television viewing is often at a fairly low level of involvement' but added that viewers 'do not always pay attention and sometimes are even asleep' (Barwise and Ehrenberg, 1990, p. 175).

Second, television and newspapers are viewed and read for a variety of reasons. Both are used extensively to provide information about everything from politics and current affairs to gardening, but they are also sources of entertainment and, more generally, relaxation. The contents of media are wide ranging and eclectic. Television offers a diversity of programming which embraces sport, soap operas, quiz shows, drama, comedy, opera, ballet and children's programming. Similarly, readers buy newspapers to consult their stars, to look at page three, to attempt the crossword, to scour the advertisements for bargains, to seek the advice of the financial page or the agony aunt about monetary or marital affairs, or simply to check the start time of their favourite radio or television programme; others use the newspaper simply to wrap up their fish and chips. Such concerns seem wholly irrelevant to discussions of 'media influence' with their quiet connotations of persuasion or even propaganda.

This chapter addresses two questions in order to examine the relationship between media and their audiences more closely and assess the impact of packaging politics on the public. First, how has the relationship between media and their audiences been conceptualised in the communications literature? Second, but more specifically, what, if any, has been the influence of media reporting of political affairs on political attitudes and behaviour?

MEDIA AND AUDIENCE RELATIONS

An exhaustive review of the literature on media effects would be a daunting task. The sheer volume of research and published material is prohibitive. An annotated bibliography dealing specifically with the effects of mass media portrayals of violence listed 784 publications, while another volume attempting a more comprehensive review of the literature cited over two thousand publications in 'the last ten years' (Cumberbatch and Howitt, 1989, p. 2). But it is not simply the scale of the enterprise which counsels caution. Research findings in this field have often been contradictory and highly contested. Some studies suggest a substantial influence for media while others argue for limited audience effects (Barker and Petley, 1997, pp. 1–12, Klapper, 1960, p. 8). Philo and Miller, for example, are 'dubious' about the 'arguments which have been advanced to suggest that television has no effect on viewers' behaviour' (Philo and Miller, 1999, p. 21) while Philo has suggested more recently that one consequence may even be the 'mass production of social ignorance' (Philo, 2002, p. 173): an idea resonant with the title of Schecter's 1998 book, *The More You Watch The Less You Know*. The impact of media on audiences remains the issue in mass communications about which 'there is least certainty and least agreement' (McQuail, 1987, p. 251). The summary conclusion of an early review of the 'media effects' literature can hardly be considered decisive in its judgement. 'Some kinds of communication', Berelson suggested, 'on some kinds of issues, brought to the attention of some kinds of people under some kinds of conditions, have some kinds of effects' (Berelson *et al.*, 1954, p. 356). Prevarication and qualification on this scale seem unlikely to move the debate forward.

Four conceptual models of the relationship between media and audiences, which developed broadly chronologically across the twentieth century, are detailed below.

'MAGIC BULLETS', 'HYPODERMICS' AND 'HAMMERS': A THEORY OF POWERFUL MEDIA

Early analyses of media invested them with powers over their audiences which approached omnipotence. From the beginning of the century until the late 1930s, the media – which at that time meant radio, newspapers and cinema – were judged to possess substantial power to mould opinions, beliefs and attitudes as well as shape the behaviour of their audiences. Media were conceived as a 'needle' which 'injected' messages into their audiences, which influenced them directly and immediately as if the opinions and attitudes of the message were a drug injected into a vein (Kraus and Davis, 1976, p. 115) – note the return of the addiction metaphor. In the words of DeFleur and Ball-Rokeach, the model 'assumed that cleverly designed stimuli would reach every individual member of the mass society via the media, that each person would perceive it in the same general manner, and that this would provoke a more or less uniform response from all' (DeFleur and Ball-Rokeach, 1982, p. 160). In 1938, when Orson Welles' version of H. G. Wells' *War Of The Worlds* was broadcast on radio, using the theatrical device of a news bulletin to announce that America had been invaded by Martians, it provoked hysteria. Over a million listeners were unable to distinguish fiction from reality, became frightened and disturbed and began to panic as they awaited the imminent demise of the world (Cantril *et al.*, 1940). For many observers the incident underscored the power of media to persuade people to accept the unbelievable.

Governments' use of broadcast propaganda during the Second World War and the reliance of the authoritarian regimes of Hitler, Mussolini and Stalin on propaganda confirmed the increasingly popular view that political leaders and elites could use the media to manipulate society.

Social scientists explored the implications of the hypodermic model by examining aspects of social as well as political behaviour. It was believed, for example, that media portayals of criminality, sexual behaviour and violence were sufficient to trigger similar socially disruptive behaviour in the audience. William Belson's classic study, *Television Violence and the Adolescent Boy*, concluded that 'high exposure to television violence increases the degree to which boys engage in serious violence'. Given his diagnosis, the prescription is simple: 'Steps should be taken as soon as possible to achieve a substantial reduction in the total amount of violence being presented on television' (Belson, 1978, p. 15).

This suggestion that media might have direct and substantial effects eventually became discredited and, in America, was dubbed derisively the 'magic-bullet' model (Cumberbatch and Howitt, 1989, p. 4). A recent, British study argued that the 'effects' model conceptualised the impact of media messages on audiences as the equivalent of hitting them over the head with a hammer (Lewis, 1990, p. 154, 1991, p. 8). With hindsight, many of the early studies seem remarkably simplistic. Contra Belson, for example, Hagell and Newburn's study revealed precisely the opposite correlation between violent behaviour and screen images of violence: namely that young offenders watched considerably less television programmes portraying violence than a control sample of 'ordinary' school children (Hagell and Newburn, 1994). These 'effects' studies assumed a very passive and uncritical audience, which was highly receptive to media messages, with little or no ability to select, reject, choose or make judgements about media messages. In this sense the model was highly deterministic. Gauntlett has been strongly critical of this tradition of audience research judging it 'to be inadequate in numerous respects, from broadest paradigm assumptions to specific methodological issues' (Gauntlett, 1996, pp. 7–8; see also Gauntlett 1995, Chapter 1 and 1997). There are other, more specific, objections and concerns.

First, effects studies tended to ignore the diversity of audiences which, as Hood reminds, includes everyone 'from the Queen to the office cleaner' (Hood, 1980, p. 23). Audiences are highly differentiated so that even when anticipated reactions to media messages occur, their nature and frequency varies reflecting individual differences of personality, interest and knowledge (DeFleur, 1970, p. 122; McQuail, 1987, p. 260). Some individuals may respond to a particular message by 'copying' it – by rioting or being violent – while others remain unaffected. But significantly, since media effects are not unitary, the model cannot distinguish, on the basis of observable behaviour, between those who have been influenced by television and those who have not. Non-violent behaviour, as much as violent behaviour, may logically be an 'effect' of television expressing a viewer's revulsion at television portrayals of violence.

Second, the hypodermic model is sociologically naive. It fails to acknowledge the social character of the audience which is fissured by cleavages of gender, class, ethnicity, age, and religious and political beliefs. Individuals' membership of particular social groups will influence their response to media messages (DeFleur, 1970, p. 123; Eldridge, Kitzinger and Willliams, 1997, p. 164).

Third, many early studies focused on the impact of television portrayals of violence, but failed to discriminate between different types of violence. The awesome attacks which Tom and Jerry routinely inflict on each other are evidently different from other forms of fictional violence or documentary scenes of war in Kosovo or Iraq. But viewers, even young viewers, can and do discriminate between them (Gunter and McLeer, 1990, p. 91). They know that some violence is not 'real' and that people are not being hurt.

Fourth, these early studies are plagued by methodological difficulties which may have resulted in the real impact of television on audiences being understated (Lewis, 1990, p. 155). When trying to assess the impact of political programmes on viewers, for example, it is virtually impossible to separate viewers who have watched a large number of political programmes from those who have watched only a few. But even if it were possible to isolate viewers in this way, the reasons which prompt people to watch political programmes in the first place may be more influential on their subsequent political behaviour than any of the political programmes they watch. It follows that any observable differences of political behaviour between high and low consumers of media political messages may have absolutely nothing to do with the impact of media, but everything to do with the initital reasons for viewing. This is the problem of the 'intervening variable' and prompts recall of the first but golden rule of social science methodology, 'correlation does not imply causality'.

Further problems arise when trying to isolate the influence of media on attitudes and behaviour from the influence of other agencies such as the family (where much viewing takes place – remember the Royle Family!) or school or work (where media are the staple diet of much conversation) (Cumberbatch and Howitt, 1989, p. 1). Klapper, in his classic review of the literature, *The Effects of Mass Communication*, summarised researchers' growing disenchantment with the hypodermic model. 'Two decades of research', he claimed, 'indicate that the tendency of persuasive mass communication to reinforce existing opinion is anything but hypodermic' (Klapper, 1960, p. 18). Gauntlett is more terse. 'Simply put' he argues 'the thesis makes little sense' (Gauntlett, 1997, p. 8): 'media effects research is generally a waste of time' (Gauntlett, 1997, p. vii).

Despite these forceful refutations, the ghost of the hypodermic model continues to stalk some of the stuffier and more reactionary corridors of power, where the televising of riots in Toxteth and St Pauls in the mid-1980s and on the Meadowell Estate in the north east in 1991 were judged to have prompted 'copy-cat' riots in other cities. The resilience of the theory to refutation by evidence and argument is testament to its congruence with deeply held 'common-sense' views about media effects. Moreover it must be remembered that scholarly studies of media may be conducted, and their findings tested and judged, within a sometimes hostile political climate. Barker and Petley, for example suggest that 'contemporary media academics are accused (usually by the pundits of the press, tabloid and broadsheet alike) of refusing to fall in behind populist, common sense, crudely behaviourist and hypodermic notions of "effects" and of peddling over-intellectualised, irresponsibly libertarian ideas derived from "fancy foreign theories"'. As a result serious work on the media by media specialists is either ignored, travestied or trashed – all in the name of 'common sense' of course' (Barker and Petley, 1997, p. 7). The existence of the National Viewers' and Listeners' Association (until recently associated with Mary Whitehouse), along with the judge's suggestion that the Bulger killers may have been influenced by the 'video nasty' *Child's Play* attest to the credibility of 'common sense' and the persistence of the effects model, long after academic assessment has consigned it to the graveyard of ideas. But advocates for such a view are to be found across the political spectrum. The hub of the feminist case against the publication of soft pornography, such as page three in the *Sun*, seems to be that these passive images of women presented as sexual objects promote physical and sexual violence against women.

THE TWO-STEP FLOW OF POLITICAL COMMUNICATION: A THEORY OF LIMITED MEDIA INFLUENCE

The publication of *The People's Choice* in 1944 by Lazarsfeld, Berelson and Gaudet, initiated a major shift in assessments of media influence. Media were no longer the persuasive Leviathans announced in the earlier studies; a considerably more modest, but complex, influence for media was now being claimed. Lazarsfeld *et al.* were trying to assess the impact of media on voting behaviour in American Presidential elections. The research methods employed by the study of the 1940 election were unambitious, but the findings were exceptional. Using a panel sample, Lazarsfeld *et al.* interviewed subjects regularly during the six months prior to the election to identify changes in political attitude and electoral preference and to see if these changes might be the consequence of media reporting of the campaign. Four significant findings were strongly at variance with the hypodermic model.

First, they discovered that voters' electoral choices were extremely resilient to media influence. More than 50 per cent of voters had decided their electoral choice in advance of media election coverage and remained faithful to that decision until polling day. Only a quarter of voters made a decision during the campaign and were therefore susceptible to media influence.

Second, the media reinforced people's existing electoral choices rather than encouraging change. Lazarsfeld *et al.* identified a process of selective exposure to media: voters listened only to those radio programmes and bought only those newspapers which endorsed their political attitudes and beliefs. 'Stability of political opinion', they argued, 'is a function of exposure to reinforcing communication' (Lazarsfeld *et al.*, 1944, pp. 88–9). The media were agents of reinforcement, not change (Blumler, 1979, p. 72; Clarke and Evans, 1983, p. 8). Third, the fairly small minority of voters who were undecided and hence possible 'converts' were the least interested in political affairs and the most minimal consumers of political and election news broadcast or published in media.

Finally, Lazarsfeld *et al.* (1944, p. 150) found that interpersonal communication was much more significant and influential in determining political views than exposure to media coverage of the election. Discussions with friends, members of the family and workmates, but especially with what they described as 'opinion leaders', were significant. Opinion leaders were trusted and respected members of social groups who tended to be more interested in political affairs, were greater consumers of political information and opinion from the media, and formed the vehicles for the transmission of media messages to other members of their immediate social group (Klapper, 1960, p. 32). They also formed a barrier against the direct influence of media on individuals. Media messages were interpreted and mediated by these opinion leaders establishing a two step flow of communications. Consequently, 'ideas often flow from radio and print to the opinion leaders and from them to the less active section of the population' (Lazarsfeld *et al.*, 1944, p. 151).

Opinion leaders are not necessarily high-status individuals but people at the centre of a communications network, 'playing a key communications role' (ibid., p. 152). A study of local party campaigning in the 1987 election reported that an election agent had constructed a detailed list of 'opinion leaders' – which included vicars, teachers, doctors, keepers of the corner shop and pub landlords – who received regular mail shots over the three years period prior to the election, to keep them informed about the party and candidate's policies (Franklin and Murphy, 1991, p. 161).

The rejection of the hypodermic model seemed complete. The tradition of two-step flow analysis initiated by Lazarsfeld *et al.* demonstrated that voters' political attitudes and beliefs were not formed by, but were resilient to, media influences. It also stressed audiences' ability to select and interpret media messages and argued that people were members of a number of social groups which structured their access to mass media and their influences upon them. The relationship between media and audience was infinitely more complex than earlier theories had imagined; the influence of media substantially less so.

But the two-step flow model eventually came to be criticised, not least for under-estimating the influence of media. Studies had tended to focus on the impact of media in the short term but neglected any consideration of longer term influences on political attitudes and behaviour. Critics argued that while television and press coverage of elections over the short period of the campaign (three to four weeks) was unlikely to prompt any Pauline conversions among the electorate, this did not deny any possibility for media influence. As Lewis observed, 'the complex set of ideological forces that create or change a person's political outlook is unlikely to be dislodged in three weeks'(Lewis, 1990, p. 157). A related criticism pointed to the use of a before-and-after methodology, which often resulted in researchers drawing inaccurate conclusions. People were asked if they had changed their mind on particular issues after exposure to media and, if they had not, it was assumed that the media had not prompted any effect. But the claim that media have *not prompted a change of mind* is not the same as the conclusion that people have *not been influenced* (Hall, 1982, p. 59).

Further criticisms stemmed from the division of audiences into active and passive members which allegedly simplified the communications process. Critics have challenged the assumption of a two-step rather than a multiple-step flow of communication (Howitt, 1982, p. 21; McQuail, 1987, p. 272), although the assertion of multi-step flow reduces even more dramatically any influence for the media (Kraus and Davis, 1976, pp. 119–22). The relationship between media and audience is complicated yet further by the suggestion that opinion 'leader' and 'follower' roles are not clearly demarcated, but may be variable and interchangeable across different topics, while many individuals may not be classifiable as either one or the other (McQuail, 1987, p. 272).

Critics have also suggested that while research within this tradition has confirmed the significance of interpersonal communication and discussion as a modifier of media influence, it has failed to demonstrate clearly that personal influence acts as an independent or oppositional source of influence on matters typically affected by mass media (Gitlin, 1978; McQuail, 1987, p. 272). McQuail also argues that direct effects from the media can occur without any mediation or intervention from opinion leaders and that on occasions where intervention by opinion leaders does occur, their effect may be to reinforce rather than counteract media influence (McQuail, ibid.).

USES AND GRATIFICATIONS: A THEORY OF WHAT PEOPLE DO WITH MEDIA

The uses-and-gratifications model of media and audience relations reversed the manner in which the issue of media effects had typically been addressed. Instead of trying to explore the various ways in which media might influence their audiences, communication scholars began to examine the different purposes for which people used mass media. The uses and gratifications approach', claimed Katz, '. . . is the program that asks the question not "what do the media do to people?" but, . . . "what do people do with the media?" ' (Katz, 1959, p. 2). Posed in this way, the power relationships between media and the audience are reversed. The media Leviathan has been toppled by the audience which uses media to gratify certain needs.

Uses and gratifications assumes an active audience composed of highly discriminating individuals who self-consciously and purposively engage with media to gratify certain needs and interests. The individual member of the audience is reduced to a set of needs; the media messages offer a variety of gratifications. The discourse of the pluralist, competitive, free market is never far away. The audience is cast in the role of the sovereign consumer selecting some goods and disregarding others from the superstore of media gratifications (Klapper, 1963; Rosengren et al., 1985; Werner and Tankard, 1988).

In *The Uses of Mass Communication* (1974), Blumler and Katz identify four major uses and gratifications which audiences derive from media. Television meets the need for *diversion*, by providing viewers with an escape from the pressures of everyday life; the need for *personal relationships* by offering companionship and conversation especially for lonely people; the need for *personal identity* by allowing individuals to contrast their own lives with those of personalities in television programming; and the need for *surveillance* by providing a source of news about a wide range of topics. McQuail offers a different typology of audience needs comprising *information, personal identity, integration* and *social interaction and entertainment* (McQuail, 1987, p. 73). Both classifications emphasise television's role as a surrogate for genuine interpersonal relationship. The argument is often illustrated by referring to viewers' deep involvement with the lives of characters in soap operas. When Bill Roach, the actor who has played Ken Barlow in *Coronation Street* for more than 40 years, appeared in court to contest a libel action against the *Sun* in 1991, members of the jury, the judge and even Roach himself, found great difficulty in separating the character attributes of the actor from his small-screen persona. As early as 1972, research studies were arguing that soap operas like *Coronation Street*, were meeting some viewers' social needs for companionship (Blumler *et al.*, 1972). The regular drinkers at the Queen Vic in Albert Square allegedly fulfil similar functions (Buckingham, 1987, p. 137). Quoting from qualitative audience research with focus groups, Taylor and Mullen suggest that the companionship which television provides is not merely 'a background "warmth" but something without which life became very difficult' (Taylor and Mullen, 1986, p. 184). Eva (72), for example, suggested that 'I'm in all day and its company for me' while Janet (32) argued that 'Television is company'; Pat (47) claimed 'It's another person living in your house all the time, isn't it? It's like having an extra person there' (Taylor and Mullan, 1986, pp. 183–4). But while some members of the audience watch *EastEnders* for companionship, others may view for entertainment, others for sheer escapism, yet others to confirm their prejudices about Londoners. The significant point here is that the same programme may gratify distinctive needs reflecting the diverse motives of individual viewers.

The uses and gratifications approach offers a sobering corrective to earlier assertions of media omnipotence, but critics argue that while it was correct to highlight the shortcomings of the 'effects' methodology, uses and gratifications studies should not have abandoned the wholly legitimate questions which that methodology failed to answer. By neglecting to address the substantive questions, uses and gratifications under-estimated media influence by investing decisions about media consumption in rational individuals. Consequently, as an intellectual tradition, it represented 'one step forward and two steps back' (Lewis, 1991, p. 14). Hart alleges the uses and gratifications approach is undermined by a circularity of reasoning; namely, the uses of media by particular audiences are the only evidence that the wants and needs, which the media are supposed to satisfy, actually exist in the first place (Hart, 1991, p. 43). Moreover, the needs which may be gratified by media are, in truth, not individual needs but needs which are 'socially structured. Individuals articulate the needs of social groups to which they belong and it is these social needs which structure their use of media' (Glover, 1984, p. 8; Hart, 1991, p. 43; Lewis, 1991, p. 16).

Critics have also challenged uses and gratifications studies for their monistic perception of human agency. Needs and desires are undoubtedly significant springboards for human action but, by themselves, they constitute an inadequate explanation of the complex motivations which inspire human decisions and judgements. Lewis offers a ribald metaphor. To suggest that audiences only see and hear those media messages that they *need* to see and hear 'is like reducing the world of sex and sexuality to the moment of orgasm' (Lewis, 1991, p. 16). Others have questioned the assumption of audience independence and autonomy. The 'needs' of the audiences are, at least in part, shaped and formed by the available diet of media output. Supply and demand are not wholly distinct and in this sense audience needs, and subsequent media choices, are made by media producers. Media consumption 'is more a matter of availability than selection' (Elliot, 1973, p. 21).

Methodological difficulties abound. There is, for example, little agreement about the basic needs which are allegedly met by media; a point well illustrated by the two distinctive classifications detailed above. The presumption of uses and gratifications that audiences purposefully select which programmes to watch or which newspapers to read is seriously undermined by studies which report the extent of unplanned viewing, or by Williams's assertions concerning the 'flow' of programmes which entices viewers to watch for longer than initially intended. Some people may watch a programme simply because it is on and they have nothing better to do. If uses and gratification theorists then suggest the programme is meeting the viewer's need for entertainment or diversion, this is rigging the argument to an extent where it becomes 'unfalsifiable'. Finally, Morley regrets the retreat from the sociological character of two-step flow theory which conceptualised relations between media and their audiences in a social context, whereas uses and gratifications' emphasis is on individuals, their needs and their motives; the very stuff of psychology (Morley, 1980, p. 13).

THE NATIONWIDE AUDIENCE: RECEIVING AND CREATING THE MEDIA MESSAGE

By the late 1970s, scholars were becoming increasingly sceptical about the very limited influence which uses and gratifications attributed to media and began to conceptualise media/audience relations in a radically different way. Stuart Hall argued that media messages are constructed jointly by broadcasters and audiences via the twin processes of encoding and decoding. News, or any media message, is not a factual representation of some external reality but an artifact, constructed by broadcasters and journalists, which presents a picture of reality shaped by distinctive and particular values (Hall, 1981, p. 276). Media messages are encoded ideologically by journalists with a distinctive or 'preferred' meaning, but audiences may decode the text with a certain latitude reflecting their own particular cultural codes which, in turn, relate to their broader social circumstances. To quote Hall:

> Broadcasters must interpret events, select the explanatory framework or
> context in which to set them, privilege or 'pre-fer' the meaning which seems

to make sense of them, and thus encode a meaning. Audiences like broadcasters, also stand in their own (very different) positions, relations and situations, have their own (again very different) relation to power, to information, to sources, and bring their own frameworks of interpretation to bear in order to get a meaning, or decode the message.

(ibid., p. 280.)

Hall's argument suggests that people do not watch television or read a newspaper with an 'open mind' but one which embraces a number of ideological predispositions. The ideological content of media output is capable of a number of interpretations, but the one which people make will reflect their existing dispositions and sociocultural circumstances. In the best Hegelian fashion, Hall has synthesised and thereby transcended the stale and allegedly contradictory antipathy of 'powerful media and passive audience', presumed by the hypodermic studies and the 'active audience but weak media' which informed uses and gratifications theory, by identifying a role for both media and audience in the construction of media messages. The analysis has important implications for studies of media and audience relations. Future analysis must consider not merely the content of media messages but the social situation of the viewer or reader. A new paradigm was established. The classic early empirical study of this reconceptualisation of media/audience relations is David Morley's study of *Nationwide*.

Morley shares Halls belief that media messages are shaped by the processes of encoding and decoding (Morley, 1980, p. 10). Audiences are not passive receivers of media messages but actively interpret them. To understand the differing interpretive frameworks viewers bring to this process, it is necessary to examine their social background and experiences, since 'decoding is determined by the socially governed distribution of cultural codes between and across different sections of the audience' (ibid., p. 18).

In his book *The Nationwide Audience*, Morley presented the findings from a study in which he showed 29 different groups, each composed of five to ten people, the same two editions of the BBC's current affairs and magazine programme *Nationwide*, initially broadcast in May 1976 and March 1977. He taped the subsequent group discussions about the programmes and the transcripts formed the basic data of the study (ibid., p. 36; Morley, 1992, Chs 3 and 4). The composition of the groups was diverse 'reflecting a wide range of ages as well as educational, occupational, social, cultural, ethnic and geographical backgrounds' (Morley, 1980, pp. 37–8).

Morley discovered that the different groups decoded the programme by making *dominant, oppositional* or *negotiated* readings of the 'text'. Certain groups (bank managers, apprentices, print managers and schoolboys) simply endorsed the *dominant* values encoded into the programme which broadly supported the status quo (ibid., pp. 105–7). But while the group supported the ideological message of the programme, it objected to the programme's presentational style or 'mode of address' which it believed was, 'patronizing' and failed to provide the group with a point of identification (ibid., pp. 106–7). Other groups (black further-education students and shop stewards) made *oppositional* readings which rejected or failed to recognise the preferred reading encoded in the programme. Group 22, an all male, white group of full-time trade-union officials, was irretrievably hostile to the values of *Nationwide*, arguing that the programme presented issues from 'an unacceptably right wing perspective' which was 'not for trade union officials but for the middle class' (ibid., p. 110). Finally, some groups (teacher-training students, trade-union officials and photography students) made a *negotiated* reading which broadly accepted the ideological position of the programme but attempted to modify it by making exceptions or qualifications in line with their own social situation (ibid., pp. 134–7).

Thus Morley argues that the encoded content of media messages, the way they are presented (their 'mode of address'), but significantly the interpretive frameworks possessed by viewers, are each vital ingredients in the construction of media messages. But social position does not directly correlate with, much less determine, the decoding of media messages. Apprentices, trade-union officials and black further-education students may share a common class position but their decodings of *Nationwide* 'are inflected in different directions by the influence of the discourses and institutions in which they are situated. In one case a tradition of mainstream working class populism, in another that of trade union and Labour party politics, in another the influence of black youth subculture' (ibid., p. 137). It follows that variations may exist within each of the three broad types of readings identified. The oppositional reading of *Nationwide* by black students was based on a sub-cultural perspective while the reading offered by shop stewards reflects a class perspective (ibid.).

The Glasgow University Media Groups' studies of media reporting of HIV/AIDS has evident affinities with Morley's work (Kitzinger, 1993, pp. 271–304; Eldridge, Kitzinger and Williams, 1997, pp. 162–7). Like Morley, Kitzinger understands the meaning of media messages to be co-constructed from the content of media messages and the diverse ways in which these messages are interpreted by audiences reflecting, in turn, aspects of their social identity shaped by gender, class, ethnicity, sexuality, age and so on. Her study involved 52 focus groups embracing 351 people aged between 14 and 81. The groups were of three kinds: first, people who might be expected to have some knowledge of HIV/AIDS (for example, doctors and social workers); second, people who were represented in media as high risk groups (young male prostitutes and drug users); finally people who had no obvious connection with HIV/AIDS (a group of civil engineers and a group of over 65-year-olds who attended the same retirement club). The groups met and discussed issues for two hours; their discussions were taped. Groups also played the 'News

Game' which involved giving them a group of photographs extracted from television news programmes about HIV/AIDS and asking group members to write a story in the style of a news item which those pictures would illustrate (Kitzinger, 1993, pp. 272–4).

Kitzinger found a significant influence for media. In the News Game sessions, members were able to reproduce news formats precisely: their stories often began 'Good evening and welcome to this evenings news' or 'news from the department of health today reveals dramatic increases in the number of people infected with the HIV/AIDS virus'. Kitzinger notes that when people were reading their stories, they even assumed the gestures of newsreaders. News stories, moreover, replicated specific messages using the language prominent in news programmes about HIV/AIDS. A picture of a young woman and her child, prompted reproduction of media phrases such as 'everyone is at risk', or 'no one is safe' or spoke of 'the innocent victims of AIDS': other stories commonly referred to phrases like 'body fluids', 'high risk groups', etc. But Kitzinger also discovered that while the media messages had a clear impact on viewers, they often lead to confusion and consequently messages about HIV transmission via body fluids for example were widely interpreted to mean that the virus could be transmitted via saliva which was not the case. Images also misled people – and dangerously. Kitzinger considers the image of what she terms the 'face of AIDS': an image prominent at the time of her research which featured the face of someone who looked very haggard, with jutting bones, sunken eyes and seemingly very ill and wasted. This image became very powerful in public perceptions and made it difficult for people to accept the Health Education Council message that people with HIV do *not* necessarily look ill – hence a rent boy's insistence that 'they do look different' (Eldridge, Kitzinger and Williams, 1997, p. 164).

Kitzinger concludes that while media were influential in shaping public attitudes towards HIV/AIDS, public reactions to media coverage of HIV/AIDS were strongly influenced by assumptions that predated the epidemic, including ideas about sexuality, gender and ethnicity. Kitzinger suggests that the power of any particular media message 'depends on how it taps into and builds on peoples' pre-existing perceptions'. Moreover, 'Audiences are active but not equal participants in the construction of meaning. They interpret what they hear and see in the context of what they already know or think ... Audiences selectively highlight, oppose or reconstruct statements and they are able to deconstruct dominant themes and to construct alternative accounts drawing on personal experience, political belief or a general critique of media or government sources' (Kitzinger, 1993, p. 300).

The wheel of media effects appears to have turned, but certainly not full circle. In the wake of the uses and gratifications theorists, the studies by Morley and Kitzinger suggest a stronger role for media: a move towards reinstating media as powerful, if not Leviathan. But this does not signal a return to the hypodermic theories. A theory of powerful media effects is certainly not quite radical chic once more, but the ghost of such studies refuses to lie down. There is a discernible creaking of coffin lids.

MEDIA AND POLITICS: FORMERS OR REFLECTORS OF PUBLIC OPINION?

In the aftermath of the 1992 General Election, politicians readily acknowledged what they believed had been the substantial influence of the British press in securing what had seemed an improbable victory for the Conservative Party. In his resignation speech Labour leader Neil Kinnock was unequivocal. 'The Conservative-supporting press', he claimed, 'has enabled the Tory party to win yet again when the Conservative party could not have secured victory for itself on the basis of its record, its programme or its character' *(Guardian*, 14 April 1992, p. 3). Many journalists agreed. The *Sun* in a famous editorial announced that 'It's the Sun wot won it' (11 April 1992) while *The Sunday Times* identified the late swing among *Sun* readers as the crucial factor which prevented Labour taking the decisive marginals like Basildon (MacArthur, 1992b). Lord McAlpine, a former Conservative Party treasurer, was in little doubt about the influence of the press on its readers and declared the editors of the pro-Conservative newspapers to be 'the heroes of this campaign' *(Sunday Telegraph*, 13 April 1992). Newspaper editors of all political persuasions, curiously sensitive to claims of partisanship, rounded forcefully on such allegations. But despite refutations from the higher echelons of the fourth estate, common sense seems to dictate that the constant 'drip, drip, drip' of tabloid disparagement targeted at the Labour Party must eventually have had an effect on support for the party.

The evidence for press influence on the electoral outcome is readily assembled. During the 1992 election, the majority of the electorate read a Conservative paper with 70 per cent of the national, daily circulation of newspapers supporting the Conservative Party; newspapers supporting the Labour Party enjoyed only 27 per cent of circulation (see Chapter 6). The extremely hostile reporting of the Labour Party in the final week of the campaign, moreover, coincided neatly with the late swing towards the Conservative Party. One study revealed an 8 per cent swing from Labour to Conservative support among readers of the pro-Conservative and vitriolically anti-Labour *Sun* in the three months prior to the election: readers of other Conservative papers revealed an equivalent swing while the electoral support of *Guardian* readers did not (Linton, 1995). Common sense rests its case.

Interestingly, by 1997 the figures for press partisanship were almost exactly the reverse of 1992 following 'the historic transformation of the hitherto "Tory press" into something altogether more unpredictable and interesting' (McNair, 2000, p. 140; Norris, 1998, p. 118). By 1997, nearly 70 per cent of the electorate was reading a paper which supported new Labour thanks, in no small part, to Rupert Murdoch's conversion to Blair's cause which triggered the significant headline 'The Sun Backs Blair' *(Sun*, 17 March 1997). Blair thanked the *Sun's* editor Stuart Higgins for the paper's 'magnificent support' which 'really did make the difference' (Greenslade in the *Guardian*, 19 May 1997). By 2001, 14 of the 19 national newspapers supported Labour giving the party a quite staggering circulation lead of 64 per cent above the Conservatives (Scammell and Harrop 2002, p. 156; Wring, 2002). The end of the Tory press seemed clear: it had been replaced by what journalist Peter Hitchen described ascerbically as 'the Tony press' (Wring, 2002, p. 84). These changes in press partisanship combined with Labour's landslide victories in 1997 and 2001 offer further and considerable, albeit prima facie, evidence in support of the common sense case for press influence.

But there is an equivalent case against any decisive influence for the press, albeit counter-intuitive (Harrop and Scammell, 1992, p. 208). The tabloid attacks on the Labour Party and Neil Kinnock in 1992 were allegedly no worse than the attacks on Michael Foot in 1983, Harold Wilson in 1964 (Preston, 1992, p. 22) or indeed on John Major in 1996 (Franklin, 1996, pp. 18–21). Many of the tabloids, moreover, gave the 1992 election story a low news salience with front page stories appearing in only five editions of the *Daily Star* and nine editions of the *Sun*. The thesis of press influence must also address the phenomenon of 'cross-reading' or 'cross-voting' where readers fail to vote for the party supported by their newspaper; 36 per cent of *Sun* readers in 1992, for example, were Labour supporters. Overstating the thesis of press influence, moreover, suited the convenience of some political and media players (McNair, 2000, p. 144). The press, for example, were convenient scapegoats for Neil Kinnock who might otherwise be obliged to acknowledge that Labour's campaign had been arrogant and misjudged; not least the infamous Sheffield celebratory rally held prior to the election. Thatcher also perhaps preferred to identify the power of the press as more electorally significant than the popularity of John Major her successor, while for Kelvin MacKenzie, the editor of the *Sun*, the claim to be 'kingmaker' represents the kind of self-serving, brash and swaggering statement which characterised his period as the tabloid's editor. It is also important to note the differing degrees of endorsement which newspapers offer the various parties: they are rarely simply 'for' or 'against' a particular party. The *Sunday Times* for example judged Labour to be 'the least worst party' (3 June 2001) while the *Sun* offered only lukewarm support for Labour compared to its previous and unconditional support for Thatcher's Conservative party. In brief, editorial declarations can range from 'staunch advocacy to the most tepid of endorsements' (Deacon and Wring, 2002. See Worcester and Mortimore, 2001, p. 157 for an analysis of the extent of individual newspaper's partisanship).

This highly contested debate about the impact of media coverage on political attitudes and behaviour continues with some authors signalling significant media effects (Newton and Brynin, 2001; Miller, 1991 and Linton, 1995) with others identifying a considerably lesser media influence (Curtice and Semetko, 1994, Norris *et al.*, 1999). Deacon and Wring

(2002), however, conclude that both advocates and critics of the 'common sense' or 'strong press thesis' might be making a too 'simple link' between press partisanship and voting behaviour: indeed they may be inverting the true character of the relationship. It is crucial to remember that newspapers are commercial, market driven organisations, with declining readerships. Newspapers need to be attentive to readers' shifting allegiances: consumers are sovereign in this market place as in others. But newspapers also entertain political ambitions (as do their editors) and seek to retain or establish influence with any new administration. Given these economic and political characteristics of newspapers, 'It is just as plausible to argue that national press affiliations follow rather than lead prevailing public opinion' (Deacon and Wring, 2002).

POLITICAL COMMUNICATION AND AUDIENCES: METHODOLOGICAL PROBLEMS

Recent academic studies of the political impact of media are relatively few; their findings are often contradictory and contentious. Both the absence and uncertainty of findings reflect, at least in part, a number of methodological difficulties (McNair, 1995, p. 29, 1999, p. 43).

First, many studies of the influence of media on politics focus on election campaigns, but this period is too short to generate the decisive shifts in political attitudes and behaviour which political scientists are trying to identify. In Britain the actual campaign (as distinct from the permanent postmodern campaign identified by Norris 1998, p. 127) is compressed into three to four weeks and studies focused on such a short time period invariably conclude that media have limited effects. But as Harrop warns, 'generalising from a brief campaign is as unjustified as exonerating cigarettes because no one gets lung cancer over the course of a three months study' (Harrop, 1987, p. 46). This limited focus, moreover, may ignore the impact of events of crucial electoral consequence immediately prior to the election, which mean 'that the result is never in doubt' (Negrine, 1989, p. 183); it may also ignore the impact of media reporting of such events. The industrial action by a number of public sector trades unions during 1978–79, dubbed by the tabloid press as 'the winter of discontent', guaranteed the Conservative Party entered the 1979 campaign with an unassailable lead. The extensive media reporting of 'Tory sleaze' prior to the 1997 election and the critical coverage of Hague's leadership in the run up to the 2001 election, offered new Labour similar electoral advantage. Such a limited focus might also ignore the influence of the press in between elections in shaping the government's agenda. David Seymour the *Mirror* group's political editor claimed that new Labour has 'followed the education, home affairs and European policies of the *Daily Mail* and the *Sun*' which he alleges is 'an agenda set by a few right wing newspapers' (Seymour, 2001, p. 14). A focus on the influence which newspapers' agendas might have for those of politicans and the public which is restricted to election periods alone, may well prove inadequate. The tendency of governments (of all political hues), moreover, to increase spending on policy advertising in the year prior to elections (see Chapter 4) is also judged (at least by critics) to give rise to electoral advantage to the governing party as well as opportunities for circumventing statutory limits on election expenditure.

Second, assessing the influence of media on voters is problematic because of the considerable changes in both media and political organisations between elections which mean that no two elections are strictly comparable. Between 1997 and 2001, for example, national press circulations dipped by 5 per cent with the tabloids (the *Sun* –8 per cent and the *Mirror* –10 per cent) suffering a particularly sharp decline: across the same period, however, the strongly Conservative supporting *Daily Mail* expanded readership by a striking 11 per cent. These circulation shifts, which suggest that more readers of tabloids might be reading Conservative supporting papers in 2001, were offset by other changes which can occur when newspapers change proprietors and partisanship between elections. Lord Hollick's ownership of the *Express*, for example, along with the appointment of editor Rosie Boycott in 1998, triggered a shift in the paper's loyal support for the Conservatives prior to the 1997 election, to active endorsement of the Labour Party (Deacon and Wring, 2002; Scammell and Harrop, 2002, p. 157). The sale of the *Express* and the *Star* to Richard Desmond in November 2000 did not result in any overall changes in the papers' partisanship but prompted the departure of Boycott and distinguished left-leaning journalists such as political editor Anthony Bevins thereby reshaping the nuances of the paper's political journalism. Worcester and Mortimore point to the complex pattern of readers shifts in partisanship following changes in the political line of the *Express*. Readers of the *Express* remained stubbornly loyal to the Conservative Party despite the change in editorial stance. In mid 2000, 45 per cent of *Express* readers expressing a preference were Conservative (15 per cent higher than the public as a whole) while 34 per cent supported Labour (16 per cent below average). By the 2001 election, the Conservative share of readers was only 10 per cent higher than the public as a whole and Labour supporters only 9 per cent lower. In brief *Express* readers 'swung disproportinately to Labour' which might signal influence for the press or it may be that 'many of its Tory readers simply switched to reading another paper altogether' (Worcester and Mortimore, 2001, pp. 160–1).

Third, it is difficult to disentangle the influence which media may exercise over political attitudes and behaviour from the influence of 'non-media' agencies such as the Church, education and the family. Deriving inspiration from Althusser, Lewis argues that these are all 'ideological apparatuses that shape the way we think' (Lewis, 1990, p. 155). But the list is potentially endless. Interpersonal communications at work, at home or in the pub, as well as the general influence of the community in which we live, must all be taken into account. It is moreover difficult to isolate the influence of particular media on political decisions. Most people are omnivorous in their consumption of media and assessing the impact of any particular diet of radio, television, newspapers and the Internet is virtually impossible (Norris, *et al.* 1999, p. 48).

Finally, as the discussion of Morley underscores, the reporting of the campaign and political events more generally will be interpreted in radically different ways by groups within the broader audience, reflecting the heterogeneity of age, class, gender, ethnicity, education and other factors which characterise them.

It is perhaps unsurprising, given these methodological problems, that evidence concerning the impact of media on political attitudes and behaviour is not over-abundant and, where it exists, tentative. But more recent studies suggest that media effects extend beyond the mere reinforcement of existing political attitudes which was too frequently the conclusion of studies conducted during the 1950s.

POLITICAL ATTITUDES AND BEHAVIOUR: THE IMPACT OF TELEVISION AND NEWSPAPERS

Four points emerge from the classic studies analysing the impact of television on political attitudes and behaviour. First, it seems that even the decision about whether or not to vote in a general election – what psephologists term 'voter turnout' – is directly related to levels of television exposure, with those who view extensively being 21 per cent more likely to vote than more moderate consumers of television election coverage (Crewe et al., 1977, pp. 38–109, Table 27). A study of first-time voters (18–24 years) in the 1970 British election confirmed that campaign communication variables, such as exposure to television reporting of the campaign and political discussions of electoral matters with friends, workmates and family, were important factors influencing turnout (Blumler and McLeod, 1974, p. 295). In 2001 the 59 per cent turnout, the lowest since 1918, was attributed to a wide range of factors but one senior journalist believed it reflected the fact that 'the level of engagement among journalists was lower than in previous elections and this transmitted itself to the electorate' (Jones, 2001, p. 585).

Second, television coverage of elections increases viewers' stock of political knowledge about parties, leaders and policies. Television election coverage is undeniably part of a process of political learning. A study of the earliest television election in 1959 reported that there 'is a very significant association between the amount of political news and propaganda an elector received through television and his better understanding of the policies the parties were putting forward' (Treneman and McQuail, 1961, p. 233). In 2001, Worcester and Mortimore confirmed that Electoral Commission research suggests that political information is the 'key driver in framing attitudes to voting' particularly among 'hard to reach groups such as young and non-white citizens', while MORI polling suggested that 'lack of information is the key reason for people saying they are undecided about who to vote for' (Worcester and Mortimore, 2001, p. 146). Paradoxically, respondents to a survey conducted after the 2001 election complained that there was too much, rather than too little, election coverage on television and in the press: they also wanted election coverage which was more candidate and policy-focused (Worcester and Mortimore, 2001, pp. 149–50).

Third, the knowledge of political and electoral matters derived from television may subsequently be used by voters when deciding which party to support. In this way, television influences viewers' political knowledge and, via knowledge, their attitudes and ultimately voting behaviour. In 2001, for example, a poll conducted by MORI and the Electoral Commission found 13 per cent of respondents claiming that election coverage on television had a 'great deal' of influence on their electoral choice with a further 36 per cent claiming a 'fair amount' of influence for television: 20 per cent suggested 'not very much' influence for television with a further 30 per cent claiming 'no' influence for television (Criddle, 2002, p. 215).

Fourth, Patterson's study of audience responses to the candidate debates in the 1976 American presidential elections suggested a considerable influence for television commentators on viewers' political attitudes. Of respondents interviewed within 12 hours of the debate, 53 per cent declared Gerald Ford the victor. But respondents interviewed 12–48 hours after the debate, who had listened to commentators' assessments of the two candidates performance, differed markedly from this view. Of this second group, 58 per cent shared the view of the overwhelming majority of television commentators that Jimmy Carter had won, citing Ford's bungling of the East European question in evidence. The belief that Carter had won the debate was particularly marked among 'heavy news users' (Patterson, 1980, p. 122, cited in Negrine, 1989, p. 190).

Miller expresses reservations about television's influence. He agrees that television was 'immensely effective at communicating party themes to the electorate' (providing information), but suggests that 'it had only a small influence on the public's issue agenda' (influencing attitudes) (Miller, 1991, p. 164). Miller illustrates the argument by pointing to the disjuncture between media and public issue agendas and the inability of the former to influence the latter to any significant extent during the campaign. Television's reluctance to feature unemployment, for example, did not diminish the persistent significance of this issue in the public's agenda. Similarly, the dramatic shift to defence during the final week of the campaign was not matched by any significant or equivalent shift in the public's concern about this issue. 'We must conclude', Miller believes, 'that television could influence but not dictate the the public agenda' (ibid., p. 165).

Miller also argues that television had little impact on trends in party support in 1987. He suggests a high degree of electoral volatility, with two-fifths of the electorate changing their voting intentions during the short three-week campaign, but argues that these changes did not reflect voters' reassessment of policies or leaders, prompted by television coverage, so much as 'tactical considerations' (Miller, et al., 1990, p. vii). He concedes, however, that television coverage may have influenced party credibility by 'publicising opinion poll findings' (Miller, 1991, p. 165). But changes in television presentation of the campaign reflected changed public priorities and preferences rather than the other way around. Television coverage followed public opinion, but did not lead it (Miller, *et al.*, 1990, p. vii).

Assessments of press influence on political knowledge, attitudes and behaviour are similarly varied, ranging from studies which suggest a limited influence for newspapers, to those which suggest their influence might be substantial (Linton, 1995; Newton, 1990; Newton and Brynin, 2001; Worcester and Mortimore, 2001). As with television there is a need for caution when evaluating the evidence. A study of local press coverage of the constituency campaigns in all elections between 1987 and 2001 revealed that most election agents believed that coverage of parties and candidates between elections was more significant for its impact on electoral outcomes than the reporting across the short three-to-four week campaign period (Franklin, 1989a, p. 214 and Franklin and Richardson, 2002, p. 37; see Chapter 7).

Initially, research suggested that the influence of newspapers was fairly limited. Harrop's analysis of post-war trends in the readership, ownership and political commitments of the British national press concludes that the net effect of newspapers' ability to reinforce readers' opinions and crystallise the electoral choices of uncommitted voters is equivalent to a modest swing of about 1 per cent (10 seats) from Labour to Conservative between elections (Harrop, 1986, p. 148). Such a swing is certainly 'not to be sniffed at', but it is 'hardly decisive' (Harrop, 1987, p. 58).

By 1990, assessments of press influence seem to have undergone a transformation. An analysis of the 1983 and 1987 elections concluded that 'there is a strong and statistically highly significant relationship between reading a newspaper which supports a particular party and voting for that party' (Newton, 1990, p. 21, see also Newton and Brynin, 2001). In 1992 a study underlined the longer-term political effects of newspapers by highlighting the 9 per cent swing to the Conservative Party among *Sun* readers, compared to only a 1 per cent swing among *Mirror* readers between mid-1991 and April 1992 (Miller, 1992, pp. 17–18). Miller's detailed study of media influence on voters in the 1987 election supported these conclusions, but the evidence is highly complex. Newspapers were influential on the political attitudes of voters during the 1987 campaign, but because the press is highly differentiated with quality and tabloid papers appealing to distinctively structured readerships, expressing differing degrees and directions of partisanship and conveying highly variable amounts of political content, their influence is far from unitary. Miller details four specific findings. First, right-wing papers enhanced their readers' images of the Conservative Party and its leader but diminished readers' images of the Labour Party and its leader. Second, press influence was modest compared to the influence of partisan commitments but developed across the campaign such that at its close, Labour identifiers who read a Conservative newspaper were 6 per cent more favourable but 6 per cent less favourable to Kinnock than Labour identifiers who did not read such a paper

(Miller, 1991, p. 197). Third, the press had 'a significant effect on voters' preferences' (ibid., p. 198). Finally, the influence of the tabloid press was particularly marked among 'politically uncommitted readers' with the Conservative lead increasing by 50 per cent among politically uncommitted readers of the *Sun* and *Star*. The tabloids seemed especially able to influence readers' voting decisions while broadsheets like the *Guardian* and the *Daily Telegraph* were influential with readers on particular issues but seemed less able to influence voting choice (ibid., pp. 198–9).

By 2001 Worcester and Mortimore's conclusion was unequivocal. 'It is clear that there is a close correlation between the papers' partisan bias and their readers' votes' they argued. 'Only the two *Express* titles, the *FT* and *The Times*, saw more of their readers vote for the major party they were "biased" against than for the one they favoured' (Worcester and Mortimore 2001, pp. 158–9). But they also counselled caution about 'assuming a causal relationship here – a newspaper's readership is not a captive audience, and such a correlation can arise just as well from voters choosing to buy a newspaper they agree with as from the paper having the power to sway the opinions of its readers' (ibid., p. 160).

MEDIA AND ELECTORS: REINFORCEMENT OR CHANGE?

Harrop is unhappy with the conclusion of studies which suggest that media influence tends to reinforce rather than change voters' political attitudes. The prominence of the 'reinforcement conclusion' in the literature derives, he argues, from posing 'an over simple question ... What are the effects of media on electors?' (Harrop, 1987, p. 45). But 'media' and 'electors' are highly heterogeneous categories. Media embrace film, radio, television, Internet and newspapers. The press may, in turn, be classified into local and national, or tabloid and broadsheet. Electors display an equivalent diversity and can be distinguished according to the strength of their political commitments, the extent of their political knowledge and the intensity of their interest in political affairs. Each of these factors might prove significant variables in enhancing or limiting media effects. In truth, the question, 'What are the effects of media on electors?' must be disaggregated into a number of distinctive inquiries before the complexities of relations between media and voters can be unravelled. Harrop argues that media influence depends on the nature of the elector, the society, the message and the type of effect which is being considered.

Media influence will be greatest among *electors* who tend not to discuss politics, have limited knowledge of political issues, tend to use media for general surveillance of the political environment rather than reinforcement of their political views and have only moderate exposure to media (ibid., p. 47). This last point is interesting since it undermines the intuitive belief that television influence is directly related to exposure; if television influences voters, more television must influence voters more! But heavy media consumption is a characteristic of people with high levels of political knowledge and interest, factors which militate against media influence (see also McQuail,1987, p. 261; Negrine, 1989, p. 184). Individuals' tendency not to discuss political issues may, of course, isolate them from alternative viewpoints and opinions which, in turn, may render them more receptive to media messages: a process acknowledged by Philo in his study of the coal dispute in 1984–5 (Philo, 1990c, p. 150).

Certain characteristics of *society* may also serve as variables for media influence. Harrop argues that media will be most influential where party and social-group loyalties are weak. The growth of partisan dealignment in Britain since the 1970s is one instance of a more generalised 'loosening' of social and political ties which create greater opportunities for media influence (Harrop, 1987, p. 48); electoral volatility and the emergence of new parties offer yet further scope for media influence (Blumler *et al.*, 1986, p. 110). The reverse proposition may also be true. In societies like Northern Ireland, where social, political and religious loyalties are deeply held, no one believes that a television or newspaper report might persuade a Sinn Fein supporter to vote for the Democratic Ulster Unionists!

The character of media *messages* is also significant for their influence on electors. Harrop (1987) claims that media messages will influence attitudes to new features of the political landscape more than to the familiar. Another feature of the message which is crucial to its potential impact on electors is its credibility. As McQuail acknowledges, 'messages stemming from an authoritative and credible source will be relatively more effective' (McQuail, 1987, p. 261). Television is considered to be a more credible source of electoral news than the press and consequently might be judged more influential (Miller, 1991, p. 129).

The influence of media is also dependent on the type of *effect* being analysed. Effects may be highly variable, but one way in which they can be distinguished is according to the time-scale on which they are measured. Some of the studies cited above concluded that the short term influence of media, measured across the brief period of the election campaign, may not be substantial, but long term cumulative effects may be greater (Hall, 1982, p. 59; Lewis, 1990, p. 157).

Alternatively, effects may be distinguished according to their focus, i.e., on an elector's information, attitudes or behaviour. The usual 'effects hierarchy' is one in which media influence is greatest on an elector's political information (cognition), followed by attitudes (affective) but which is least evident on behaviour (connotative). It follows that studies seeking to identify media influences on political behaviour were exploring merely the tip of the effect's iceberg. McQuail suggests this pattern of effects, moreover, presumes an individual who is highly motivated and displays high levels of interest and involvement. For an individual with low involvement (common in many television viewing situations) the sequence may be from cognition directly to behaviour, with attitude changes occurring *ex post* to make opinions and beliefs congruent with behaviour (McQuail, 1987, p. 261). In such circumstances it is attempts to identify and measure attitude changes which might fail to note media effects.

Finally, effects may be distinguished according to their nature. One effect of media on electors may be to help those who are unclear about their electoral choice to crystallise their opinions into a firm decision. The influence of media may, however, be to reinforce viewers in their existing political beliefs while the most extensive media influence results in changes to political attitudes or behaviour. This is the least likely of media effects. The nature of media effects is consequently a good deal more complex than answers to the simple inquiry, 'What are the effects of media on electors?' might imagine.

MEDIA, AUDIENCES AND THE PACKAGING OF POLITICS

The analysis of media influences on electors must consider the complex nature of electors and the extent of their political knowledge, interest and commitments, as well as the strength of social and political loyalties within the broader political community. The credibility, authority and 'novelty' of the media message is also significant. Whether the effect to be measured is on political information, attitudes or behaviour, whether the effect is short or long term or whether the effect serves to reinforce or change existing views, must also be assessed. The size and variegated character of the audience and the variable impact of different media on audiences must also be taken into account. Additionally, it is important to consider the extent of audience involvement with particular programmes and newspaper articles and their motives for watching or reading the particular text. It is also salutary to remember that election coverage is considered uninteresting by large sections of both television and newspaper audiences, whose first reaction may be to switch off or turn to the crossword.

But these are only a few of the problems to be confronted when assessing media influence on audiences. It is, for example, practically impossible to isolate the effects of media from other influences on voters' choices. More significantly, it is crucial to remember that media do not create 'effects' in audiences according to any simple 'stimulus/response' model. Morley (1992) has illustrated that audiences are complicitous with media in generating 'messages'. Media messages are the result of a complex interaction between media content and readers who bring distinctive interpretive frameworks to the decoding process which reflect the particularities of their social and cultural backgrounds and experiences. As Newton observed, by playing with the words of a cliche, while we may not believe all that we read in the papers, we may tend to read in them what we believe (Newton, 1990). This complexity does not necessarily lead, however, to Berelson *et al.*'s ambiguous conclusion that 'some kinds of communication, on some kinds of issues, brought to the attention of some kinds of people under some kinds of conditions, have some kinds of effects' (Berelson *et al.*, 1954, p. 356). Certain trends are evident.

A number of studies reveal that television influences voters' political knowledge, attitudes and behaviour, in both the short and long term. Television influences levels of voter turn-out, helps viewers to make their electoral choices and is especially influential with certain categories of voters who may be 'undecided', 'floating' or 'new' voters. Because television is subject to statutory controls, coverage is reatively even-handed and consequently television's influence is greater on political knowledge than attitudes. But British broadcasting is undergoing radical changes with evident implications for the influence of political broadcasting.

The broadcasting philosophy implemented by the Broadcasting Acts 1990, 1996 and 2003 prefers a system driven by market considerations and regulated with a 'lighter touch': in the 2003 Act the touch become as light as a feather! In this new commercial environment, the extent of political programming in the broadcast schedule, broadcasters' commitments to the public service tradition of broadcasting and the very character of public service broadcasting are changing. The growth of a multi-channel broadcasting environment replete with digital, cable and satellite channels, moreover, signals the development of 'narrowcasting' with specific channels appealing to closely identified audiences. Television audiences, like newspaper readerships, will become highly differentiated, with specific messages targeted at distinctive audiences. On commercial channels such as Channel 3 and Channel 5, which are increasingly 'ratings-driven' and chase large audiences and high advertising revenues, pressures on political broadcasting are likely to be severe. A number of recent studies are beginning to catalogue striking reductions in the amount of broadcasting time devoted to documentary programming (Campaign for Quality Television 1998) current affairs (Barnett and Seymour, 1999; Barnett, et al., 2001) and parliamentary programming (Franklin, 1995) while other studies point to the declining quality of much news and current affairs output signalling a decline in investigative journalism and foreign coverage (Franklin, 1997; Sampson, 1996). On other channels, perhaps the news and current affairs subscription channels, programming will increase. The latter, however, are likely to be supported by the most politically well informed and highly committed viewers who are least influenced by television. But the commercial channels where the quality and independence of political and electoral coverage may become less apparent than is currently the case will be watched by those people which studies suggest are most vulnerable to media influence. Broadcasting's common pasture of quality news and current affairs provision is likely to be 'enclosed' by market forces. Television's impact on electors may be considered likely to grow.

Newspapers already serve the needs of highly differentiated readerships. The influence of tabloids, with their clear partisanship, but spartan provision of political information, tends to be on readers' political attitudes. Conversely, the qualities tend to confine opinions to editorials with the bulk of reporting offering copious political information which readers can use to help to make political choices: online editions of broadsheet papers provide further extensive news coverage of political affairs. Newspaper circulations have experienced a long-term decline since 1945 and the expansion of television as the major source of most people's news in the short term is likely to confirm that trend. In these circumstances of expansive, but deregulated, television news serving increasingly differentiated audiences, combined with slowly dwindling alternative sources of news provided by print journalism, it seems likely that the influence of media on the political knowledge, attitudes and behaviour of the public will increase. The conditions are ripe; the packaging of politics seems certain to flourish.

REFERENCES

Adams, B. (1974) 'The council newspaper: A Public Interest', *Municipal Review*, vol. 45, November, pp. 252–54.

Ahmed, K. (1998) 'Broadcast Threat Angers Labour' *Guardian*, 21 January, p. 8.

Aitken, I. (1991) 'Mrs T's blunt instrument', *Guardian*, 16 May.

Allen, R. (1986) 'Working within the Local Government Act 1986'. Unpublished paper presented to the Institute of Public Relations Local Government Group annual conference, Wolverhampton.

Alvarado, M., Gutch, R. and Wollen, T. (1987) *Learning the Media: an Introduction to Media Teaching*, London and Basingstoke: Macmillan.

Armstrong, S. (2000) 'Poster Power' *Guardian*, 27 November, pp. 8–9.

Article 19 (1989) *No Comment: Censorship, Secrecy and the Irish Troubles*, The International Centre on Censorship, London.

Ashley, J. (2002) 'Puttnam is right to want broadcasting to stay British' *Guardian*, 31 July, p. 16.

Ashley, J. (2003) 'The Knives Are Out But The Master of Spin Will Survive' *Guardian*, 16 January, p. 24.

Atkinson, M. (1984) *Our Masters' Voices*, London: Routledge.

Audit Commission (1995) *Talk Back: Local Authority Communication With Citizens*, London: HMSO.

Barbour, R.S. and Kitzinger, J. (1999) *Developing Focus Group Research*, London: Sage.

Bains (1972) *The New Local Authority: Management and Structure* (The Bains Report), London: HMSO.

Baird, R. (1997) 'Keeping an eye on the COI' *Press Gazette*, 19 September, p. 13.

Baistow, T. (1985) *Fourth Rate Estate*, London: Comedia.

Ballinger, C. (2002) 'The Local Battle, The Cyber Battle' in Butler, D. and Kavanagh, D. (eds) *The British General Election of 2001*, London: Palgrave, pp. 208–34.

Barker, M. and Petley, J. (1997) *Ill Effects: the Media /Violence Debate* London: Routledge.

Barnados (1993) *HIV and AIDS: Who's Telling the Children?* London: Barnados.

Barnett, S. (1992) 'Hijacked! Television and politics during the election', *British Journalism Review*, vol. 3 no. 2, pp. 17–19.

Barnett, S. and Gaber, I. (1991) 'Televising Parliament: some unexplored consequences'. Paper presented to International Television Studies Conference, London, July.

Barnett, S. and Gaber, I. (2001) *Westminster Tales: The Twenty First Century Crisis in Political Journalism*, London: Continuum.

Barnett, S. and Seymour, E. (1999) *A Shrinking Iceberg Slowly Travelling South: Changing Trends in British Television – A Case Study of Drama and Current Affairs*, London Campaign for Quality Television.

Barnett, S., Seymour, E. and Gaber, I. (2000) *From Callaghan to Kosovo: Changing Trends in British Television News 1975–1999*, University of Westminster.

Bartle, S. and Griffiths, D. (2001) *Political Communications Transformed: From Morrison to Mandelson*, Basingstoke: Palgrave.

Barwise, P. and Ehrenberg, A. (1990) *Television and its Audience*, London and Beverly Hills, CA: Sage.

Bayley, S. (1998) *Labour Camp: The Failure of Style Over Substance*, London: BT Batsford.

BBC (1992) *Expanding Choice: The BBC's Role in the New Broadcasting System*, London: BBC.

BBC (1993) *Responding to the Green Paper*, London: BBC.

BBC/ITC/Radio Authority/S4C (1998) *Consultation Paper on the Reform of Party Political Broadcasting*, London, January.

Bell, T. (1982) 'The Conservative's advertising campaign', in R. Worcester and M. Harrop (eds) *Political Communications*, London: Allen & Unwin.

Belson, W. (1978) *Television Violence and the Adolescent Boy*, Farnborough: Saxon House.

Benfield, C. (1987) 'Taking notice of national security', *UK Press Gazette*, 19 October, p. 12.

Benn, T. (2001) 'The Media and The Political Process' James Cameron Lecture 2001 in Stephenson, H. (ed.) *Media Voices: The James Cameron Memorial Lectures*, London: Politicos, pp. 327–45.

Benn, T. (1994) *Years of Hope: Diaries, Papers and Letters 1940–1962*, London: Hutchman.

Berelson, B., Lazarsfeld, P. and McPhee W. (1954) *Voting*, Chicago, IL: University of Chicago Press.

The Broadcasting Committee Report, Lord Beveridge (Chair) 1951, Cmd 8116, Cmd 8117, ix, I, pp. vii–327.

Bevins, A. (1990) 'The crippling of the Scribes', *British Journalism Review*, vol. 1, no. 2, pp. 13–18.

Birrell, I. and Hughes, D. (1989) 'Row grows over £50 million sell-off ads', *The Sunday Times*, 8 January.

Birt, J. (1993) *The BBC*, The Royal Television Society Fleming Memorial Lecture, 30 March, London: BBC.

Blair, T. (1989) 'Privatization advertising: a report'. Unpublished report by the then Shadow Spokesperson for Trade and Industry.

Blumler, J. G. (1967) 'Parliament and television', *Encounter*, vol. 28, no. 3, pp. 52–56.

Blumler, J. G. (1979) 'An overview of recent research into the impact of broadcasting in democratic politics' in M. J. Clark (ed.) *Politics and the Media: Film and Television for the Political Scientist and the Historian*, Oxford: Pergamon Press.

Blumler, J. G. (1981) 'Political communication: democratic theory and broadcast practice', *University of Leeds Review*, pp. 43–62.

Blumler, J. G. (1984) 'The Sound of Parliament', *Parliamentary Affairs*, pp. 250–67.

Blumler, J. G. (1990) 'The modern publicity process', in M. Ferguson (ed.) *Political Communication: The New Imperatives*, London: Sage, pp. 101–14.

Blumler, J. G. (1991) 'Parliamentary communication in Britain'. Paper presented to the Conference on Parliamentary Information in the 1990s: The Italian Case and the European Situation, 6–7 November, Rome.

Blumler, J. G. (1992) *Television and the Public Interest: Vulnerable Values in West European Broadcasting*, London: Sage.

Blumler, J.G. and Coleman, S. (2001) *Realising Democracy Online: A Civic Commons in Cyberspace*, London: IPPR/Citizens Online Research Publication.

Blumler, J. G. and Gurevitch, M. (1975) 'Towards a comparative framework for political communications research', in S. Chaffe (ed.) *Political Communication: Issues and Strategies for Research*, (vol. iv), London and Beverly Hills, CA: Sage.

Blumler, J. G. and Gurevitch, M. (1981) 'Politicians and the press: an essay on role relationships', in D. Nimmo and K. Saunders (eds) *Handbook of Political Communication*, London, and Beverly Hills, CA: Sage. pp. 467–97.

Blumler, J. G. and Gurevitch M. (1986) 'Journalists' orientation to political institutions: the case of parliamentary broadcasting', in P. Golding, G. Murdock and P. Schlesinger (eds) *Communicating Politics*, Leicester: Leicester University Press.

Blumler, J.G. and Gurevitch, M. (1995) *The Crisis In Public Communications*, London: Routledge.

Blumler, J.G. and Gurevitch, M. (1998) 'Change in the Air: Campaign Journalism at the BBC' in Crewe, I. Gosschalk, B. and Bartle, J. (eds) *Political Communications: Why Labour Won the General Election of 1997*, London: Cass, pp. 176–194.

Blumler, J. G. and Gurevitch, M. (2000) 'Rethinking the Study of Political Communication' in Curran, J and Gurevitch, M. (eds) *Mass Media and Society*. 3rd Edition. London: Edward Arnold.

Blumler, J. G. and Katz, E. (1974) *The Uses of Mass Communications*, London, and Beverly Hills, CA: Sage.

Blumler, J. G. and Kavanagh, D. (1999) 'The Third Age of Political Communication: Influences and Features' in *Political Communication*, vol. 16 no 3, pp. 209–30.

Blumler J. G. and McLeod, J. (1974) 'Communication and voter turnout in Britain', in T. Leggatt (ed.) *Sociological Theory and Survey Research: Institutional Change and Social Policy in Great Britain*, London, and Beverly Hills: Sage, CA, pp. 265–312.

Blumler, J. G. and McQuail, D. (1968) *Television in Politics*, Faber & Faber: London.

Blumler, J. G., McQuail, D. and Brown, R. (1972) 'The television audience: a revised perspective', in D. McQuail (ed.) *The Sociology of Mass Communications*, Penguin, Harmondsworth, pp. 136–66.

Blumler, J. G. and Nossiter, T. (eds) (1991) *Broadcasting Finance in Transition: A Comparative Handbook*, Oxford: Oxford University Press.

Blumler, J., Gurevitch, M. and Nossiter, T. (1986) 'Setting the television news agenda: campaign observation at the BBC', in I. Crewe and M. Harrop (eds) *Political Communications: The General Election of 1983*, Cambridge: Cambridge University Press, pp. 104–24.

Blumler, J., Gurevitch, M. and Nossiter, T. (1989) 'The earnest vs. the determined', in I.

Crewe and M. Harrop (eds) *Political Communications: The General Election Campaign of 1987*, Cambridge: Cambridge University Press, pp. 157–75.

Bolton, R. (1990) *Death on the Rock and Other Stories*, London: W. H. Allen.

Boulton, A. (1998) 'Television and the 1997 General Election: A View from Sky News' in Crewe, I., Gosschalk, B. and Bartle, J. (eds) *Political Communications: Why Labour Won the General Election of 1997*, London: Cass, pp. 195–204.

Boulton, D. (1991) *The Third Age of Broadcasting*, London: Institute for Public Policy Research.

Bovill, M. (1991) *Audience Reactions to Parliamentary Television – An Update*, London: BBC Special Projects.

Bovill, M., McGregor, R. and Wober, M. (1992) 'Audience reactions to parliamentary television', in *Televising Democracies*, London: Routledge. pp. 149–70.

Bradlee, B. (1987) 'Why the press must confront all lies', *UK Press Gazette*, 4 May, p. 44.

'Breaking the silence at County Hall' (1986) *PR Week*, 19 November, p. 14.

Brennen, B. (2000) 'Communication and Freedom: An Althusserian reading of media/government relations' in *Javnost/The Public*, vol. 7, no. 4, pp. 5–16

Brignull, T. (1992) 'Sales pitches more suited to 60 second slots', *Guardian*, 11 April, p. 8. *The Broadcasting Act 1990*, London: HMSO.

Buckingham, D. (1987) *Public Secrets: Eastenders and its Audience*, London: BM.

Bull, P. and Mayer, K. (1988) 'Interventions in political interviews: a study of Margaret Thatcher and Neil Kinnock', *Journal of Language and Social Psychology*, vol. 7, no. 1, pp. 44–5.

Burke, R. (1970) *The Murky Cloak: Local Authority Press Relations*, Croydon: Charles Knight.

Butler, D. and Kavanagh, D. (1981) *The British General Election of 1979*, London: Macmillan.

Butler, D. and Kavanagh, D. (1984) *The British General Election of 1983*, London: Macmillan.

Butler, D. and Kavanagh, D. (1988) *The British General Election of 1987*, London: Macmillan.

Butler, D. and Kavanagh, D. (1992) *The British General Election of 1992*, London: Macmillan.

Butler, D. and Kavanagh, D. (2002) *The British General Election of 2001*, London: Palgrave.

Butler, D. and Rose, R. (1960) *The British General Election Of 1959*, London: Macmillan.

Cabinet Office (1997) *Guidance on the Working of the Government Information Service*, London: HMSO.

Calcutt, D. (1993) *Review of Press Self-Regulation*, Cmnd 2135, London: Department of National Heritage. January.

Campaign for Quality Television (1998) *Serious Documentaries on ITV*, London: The Campaign for Quality Television Ltd.

Campbell, A. (2002) 'Time to Bury Spin' in *British Journalism Review*, vol. 13, no. 4, pp. 15–23.

Campbell, A. Harrop, A. and Thompson, B. (1999) 'Towards the Virtual Parliament: What Computers Can Do for MPs' in *Parliamentary Affairs*, vol. 52, no. 3, pp. 388–403.

Campbell, D. (1988) 'BBC's Zircon programme and the role of Colonel Protheroe', *UK Press Gazette*, 28 November, p. 7.

Cantril, H., Caudet, H. and Hertzog, H. (1940) *The Invasion from Mars*, Princeton, NJ: Princeton University Press.

Carroll, R. (1998) 'Producers "Bombarded" With Political Storylines' *Guardian*, 17 September 1998, p. 4.

Carty, R. K. and Eagles, M. (2000) 'Is There A Local Dimension to Modern Election Campaigns? Party Activists' Perceptions of the Media and Electoral Coverage' in *Political Communication*, vol. 17, no. 3, pp. 279–95.

Central Office of Information (2001) Annual Reports and Accounts 2000–2001 HC53 London: HMSO.

Cassell, M. (1988) 'Government advertising: Labour alleges partiality', *The Financial Times*, 13 December.

Chaudhuri, A. (1986) 'Government gets tough on council political publicity', *PR Week*, 27 November.

Churchill, D. (1989) 'The really big spenders', *The Financial Times*, 27 April, p. 15.

Clark, F. (1970) *The Central Office of Information*, London: Allen & Unwin.

Clarke, P. and Evans, S. (1983) *Covering Campaigns: Journalism in Congressional Elections*, Stanford, CA: Stanford University Press.

Cobb, R. (1989a) 'Ask no questions, tell no lies', *PR Week*, 2 February, pp. 12–13.

Cobb, R. (1989b) 'Behind Big Brother' *PR Week*. 13 February, pp. 14–15.

Cobb, R. (1989c) 'PR has radio taped', *PR Week*, 20 April, pp. 12–13.

Cockerell, M. (1988a) 'The sincerity machine', *PR Week*, 17–23 November, pp. 13–18.

Cockerell, M. (1988b) *Live from Number Ten*, London: Faber & Faber.

Cockerell, M. (1992) 'Armchair fever', *The Independent Magazine*, 14 March, pp. 32–6.

Cockerell, M. (2000) 'Lifting the Lid off Spin' in *British Journalism Review*, vol. 11, no. 3, pp. 6–15.

Cockerell, M. (2001) 'Alastair Campbell: Tony Blair's Press Secretary', *Independent on Sunday*, 15 April, p. 15.

Cockerell, M. (2003) 'Are These Men To Blame For Making Us Sick of Politics?' *Guardian*, 4 February, p. 7.

Cockerell, M., Hennessey, P. and Walker, D. (1984) *Sources close to the Prime Minister: Inside the Hidden World of the News Manipulators*, London: Macmillan.

Cohen, N. (1999a) *Cruel Britannia: Reports on the Sinister and the Preposterous*, London: Verso.

Cohen, N. (1999b) 'An Explosion Of Puffery', *New Statesman*, 29 November, pp. 14–15.

Coleman, S. (1999) *Electronic Media, Parliament and the People*, London: Hansard Society.

Coleman, S. (1999a) 'Westminster in the Information Age', in *Parliamentary Affairs*, vol. 52, no. 3, pp. 371–88.

Coleman, S. (2001) 2001: Cyber Space Odyssey: The Internet in the UK Election Hansard Society website, www.hansard-society.org.uk/cyberodyssey.htm.

Coleman, S. (2001a) 'Online Campaigning' in Norris, P. (ed.) *Britain Votes 2001*, Oxford: Oxford University Press, pp. 115–24.

Coleman, S., Taylor, J. and Van de Donk, W. (1999) 'Parliament in the Age of the Internet' in *Parliamentary Affairs*, vol. 52, no. 3, pp. 365–70.

Coles, J. (1992) 'The constant appeal of the political poster', *Guardian*, 25 April, p. 25.

Collet, P. and Lamb, R. (1985) *Watching People Watching Television*, London: IBA Report.

Cook, T. (1989) *Making Laws and Making News*, Washington, DC: The Brookings Institute.

Corner, M. (1988) 'Horrifying tale of creeping secrecy', *UK Press Gazette*, 19 September, pp. 14–15.

Cowley, A. (1996) 'New Value of Public Relations in Local Government' in *Local Government Chronicle*, 12 July, pp. 8–9.

Cowley, P. (2001) 'Blair's Lapdog' *Parliamentary Affairs*, vol. 54, no. 6, pp. 815–27.

Cozens, C. (2001) 'Take A Proper Gander', *Guardian*, 5 May, p. 6.

Crain, W. M. and Goff, B. L. (1986) 'Televising legislatures: an economic analysis', *Journal of Law and Economics*, pp. 405–21.

Crewe, I. (1986) 'Saturation polling, the media and the 1983 election', in I. Crewe and M. Harrop (eds) *Political Communication: The General Election of 1983*, Cambridge: Cambridge University Press.

Crewe, I. (1987) 'The campaign confusion', *New Society*, 8 May, p. 11.

Crewe, I. (1992) 'A nation of liars? The failure of opinion polls in the British election of 1992'. Paper presented to the Annual Conference of the American Political Science Association, 3–6 September, Chicago.

Crewe, I. (2001) 'The Opinion Polls: Still Biased to Labour' in Norris, P. (ed.) *Britain Votes 2001*, Oxford: Oxford University Press and the Hansard Society.

Crewe I., Fox, T. and Alt, J. (1977) 'Non-voting in British general elections 1966–October 1974', in C. Crouch (ed.) *British Political Sociology Yearbook*, vol. 3, London: Croom Helm. pp. 38–109.

Crewe, I. and Harrop, M. (eds) (1986) *Political Communications: The General Election Campaign of 1983*, Cambridge: Cambridge University Press.

Crewe, I. and Harrop, M. (eds) (1989) *Political Communications: The General Election Campaign of 1987*, Cambridge: Cambridge University Press.

Criddle, B. (2002) 'MPs and Candidates' in Butler, D. and Kavanagh, D. *The British General Election of 2001*, London: Palgrave, pp. 182–207.

Cumberbatch, G. and Howitt, D. (1989) *A Measure of Uncertainty: The Effects of the Mass Media*, London: John Libbey.

Cumberbatch, G., Brown, B. and Skelton, J. (1992) 'Politicians' reactions to parliamentary broadcasting', in B. Franklin (ed.) *Televising Democracies*, London: Routledge. pp. 203–21.

Cunningham, J. (1985) 'Labour pledge to repeal publicity restrictions', *Local Government Chronicle*, 22 November, p. 1317.

Curran, J. (1990) 'The new revisionism in mass communication research: a reappraisal', *European Journal of Communications*, vol. 5, pp. 134–64.

Curran, J. and Seaton, J. (1988) *Power without Responsibility: The Press and Broadcasting in Britain* (3rd ed.), London: Routledge.

Curtice, J. and Semetko, H. (1994) 'Does It Matter What The Papers Say?' in Heath, A., Jowell, R., Curtice, J. and Taylor, B. (eds) *Labour's Last Chance: The 1992 Election and Beyond*, Aldershot: Dartmouth.

Curtis, L. and Jempson, M. (1993) *Interference on the Airwaves: Ireland, the Media and the Broadcasting Ban*, London: Campaign for Press and Broadcasting Freedom.

Damon, D. (2001) 'The Broadcasters' Election ' in *Journalism Studies*, vol. 2, no. 4, pp. 596–601.

Davis, A (2002) *Public Relations Democracy: Public Relations, Politics and the Mass Media In Britain*, London: Sage.

Day, R. (1963) *The Case for Televising Parliament*, London: Hansard Society.

Day, R. (1989) 'On political interviews', in I. Crewe and N. Harrop (eds) *Political Communications: The General Election Campaign of 1987*, Cambridge: Cambridge University Press, pp. 126–37.

Deacon, D. (1999) 'Charitable Images: the construction of voluntary sector news' in Franklin, B. (ed) *Social Policy, the Media and Misrepresentation*, London: Routledge, pp. 51–68.

Deacon, D. and Golding, P. (1991) When ideology fails: the flagship of Thatcherism and the British local and national media', *European Journal of Communication*, vol. 6, no. 3, September, pp. 291–315.

Deacon D. and Golding, P. (1994) *Taxation and Representation: The Media, Political Communication and the Poll Tax*, London: John Libbey.

Deacon, D. and Wring, D. (2002) 'Partisan De-Alignment and the British Press' in Bartle, J., Mortimore, R. and Atkinson, S. (eds) *Political Communications: The British General Election of 2001*, London: Frank Cass.

Deacon, D. Golding, P. and Billig, M. (2001) 'Press and Broadcasting: "Real Issues" and Real Coverage' in Norris, P. (ed) *Britain Votes 2001*, Oxford: Oxford University Press.

DeFleur, M. (1970) *Theories of Mass Communication*, New York: David McKay.

DeFleur, M. and Ball-Rokeach, S. (1982) *Theories of Mass Communication* (4th edn), New York: Longman.

Delmar, R. and Nowell-Smith, G. (1987) Watching 'teszelin', in P. Simpson (ed.) *Parents Talking Television: Television in the Home*, London: Comedia.

Denver, D. and Bochel, J. M. (1977) 'Political communication: Scottish local newspapers and the general election of February 1974', *The Scottish Journal of Sociology*, vol. 2, no. 1, pp. 11–30.

Denver, D. and Hands, G. (1992) 'Constituency campaigning', *Parliamentary Affairs*, vol. 45, no. 2, pp. 528–45.

Denver, D. and Hands, G. (1997) *Modern Constituency Electioneering: Local Campaigning in the 1992 General Election*, London: Frank Cass.

Denver, D. and Hands G. (1998) 'Constituency Campaigning in the 1997 General Election: Party Effort and Electoral Effect' in Crewe, I., Gosschalk, B. and Bartle, J. (eds) *Political Communications: Why Labour Won the General Election of 1997*, London: Frank Cass, pp. 75–92.

Department of Environment (1975) *Publicity for the Work of Local Authorities*, Circular 45/75, HMSO, London.

DfEE (1998) *National Year of Reading Update*, Issues 1–8, January to October 1998.

DfEE (1998a) *National Year of Reading How To Get Involved*, London: DfEE.

DTI and DCMS (2000) *A New Future for Communications*, Cm 5010, London: HMSO.

Downey, J (2001) 'In Search of the Net Election', *Journalism Studies*, vol. 2, no. 4, pp. 604–10.

Dutton, B. (1986) *The Media*, Harlow: Longman.

Dyer, G. (1982) *Advertising as Communication*, Methuen, London.

'Edinburgh runs risk of court action', *PR Week*, 18 December 1986.

Ehrenreich, B. (1991) 'Spudding Out' in *The Worst Years of Our Lives: Irreverent Notes From A Decade of Greed*, New York: Harper Perennial, pp. 15–18.

Eldridge, J. (1996) *Getting The Message: News, Truth and Power*, London: Routledge.

Eldridge, J., Kitzinger, J. and Williams, K. (1997) *The Mass Media and Power in Britain*, Oxford: Oxford University Press.

Electoral Commission (2002) *Party Political Broadcasting Consultation Paper*, London: Electoral Commission, June.

Electoral Commission (2003) *Party Political Broadcasting Report and Recommendations*, London: Electoral Commission, January.

Elliot, P. (1973) *Uses and Gratifications: A Critique and a Sociological Alternative*, Centre for Mass Communications Research, University of Leicester.

Elliott, V. (1988) 'Labour attack on Tory propaganda spending', *Sunday Telegraph*, 10 January, p. 3.

Ericson, R.V., Baranek, P. and Chan, J. (1989) *Negotiating Control: A Study of News Sources*, Milton Keynes: Open University Press.

Esser, F. Reinemann, C. and Fan, D. (2000) 'Spin Doctoring in British and German Election Campaigns: How the Press is being Confronted with a New Quality of Political PR' in *European Journal of Communication*, vol. 15, no. 2, pp. 209–39.

Esser, F., Reinemann, C. and Fan, D. (2001) 'Spin Doctors in the United States, Great Britain, and Germany. Metacoverage about Media Manipulation', in *The Harvard International Journal of Press/Politics*, vol. 6, no. 1, pp. 16–45.

Etzioni-Halevy, A. (1987) *National Broadcasting Under Seige: A Comparative Study of Australia, Britain, Israel and West Germany*, Basingstoke and London: Macmillan.

Evans, H. (1984) *Good Times, Bad Times*, London: Coronet.

Evans, L. (1966) 'The constitutional importance of the information officer', *Local Government Chronicle*, 29 January, pp. 2–5.

Evans, L. (1973) *The Communications Gap*, Charles Knight, Croydon.

Eysenck, H. and Nias, D. (1980) *Sex, Violence and the Media*, London: Paladin.

Farhi, P. (1997) 'Time for a public service renouncement: Clinton's anti-drug campaign', *Washington Post*, 12 March, 10C.

Farrell, D., Kolodny, R. and Medvic, S. (2001) 'Parties and Campaign Professionals in a Digital Age' in *Press/Politics*, vol. 6, no. 4, pp. 11–30, Harvard: MIT Press.

Fawcett, L. (2001) *Political Communication and Devolution in Northern Ireland*, End of Award Report to ESRC Award, L327253040.

Fedorcio, D., Heaton, P. and Madden, K. (1991) *Public Relations in Local Government*, Harlow: Longman.

First Report of the Select Committeee on Televising of Proceedings of the House (1989–90) vol. 1, Cmnd 265–1, 3 July, London: HMSO.

First Report of the Select Committee on Broadcasting (1990–91), 12 March, London: HMSO.

Fisk, R. (2001) 'Top Hack Blasts Local Rags' www.independent.co.uk/story.jsp?story=87307.

Fletcher, M. (1995) *Managing Local Communications*, London: Kogan Page.

Fletcher, W. (2000) 'The Ads That Don't Add Up', *Guardian*, 4 December, p. 23.

Foley, M. (1993) 'The Political Lobby System' in *Irish Communication Review*, vol. 3, pp. 21–33.

Forbes, D. 'Prime time propaganda: How the White House secretly hooked network TV on its anti-drug message – A *Salon* special report' 113, January http://www.salon.com/news/feature/2000/01/13/drugs/index.html.

Fox, D. (1990) 'Questioning politicians', *TV Week*, 12–18 September, pp. 1822.

Fountain, N. (1993) 'Vote for me I'm a TV celeb', *Guardian*, 31 May, pp. 1415.

Franklin, B. (1986a) 'A leap in the dark: MPs' objections to televising Parliament', *Parliamentary Affairs*, July, pp. 284–97.

Franklin, B. (1986b) 'Public relations, the local press and the coverage of local government', *Local Government Studies*, July/August, pp. 25–33.

Franklin, B. (1987a) 'Local government public relations: the changing institutional and statutory environment 1974–87', *Public Relations*, Winter, pp. 26–30.

Franklin, B. (1987b) 'The metropolitan counties campaign against abolition', *Local Government Studies*, July/August, pp. 30–51.

Franklin, B. (1987c) 'Local government PR: press, public or poor relation?', *Local Government Chronicle*, March.

Franklin, B. (1987d) 'The public image of local government public relations', *Local Government Chronicle*, 9 October.

Franklin, B. (1988a) The TV debate', *New Society*, 15 January, pp. 20–22.

Franklin, B. (1988b) *Public Relations Activities in Local Governnment*, Croydon: Charles Knight.

Franklin, B. (1988c) 'Are publicity goal posts moved by partisans?', *Local Government Chronicle*, 26 August, pp. 18–19.

Franklin, B. (1988d) 'The Local Government Act 1986', *Public Relations*, Spring, pp. 16–21.

Franklin, B. (1989a) 'Local parties, local media and the constituency campaign', in Crewe, I. and Harrop, M. (eds) *Political Communication: The General Election of 1987*, Cambridge: Cambridge University Press, pp. 211–21.

Franklin, B. (1989b) 'Televising legislatures: the British and American experiences', *Parliamentary Affairs*, October, pp. 485–503.

Franklin, B. (1990) 'Parliamentary television in the regions', *Television Week*, October, pp. 10–14.

Franklin, B. (1991) Watchdog or lapdog? Local press/politician relations in West Yorkshire', *Local Government Studies*, September/October, p. 15–32.

Franklin, B. (ed.) (1992a) *Televising Democracies*, London: Routledge.

Franklin, B. (1992b) 'Commons television in the regions: creative broadcasting in a constrained environment', in B. Franklin (ed.) *Televising Democracies*, London: Routledge, pp. 178–203.

Franklin, B. (1992c) 'Local journalists hold the ring', *British Journalism Review*, vol. 3, no. 4, pp. 14–20.

Franklin, B. (1994) *Packaging Politics; Political Communication in Britain's Media Democracy*, London: Edward Arnold.

Franklin, B. (1995) 'Have You Read That? A review of political communications research 1990–1994', *Political Communication*, Summer 1995, vol. 12, no. 2, pp. 223–39.

Franklin, B. (1996) 'The Sun Won't Shine on Mr Major', *Parliamentary Brief*, March, pp. 18–21.

Franklin, B. (1996a) 'An Obituary for the Press Gallery', *Parliamentary Brief*, vol. 4, no. 4, pp. 13–15.

Franklin, B. (1996b) 'Keeping It Bright, Light and Trite: Changing newspaper reporting of Parliament', *Parliamentary Affairs*, Jan/Feb, pp. 57–78.

Franklin, B. (1997) *Newszak and News Media*, London: Arnold.

Franklin, B. (1998) *Tough on Soundbites, Tough on the Causes of Soundbites: New Labour and News Management*, London: The Catalyst Trust.

Franklin, B. (1999) (ed) *Social Policy the Media and Misrepresentation*, London: Routledge.

Franklin, B. (2000) 'The Hand of History: New Labour, News Management and Governance' in Ludlam, S. and Smith, S. (eds) *New Labour: Power, Politics, Policy*, London: Macmillan.

Franklin, B. (2001) *British Television Policy: A Reader*, London: Routledge.

Franklin, B. (2003) 'A Good Day To Bury Bad News: Journalists, Sources and the Packaging of Politics' in Cottle, S. (ed) *News, Power and Public Relations*, London: Sage, pp. 45–62.

Franklin, B. (2003) 'A Damascene Conversion? New Labour and Media Relations' In S. Ludlam and Smith, M. (eds) *New Labour in Government: Power, Politics, Policy*, London: Palgrave.

Franklin, B. and Murphy, D. (1991) *What News? The Market, Politics and the Local Press*, London: Routledge.

Franklin, B. and Murphy, D. (1998) *Making the Local News: Local Journalism in Context*, London: Routledge.

Franklin, B. and Parry, J. (1998) 'Old Habits Die Hard: Journalism's Changing Professional Commitments and Local Newspaper Reporting of the 1997 General Election' In Franklin, B. and Murphy, D. (eds) *Making the Local News: Local Journalism in Context*, London: Routledge, pp. 209–28.

Franklin, B. And Richardson, J. (2002) 'A Journalist's Duty? Continuity and change in local newspaper reporting of recent UK general elections' in *Journalism Studies*, vol. 3, no. 1, pp. 35–52.

Franklin, R. and Richardson, J. (2002) 'Priming the parish pump: Political marketing and news management in local political communication networks' in *Journal of Political Marketing*, vol. 1, no. 1, pp. 117–48.

Franklin, B. and Richardson, J. (2003) 'Dear Editor: Race and Letters about the 2001 General Election' in *Political Quarterly*.

Franklin, B. and Turk, J. V. S. (1988) 'Information subsidies: agenda setting traditions', *Public Relations Review*, Spring, pp. 29–41.

Franks, S. and Vandermark, A. (1995) 'Televising Parliament Five Years On' in *Parliamentary Affairs*, vol. 48, no. 1, pp. 57–71.

Gaber, I. (1998) 'A World Of Dogs and Lamp-posts', *New Statesman*, 19 June, p. 14.

Gaber, I. (2000) 'Lies, Damn Lies and Political Spin' in *British Journalism Review*, vol. 11, no. 1, pp. 60–70.

Gaber, I. (2001) 'E-lectin Gets the Vote', *Guardian*, 30 July 2001, pp. 38–9.

Gale, R. (1988) 'The argument for televising the British House of Commons', *The Parliamentarian*, July, pp. 151–3.

Gale, R. (1992) 'A sceptic's judgement of television broadcasting', in B. Franklin *Televising Democracies*, London: Routledge. pp. 100–16.

Gandy, O. (1982) 'Beyond Agenda Setting: Information Subsidies and Public Policy', New York: Ablex.

Gardner, C. (1986) 'How they buy the bulletins', *Guardian*, 17 September.

Garner, B. and Short. J. (1998) 'Hungry media need fast food: The role of the Central Office of Information' in Franklin, B. and Murphy, D. (eds) *Making the Local News: Local Journalism in Context*, London: Routledge, pp. 170–83.

Gauntlett, D. (1995) *Moving Experiences: Understanding Television's Influences and Effects*, London: John Libbey.

Gauntlett, D. (1996) *Video Critical: Children, the Environment and Media Power*, London: John Libbey.

Gauntlett, D. (1997) 'Ten Things Wrong With the "Effects" Model' in Dickinson, R., Harindranath, R. and Linne, O. (eds) *Approaches To Audiences*, London: Arnold.

Gibson, O. (2001) 'MP.Com', *Guardian*, 7 January, pp. 42–43.

Gibson, R. and Ward, S.(2001) "Open All Hours'? Political Parties and Online Technologies', unpublished paper for IPPR Conference, 20 June 2001.

Gitlin, T. (1978) 'Media sociology: the dominant paradigm', *Theory and Society*, vol. 6, no. 2, pp. 205–55.

Goddard, P., Scammel, M. and Semetko, H. (1998) 'Too Much of a Good Thing? Television in the 1997 Election Campaign' in Crewe, I., Gosschalk, B. and Bartle, J. (eds) *Political Communications: Why Labour Won the General Election of 1997*, London: Cass, pp. 176–94.

Goldenberg, E. and Traugott, M. (1984) *Campaigning for Congress*, Congress Quarterly Press, Washington, DC.

Goldie, G. W. (1977) *Facing the Nation: Television and Politics 1936–1976*, London: The Bodley Head.

Golding, P. (1989) 'Limits to Leviathan: the local press and the Poll Tax', paper presented to the Political Studies Association Annual Conference, University of Warwick, 6 April.

Golding, P. (1990) 'Political communication and citizenship: the media and democracy in an inegalitarian social order', in M. Ferguson (ed.) *Political Communication: The New Imperatives*, London and Beverly Hills, CA: Sage, pp. 84–101.

Golding, P. (2001) 'When What is Unsaid In The News', *Guardian*, 28 May, p. 7.

Golding, P. and Deacon, D. (1991) When ideology fails: local press and the so-called Poll Tax', paper presented to the Annual Conference of the Political Studies Association, University of Lancaster, 15 April.

Golding, P. and Deacon, D. (2001) 'An Election That Many Watched But Few Enjoyed', *Guardian*, 12 June, p. 5.

Golding, P., Billig, M., Deacon, D. and Middleton, S. (1992) 'Two shows for the price of one', *British Journalism Review*, vol. 3, no. 2, pp. 6–10.

Gould, Philip, (1998): *The Unfinished Revolution. How the Modernisers Served the Labour Party.* London: Little Brown.

Gould, P., Herd, R, and Powell, C. (1989) 'The Labour Party's campaign communications', in I. Crewe and M. Harrop (eds) *Political Communications: The General Election of 1987*, Cambridge: Cambridge University Press, pp. 72–87.

'Government ads: counting the cost' (1991) *Labour Research*, November, pp. 7–8.

Government Information and Communications Service (1997) *A Working Guide for Government Information Officers*, London: GICS.

Grant, D. (2002) 'Defamation and the Internet: Principles for a unified Australian (and world) online defamation law' in *Journalism Studies*, vol. 3, no. 1, pp. 115–32.

Gray, P. (1981) *Communication Behaviour*, Leicester: Centre for Mass Communication Research.

Grice, A. (1988) 'Government advertising: propaganda or publicity?', *The Sunday Times*, 4 September.

Grist, J. (1992) 'As long as a piece of string: the role of the Supervisor of Broadcasting', in B. Franklin (ed.) *Televising Democracies*, London: Routledge. pp. 29–41.

Gunter, B. and McLeer, J. (1990) Children and Television: The One Eyed Monster, London: Routledge.

Gunter, B. and Svennevig, M. (1987) *Behind and in Front of the Screen*, London: John Libbey.

Gunter, B. and Winstone, P. (1993) *Television: The Public's View 1992*, London: John Libbey.

Gutch, R. and Percival, R. (1986) *Publish and not be Damned: A Guide to Part Two of the 1986 Local Government Act for Voluntary Organisations*, London: NCVO.

Hagell, A. and Newburn, T. (1994) *Young Offenders and the Media: Viewing Habits and Preferences*, London: London Policy Institute.

Hagerty, B. (2000) 'Cap'n Spin Does Lose His Rag' An Interview with Alastair Campbell in *British Journalism Review*, vol. 11, no. 2, pp. 7–20.

Hagerty, B. (2000) 'The Sheep Sheared', *Press Gazette*, 21 July, p. 3.

Hall, S. (1981) The structured communication of events', in D. Potter (ed.) *Society and the Social Sciences*, London: Routledge & Kegan Paul.

Hall, S. (1982) 'The rediscovery of ideology: return of the repressed in media studies', in M. Gurevitch, T. Bennet, J. Curran and J. Woollacot (eds) *Culture, Society and the Media*, London: Methuen.

Hall-Jamieson, K. (1984) *Packaging the Presidency*, Oxford: Oxford University Press.

Hall-Jamieson, K. (1992) *Dirty Politics: Deception, Distraction and Democracy*, Oxford and New York: Oxford University Press.

Hanna, V. (1992) 'Agenda battle draw a victory for voters', *Guardian*, 9 April, p. 16.

Hammond, S. (2000) Reaching the Regions: Government Communications and the Regional Media, Unpublished MA thesis, Trinity and All Saints University College, Leeds.

Hardy, E. (1983) The Northern Ireland Office and the Press. Unpublished dissertation, Queen's University, Belfast.

Hargreaves, I. and Thomas, A. (2002) *Old News, New News*, London: ITC/BSC.

Hargreaves, R. (1988) 'ITV unhappy with Commons TV plans', *Broadcast*, 31 March, p. 3.

Harris, M. (1986) 'The last days of the mets', *New Society*, 21 March, pp. 494–5.

Harris, R. (1983) *Gotcha: The Media, the Government and the Falklands Crisis*, London: Faber & Faber.

Harris, R. (1989) 'Money spent like water', *The Sunday Times*, 30 April.

Harris, R. (1990) *Good and Faithful Servant*, London: Faber & Faber.

Harrison, M. (1992) 'Politics on the air' in D. Butler and D. Kavanagh (eds) *The British General Election of 1992*, London: Macmillan. pp. 155–80.

Harrison, M. (1997) 'Politics on the Air' in Butler, D. and Kavanagh, D. *The British General Election of 1997* London: Macmillan. pp. 133–55.

Harrison, M. (2002) 'Politics on the Air' in Butler, D. and Kavanagh, D. (eds) *The British General Election of 2001*, London: Palgrave, pp. 132–55.

Harrison, S. (1998) 'The Local Government Agenda: News From the Town Hall' in Franklin, B. and Murphy, D. (eds) *Making the Local News: Local Journalism in Context*, London: Routledge, pp. 157–69.

Harrison, S. (1995) *Public Relations: An Introduction*, London: Routledge.

Harrop, M. (1986) 'The press and post-war elections', in I. Crewe and M. Harrop (eds) *Political Communications: The General Election of 1983*, Cambridge: Cambridge University Press, pp. 137–50.

Harrop, M. (1987) 'Voters' in J. Seaton and B. Pimlott (eds) *The Media in British Politics*, Aldershot: Gower, pp. 45–64.

Harrop, M. (1990) 'Political Marketing' *Parliamentary Affairs*, vol. 43, pp. 277–91.

Harrop, M. and Scammell, M. (1992) 'A tabloid war' in D. Butler and D. Kavanagh (eds.) *The British General Election of 1992*, London: Macmillan, pp. 180–210.

Hart, A. (1991) *Understanding the Media: A Practical Guide*, London: Routledge.

Hattersley, R. (1988) 'Read my lips', *The Listener*, 15 December, pp. 18–19.

Hattersley, R. (1998) 'Let's Hear It For Tony … Or Else', *Observer Review*, 22 February, pp. 3–4.

Hattersley, R. (2001) 'The Unholy Alliance: the relationship between Members of Parliament and the press' James Cameron Lecture 1996 in Stephenson, H. (ed) *Media Voices: The James Cameron Memorial Lectures*, London: Politicos, pp. 227–45.

HC Debs, Vol. 87, Cols 277–366, 20 November 1985. Bill introduced by Dame Janet Fookes to televise the proceedings of the House.

HC Debs, Vol. 127, Cols 194–288, 9 February 1988. Bill introduced by Antony Nelson approving the principle of an experiment in televising proceedings and calling for the establishment of a select committee.

HC Debs, Vol. 154, Cols 607–660, 12 June, 1989. Motion to approve the report of the select committee on televising of proceedings.

HC Debs, Vol. 176, Cols 1223–1276, 19 July 1990. Debate of the Report of the Select Committee on Televising of Proceedings of the House approving the committee report and agreeing in principle that televising of proceedings of the House should now continue indefinitely.

HC Debs, Vol. 361, Col 467 Debate on the Fourth Report of the Select Committee on Public Administration.

HC 1065 Committee Session 2001–2, 16 July 2002 http://www.parliament.the-stationery-office.co.uk/pa/cm200102/cmselect/cmliaison/1065

Heathcote, C. (1986) 'The disappearing council reporter', *Newstime*, September, pp. 9–13.

Heaton, L. (1988) When does information become propaganda?', *The Listener*, 10 March, pp. 8–9.

Hedley, R. (1986) 'Council gag – protest grows', *Local Government Chronicle*, 27 January.

Hedley, R. (1987) 'Publicity should not attack morals', *Local Government Chronicle*, 23 January, p. 5.

Henderson, L. (2002) 'Social Issue Story Lies in British Soap Operas'. Unpublished PhD thesis, Glasgow Media Group, Glasgow University.

Hennessy, P. (1987) 'Lighting a fuse which will blow up the system', *UK Press Gazette*, 13 April, p. 14.

Hennessy, P. and Walker, D. (1987) 'The Lobby', in J. Seaton and B. Pimlott (eds) *The Media in British Politics*, Aldershot: Gower.

Henry, C. (1991) 'Political adverts need not be true', *Guardian*, 3 August, p. 1.

Herman, E. S. and Chomsky, N. (1988) *Manufacturing Consent: the Political Economy of the Mass Media*, New York: Pantheon.

Hess, S. (1984) *The Government/Press Connection: Press Officers and their Offices*, Washington, DC: The Brookings Institute.

Hetherington, A., Ryle, M. and Weaver, K. (1990) *Cameras in the Commons*, London: Hansard Society.

Hewitt, P. and Mandelson, P. (1989) 'The Labour campaign', in I. Crewe and M. Harrop (eds) *Political Communications: The General Election Campaign of 1987*, Cambridge: Cambridge University Press, pp. 49–55.

Hill, D. (1966) 'Democracy in local government: A study in participation and communication'. PhD thesis, University of Leeds.

Hill, D. (1992) 'Election of yawning gaps', *Guardian*, 6 April, p. 29.

Hill, P. (1998) 'The BBC Backs Away From Parliament', *British Journalism Review*, vol. 9, no. 2, pp. 16–22.

Hill, P. (1993) 'Parliamentary Broadcasting – From TWIW to YIP', *British Journalism Review*, vol. 4, no. 4, pp. 39–44.

Hillyard, M. and Percy-Smith, J. (1988) *The Coercive State*, London: Collins.

Hodge, M. (1986) 'Bill to end free flow of information', *Local Government Chronicle*, 31 January, p. 124.

Hodgson, J. (2001) 'A Gentlemen's Agreement', *Guardian*, 1 October, p. 10.

Hoggart, S. (2002) *Playing to the Gallery: Parliamentary Sketches from Blair Year Zero*, London: Atlantic Books.

Hoggart, S. (2002) 'Open Briefing Not Brief Enough', *Guardian*, 15 October, p. 10.

Holines, P. (1987) 'Courting controversy at Derby's County Hall', *PR Week*, 7–13 May, pp. 6–7.

Hollingsworth, M. (1986) *The Press and Political Dissent: A Question of Censorship*, London: Pluto Press.

Hollins, T. (1981) 'The presentations of politics: the place of party publicity, broadcasting and film in British politics 1918–39'. Unpublished PhD thesis, University of Leeds.

Holt, R. and Turner, J. (1968) *Political Parties in Action: The Battle for Baron's Court*, London: Collier MacMillan.

Hood, S. (1980) *On Television*, London: Pluto Press.

Horgan, J. (2001) '"Government Sources Said Last Night …" the development of the parliamentary press lobby in modern Ireland' in Morgan, H. (ed) *Information, Media and Power through the Ages*, Dublin: University College Dublin Press, pp. 259–71.

Horsnall, M. (1991) 'Major has complained to the BBC', *The Times*, 12 October.

Hurd, D. (1988) 'Secrets: more light, less heat', *UK Press Gazette*, 12 December, p. 7.

Hutton Inquiry http://www.the-hutton-inquiry.org.uk.

Ingham, B. (1990) 'Government and media: Coexistence and tension'. Unpublished lecture delivered at Trinity and All Saints College, Leeds, 22 November.

Ingham, B. (1991) *Kill the Messenger*, London: HarperCollins.

Ingham, B. (2001) 'Spin and the UK General Election 2001' in *Journalism Studies*, vol. 2, no. 4, pp. 585–90.

Ingham, B. (2003) *The Wages of Spin*, London: John Murray.

Institute of Public Relations Local Government Group (1986) *Public Relations in Local Government*, London.

ITC (2001) *Election 2001: Viewers' Responses to the Television Coverage*, London: ITC.

ITN (1985) 'Their Lordships' House: audience statistics'. Unpublished report.

James, H. (1982) 'The role of the Central Office of Information', in A. May and K. Rowan (eds) *Inside Information: The British Government and the Media*, London: Constable.

Janosik, E. (1968) *Constituency Labour Parties in Britain*, London: Pall Mall Press. pp. 62–85.

Johnston, R. (1987) *Money and Voters: Constituency Campaign Spending and Election Results*, London: Croom Helm.

Jones, B. (1992) 'Broadcasters, politicians and the political interview', in B. Jones and L. Robins (eds) *Two Decades in British Politics*, Manchester: Manchester University Press, pp. 53–79.

Jones, H. (1989) 'Ingham's new post draws the old shots', *The Sunday Times*, 12 February.

Jones, N. (1989) 'The Lobby system: inside or outside', *UK Press Gazette*, pp. 12–13.

Jones, N. (1991a) 'The hundred day honeymoon', *Guardian*, 4 May.

Jones, N. (1991b) 'Oh yes but whose line is it anyway', *Guardian*, 24 June.

Jones, N. (1995) *Soundbites and Spindoctors: How Politics Manipulate the Media – And Vice Versa*, London: Cassell.

Jones, N. (1999) *Sultans of Spin. The Media and the New Labour Government*, London: Victor Gollancz.

Jones, N. (2001) *The Control Freaks: How New Labour Gets its Own Way*, London: Politicos.

Jones, N. (2001a) 'Election 2001' *Journalism Studies*, vol. 2, no. 4, pp. 601–3.

Jones, N. (2002) *The Control Freaks: How New Labour Gets its Own Way*, London: Politicos, Second Edition.

Jones, N. (2002a) 'Spin city' in *Politicos*, vol. 1, no. 1, Summer 2002, pp. 6–7.

Jones, N. (2003) 'Can Alastair Open Closed Doors?' *British Journalism Review*, vol. 14, no. 3, pp. 45–51.

Kaid, L. L. and Holtz-Bacha, C. (1995) *Political Advertising in Western Democracies*, London: Sage.

Kampfner, J. (2000) 'My Life In Spin City', *Guardian*, 6 November, p. 2.

Katz, E. (1959) 'Mass communication research and the study of popular culture', *Studies in Public Communication*, vol. 2, pp. 1–27.

Katz, E. and Lazarsfeld, P. (1955) *Personal Influence*, Glencoe, IL: Free Press.

Katz, I. (1992) 'Posters that fail to stick', *Guardian*, 13 April, p. 23.

Kaufman, G. (2003) 'BBC's Youth Politics Show is a Smart-Casual Turn-Off', *Guardian*, 24 February, p. 8.

Kavanagh, D. (1970) *Constituency Electioneering in Britain*, London: Longman.

Kavanagh, D. (1995) *Election Campaigning; The New Marketing of Politics*, Oxford: Blackwell.

Kavanagh, D. and Seldon, A. (2000) *The Powers Behind The Prime Minister*, London: HarperCollins.

Kavanagh, T. (2002) 'Don't be fooled by this death', *British Journalism Review*, vol. 13, no. 2, pp. 14–18.

Keane, F. (1996) *Letter To Daniel: Despatches from the Heart*, London: BBC.

Kellner, P. (1983) 'The Lobby, official secrets and good government', *Parliamentary Affairs*, vol. 36, no. 3, Summer, pp. 275–82.

Kelly, T. (1990) 'ITC code a recipe for endless litigation', *UK Press Gazette*, 3 December, p. 16.

Kemp, A. (1989) 'The parliamentary Lobby: informal and indispensable', *UK Press Gazette*, 19 June, p. 7.

Kennedy, C. and Culey, C. (1992) 'Televising the House: the view from the third party', in B. Franklin (ed.) *Televising Democracies*, London: Routledge. pp. 116–29.

King, A. and Sloman, A. (1982) 'The Westminster Lobby correspondents', in A. May and K. Rowan (eds) *Inside Information: British Government and the Media*, London: Constable, pp. 174–8.

Kitzinger, J. (1990) 'Audience understandings of AIDS media messages: a discussion of methods', *Journal of Sociology of Health and Illness*, vol. 12, no. 3, pp. 319–35.

Kitzinger, J. (1993) 'Understanding AIDS: researching audience perceptions of Acquired Immune Deficiency Disease' in Eldridge, J. (ed.) *Getting The Message: News, Truth and Power*, London: Routledge.

Klaehn, J. (2002) 'A Critical Review and Assesment of Herman and Chomsky's "Propaganda Model" ' in *European Journal of Communication*, vol. 17, no. 2, pp. 147–82.

Klapper, J. (1960) *The Effects Of Mass Communication*, New York: Free Press.

Kraus, S. and Davis, D. (1976) *The Effects of Mass Communication on Political Behavior*, Philadelphia, PA: Pennsylvania State University Press.

Kurtz, H. (1998) *Spin Cycle*, New York: Free Press.

Lacey, M. (2000) 'In trade-off with TV networks, drug office is reviewing scripts', *New York Times*, 14 January, 1A.

Larsson, L. (2002) 'Journalists and Politicians: A Relationship Requiring Manoeuvering Space', in *Journalism Studies*, vol. 3, no. 1, pp. 21–34.

Lawson, M. (1990) 'Raising an eyebrow', *Independent Magazine*, 24 February, pp. 28–36.

Lawson, M. (1992) 'The writing on the wall', *Independent Magazine*, 14 March, pp. 24–8.

Lazarsfeld, P., Berelson, B. and Gaudet, H. (1944) *The People's Choice*, New York: Duell, Sloan & Pearce.

Leapman, M. (2001) ' 'Trevor Kavanagh', *New Statesman*, 9 April, pp. 18–19.

Leaton Gray, J. (1992) 'The Committees and the Cameras: Romeo and Juliet or Cinderella and Prince Charming', in B. Franklin (ed.) *Televising Democracies*, London: Routledge. pp. 60–85.

Leigh, D. (1988) 'The fight for information: a tough job getting tougher', *UK Press Gazette*, 7 November, p. 7.

Lennon, P. (1991) 'The spin doctors' new bag', *Guardian*, 25 February, p. 25.

Lepkowska, D (1998) 'Celebrities Booked to Improve Literacy', *Times Educational Supplement*, 13 March.

Lewis, J. (1990) 'Are you receiving me?', in A. Goodwin and G. Whannel (eds) *Understanding Television*, London: Routledge.

Lewis, J. (1991) *The Ideological Octopus: An Exploration of Television and Its Audience*, London: Routledge.

Lewis, P. and Booth, J. (1989) *The Invisible Medium: Public Commercial and Community Radio*, London: Macmillan.

Liddle, R. (2003) 'Hands off the BBC', *British Journalism Review*, vol. 14, no. 3, pp. 6–10.

Linton, M. (1995) 'Sun Powered Politics', *Guardian*, 30 October, pp. 14–16.

The Local Government Act 1986, London: HMSO.

The Local Government Act 1988, London: HMSO.

Lloyd, J. (1997) 'A Dangerous Web They Spin', in *New Statesman*, 24 October, pp. 11–13.

MacArthur, B. (1989) 'Lobby assassination by hint and innuendo', *The Sunday Times*, 4 June.

MacArthur, B. (1992a) 'The British keep reading despite the box', *British Journalism Review*, vol. 3, no. 4, pp. 65–6.

MacArthur, B. (1992b) 'Perhaps it was the Sun "wot won it" for John Major', *The Sunday Times*, 12 April.

MacAskill, E. (1997) 'Cabinet Watch' in *Red Pepper*, September, p. 34.

Macdonagh, M. (n. d.) *The Reporters Gallery*, London: Hodder & Stoughton.

Macintyre, D. (2001) 'The 2001 General Election: A Journalist's Diary' in *Journalism Studies*, vol. 2, no. 4, pp. 590–6.

Mackey, S. (1994) 'Controversy in Town Hall Public Relations', Unpublished PhD, Deakin University, Australia.

Mancini, P. (1993) 'Between trust and suspicion: how political journalists solve the dilemma', *European Journal Of Communication*, vol. 8, no. 1, March, pp. 33–53.

Mandelson, P (1997) 'Coordinating Government Policy' A speech delivered to the Conference 'Modernising the Policy Process', at Regent's Park Hotel 16 September.

Mandelson, P. (2002) *The Blair Revolution Revisited*, London: Politicos.

Marr, A. (2001) 'The Retreat of the Spin Doctors', *British Journalism Review*, vol. 12, no. 2, pp. 6–12.

Masterman, L. (1987) *Television and the Bombing of Libya*, London: MK Media Press,

Mathias, G. (1993) 'Competing with impartiality', *British Journalism Review*, vol. 4, no 1, pp. 16–20.

McAllister, I. (1985) 'Campaign activities and electoral outcomes in Britain 1979 and 1983', *Public Opinion Quarterly*, Winter, vol. 49, no. 4, pp. 489–503.

McGwire, S. (1997) 'Dance to the Music of Spin', *New Statesman*, 17 October, p. 11.

McKie, D. (1982) 'The Lobby and other matters', in A. May and K. Rowan (eds) *Inside Information: British Government and the Media*, London: Constable, pp. 178–82.

McKie, D. (1998) 'Swingers, Clingers, Waverers and Quaverers: The Tabloid Press in the 1997 General Election' in Crewe, I. Gosschalk, B. and Bartle, J (eds) *Political Communications: Why Labour Won the General Election of 1997*, London: Cass, pp. 115–30.

McKie, D. (1999) *Media Coverage of Parliament*, London: Hansard.

McManus, J. (1994) *Market Driven Journalism*, London: Sage.

McNair, B. (1995) *An Introduction to Political Communication*, London: Routledge.

McNair, B. (2000) *Journalism and Democracy. An Evaluation of the Political Public Sphere.* London: Routledge.

McNair, B., Hibberd, M. and Schlesinger, P. (2002) 'Public Access Broadcasting and Democratic Participation in the Age of Mediated Politics' in *Journalism Studies*, vol. 3, no. 3, pp. 407–22.

McNamara, M. (1992) 'How to unwrap the political packaging', *UK Press Gazette*, 30 March, p. 10.

McQuail, D. (1987) *Mass Communication Theory: An Introduction* (2nd edn), London: Sage.

Milburn, M. and Brown, J. (1997) 'Adwatch: Covering Campaign Ads' in Norris, P. (ed) *Politics and the Press: The News Media and their Influences*, Boulder, Colorado: Lynne Reinner Publishers, pp. 165–82.

Miller, D. (1990) 'The History Behind A Mistake', *British Journalism Review*, vol. 1, no. 2, pp. 34–44.

Miller, D.(1994) *Don't Mention The War: Northern Ireland, Propaganda and the Media*, London: Pluto.

Miller, D. (1996) 'The Northern Ireland Information Service and the Media: Aims, strategy, tactics' in Rolston,B and Miller, D. (eds) *War and Words: The Northern Ireland Media Reader*, Belfast: Pale Publications, pp. 208–35.

Miller, D. and Philo, G. (1999) 'The Effective Media' in Philo, G. (ed) *Message Received*, London: Longman, pp. 21–32.

Miller, W. (1991) *Media and Voters*, Oxford: Clarendon Press.

Miller, W. (1992) 'I am what I read', *New Statesman and Society*, 24 April, pp. 17–18.

Miller, W., Clarke, H. D., Harrop, M., Leduc, L. and Whiteley, P. (1990) *How Voters Change: The 1987 British Election Campaign in Perspective*, Oxford: Clarendon Press.

Milne, A. (1988) *DC: The Memoirs of a British Broadcaster,* London: Hodder & Stoughton.

Milne, S. and McGuire, K. (2001) 'Hack Watch', *Guardian,* 22 January, pp. 2–3.

Mitchell, A. (1982) 'The local campaign, 1977–9', in R. Worcester and M. Harrop (eds) *Political Communication: The General Election Campaign of 1979,* London: Allen & Unwin, pp. 36–42.

Mitchell, A. (1988) 'Commons television', *Broadcast,* 22 July, p. 15.

Mitchell, A. (1992) 'Televising the Commons: a backbencher's view', in B. Franklin, (ed.) *Televising Democracies,* London: Routledge, pp. 85–100.

Mitchell, A. (1995) 'Beyond Televising Parliament: Taking Parliament to the people' in *Parliamentary Affairs,* vol. 43, no. 1, p. 2.

Morgan, D. (1991) 'Media-Government relations: the right to manage information versus the right to know', *Parliamentary Affairs,* November/December, pp. 531–41.

Morgan, J. (2000) 'Rusbridger on the Record Against Secret Spinning', *Press Gazette,* 21 July, p. 1.

Morley, D. (1980) *The Nationwide Audience: Structure and Decoding,* London: BFI.

Morley, D. (1992) *Television, Audiences and Cultural Studies,* London: Routledge.

Morrison, D. and Tumber, H. (1988) *Journalists at War,* London: Sage.

Morrison, J. and McSmith, A. (2003) 'Ministers Accused of Threatening the BBC', *Independent on Sunday,* 17 July, p. 1.

Mountfield, Lord (1997) *Report of the Working Group on the Government Information Service,* Cabinet Office, HMSO.

Mullen, B. (1997) *Consuming Television: Television and its Audiences,* Oxford: Blackwell.

Murgach, J. (1978) *Abuse of Power,* London.

Murgach, J. (1981) *Anatomy of Power,* London.

Myers, K. (1985) 'Mandelson's overtures for a Labour victory', *Guardian,* 25 November, p. 13.

Myers, K. (1986) *Understains: The Sense and Seduction of Advertising,* London: Comedia.

NALGO (1947) *Report on Relations between Local Government and the Community,* March, London.

Nariman, H.E. (1993) *Soap Operas for Social Change: Towards a Methodology for Entertainment – Education Television,* Westport, Conn: Praeger.

National Audit Office (1989) *Publicity Services for Government Departments*, London, 1 December.

Negrine, R. (1989) *Politics and the Mass Media in Britain*, London: Routledge.

Negrine, R (1996) *The Communication of Politics*, London: Sage.

Negrine, R (1998) *Parliament and the Media: A Study of Britain, Germany and France*, London: Pinter.

Nelson, A. (1988) 'The argument for televising the British House of Commons', *The Parliamentarian*, vol. 6, July, pp. 148–51.

Neveu, E. (2002) 'The Local Press and Farmers' Protests in Brittany: Proximity and Distance in the Local Newspaper Coverage of a Social Movement' in *Journalism Studies*, vol. 3, no. 1, pp. 53–68.

Newton, K. (1990) 'Do people read everything they believe in the papers? Newspapers and voters in the 1983 and 1987 general elections'. Paper presented to the Conference on Elections, Parties and Public Opinion in Britain, University of Essex, 22–23 September.

Newton, K. and Artingstall, S. (1992) 'Government and private censorship in nine Western nations in the 1970s and 1980s'. Unpublished paper, Department of Government, University of Essex.

Newton, K. and Brynin, M. (2001) 'The National Press and Party Voting in the UK', *Political Studies*, vol. 49, pp. 265–85.

Norris, P. (1997) 'Introduction: The Rise of the Postmodern Political Communications' in Norris, P. (ed.) *Politics and the Press: The News Media and their Influences*, Boulder, Colorado: Lynne Reinner Publishers, pp. 1–22.

Norris, P. (1998) 'The Battle For the Campaign Agenda' in King, A. (ed.) *New Labour Triumphs: Britain at The Polls*, New Jersey: Chatham House.

Norris, P. (2000) *A Virtuous Circle: Political Communication in Post Industrial Democracies*, New York: Cambridge University Press.

Norris, P., Curtice, J., Sanders, D., Scammell, M. and Semetko, H. (1999) *On Message. Communicating the Campaign*, London: Sage.

Norton-Taylor, R. and Black, I. (1997) 'The Ministry of Spin', *Guardian*, 15 September, p. 17.

Nossiter, T. (1986) 'British television: a mixed economy', in *Research on the Range and Quality of Broadcasting Services*, West Yorkshire Media in Politics Group, London: HMSO.

Oborne, P. (1999) *Alastair Campbell, New Labour and the Rise of the Media Class*, London: Aurum Press.

Oborne, P. (2002) 'A Flea In The Government's Ear', in *British Journalism Review*, vol. 13, no. 4, pp. 32–40.

O'Donnell, T. (1992) 'Europe on the move: the travelling Parliamentary Show', in B. Franklin (ed.) *Televising Democracies*, London: Routledge, pp. 254–69.

Ogilvy-Webb, M. (1965) *The Government Explains*, London: Allen & Unwin.

O'Sullivan, T. (1989) Why Labour's not sold on the sell offs', *PR Week*, 11 May, p. 5.

O'Sullivan, T. (1991) 'Tories take PR advice', *PR Week*, 12 September, p. 1.

Panorama (2002) 'Tony in Adland', 26 May.

Parris, M. (2002) *Chance Witness: An Outsider's Life in Politics*, London: Viking.

Pateman, C. (1979) *The Problem of Political Obligation: A Critical Analysis of Liberal Theory*, Brisbane: Wiley.

Patterson, T. (1980) *The Mass Media Election*, New York: Praeger.

Perkins, A. (2003) 'BBC Urged Not to Dumb Down Politics Shows', *Guardian*, 20 January, p. 6.

Peshchek, D. (1987) 'The Art of Communication', *Local Government Chronicle*, 6 December, p. 17.

Petley, J. and Finn, C. (1989) 'The edge of darkness', *Broadcast*, 24 February, pp. 20–23.

Phillips, M. (1992) 'The Seige of Our Screens', *Guardian*, 17 February, p. 29.

The Phillis Inquiry (Government Communications Review) http://www.gcreview.gov.uk.

Philo, G. (1990a) 'Striking effects', *The Listener*, 12 July, pp. 8–9.

Philo, G. (1990b) 'Seeing is believing', *Guardian*, 4 June, p. 23.

Philo, G. (1990c) *Seeing and Believing: The Influence of Television*, London: Routledge.

Philo, G. (1999) *Message Received*, London: Longmans.

Philo, G. (2002) 'Television News and Audience Understandings of War, Conflict and Disaster', in *Journalism Studies*, vol. 3, no. 2, pp. 173–86.

Philo, G. and Miller, D. (1999) 'The Effective Media' in G. Philo (ed.) *Message Received*, London: Longman. pp. 21–33.

Pilger, J. (1990) 'A code for charlatans', *Guardian*, 8 October, p. 25.

Pipkin, R. (2001) 'The Party Election Broadcast: A Sleeping Giant or an Old Pair of Shoes?', Paper delivered to the Annual Conference of the Elections, Public Opinion and Parties Specialist Group of the Political Studies Association, UK, 15 September.

Ponting, C. (1988) 'A fundamentally new approach to controlling information', *UK Press Gazette*, 31 October, p. 15.

Ponting, S. (1989) 'Nothing changes in this tradition of secrecy', *UK Press Gazette*, 20 March.

Porter, H. (1985) *Lies, Damned Lies and Some Exclusives*, London: Hodder & Stoughton.

Postman, N. (1987) *Amusing Ourselves to Death: Public Discourse in the Age of Show Business*, London: Methuen.

Powell, C. (2001) 'The Men Who Made Politics Boring Again', *Guardian*, 23 October, pp. 4–5.

Preston, P. (2001) 'What That Email Said', *Guardian*, 15 October, p. 17.

Protheroe, A. (1987) 'The use and abuse of the Official Secrets Act, *The Listener*, 12 February, pp. 4–5.

Protheroe, A. (1988) 'A flak catcher's survival guide to good journalism', *UK Press Gazette*, 14 November, p. 11.

Rawnsley, A. (2000) *Servants of the People. The Inside Story of New Labour*. London: Hamish Hamilton.

Redcliffe-Maud (1974) *The Royal Commission on Local Government in England* (Cmd 4040) London: HMSO.

Richardson, T. (1988) *Public Relations in Local Government*, London: Heinemann.

Riddell, P. (1988) 'Money used for party propaganda', *The Financial Times*, 30 March, p. 2.

Riddell, P. (1992) 'Media manipulation much exaggerated', *British Journalism Review*, vol. 3, no. 2, pp. 11–17.

Riddell, P. (1998) 'Members and Millbank, The Media and Parliament' in Seaton, J. (ed.) *Politics and the Media. Harlots and Prerogatives at the Turn of the Millennium*, Oxford: Blackwell, pp. 8–18.

Riddell, P. (1999) 'A Shift of Power and Influence', *British Journalism Review*, vol. 10, no. 3, pp. 26–33.

Root, J. (1986) *Open the Box*, London: Comedia.

Rose, D. (2002) 'Lobby Chief supports co-chair compromise', *Press Gazette*, 10 May 2002, p. 5.

Rose, D. (2003) 'MPs Criticise Changes to BBC's Political Coverage', *Press Gazette*, 17 January, p. 4.

Rose, D. (2003) 'Blair's television briefings branded a "waste of time"', *Press Gazette*, 16 May, p. 6.

Rosenbawm, M. (1997) *From Soap Box to Spin Doctor: Party Political Campaigning in Britain Since 1945*, London: Macmillan.

Rosengren, K., Wemer, L. and Palmgreen, P. (eds) (1985) *Media Gratifications Research: Current Perspectives*, London and Beverly Hills, CA: Sage.

Roth, A. (1999) 'The Lobby's 'Dying Gasps'?' *British Journalism Review*, vol. 10, no. 3, pp. 21–5.

Routledge, P. (2001) 'It May Pay But Journalism It Ain't', *British Journalism Review*, vol. 12, no. 4, pp. 31–6.

Roxburgh, I. (1987) 'Publicity code to render councils mute', *Local Government Chronicle*, 27 November, p. 9.

Rusbridger, A. (2000) 'No More Ghostly Voices', *Guardian*, 15 July, p. 20.

Ryan, T. (1986) 'Labour and the media in Britain 1929–1939. A study of the attitudes of the Labour movement towards the new media film and radio and its attempts to use them for political purposes'. Unpublished PhD Thesis (2 Volumes), University of Leeds.

Ryle, M. (1991) 'Televising the House of Commons', *Parliamentary Affairs*, vol. 44, no. 2, pp. 185–207.

Sadler, P. (2001) *National Security and the D Notice System*, Hampshire: Ashgate.

Sambrook, C. (1992) 'Selling the party', *Marketing*, 12 March, pp. 17–20.

Sampson, A. (1996) 'The Crisis at the heart of Our Media', *British Journalism Review*, vol. 7, no. 3, pp. 42–56.

Scammell, M. (1991) 'The impact of marketing and public relations on modern British politics'. Unpublished PhD thesis, University of London.

Scammell, M. (1990) 'Political advertising and the broadcasting revolution', *Political Quarterly*, pp. 200–13.

Scammell, M. (1995) *Designer Politics. How Elections are won*, Basingstoke: Macmillan.

Scammell, M. and Harrop, M. (1997) 'The Press' in Butler, D. and Kavanagh, D. *The British General Election of 1997*, London: Macmillan.

Scammel, M. and Harrop, M. (2002) 'The Press Disarmed' in Butler, D. and Kavanagh, D. (eds) *The British General Election of 2001*, London: Palgrave, pp. 156–81.

Scammell, M. and Semetko, H. (1995) 'Political Advertising on Television: The British Experience' in Kaid, L. L. and Holtz-Bacha, C. (eds) *Political Advertising in Western Democracies*, London: Sage, pp. 19–42.

Schatz, H. (1992) 'Televising the Bundestag', in B. Franklin, (ed.) *Televising Democracies*, London: Routledge, pp. 234–54.

Shaeffer, S. (2000) 'Campaign To Make Young "Think Twice" before Sex', *Telegraph*, 10 October, p. 4.

Schechter, D. (1998) *The More You Watch, the Less You know*, New York: Seven Stories Press.

Scheslinger, P., Miller, D. and Dinan, W. (2001) *Open Scotland: Journalists, Spin Doctors and Lobbyists*, Edinburgh: Polygon.

Seaton, J. (ed.) (1998) *Politics and the Media: Harlots and Prerogatives at the Turn of the Millennium*. Oxford: Blackwell.

Seaton, J. and Pimlott, B. (eds) (1987) *The Media in British Politics*, Aldershot: Avebury.

Select Committee on Public Administration (1998) *The Government Information and Communications Service: Report and Proceedings of the Select Committee together with Minutes of Evidence and Appendices*, London: HMSO, HC770.

Select Committee on Public Administration (1999) *Government Response to the Sixth Report From the Select Committee on Public Administrations (session 1997–98) On the Government Information and Communications Service*, 19 January, London: HMSO.

Select Committee on Public Administration (2001) *Special Advisers: Boon or Bane? Fourth Report together with the proceedings of the Committee and Appendices*, 13 March, London: HMSO, HC293.

Select Committee on Public Administration Press Release, 30 March 1998.

Seymour-Ure, C. (1968) *The Press, Politics and the Public*, London: Methuen.

Seymour-Ure, C. (1974) *The Political Impact of the Mass Media*, London: Constable.

Seymour-Ure, C. (1991) *The British Press and Broadcasting Since 1945*, Oxford: Blackwell.

Seymour-Ure, C. (1998) 'Leaders and Leading Articles: The Characterisation of John Major and Tony Blair in the Editorials of the National Daily Press' in Crewe, I., Gosschalk, B. and Bartle, J. (eds) *Political Communications: Why Labour Won the General Election of 1997*, London: Cass, pp. 131–48.

Seymour-Ure, C. (2000) 'Prime Ministers' and Presidents' News Operations: What Effects on the Job?' in Tumber, H. (ed.) *Media Power, Professionals and Policy*, London: Routledge, pp. 151–66.

Seymour-Ure, C. (2002) 'New Labour and The Media' in King, A. (ed.) *Britain at The Polls 2001*, London: Chatham House, pp. 117–42.

Sharkey, J. (1989) 'Saatchis and the 1987 election', in I. Crewe and M. Harrop (eds) *Political Communications: The General Election of 1987*, Cambridge: Cambridge University Press, pp. 63–72.

Sherman, J. (2002) 'Whitehall Chief Tells Blair to curb advisers' powers', *The Times*, 27 March, p. 10.

Skeffington (1975) *Report of the Committee on Public Participation in Planning*, London: HMSO.

Snow, J. (1999) 'We've been televising Parliament for 10 years, so why are dull pictures like these still the best we can do?', *Guardian*, 19 July.

Sobol, S. (1980) 'Community perceptions of local government: an empirical evaluation of the role of public relations as a management function in English local government'. Unpublished Phd thesis, University of Bradford.

Society of County and Regional Public Relations Officers (1985) The public image of local government, *County Councils Gazette*, January, p. 310.

Society of County and Regional Public Relations Officers (1986) Unpublished letter dated 13 January to the Department of the Environment concerning the code of practice.

Sparrow, J. (2003) *Obscure Scribblers: A History of Parliamentary Journalism*, London: Politicos.

Stanyer, J. (2001) *The Creation of Political News: Television and British Party Political Conferences*, Brighton: Sussex: Academic Press.

Straw, E. (1998) *Relative Values*, London: Demos.

Straw, J. (1993) 'Parliament on the Spike', *British Journalism Review*, vol. 4, no. 4, pp. 45–54.

Straw, J. (1999) 'Wanted: One Bold Editor', in *British Journalism Review*, vol. 10, no. 1, pp. 29–34.

Street, J. (2001) *Mass Media, Politics and Democracy*, London: Palgrave.

Sussman, L. D. (2001) 'The Internet in Flux' in Freedom House *Press Freedom Survey 2001*, pp. 1–4, www.freedomhouse.org/pfs2001/pfs2001.pdf.

Swingewood, D. (1988a) 'Backlash threatened as Hurd ban bites', *UK Press Gazette*, 24 October, p. 1.

Swingewood, D. (1988b) 'D-notice chief tried to delay Wilson plot blow, *UK Press Gazette*, 7 November, p. 3.

Swingewood, D. (1988c) 'Press may be muzzled by Secrets Act reform', *UK Press Gazette*, 7 November, p. 5.

Taras, D. (1996) 'The New and Old Worlds: Media Coverage and Legislative Politics in Canada', Unpublished paper.

Taylor, L. and Mullen, B. (1986) *Uninvited Guests: The Intimate Secrets of Television and Radio*, London: Chatto and Windus.

Tebbit, N. (1989) 'The Conservative campaign', in I. Crewe and M. Harrop (eds) *Political Communications: The General Election Campaign of 1987*, Cambridge: Cambridge University Press, pp. 43–9.

Theaker, A. (2001) *The Public Relations Handbook*, London: Routledge.

Thomson, A. (1989) *Margaret Thatcher: The Woman Within*, W.H. Allen: London.

Timmins, N. (1997) 'Blair Aide Calls on Whitehall to Raise its PR Game', *The Financial Times*, 9 October, p. 2.

Tomlin, J. (2001) 'BBC Relations With Labour "Very Fragile" Says Damazer', *Press Gazette*, 22 June, p. 2.

Tomlin, J. and Morgan, J. (2001) 'Poll Voted a Turn-Off By Viewers and Readers', *Press Gazette*, 8 June, p. 1.

Toolis, K. (1998) 'The Enforcer', *Guardian Weekend*, 4 April, pp. 29–36.

Toynbee, P. (2001) 'Basking in the Sun', *Guardian*, 9 March, p. 17.

Travis, A. and Silverman, A. (2002) 'Whitehall Spin Machine Expanded', *Guardian*, 3 August, p. 2.

Traynor, I. (1998) 'Peter's Passions', *Guardian*, 16 March 1998, p. 8.

Trenaman, J. and McQuail, D. (1961) *Television and the Political Image*, London: Methuen.

Tunstall, J. (1970) *The Westminster Lobby Correspondents: A Sociological Study of National Political Journalism*, London: Routledge & Kegan Paul.

Tunstall, J. (1983) *The Media in Britain*, London: Constable.

Tusa, J. (2003) 'Don't Attack the BBC, You Can't Win', *Guardian*, 22 July, p. 22.

Tutt, B. (1992) 'Televising the Commons: a full "balanced and fair account" of the work of the House', in B. Franklin, (ed.) *Televising Democracies*, London: Routledge, pp. 129–49.

UCLA Centre for Communication Policy (2000) *The UCLA Internet Report: Surveying the Digital Future*, www.ccp.ucla.edu/ucla-internet.pdf.

UK Press Gazette (1988) 'Delay tactics may hinder start of TV in Commons', 27 June, p. 3.

Vanston, P. and Sykes, R. (2001) *Communications in Local Government: A Survey of Local Authorities*, London: Local Government Association.

Waddle, K. (1989) 'Ancient and modern: innovations in electioneering at the constituency level', in I. Crewe and M. Harrop (eds) *Political Communications: The General Election Campaign of 1987*, Cambridge: Cambridge University Press, pp. 29–41.

Walker, D. (1998) 'Getting The Choir Singing From The Same Sheet', *Guardian*, 6 August, p. 17.

Walker, M. (1993) What the spin doctor ordered', *Guardian*, 2 July, pp. 25–6.

Ward, L. (2000) 'Blair Launches No 10 Website', *Guardian*, 12 February, p. 5.

Ward, S. and Gibson, R. (1998) 'The First Internet Election? UK Political Parties and Campaigning in Cyberspace', in Crewe, I., Gosschalk, B. and Bartle, J. (eds) *Political Communications: Why Labour Won the General Election of 1997*, London: Cass, pp. 93–114.

Warden, J. (1988) 'Mr Lawson: here's what you said', *UK Press Gazette*, 14 November, p. 5.

Watson, R. (1999) 'Blair Looks For New Medium To Deliver Message', 6 March, p. 20.

Watt, R. (2001) 'Blair in Row as Whitehall Adverts Soar by 157%', *Guardian*, 26 April, p. 13.

Watt, N. (2001a) 'Tories in Scare Tactics Row', *Guardian*, 16 May, p. 13.

Watt, N. (2001b) 'Storm At New Tory Film', *Guardian*, 25 May, p. 15.

Watt, N. and Tempest, M. (2001) 'Hague's Tories Outspent Rivals in 2001 Poll Fiasco', *Guardian*, 27 November, p. 14.

Waugh, P. (2002) 'Campbell in control of government advertising', *Independent*, 25 May, p. 5.

Weatherill, B. (1992) Foreward to Franklin, B. (1992a) *Televising Democracies*, London: Routledge, pp. xiii–xvi.

Wells, M. (2002) 'Peers Warn No 10 on Media Ownership Plans', *Guardian*, 1 August, p. 6.

Werner, J. and Tankard, J. (1988) *Communication Theories*, New York: Longman.

West, R. (1963) *PR the Fifth Estate: An Enquiry into Public Relations in Great Britain Today*, London: Mayflower Books.

Wheatley (1969) *Report of the Royal Commission on Local Government in Scotland* (Cmd 4150) London: HMSO.

White, M. (1991) 'Labour attacks tax cost of charter propaganda', *Guardian*, 24 July.

White, M. (1992) 'Knives are out for Labour media team', *Guardian*, 18 June, p. 7.

White, M. (1999) 'Want to find out what's really going on in British politics? Read a women's magazine', *Guardian*, G2 February, pp. 2–3.

White, M. (2000) 'Inside Story Of A Campbell Briefing', *Guardian*, 15 March, p. 12.

White, M. (2002) 'Labour 'broke rules' on pre-election spending', *Guardian*, 25 May, p. 9

White, M. (2002) 'Major Surgery For Labour's Spin Doctors', *Guardian*, 3 May, p. 1.

White, M. (2002) 'Squaring Up To A Century Of Spin', *Guardian*, 3 May, p. 8.

White, M. (2002) 'Fear and Loathing in the Lobby', *Guardian*, 16 December, pp. 2–3.

White, M. (2003) 'Bong! Time To Go Home', *Guardian*, 6 January, p. 6.

White, M. and MacAskill, E. (1999) 'His Master's Voice', *Guardian*, 26 January, pp. 2–3.

Whiteley, P. and Seyd, P. (1992) 'Labour's vote and local activism: the impact of local constituency campaigns', *Parliamentary Affairs*, October, pp. 582–95.

Widdicombe, D. (1985) *Committee of Enquiry into the Conduct of Local Authority Business: Interim Report*, 31 July, London: HMSO.

Wildy, T. (1986) 'From MoI to COI – publicity and propaganda in Britain, 1945–1951: the National Health and the insurance campaigns of 1948', *Historical Journal of Film, Radio and Television*, vol. 6, no. 1, pp. 3–19.

Wildy, T. (1985) 'Propaganda and Social Policy in Britain 1945–51: Publicity for the Social Legislation of the Labour Government'. Unpublished PhD thesis, University of Leeds.

Williams, A. (1996) 'The Media, The Hierarchy of Information and the Reliance on Official Sources'. Unpublished MA thesis, Department of Journalism Studies, University of Sheffield.

Williams, G. (1992) 'The rat pack hacks', *Free Press*, March/April, pp. 4–6.

Williams, G. (1993) 'ITV down the tube', *Free Press*, March/April, p. 7 (Campaign for Press and Broadcasting Freedom, London).

Williams, M. (2000) 'The Impact of Mountfield: A Detailed Analysis in the Department for Education and Employment'. Unpublished MA Thesis, Department of Public Media, Trinity and All Saints University College.

Williams, R. (1974) *Television, Technology and Cultural Form*, Glasgow: Fontana.

Willings (1992) *Willings Press Guide* 1992 (118th ed.), Sussex: Reed Information Services.

Wilkinson, N. (2002) 'The Defence Press and Broadcasting Committee' in *Pennant Magazine* on www.dnotice.org.uk/articles.htm.

Willmott, N. (1986) 'Party broadcasts', *Invision*, November, pp. 99–125.

Wilson, B. (1996) 'This Time He's Gone Too Far', *Daily Telegraph*, 1 November.

Wilson, D. and Game, C. (2002) *Local Government in the United Kingdom*, London: Palgrave.

Windlesham, Lord and Rampton, R. (1989) *The Windlesham/Rampton Report on Death on the Rock*, London: Faber & Faber.

Winn, M. (1977) *The Plug in Drug: Television, Children and the Family*, New York: Viking Press.

Wintour, C. (1991) 'Kinnock tries to end propaganda feud', *Guardian*, 30 May, p. 2.

Wintour, P. (1991) 'Campaign veteran applies pressure', *Guardian*, 16 March, p. 3.

Wintour, P. (1992) 'Labour sifts through ashes of defeat', *Guardian*, 17 June, p. 6.

Wintour, P (1999) 'Parliament on TV Leaves Viewers in the Cold', *Independent*, 19 July, p. 1.

Wintour, P. (2001) 'New Blow For Hague As Sun Sets On The Tories', *Guardian*, 9 March, p. 12.

Wober, M. (1992) *Televising the Election: A Preliminary Report on Knowledge, News Use and Attitudes in Three parts of the United Kingdom*, London: ITC.

Woffinden, B. (1988) 'Commons pursuit', *Broadcast*, 3 November, pp. 12–13.

Woffinden, B. (1989) Vision of the future', *The Listener*, 19 January, pp. 6–7.

Worcester, R. (1991) *British Public Opinion*, Oxford: Blackwell.

Worcester, R. (1998) 'The Media and the Polls: Pundits, Polls and Prognostications in British General Elections' in Crewe, I., Gosschalk, B. and Bartle, J. (eds) *Political Communications: Why Labour Won the General Election of 1997*, London: Cass, pp. 53–75.

Worcester, R. and Mortimore, R. (2001) *Explaining Labour's Second Landslide*, London: Politicos.

Wring, D. (1997) 'Political Marketing and the Labour Party'. Unpublished PhD thesis, Cambridge: Cambridge University Press.

Wring, D. (2002) 'The 'Tony' Press: Media Coverage of the Election Campaign', in Geddes, A. and J. Tongue (eds) *Labour's Second Landslide*, Manchester: Manchester University Press, pp. 84–100.

Young, H. (1989) *One of Us*, London: Macmillan.

Young, H. (1992) 'Politics without people', *Guardian*, 25 March, p. 23.

Young, H. (1999) 'A Shocking Appointment', *Guardian*, 25 June, p. 18.

Young, H. (2003) 'Every Prime Minister must have an Alastair Campbell', *Guardian*, 29 July, p. 20.

INDEX